Wisdom of Love

Wisdom of Love

Philosophical Implications of 1st Corinthians 13.

JOHN CORRY

WISDOM OF LOVE
PHILOSOPHICAL IMPLICATIONS OF 1ST CORINTHIANS 13.

NRSV
Scripture quotations marked NRSV are taken from the New Revised Standard Version of the Bible, Copyright © 1989, by the Division of Christian Education of the National Council of the Churches of Christ in the United States of America. Used by permission. All rights reserved. Website

iUniverse books may be ordered through booksellers or by contacting:

iUniverse
1663 Liberty Drive
Bloomington, IN 47403
www.iuniverse.com
1-800-Authors (1-800-288-4677)

ISBN: 978-1-5320-6123-3 (sc)
ISBN: 978-1-5320-6124-0 (e)

Print information available on the last page.

iUniverse rev. date: 10/27/2018

Dedicated to

the nurses, doctors, and paramedics at Chester Co. Memorial Hospital, West Chester, Pa.; Betty and Steve who read and commented throughout the writing. Dr. Jay Clark and Dr. Wayne Benenson who edited and shared their responses throughout the writing; our family of twenty two children and grandchildren Steve through Megan. Middletown (Chester Co., PA) & Albuquerque (NM) Friends Meetings. The Norbertines at Daylesford Abby, Paoli, Pa., and Maria de la Vid, Albuquerque. And finally my mom and dad: Esther White Corry (Yoh) and John Pitts Corry, who first introduced me to Paul's amazing love.

1st Corinthians 13 (NRSV)

"If I speak in the tongues of mortals and angels, but do not have love, I am a noisy gong or a clanging cymbal. And if I have prophetic powers and understand all mysteries and all knowledge, and if I have all faith, so as to remove mountains, but do not have love, I am nothing. If I give away all my possessions, and if I hand over my body to be burned, but do not have love, I gain nothing.

Love is patient; love is kind; love is not envious or boastful or arrogant or rude. It does not insist on its own way; it is not irritable or resentful; it does not rejoice in wrongdoing, but rejoices in the truth. It bears all things, believes all things, hopes all things, endures all things.

Love never ends. But as for prophecies, they will come to an end; as for tongues, they will cease; as for knowledge, it will come to an end. For we know only in part, and we prophesy only in part; but when the complete comes, the partial will come to an end. I was a child, I spoke like a child, I thought like a child, I reasoned like a child; when I became an adult, I put an end to childish ways.

For now we see in a mirror, dimly, but then we will see face to face. Now I know only in part; then I will know fully, even as I have been fully known. And now faith, hope and love abide, these three; and the greatest of these is love."

"If philosophy is the love of wisdom, it is also
and primarily, the wisdom of love."

Emmanel Levinas, French Jewish Philosopher

Contents

PARTII— PAUL'S LOVE AND CAPITALISM

PARTIII— PAUL'S LOVE AND WAR

Introduction

I

Last spring after my first heart attack I spent the night in the ER at our local hospital. Seven to seven. With no rooms available I could not be moved and as the hours passed I was unable to sleep. All around me the sounds of pain and fear: an intestine with a tiny pinprick, a broken hip, a child screaming. For several hours I lay awake alternately agonizing over and trying to ignore, the unsettling sounds around me; as well as the whisperings of my own nervous heart. Then I heard other sounds. Quieter, gentler.

"We'll have you in for the operation in forty minutes. They're clearing the room now."

"It's OK dad. We're with you. It's going to be all right."

"Can I get you some water? Do you need another painkiller?"
"Mommy's here."

These were voices of concern, the murmur of human beings caring for each other and suddenly I realized the struggle was not about pain and death, but about caring and not caring. The fear and groans still echoed, but even if every person died that night love wins. Do you understand? Love wins! The Ocean of Light covers the Ocean of

Darkness! Love wins! I fell asleep almost at once lulled by the soothing sounds of love.

Three years later I am still reflecting on the implications of this riveting experience. It has changed the way I feel visiting the nursing home to visit Betty's mother, Nell, where I sense the same caring helpfulness, the same atmosphere of love in the caring staff, visiting relatives, and old people who created a loving community among themselves. When I see our children raising their own kids; changing diapers, giving up their evenings and weekends to feed, talk and play with their children, I again encounter the presence of this animating energy that bonds one human to another. Reading the paper I follow with interest efforts in Israel and Northern Ireland to bring an end to that bitter conflict between neighbors; and the work of ex-president Jimmy Carter and other volunteers helping build new homes with the poor. I notice the way people treat each other. The way Betty and I interact. Stepping back, listening to someone else's opinion; offering encouragement for a new job, visiting a neighbor when they return from the hospital, bringing in meals. In the daily events close at hand and at a distance I see on the margins of life, the little kindnesses that had seemed so inconsequential. The riveting public events: elections, wars, the ongoing media featured scandals and personal tragedies no longer focus my interest; no longer compel my response. When I look more closely at the marginalized interactions between ordinary citizens I see the same signs of love I experienced in the ER. Even in the midst of the pettiness and posturing so evident in myself and in others around me, I seem to be looking at life from another perspective; one where fear and concern for self have been diminished. Even overcome.

II

Was the revelation in the ER a fleeting experience? Or has it an enduring significance? As a philosophy major at Haverford college, who has kept an interest in how the human mind has organized its experience in various comprehensive ways producing theories of reality as diverse as those of Plato, Hume, Kierkegaard, Marx and Derrida, I'm captivated by the idea that my ER experience might be of some philosophic significance. Could it be the love I'd experienced in the ER might survive, even prevail, in the philosophic marketplace? Could it be philosophy – Plato's love of wisdom – is as Levinas, the French Jewish philosopher, suggests primarily the wisdom of love? Is there a wisdom in love, a logic to love, that might be traced in human thought as well as in the lives of saints and ordinary citizens? William James in 1907 had spoken of the diversity of strong philosophic personalities who rose above the eclectic mix of inconsistencies that compose the philosophy of the ordinary citizen.

> "Most of us have no very definite intellectual temperament, we are a mixture of opposite ingredients, each one present very moderately. We hardly know our own preferences in abstract matters… but the one thing that has counted so far in philosophy is that a [person] should see things, see them straight in [their] own peculiar way, and be dissatisfied with any opposite way of seeing them." (*Pragmatism*, p. 11-12)

My peculiar intent is to see the human endeavor from A to Z, from its theoretical aspects to its practical application, from the point of view of the love I experienced in the ER - and to be dissatisfied with any intervening or obstructing view. As any thinker might in presenting a thesis for general consideration, I am like a young stag lowering its antlers to challenge the prevailing authorities.

Unlike literature and the other arts, philosophy is about agreements and disagreements. If one line of thought, one truth-claim, is valid – or probable, or appropriate, or verifiable, or whatever criterion is favored at the moment – other truth-claims are invalid. The logic of philosophic truth insists that if premise X is right, premise Y and Z are wrong. If Plato is right then Kant and Hegel are wrong. If Kant is right then Hegel is wrong. Philosophy is a series of ongoing arguments about the nature of reality. When I defend, as I will in the first chapter, Paul's

Love expressed in *1st Corinthians 13* as the primary truth of existence rather than Being, power, God, self, freedom, or science, I'm saying anyone who doesn't agree is wrong. That doesn't mean I'm mad at Plato or Kant or that I think, God forbid I'm a better philosopher. It's just the way philosophy is played. If you don't think you're right, i.e. that your premise is right and that therefore the other options are incomplete, distorted, or plain wrong you won't last long. Like playground basketball; you win you keep playing. Lose and you sit out. Of course if you lose in one era, like the American pragmatists and Nietzsche did for a while, there's always the chance you'll return to favor in another era.

Frankly I'm not much of a philosopher. For fifteen years I'd written mostly poetry, but I do think I'm right on the critical significance of love. And if I believe that I have to present my case and be prepared to defend my position. Some friends who've already read Part I have suggested I go easy on the philosophy and concentrate on my own experience and conclusions. Though I have edited a bit to be more accessible to the general reader I've decided against this approach for two reasons. First I really do think in philosophic terms – those I can understand. The philosophers I began studying in college and who have accompanied me ever since: Plato, Descartes, Kant, James, Martin Buber, Nietzsche, Sartre, and Kierkegaard are real figures for me, inner companions who offer their perspectives on the events of my life.

These cultural icons, combined with the contemporary thinkers I've enjoyed over the last ten years as a respite from the rigors of writing poetry, eventually goaded me into a response. After years of listening attentively to the acknowledged experts I could restrain myself no longer. I had to break in and exclaim, "No! No! No! You've missed the main point. Start over. Start with what Paul puts first, then your arguments and insights will fall into place." Whether I'm right or not remains to be seen but that's one reason I reference philosophy as we go along.

The second reason is because while anecdotal evidence may be emotionally compelling and more easily understood by the general reader, comprehensive ideas have always shaped our culture. Literature entertains and deeply enriches our lives but ideas and arguments – philosophy – shape the economic, political and religious institutions around us. Think of Plato's and Aristotle's effect on Western religious, scientific and political life. Compared to the marvels of Greek literature and art. Contrast the influence of Homer or Sophocles with Aristotle's or Plato's. Think of Descartes', Hume's and Kant's decisive role in creating the Enlightenment that has shaped the modern world. Or Adam Smith, John Locke, Rousseau, Hegel and Marx and their impact on our economic and political institutions. In religion Paul, Augustine, Luther and today's Karl Barth, and the Feminist and the Liberation theologians are the theological authorities rather than the saintly believers: Dr. King, Mother Teresa, and Dorothy Day. Even scientists - Newton, Darwin, Freud, and Einstein - when they present truth-claims about reality are acting as philosophers.

Since comprehensive thinking about reality – philosophy of one sort or another – is the critical cultural mode for challenging the established truths which shape our society I've turned to philosophy to present my case for love as the primal energy, the foundational premise, for our time. That is, I think, quite a revolutionary claim and I look forward to arguing it as passionately and cogently as I can.

III

In addition to presenting philosophy as the wisdom of love, I would convey through the text the taste and feel of the love that has burned its way into my life and my awareness of the way the world works. Karl Barth, Augustine and more recently, Catherine LaCungna, have spoken of the need for theology, the study of God, to convey the joyous reality of its subject. Books on humor should make us laugh, or at least smile. Writings on love should convey the awesome animating power of the subject itself. It is not enough to present the wisdom of love as credible line of thought; the text must also leave the reader with a renewed sense of being in touch with the most compelling component of human life. It must move the heart as well as the mind. If, on the other hand, my writing elicits only an emotional response I will have failed to trace the influence of love as it presses its way into every aspect of human existence; not only in personal relationships and religion, but in business, politics, and the military establishment as well.

IV

Preparing to explore the philosophic implications of the love I experienced in the ER – of what beginning with chapter one I shall call Paul's Love – I'm mindful of the expectations of two distinct audiences. On the one hand I hope to be relevant to the philosophical tradition that contemporary philosophers might ponder the decisive role love (restricted to an activist reading of Paul's Love in *1 Corinthians 13*) might play in their own thinking. On the other hand I hope to interest the general reader who ponders, as Gauguin did, the central enigmas of existence. Where Do We Come From? What Are We? Where Are We Going?

I realize that this may be asking a lot of both groups. Philosophers will need to be patient while I share some fairly elementary philosophical concepts. The general reader will need to be patient with the sometimes confusing and sketchy references to Levinas' the "Other", pragmatic choice, and Kierkegaard's subjective truth. And the oddly argumentative tone the text assumes at times. Not nearly precise enough I would think to satisfy the exacting demands of professional philosophers. The tension between the hard thinking required to follow the unfolding argument and the emotional and imaginative content I've used to illustrate the unfolding thesis seems to me essential to the work as a whole. I'm writing about the most compelling reality in the entire universe. To grasp its driving power in conceptual, or at least quasi-conceptual terms will require patience and a condition of mind that embraces the extremes of logical reasoning and strong feeling in one text.

Adjusting to this ongoing interplay between thinking and feeling will, I think, be one of the major challenges the work makes on the reader.

As I look back over Part I find my thought does not unfold as much philosophy does, moving from one point to the next in an orderly and logical way. I don't seem able to move easily from premise to supportive arguments to the culminating conclusion. Rather my mind seems to explore one issue, one dilemma, at a time before moving on. Focusing on a major concept such as Other, Choice, Gift and seed I tend to weave rational arguments, personal experiences, and imaginative analogies together, as I explore the various possibilities within each issue. If one fails to keep in mind the overriding issue or dilemma, often presented in Part I in a single chapter, one may find it hard to follow. Like a hunting dog tracking the scent of its prey my thought pursues its prey through the tangled byways of human reasoning, darting here and there, intoxicated by the primal scent of patient love that Paul's exalts in *Corinthian 13*.

As a poet I was trained to gather elliptic incongruities under one general image, incident or theme – tree, loss, first love, or death. A whole poem would often explore one mysteriously unnamed central incident or image. Writing Part I I became aware that each hub concept – "Other", "Choice" etc. – was meant to overlap and support its neighboring concepts, and that the four hub concepts taken together were intended to illuminate the elusiveness obviousness of Paul's Love. Given the philosophically puzzling central concept of Paul's Love I do not find this an unworkable approach. If love like sunlight is pervasive, life-supporting, and elusive it does not yield the secrets of its origins and movement to only one approach in Plato's cave-clouded world. It must be courted tenderly with all the human faculties at our disposal. And when we have finished we shall discover we have only uncovered what was obvious all along.

V

I've tried to be mindful of the general reader by going light on footnotes and extensive philosophic references, though I couldn't resist framing the major concerns of many chapters with relevant quotes.

Unlike many philosophers I have not critiqued my relevant predecessors: Plato, Descartes, William James, and Kierkegaard among others, before coming at long last to my own arguments. Though I rely heavily on the insights of those and others the wisdom of love has pursued its own course in my thinking exploring Paul's Love in Part I in relation to the individual, in Part II in relation to our economic system, capitalism, and in Part III to the military establishment.

While the arguments presented may fail to adequately illuminate my momentous topic I would hope that others would take up the task. If love is to be more than a devotional ornament, like the absurdly small cross at the top of certain church spires, it will take fresh thought and an innovative attitude by many disciplines to begin to see love as the foundation on which everything else depends.

A few final words about methodology. First, I have occasionally utilized contemporary events – personal in Part I and public in Parts II and III – to clarify my line of thought. While I may have misjudged contemporary events; failing to foresee for example the eventual outcome of Bush's current War on Terrorism, or my ongoing relationship with family and friends, still my responses to these events may serve the purposes of the larger argument. In making my case for love I have opted to utilize the immediacy of unfolding daily life, rather than depending on scholarly hindsight, which edits out current misjudgments and archaic references.

Second, I had hoped to think through the successive stages of my argument from premise to conclusion before I began writing; hanging my ideas like wash on a clothesline to be taken up sequentially, being aware from the beginning of the overall structure of the book. That way I might have balanced the validity of one section, one stage in the argument against the others. Unfortunately my mind failed to cooperate and I've had to settle for a more piece meal approach, thinking through the validity of one chapter at a time, before moving on to the next. Still I'm hopeful an elusive consistency will thread its way through the various stages of my developing thought on love.

Often it seemed as though I was crossing a turbulent river one tippy stone at a time, having to secure my footing on one stone before looking up for the option that might become my next step. In the beginning as I looked across the river at the variety of available stepping stones I had a rough idea of the path I wished to take. But as I move from stone to stone I find certain stones not as secure as I'd assumed and I've had to move in new directions. In the beginning looking to either side I could see well traveled pathways across the river. The stones were placed within easy stepping distance of one another. Upstream on the higher ground, to my right, I sensed the initial rocks had names like Order, Truth, Spirit, Beauty, Goodness, and God. To my left downstream the rocks were labeled less idealistically: the knowing self, the will to power, the repressed unconscious, and so on. I also had the sense that though others had crossed the river before me there was no clear pathway leading from my rock across the turbulent waters; that I would have to make my way alone. The rock I'm standing on, my anecdotal experience in the ER, is not so large and grand as those to my right, nor so gritty and firm as those to my left. By comparison mine is a slight rock which wobbles when I put my weight on it and before I quite know what is happening I'm impelled to stretch out for the next rock and the next. Soon I am out in the rushing stream more quickly than I'd planned. As I move across the river, rock by rock, I find my path does not allow for the security of being certain that each stone is the best stone, or only stone, that would take us - for we are I trust on a common journey - across the river. Still I am exhilarated to begin the journey, and I trust that one stone will lead to the next and that somehow we will find our way across the rushing waters.

Part I

Paul's Love and the Individual

Chapter

I

Paul's Love

"Great ideas, it has been said, come into the world as gently as doves. Perhaps then, if we listen attentively we shall hear, amid the uproar of empires and nations, the gentle stirrings of life and hope."

Camus (*Resistance.*. P. 272)

"All you need is love; love is all you need."

The Beatles

I

If love is foundational, greater than faith and hope which without love are as nothing as Paul in *I Corinthians 13* proclaims, then everything else is secondary, contingent, unessential. Let us look briefly at what Paul puts in second place. "Tongues of mortals and angels"? Archaic at best. Irrelevant to our post-modern worldview. "Prophetic powers"? Bit vague. Suggestive perhaps. Intuitive insight into the trends that carry us into the future? In science? Business? Political changes? "And understand all mysteries"? The unconscious mysteries explored by Jung and Freud? The mystery of our quest for inner fulfillment, inner worth? The elusive nuances of the human condition etched by artists, writers and poets?

"...And all knowledge." Of the seen, sensed, and measurable world around us? Our scientific worldview? Archeology, biology, psychology, cyberspace, outer space, inner space? Mathematics, philosophy, economics? Einstein, Plank, Marx, Adam Smith, and their varied disciples?... Pause. Reflect. Take a deep breath. With a few lines it seems Paul has brushed to one side the entire modern range of mysteries and hard earned Enlightenment-based knowledge. Not that he disputes the validity of our world view. How could he, a first century Judeo-Christian Roman, challenge our scientific data? But he does insist that they are secondary, contingent, and ultimately unessential.

Paul moves on. "If I have all faith so as to move mountains, but do not have love, I am nothing". Think of it! Paul who'd had the most riveting experience of the risen Christ in the entire Christian tradition; who'd suffered imprisonment, decades of privation and abuse and would ultimately be beheaded (probably)for preaching the risen Lord Jesus in opposition to the reigning Lord Caesar, put all that behind love. All the theologies (including Paul's own cogently argued in *Romans, Galatians*, and elsewhere),creeds, church services, bible study, holy days, outreach programs, relief efforts, evangelism, private prayers and devotions that relate to Jesus the sum and substance of our faith, are put behind love. A faith Paul says that is as nothing without love.

At this point I sense believers and humanists who've been suspicious of Christianity, or of certain elements in Christianity, reviving their interest in Paul. Still recovering from having their valued mysteries of the inner quest, and/or outer scientific certainties - the whole worldview of the post-modern era - abruptly brushed aside, the post-modern critics of Christianity may be excused for gloating a bit. "That's what we've been saying all along! Look at the Crusades, the Holocaust, the... They (Christians) talk about love but their record, even with Francis of Assisi and Mother Teresa is simply horrendous." And Paul seems to agree.

But Paul is not finished. "If I give away all my possessions" (as Jesus suggested to the rich young man) and "give my body over to be burned but do not have love, I gain nothing". Even concern for the poor and martyrdom, for whatever noble purpose, without love, is again as nothing. Let us be clear here. I am reading Paul to mean that even the heroic emancipatory efforts of our century; for civil rights, women's rights, gay and lesbian rights; church reforms of Vatican II; protests for democracy and economic justice for the world's poor, and countless individual acts of mercy, are as nothing without love. Worthless, misleading, divisive, distracting. As nothing. That is what Paul's words say to our modern condition. Which is not to deny of course, that like any text, *Corinthians 13* had a more restricted local setting, directed originally, in Paul's case, to certain squabbling factions in the church at Corinth in the late first century. What Paul's words tell us today however, is that no effort; right, left, center, conservative, moderate, liberal, radical, traditional, evangelical, revolutionary, avant guard, New Age - whatever - may entertain an agenda that moves outside the primary motivation of love. No grievance, no injustice, no suffering, however long standing, however horrendous, may set aside this clear word that champions love as the primary and essential component of our intentions and actions. Paul is not saying that anger, righteous outrage, sorrow, and pain; even resentment, jealousy, and a host of lesser emotions play no role in our critical choices. but that when push comes to shove only love - not prophetic powers, insight into mysteries, knowledge, faith, concern for the poor, the environment, the marginalized, the willingness to sacrifice and even die for one's cause - is worthy of our allegiance. When all the vicissitudes of our culture and personal lives would encroach on our intent, our will, only love can be trusted. Like a solar system without a sun, without love nothing on our planet lives, nothing survives. Without love there is only darkness and death - nothing.

What is this love that Paul so prizes; even above his own deepest spiritual experiences? His own life work of preaching the gospel. Is it interwoven with the other enduring elements (faith and hope - and to a lesser extent mystery and knowledge)? Is love linked to Jesus? To one's faith in Jesus? Not necessarily. "Love is patient. Love is kind. Love is not envious or boastful or arrogant or rude." Nothing about having to accept Jesus in that. Seems open to everyone. "It does not insist on one's way." Do we? Insist on our own way in our interactions with others? In actions taken as part of our faith or non-faith community? In our outreach to others? Our printed material, our preaching, our collective action, do we make our witness in a loving way? Leaving it to the presumed good sense, and good will of those with whom we would dialogue, to accept or not, our witness to the truth as we understand it? Are we irritable, or resentful when others reject our plans, our precious sharings, our deepest hopes and convictions? In any case there seem to be no strings attached to Paul's Love. We are not to insist on our own way. Are not to be irritable or resentful, boastful or arrogant. Our love is to be open to all, unconditional, and generous hearted. Unrestricted by theological requirements. Whether or not one believes, as Paul and I do, in the imminent royal return of God- as-Jesus to usher in the cosmic Springtime, the rule of God on earth, or any other staple of Christian belief, one may be patient and kind.

Not that Paul dismisses the specific beliefs of Christianity. Love he continues "Bears all things, believes all things, hopes all things, and endures all things." Bit vague but I take Paul to be referring here to his own belief in all the things taught and believed about Jesus by Christians of his own time, especially the council with Peter, James and others, in Jerusalem. Love bears the trials and tribulations of adhering to the disciples' common hope for a cosmic coming to life of love over the whole earth with God-as-Christ's return. Love also is able to endure the testing of the faith in persecution even unto execution. Here again love is seen to be the basis, the enabling agent, of our faith, our hope for God's future on earth, and our possible martyrdom. Only as these stables of Christianity are infused with love are faith, hope and martyrdom of any value at all. In short Paul privileges love above everything common to humanity, even his own faith and hope in the risen Christ.

While he does not, in the text before us, make love dependent on his experiences of Jesus, elsewhere Paul sees love permeating the major Christian realities including the Cross and Resurrection, the impending Kingdom of God, and martyrdom at the hands of the Romans. And yet the love he champions in *Corinthians*, toward the end of *Romans,* and elsewhere as well is easily recognized by all; plain and simple garden variety love - patient, kind, gentle, attentive to other's needs before one's own.

II

Where in today's world can one find such teaching on the primacy of love over the specifics of traditional religious beliefs? Almost everywhere. At popular and academic levels love is widely viewed as the *sin quo none* of any cultural worldview, of any responsible non-fundamentalist mindset. Those who's worldview echoes *Corthinians 1st 13* include Tenzin Gyatso, the 14th Dalai Lama and ecumenically-minded religious pluralists like John Hicks the innovative Anglican theologian and Hans Kung, a feisty Vatican II Catholic scholar. At the political level Gandhi's non-violent campaign for Indian independence is the most striking example of the effectiveness of love acting collectively in our century. In any century. Growing out of a radically compassionate reading of the Hindu scriptures, wedded to insights from Thoreau, Tolstoy and Jesus, Gandhi's work stands in mute opposition to the turbulent waves of violence and counter violence that have swept over the twentieth century. Perhaps the words of the Dalai Lama best express this emerging vision of the centrality of love for our time.

"Whether you believe in God or not does not matter so much, whether you believe in Buddha or not does not matter so much; as a Buddhist, whether you believe in re-incarnation or not does not matter so much. If as a Buddhist you try to implement, practice compassion, even if you do not place much emphasis on the Buddha, it is right. For a Christian, if you try to practice this love there is no need for much emphasis on other philosophical matters. I say this in a friendly way... Thus if you consider the essence of religion, there is not much difference."

Mindful that what the Dalai Lama refers to as "philosophical matters" are for Paul the enduring realities of faith and hope which will need more attention later, I still resonate to the privileging of love that the Dali Lama places above his other Buddhist beliefs. Just as Paul placed love above his other Christian beliefs.

Chapter

II

Paul's Love: The Philosopher's Cornerstone?

"In the world of knowledge the idea of the good appears last of all, and is seen only with an effort… This is the power upon which he who would act rationally either public or private life must have his eyes fixed."

Plato (#517 *Republic*)

"Once in a lifetime we must demolish everything completely and start again right from the foundation."

Descartes

I

If Paul's Love is to be valued above knowledge and faith as the primary fact of existence its relation to the five cornerstones of traditional philosophy must be clarified. Otherwise Paul's Love ends up being defined not as the one essential truth that *Corinthians 13* proclaims, but as an adjunct to a more primal reality. Love needs its own philosophic credibility to protect it from the corroding influence of well-meaning friends who are ultimately committed to other agendas. A knowledgeable friend with whom I shared my concern for making love philosophically creditable was intrigued with the effort, but said it was all muscle and no bone. That it lacked a skeleton; structure. The task at hand is to provide such a structure by giving the fleshy body of Paul's Love the bones to stand, to move, and begin to effectively engage the compelling figures who shape our contentious post-modern discussion.

If we would make Paul's Love the cornerstone of a revised philosophical line of thought, we must first understand how philosophy views reality. Modern and post- modern thinkers view Hume's fleeting sense data, what William James called the "blooming, buzzing confusion" of existence, from their own varied perspectives. The more earthy realities: economic life (Marx), the will-to-power(Nietzsche), and the shadowy psycho-sexual realms (Freud) each have their contemporary advocates. More recent philosophers, notably continental Europeans: Heidegger and Sartre, Derrida, Gadamer, Foucault, Habermas, and Kristeva, and the Anglo- Americans: Bertram Russell, Wittgenstein, Popper, Rorty and Rawls, have wrestled with existential, linguistic and hermeneutic issues, political concerns and scientific innovations, which we will not pause to consider, except to note Paul's claim that love outlasts all mysteries and all knowledge, of whatever era.

Rather we'll turn our attention to the legacy that traditional philosophy has left us, for it is here we discover the five fundamental patterns of thought that have shaped all subsequent philosophic thinking. These five responses to the question "What is reality?" provide the basic assumptions on which later lines of thought were to be developed. Descartes, the early Enlightenment mathematician and philosopher, first articulated the idealist position that still pervades continental philosophy i.e. that the knowing self, the conscious mind and its ideas, is the foundation of all knowable reality. Known as the father of modern philosophy Descartes' view that consciousness is the primal reality has outlasted his own theocentric beliefs and the challenge of other philosophers ever since. If he has no dutiful offspring (except in France where he is taught in every school) Descartes is an archetypal figure whose body-mind split still haunts the corridors of modern and post-modern academia. By divorcing philosophy from the classical certainties of Plato and Aristotle

Descartes' doubting consciousness raises the issues peculiar to modern and post- modern thinkers.

Materialists on the other hand focus not on Descartes' interior realm of consciousness and reason, but on the observable physical world. They focus on the outer world (Descartes' "body") rather than the inner self; on what we know rather than how we know. Scientific and political philosophers explore, respectively, reality in the various patterns of nature and history. Utilizing the framework provided by Aristotle (minus the Unmoved Mover, God), and modified by Bacon, Comte, Einstein, and others, the scientific world view explores reality in the observable and, more importantly, the measurable universe around us.

Unlike Plato Aristotle was fascinated by the workings of the natural world. That he failed to adequately appreciate the role of accurate measurement (mathematics) and experimentation, does not diminish the contribution he made in establishing close observation and reason as essential tools in understanding reality. His detailed studies in zoology, biology, astronomy, and other nascent sciences initiated the scientific approach to knowledge that is still with us.

Moving from nature to history socio-political philosophers such as Adam Smith, Locke and Rousseau, Hegel and Marx, helped shape the forms of economic and political life we live under today. Together scientific and political philosophies comprise the non-theistic broadly materialist worldview.

II

Neither of these options, Idealism or Materialism in a broad and general sense, precludes the possibility that both the knowing self and the measurable universe are encompassed by an even wider reality, but each of the first two options by denying the existence of a wider realm presents a one-story, humanistic, view of reality. Many humanist thinkers explore both aspects of this one-story reality; nature and history on one side and the individual's perception of reality (consciousness) on the other. No one is totally discounting the presence of either aspect in human experience, but in general contemporary philosophy divides along lines that favor one or the other – or perhaps three – of the humanistic options. In the third option the great German philosopher Heidegger returns to Being within which particular beings (chairs, trees, people, objects ad infinitum) exist, much as earlier thinkers saw the Supreme Being, God, above all, present in all and through all. While the early Heidegger dismisses the notion that Being is "above all", i.e. is separate from Dasein – "being there" in time, the later Heidegger takes a more puzzling, even mystical turn. Being becomes Non-Being and if not above all is certainly distinct from the totality of beings. But Heidegger's line of thought which views Being, first explored by the pre-Socratic Greeks, as the root concern and mystery of human existence, must wait a bit till the first two options have been mentioned briefly.

Both Anglo-American analytic (broadly materialist) and continental philosophers(subjective idealists of one sort or another) derive reality from the Scotch philosopher David Hume's refinement of Descartes' knowing self into its essential components: kaleidoscopic sense impressions, or sense data. Hume isolated sense date, the primary stuff of reality, apart from the unsupported assumption of a real world out there (strict Materialism), or an equally invalid, to Hume, realm of interior consciousness (Idealism). Analytical philosophers pursued aspects of Hume's thought in either a scientific-mathematical, or a language- oriented direction. The latter group, including thinkers like Wittgenstein (with Heidegger the other great 20th century philosopher), G.E. Moore (the great disciple of common sense and sensible sentences),

John Searle, and professional linguist Norm Chomsky, who uncovered universal forms of thought common to all languages, all explored language as the quintessential medium which shaped our thinking in all other areas. Others analytic thinkers like Gottlob Frege, Bertam Russell, and the once fashionable Logical Positivists under A.J. Ayer, leaned heavily on mathematics and science to supply the credible information which language utilized for the benefit of society at large. Making accurate fact based statements about what was really the case motivated the analytic anti-philosophers to eliminate the fanciful fluff of Existential angst, God, and murky probes into the human condition. "No truth but in things," as Williams Carlos Williams put it, or linguistically, no sentences without verifiable references. All prose; no poetry. And no unverifiable prose.

Continental thinkers on the other hand explored the subjective realities associated first with Kant's critique of Hume, and later with Existentialism and Phenomenology. Kant argued that Hume's bits and pieces of reality had already been shaped and organized by the human mind itself to confirm to the innate categories of space, time, plurality, sequence, cause and effect etc. These cookie cutters of the unknowable dough of reality (the thing-in-itself) were in place Kant argued prior to any sense data coming from the outside world. If there was indeed an outside world, which for practical purposes Kant assumed, but could not prove existed. If you doubt this odd way of looking at the world, try to think of a scientific fact or an historical event, or an event from your life today that is *not* shaped by location and time, sequence and cause and effect. In any case Anglo- American analytical and continental more humanistic philosophy; one broadly materialist, the other subjective, inwardly oriented, Idealism, have divided philosophy for most of the 20th century into two contentious factions.

Then, as the master of dialectical thought Hegel might have predicted, once the two positions were established thinkers like Paul Ricoeur, a subtly nuanced hermeneutic French philosopher, and the two Richards, Rorty and Bernstein (one time Haverford professor) the American neo-pragmatists, sought to reconcile the differences in a new paradigm. The newer reconciling lines of thought attempt to unite the primary reality of Descartes's updated knowing self on the one side with insights from the scientific and linguistic lines of thought on the other.

I mention these efforts merely to suggest the dialectical process constantly at work – at play? – in philosophy. After all without new truth claims that state some other philosopher is wrong; in fact that everyone else in one way or another is wrong the philosopher is out of business. One thinker may admit to being influenced by another but no philosopher can rubber stamp another's line of thought and be a true philosopher. If lasting truth is the avowed goal of philosophy the hidden agenda is change. Modifying, updating, or revolutionizing the truth, leaving room for new thinkers to make their unique contributions.

But is philosophy like art or fashion about making a personal statement? Finding one's voice? Or is it about getting it right? Even if someone else has gotten there first? Let's assume everyone can agree that one philosopher, say Plato, did get it right. They'd have to declare a moratorium on new truth claims after Plato. If Plato was right, and he did cover a full range of philosophic issues, there'd be no need for neo-Platonists or Aristotle or anyone else to update the truth. Simply learn Plato. But even assuming Plato was right, that his views were the truth, the whole truth, and nothing but the truth, thinking is then reduced to rote learning. But if philosophy is memorizing someone else's ideas one isn't thinking at all. One is simply at copier, a printer, for a dead philosopher's sacred text. Philosophy has killed thinking! And no one would have been thinking since Plato. So the only way to think is to deny truth – so one can think? Ah but since we're pondering this puzzling conundrum – does truth kill thinking? and conversely does thinking kill truth? – we are in fact thinking. In any event it's time to return to the business at hand.

The third humanistic option rediscovered by Heidegger among the pre-Socratics, asks the question, "What is reality made of?" Passing over earlier answers: fire, earth, water and air; atoms; everything changes like a flowing river (Heraclitus), nothing changes (Parmenides), Heidegger sees Being that encompasses every individual being as the ultimate and ordinary reality. Whatever is, Is, including the ways we respond to living in the world; either following conventional wisdom "They", or becoming an authentic individual. His truth claim lies somewhere between self-centered, subjective Idealism and a broad Materialism in constant contact with the outer world. Heidegger's notion of human existence – Dasein – views the individual as thrown into the world without a clue where she came from or where she is heading.

To repeat myself Heidegger's Being-in-the-world, which combines aspects of both the conventional subjective and objective approach to reality, incorporates philosophically marginal aspects of existence that Kierkegaard and later Husserl, the seminal German phenomenologist and Heidegger's mentor had explored.

Kierkegaard had traced the role of elusive states of Dasein such as anxiety, dread and faith, while Husserl monitored the intentional activities of consciousness. Heidegger grounded these two somewhat one-sided investigations – Kierkegaard's into the metaphysics of mood and Husserl's perceptual rationality – in Being (Dasein for humans) where, so Heidegger claimed, Western philosophy had begun with the pre-Socratic Greeks. Balancing the inner, subjective mindset of Descartes and Kant, and the objective mindset favored by materialists (both scientific and political) Heidegger's Being (both person focused, Dasein, and later pure Being (aka Non-Being) encompassing everything that is, represents a third major non- theistic option.

III

While religiously minded philosophers, a distinct minority today, accept a good portion of the humanist world view, they envision a wider reality within which the self, nature, and history find their place. Theirs is a two story reality; one seen and measureable; the other secluded but pervasive for those who stumble into sacred space and time interwoven into our down to earth world. These theologians (philosophers who study God) tend to view reality in either of two ways. Both ways claim that a creative and loving non-sensate, invisible higher power, God, created and sustains the creation. Those who perceive the Creator as distant and distinct from the sensate creation tend to think in Platonic terms. Protestants (following Luther), and many Christian, Jewish, and Islamic fundamentalists who sharply distinguish the sovereign source, God – and God's chosen faith community – from the sinful fallen creation, adhere to patterns of thought first explored by Plato. And later Plotinus, a remarkable Egyptian Roman thinker who condensed Plato's Forms of Truth, Justice, and Beauty into one source, God.

Other believers who see God present in, and working through, a less fallen, less sinful creation tend toward Aristotelian patterns of thought. Catholics and liberal Protestants including Quakers, who see grace building on nature(or rather on what reason can tell us about nature)adhere to the Aristotelian mode; even for Catholics whose ties to such thinking through Aquinas, have been modified by more modern Catholic theologians including some of my favorites: Karl Rahner, David Tracy, Elizabeth Fiorenza, and Catherine LaCunga.

To repeat myself for emphasis Plato saw transcendent truth drawing a deluded and passion-ridden humanity to itself beyond the confines of our cave-like earthy existence. Plato sees his task as a philosopher to act as a midwife helping deliver the truth buried in his unenlightened dialog partners so they too might experience the transcendent Forms of Truth, Justice, and Beauty. Aristotle, a true scientist- ethicist-philosopher fascinated by the development evident in all living organisms looked for Truth not above and apart from creation, but embedded in the creation; impersonal Unmoved Mover, the ever present First Cause. My memory is unclear on whether the Unmoved Mover who started things off is still operative in the unfolding creation, natural and human.

Aristotle's developmental - teleological - tendencies inherent in all living things, reinforced by human choices express the basic striving for goodness and life that Plato situated in a more transcendent realm, apart from this world of decay and illusion. Later of course Thomas Aquinas transformed Aristotle's Unmoved Mover into the more personal and loving Trinitarian God worshipped by Christians today. While this image of a personal, loving, but also ultimately judging God, replaced the earlier Platonic and Aristotelian patterns of thought, their legacy remains, creating tension at times between different factions of Christianity.

IV

The five patterns of thought already mentioned, three humanistic, two theo-centric, represent traditional responses to our original question, "What is reality?"

Certainly the wisdom of love is not currently considered a proper topic for philosophical discussion. In the *Cambridge Dictionary of Philosophy* (1995) metaphysics, "The philosophical investigation of the nature, constitution, and structure of reality" makes no mention in five and a half columns of love. If we look up the relevant topics we find: Idealism, 4 columns and 5 related topics; Materialism, see Philosophy of Mind about ten columns, Philosophy of Science 7½ columns with 9 related topics; political philosophy 4 columns and 5 related topics; Being under Heidegger, metaphysics and transcendentals 13 columns, Philosophy of Religion 8½ columns with 9 references. Love, see Divine Command ethics, 1 column. No related topics.

Of course it might be argued that philosophy has been talking about love all along – that it's woven into the fabric of each approach. And to some extent I think that's true. One of the great hopes I have is that the various philosophical lines of thought can be reexamined in light of *1 Corinthians 13*. But I do find it curious that philosophers who pride themselves on using precise language should have overlooked – or misread – such a major component of reality. If they meant love why not say love? Love as Paul defines love in *1st Corinthians 13*.

While each of the five options mentioned incorporates Paul's Love into its own worldview I question whether any one of them captures the pervasive love that Paul champions in *Corinthians 13*. No matter how much or how little each philosophy may value Paul's Love, each has a prior commitment to another Archimedes' principle on which the world turns. Idealism to the knowing, and for many post-modern thinkers, skeptical doubting, mind; Materialism to the physical realm (in its scientific and political aspects); Heidegger to quasi-phenomenological Being. Plato and Plotinus to the transcendental realm dimly reflected in our shadowy earthly life, and Aristotle to the Unmoved Mover, First Cause, working within creation, which Aquinas updated to the loving

15

personal God of Christian belief. Before moving into uncharted waters I might remind the reader that while Paul believes God is loving and kind, he clearly does not equate faith and love. Love as I've argued must have in today's world its own mystic, its own philosophical rationale.

I trust it's clear before we move on I'm grounding my argument for Paul's Love solely on love as defined by *Corinthians 13*. I'm suggesting that if you read *Corinthians 13* as making a truth claim about reality then love as Paul defines it – patient and kind – must take precedent over knowledge, prophecy, even faith. If *Corinthians 13* is read purely as a devotional exercise, or an emotive expression reflecting Paul's hopeful, euphoric, state of mind, or his one time response to certain internal controversies in the Corinthian fellowship, then my thesis falls apart and love can be relegated to its traditional domestic and devotional role. Without intruding on philosophical or public affairs.

Ah but some might say, "Isn't God patient and kind? Isn't God the philosophical cornerstone you've been looking for?" Certainly all Christians would agree, but Paul would say "Yes, God is patient and kind, but what's not certain is whether believers (those with faith) are patient and kind." It is not God's Love Paul questions but the love of devout believers. Having faith in a loving God is not enough to insure that the believer herself is loving. Which Paul makes clear writing, "If I have all faith, so as to remove mountains, but do not have love, I am nothing."

I realize not all authorities define love as Paul does. Classical distinctions were made between eros, filios and agape; between sacred and profane love; love of family, an individual, or one's church or nation, but these distinctions are not mentioned in *Corinthians 13*. I'm not trying to deal with love in all its varied manifestations, but to focus on the love Paul chose to champion in *Corinthians*. I realize biblical scholarship disowns the single passage proof text. I agree one would need to sift and weigh a number of passages and other sources to compose a strong reading of Paul's views on love, which I find in similar passages spread throughout the letters especially toward the end of Romans, but I'm not a biblical scholar trying to assess Paul's comprehensive understanding of love. It is not Paul but the text of

Corinthians 13 I take as our starting place. I am taking *Corinthians 13* at face value and pursuing the implications of those compelling words in a philosophical setting, without assuming a Christian framework or outcome. Which I would suggest is entirely consistent with Paul's own views expressed in our short passage.

V

Before turning to Paul's Love as the foundational assumption about reality, we might dwell for a moment on the general nature of primary assumptions. A major task in itself. Without unduly prolonging the prelude I would make two points. First, primary assumptions must be both comprehensive and visceral. On the one hand the foundational assumption must be broad enough to explain, or at least wrestle with, all other facets of existence. A religious option must wrestle with the troublesome realities of evil and a materialistic world view. An idealist must explain how the physical world can seem to exist in its own right, apart from human consciousness. The scientific materialist can explain and measure physical phenomena rather well. He or she has a harder time with intangible phenomena like free will, resentment, joy, and Paul's Love. And why human perception, the mind, is the only available medium for processing information about the measurable real universe. They are also hard pressed to explain the motivation for figures like Gandhi, Francis and Clare of Assisi, Dr. King, and Mother Teresa, who attribute their admittedly remarkable lives of service to others to a scientifically problematic God. The argument of the saints. Of course many religious scientists exploring God's wondrous creation aren't troubled by these issues.

Heidegger's claim that Being is the source and mystery of existence; human and non-human, faces several objections. One from believers who claim, Being (especially his later upgrade of Being to Non-Being) is another name for the traditional God – minus God's personal touch in dealing with fallible human beings. A second objection comes from analytical thinkers who think Heidegger is the most wordy, fuzzy minded, overrated philosopher of the century, and finally everyone is suspicious of a thinker who supported Hitler, failed to support his Jewish colleagues, and who after the war refused to clarify his connection to the Third Reich. Which should not detract in my opinion from the claim that Heidegger has raised issues on the nature of existence that are still relevant today. Of the five traditional cornerstones of philosophy his exploration of Being – as the intensely personal and perceptive Dasein (Being-for-me) and the broader, cosmic, Being in itself, seems to me the most congenial meeting ground for postmodern humanists and religious philosophers.

Besides being comprehensive a primary philosophical truth claim must be personally important to the author and the reader. It must be compelling, visceral; like an ax blow, that as Kafka said strikes at the heart. The primary assumption must be the most critical component in a person's life; something which will affect not only way the way she thinks, but that also shapes her core values, and the way she interacts with her neighbors. Near and far.

VI

Let us take Descartes, the "Father of modern philosophy", as an example of a gifted thinker who left Paul's Love to one side as he took a fresh look at the bookish, logic-laced, scholastic philosophy of the time. Torn between the traditional Catholic worldview of the late medieval period and the emerging interest in science, mathematics, geometry, and unfettered reason in general, Descartes wrestles with the age old philosophical questions. What is reality? And how can I be sure my view of reality is reliable? What assurance do I have that what I've been taught as true is really true? Can I trust my senses and reason apart from what I've learned from the theologians on one side and the emerging scientists to give me accurate information on the nature of reality?

Let us picture Descartes as a middle-aged Frenchman in his secluded study, somewhere in Holland, sitting alone by the fire in his dressing gown. Thinking. Then thinking some more, searching for a first principle, a cornerstone on which to base his thinking and life, Descartes is overwhelmed by the insight that when he has doubted everything else he cannot doubt that he is doubting! 'I doubt... I think! Therefore I must exist!' He has found his primary assumption and the rest of his life is spent reflecting on the implications of this insight; testing it against the prevailing philosophic assumptions. He invites the reigning authorities: theologians, scientists, and philosophers - including the dour Englishman Thomas Hobbes, to critique his work. After consolation with the authorities - whose input is generally ignored - Descartes worked out a comprehensive and compelling philosophy wrestling with all aspects of existence. All based in his mind on his primal self-validating premise — I doubt, I think, I exist.

Certainly one may question the consequences that flow from Descartes initial insight, i.e. the still controversial mind-body, matter-mental, subjective-objective dichotomy which philosophers are still trying to resolve, but apart from the consequences - discussed from a variety of perspectives - Descartes' initial insight deserves our attention.

Miraculously Descartes' philosophy has survived devastating criticism. The bête noire of contemporary philosophers he is still being refuted and discussed. Because I believe professional philosophers and ordinary thinkers can relate to his primary assumption, whatever the troubling consequences may be. We have all sat somewhere alone and pondered the reality or unreality of life around us. We have all sensed that magical moment when the reality of our own thinking enlivens our whole being. For many it comes in adolescence as we move from a child's adult dependent mind set to an independent adult consciousness. Beginning with this sense of being alive, existing in a new way, as a doubting, thinking, conscious, individual, I can understand how one might view the wider world differently. For the first time the relation to one's environment, even one's own body becomes problematic. The visible limbs are no longer identical with my sense of who I am. Is my arm me? Or my leg? Or the brain in my head? Or am "I" my conscious self, my real self, more than my body parts? More than my brain? If I'm not the body I've lived in all my life who am I? Where do these odd thoughts come from? These intangible images I cannot touch or measure? Somehow after considering Descartes' dilemma a slight gap opens between the lived reality of my thinking self and my visible active physical self. Resist as I might the horrors of a mind-body split, Descartes' experience recounted in the *First Meditation*, becomes at least understandable.

The same would be true I believe of the other options we've mentioned. They have persisted in the general culture and in philosophic discourse because they each present believable assumptions about the nature of existence. Williams Carlos William's "No truth but in things" speaks for the materialist's visceral insight, while Auden's "Some things can't be seen with a microscope" opens the window to a religious dimension to reality. But our question is, are they – any of them – the most comprehensive, most visceral option available?

VII

Think of Descartes in his study, shocked and amazed at the riveting revelation that he exists! As a doubting, thinking, conscious being! A whole new line of thought opens before him. He begins tentatively at first, but growing in confidence to speak a new language. A language that will soon sweep the contemporary late medieval scholasticism of Aristotle and Aquinas from the universities and permeate the consciousness of generations of ordinary citizens. But is the doubting consciousness, the immeasurable mind in a tangible body really the primary reality in Descartes' life? Did he not exist the day, the week, before his great insight?

What carried Descartes up to the great discovery "I think, therefore I exist!"? The physical world certainly, as materialists will be quick to point out. His brain and nervous system developed and provided the mechanics for bodily movement and thought, without which there could have been no consciousness, no knowing mind.

No need to postulate a ghost in the machine, a subjective presence that animates his unified physical nature. Reality ultimately derives from and depends on the physical reality that science explores. Ah, but a believer might interrupt, what of Descartes' spiritual nature? Is he not, as are we all, a human being created by a merciful Creator? A child of God? Or at least, for many post-Christians, a child of the unseen transcendent Universe? A living soul. Testimonial, scriptural and reasoned philosophic evidence might then be offered for a variety of theo-centric (or non-theo-centric Buddhist) options that challenge Descartes philosophy. Later Idealists (those basing reality on ideas, or at least on human consciousness, or human "existence", or human something - anything rather than mindless materialism) and Heidegger have their own objections and yet, despite strong criticism from many quarters Descartes *and each of the other four traditional cornerstones of Western thought* has persisted in the general culture and in philosophic discourse because they represent valid and fruitful ways of perceiving our blooming buzzing reality. Each option is inclusive and compelling enough to either explain, or seriously wrestle with, the problematic issues of existence. And yet each option must, according to *Corinthians 13*, defer to another foundational assumption.

Returning to the middle aged Descartes reflecting alone in his snow bound Dutch study, let us picture his life run backwards, like a film in reverse. First Descartes as a mature adult among his scientific and liberal Catholic friends: Plemp the anatomy savant; Father Mersenni a former schoolmate and philosopher-priest who worked tirelessly on Descartes' behalf gathering the learned authorities of the day – including the dour English philosopher Thomas Hobbes – to publicly engage his friend's revolutionary ideas; Cardinal Beruille who encouraged Descartes to pursue his philosophy of a God-centered mechanical, scientific universe. God the clock maker, the blessed Holy Ghost in the machine. Then going back a few years, the great sadness of his life; losing his beloved illegitimate daughter, Francine when she was five to scarlet fever while he was finishing his monumental work, *Meditations on First Philosophy*. Back again to his early twenties meeting Issac Beeckman, the Dutch mathematician-scientist, a close friend and mentor who first awakened Rene's slumbering intellect to ask unconventional questions. Another shift and we're watching Descartes during the adolescent years being taught Aristotelian scholasticism by kindly Jesuits who made "hardly

any distinction between the humblest and those of higher birth."
(*Cambridge Dictionary*. 3. 224) Descartes valued his time at La Fleche
in Anjou which he considered, "One of the best schools in Europe."
Further back we see little Rene with his older sister Jeanne playing with
childhood friends, taking his first steps as a toddler towards his father's
or more likely his grandmother's or his favorite nurse's waiting arms.

Another shift and Rene is being fed at the wet nurse's breast, and
then further back the mucous covered small head breaks into the cold
air between his mother's sweaty thighs, before the scene shifts to the soft
tunnel of conception and delivery into the womb where the nameless
Rene waits and begins to swell his mother's body. A frail caring woman
who died soon after giving birth to Descartes.

What I'm suggesting of course is that Descartes exists not only,
or not primarily, because he thinks but because a lot of people cared
for him; from the passionate act of intentional love that initiated his
existence in his mother's womb throughout childhood and later life,
until he was in a position some thirty years later to celebrate his existence
as a thinking being sitting alone in a Dutch cottage. Leaving love
aside we may credit Descartes' existence to the physical circumstances
of his birth and development, or we may assume as I would, that a
compassionate Creator brought Descartes into life. Deferring to those
who would not make that assumption I would return to *Corinthian 13*
and say that at least there can be agreement that Descartes exists because
he was loved. If not fully by a rather distant father who cared for Rene's
material and educational needs more than his emotional needs, then by
a caring grandmother, a much admired older sister, and a devoted nurse.
And later by playmates, schoolmates, teachers, good friends, fellow
scientists, churchmen, and philosophers. Through a rather difficult and
sickly childhood Rene received the care and support needed to pursue
his scientific and philosophical interests. Interests vital to Descartes and
that he believed to be of benefit to his fellow human beings.

Relations with his family while not openly unpleasant were not
generally cordial. He did not attend most family events nor his father's
funeral, but for all his shortcomings Descartes throughout his life was
in contact with people who admired and loved him. They, and he,

were not always kind and patient; the world around Descartes was not always kind and patient, but there was enough support that as he grew into maturity Descartes was able to love others and receive their love. His pioneering work in analytic geometry, optics, and philosophy was intended to be of benefit to his fellow human beings. Of all the contributing factors at work in Descartes' life – his physical nature, his doubting mind, the possibility of his being (as he believed) the child of a merciful God – the most critical, most lasting, most significant factor was Paul's patient and caring love. We too exist because like Descartes we are cared for and loved by others. Each of us can say "I am loved; therefore I exist."

Chapter

III

Building on a New Foundation

"The face in its nakedness as a face presents to me the destitution of the poor one and the stranger; but this poverty and exile which appeals to my powers, addresses me as an equal. He comes to join me."

Emanuel Levinas

"To the human being the world is twofold in accord with her twofold nature. The attitude of the human being is twofold, in accordance with the twofold nature of the primary words which she speaks.

The primary words are not isolated words, but are combined words. The one primary word is the combination

I-Thou.

The other primary word is I-It."

Martin Buber

I

While Paul's description of love focuses on the effect of love on the one doing the loving - being patient, kind, not arrogant etc. - the implied emphasis is on the one being loved. Love is thinking about the other person's welfare rather than one's own welfare. One is kind not rude to another; one is not arrogant or boastful about one's own achievements and interests. One listens to and cares about the other person, rather than seeking to advance one's own agenda. Love does not insist on one's own way but defers to the other person's interests and plans.

Though many post-modern thinkers have resonated to Paul's concern for the other person none has been as relentless in placing the Other at the center of their philosophic concern as the French Jewish philosopher, Emmanuel Levinas. By "Other" Levinas indicates whatever is not Descartes' thinking self, i.e. those realities that intrude on the individual's self-awareness: the physical world, illness, death, God, and equally important other people, other faces. Levinas is not just saying that ethically or religiously one is responsible for one's neighbor, but that reality itself is knowing that my neighbor - contrary to my immediate understanding and Western philosophy – is more real than I am! Levinas locates authenticity, what he calls infinity, not in the individual knowing self as Descartes did, but in the one who is different from me, the one who "interrupts my spontaneity". Reality begins not with my perspective, myself, my soul, my consciousness, but with the face in front of me today who by her, by his, very presence alters my thinking, my life. This face is to be responded to in two ways, first with "love and respect... [which] belong to our private activities," and secondly and of equal or greater importance for Levinas, with justice – especially economic justice. Putting aside [bracketing] for now the complex issues arising from Levinas' contrasting of private love and public justice it's clear that Levinas would move philosophy from the a self-centered or science based philosophy to focus on the Other, especially the Other face.

In philosophic terms metaphysics (the study of first principles) has become, with Levinas, ethical rather than noetic. "You" rather than "I" is Levinas's center of attention. Only through accepting responsible for the other person can we approach the infinite intangible God. Nor is the neighbor to be embraced in an intuitively inclusive way which emphasizes sameness and unity. What interests Levinas is not that human beings are like one another but that the individual I meet today is radically other than I am. This otherness, this difference between us is what breaks open my self-centered, self-contained mind set.

The visceral sense of the reality of the other person's importance over my own runs, of course, counter to the ego-centric ethos of any competitive culture that favors self preservation over the needs of one's neighbor. It means to become a person who, as Bonhoffer says of Jesus, lives for others.

The limitation of Levinas' thought from the perspective of Paul's Love is that by focusing on the Other one risks replacing one abstract concept – the self, the ego – with another – the Other. Engaged in the formidable task of defending his revolutionary notion of a new cornerstone for philosophy the complexities of Levinas's thought occasionally obscure the simple reality of the human faces he would privilege. Reading Levinas I sense I am again dealing with abstractions rather than human beings, and I often lose sight of the human face which disappears in a flurry of densely reasoned explanations and arguments.

A second limitation from the standpoint of Paul's Love is that for Levianas "Law takes precedence over charity" i.e. that love and sympathy are viewed as private, domestic, and dangerous factors in political life. By Other Levinas means to present us with the reality of our injustice to our neighbor, not stopping short with the *amorous dialogue* "Love" which, without justice, especially economic justice, "is but a pious intention oblivious to real evil." (*Entre Nous*, P. 21) Again, I would defer wrestling with the issue Levinas raises of the relation of Paul's Love to justice until we've explored love in its more domestic setting, i.e. in the relationships between individuals. Then I trust we shall find Paul's Love in its socio-political aspects far more significant than Levinas supposes.

While Levinas's focus on the Other person is critical to any philosophical understanding of Paul's Love, Levinas does not, to my mind, move us to walk in the ways of love. Talk of responsibility for our neighbor sets the stage for but does not convey the energizing reality of Paul's Love. Like Plato of the *Republic* and contemporary political philosophers such as Hannah Arendt and John Rawls, Levinas finds it easier to speak of justice and law (the right relationship between human beings) than of Paul's Love. In a world awash with sloppy notions of love I understand his concern to place his philosophy on firmer ground. Turning from contemporary notions of the evolving self, the fulfilled self, Levinas renews a much neglected prophetic cry from the heart in favor of the stranger, the orphan, the marginalized, but I miss the energizing influence of the patient, long suffering tender compassion Paul champions in *Corinthians 13*.

II

A second philosopher who speaks movingly of the Other is Martin Buber the dialogical, mystical Jewish theologian who has been a lifelong spiritual companion. I met Dr. Buber at Haverford college in my senior year when he visited as a guest of Douglas Steere, my Quaker mentor in philosophy. The memory of Dr. Buber's small frame and alert caring eyes that turned so carefully toward us budding philosophers to reflect on our concerns before responding, has stayed with me. Like Dorothy

Day, co-founder of the *Catholic Worker*, Buber's eyes spoke of a world that was foreign to me. A world I now sense around me of infinite caring. At the time, along with my fellow philosophers-in-training, I challenged Buber's thought, bewildered by his elliptic pronouncements which punctuated the flow of his more reasoned arguments. A pragmatist, immersed in Dewey, I was puzzled by Buber's illogical lapses. In dialogue with students his answers often seemed beside the point, but on reflection I sense he was responding to the questions that lay behind our stated concerns. At his first Quaker meeting, which all students at the time were required to attend every Thursday morning, Buber spoke briefly on the way we talk to one another; how we must cherish – must relish – the partner with whom we dialogue in pursuit of truth. He said that as we talk and argue, agree and disagree, the truth would be raised up between us. He said it was in the dialogue, in listening to the other person and presenting of our more authentic selves through our arguments - not in the conclusions we reached - that life stirred. It was in the give and take of serious dialogue on truth that the ultimate and sustaining Thou, G-D, was able to permeate – to visit - our conversation.

Later Buber's I-Thou dialogical philosophy became a permanent component of my evolving Christian theology. With others and in my prayer life, I found myself listening more attentively to my seen and unseen partner cherishing as Buber and Steere did the Thou, in conversation or in prayer, who opened me to a realm beyond my own self-centered fears and hopes. I began to see the visceral connection between my neighbor and our common creator, and I recalled the Quaker insight that there is that of God in every human being. But when I considered the wider world, the world of science and politics, Buber's dialogical model seemed limiting. Not all problems were resolvable by attentive listening; by what Levinas called, the "intimate society... the false totality... of the I and thou", which I came to agree did shut out the third party, the others who sought our attention, while we were engaged in a private conversation. What does cherishing the Thou mean for example in the voting booth? Or joining others in political action that favors one group at the expense of another group?

The poor for example over an entrenched socio-economic system that favors one class of citizens.

Despite reservations the insights of both Levinas and Buber have become an integral part of my thinking as I ponder Paul's Love in a philosophical setting. Viewed in the light of Paul's Love, I find Buber's I-Thou formulation (contrasted to, or at times complimented by, the I-It relationship) more inclusive, more congenial, than the sharp dichotomy Levinas makes between the self and the Other. Buber's thought and tone allows us to embrace the mystery of the Thou (in God and Others) through the eyes of the more philosophically familiar knowing self. Levinas, a passionate ethical prophet is more concerned to confront the philosophic mind in its own terms, and pushes Buber's relational I-Thou formulation to it's logical (or one logical) limit, virtually eliminating the I, the ego, as an ontological reality. And raising more sharply than Buber the social dimensions of love, justice and evil. Since both thinkers direct attention to the other person and the Divine Nature as the primal reality rather than Descartes' self- knowing self both may prove useful in making Paul's insights credible to our post- modern sensibilities.

Levinas and Buber also allude to the decisive role Paul's Love plays in mediating the ego and the Other; the I and the Thou. Levinas while suspicious of love as a private coupling that distracts attention from social justice does suggest the I-Thou relationship may have a role in creating viable social structures. Drawing on Heideger's intersubjectivity, Levinas writes, "Intersubjectivity is a coexistence, a WE prior to the I and the Other... The face to face both announces a society, and permits the maintaining of a separated I." (*Totality and Infinity*, p. 68)). The intersubjective WE which places the I and the Other in a social setting allows Paul's patience and kindness to operate between individuals while, simultaneously, sustaining the social fabric. Not a conclusive endorsement but suggestive.

Buber views love as more directly involved, saying "Love does not cling to the I in such a way as to have the Thou only for its 'content', its object; but love is *between* I and Thou. The person that does not know this does not know love." In other words Paul's Love is the decisive animating agent between the I and the Thou. Without love there is no dialogical relation. Nor does Buber's love neglect the practicalities that flow from love. "Helping, healing, educating, raising up, saving… Love is responsibility of an I for a Thou." (*I and Thou*, p 14-15) In Heidegger's and Levinas' intersubjective WE and Buber's *between* there are the stirrings of a more systematic investigation of Paul's Love.

We must not assume the I-Thou relation is free from the range of human emotions and strategies associated with any relationship. What is asserted is that Paul's Love is the essential component – often unmentioned – of any lasting relationship. All other components: attraction, anger, obligation, convenience, resentment, and passion, are so *Corinthians 13* implies secondary. Only patience and kindness survive time's swirling currents. As we seek to become a mutually caring WE, to cherish others in our lives as Thous we find ourselves immersed in a variety of other attitudes which *Corinthians 13* does not take time to clarify or evaluate. It's as if Paul's Love looking into the tangled nest of feelings, fears, intentions and aspirations that compromise our relationships should point to certain small twigs saying "These will last. Continue to weave and reweave them into your nest until one day you will hear the rustle of wings descending."

Philosophically then we may assume that while Paul's Love acts as the sustaining agent between the I and the Thou, it's the Other on whom the I focuses its attention. Paul's Love acting through the knowing self, Buber's I, reaches out to the Other, and yet Paul's Love retains its own reality distinct from the Buber's I-It, I-Thou *and* its significant companions, faith and hope. Like sunlight that animates varied forms of life, Paul's Love illuminates the I-Thou as it relates to other human beings and to the Divine Nature.

III

In the Introduction I suggested we complement a philosophic exploration of Paul's Love with "the taste and feel of the love that has burned its way into my life." As long as we're able to love others - being attentive, kind and patient to those around us - we are able to live out what the Dalai Lama, Paul, Levinas (with reservations), and Buber have identified as the source of all light for our otherwise dark human existence. We have begun to walk in the light of Paul's Love, and at first the world grows wondrously bright around us, until the grim realities of life on our troubled planet challenge our new venture. Discouraged we may return to *Corinthians 13* where Paul tells us that "Love bears all things, believes all things, hopes all things, endures all things. Love never ends." What more encouragement do we need? Whatever the obstacles Paul clearly urges us to press on. He doesn't say there won't be obstacles; that love will win every battle, or change every heart. Or any hearts at all! He doesn't address the issue of love's effectiveness directly, but he does suggest love is not a utilitarian value to be measured by its results. Like a pauper certain of his future inheritance we may spend love lavishly, trusting our debt will be covered; that our inheritance is secure.

And so, if we choose Paul's love as our guide we're on our way at last. We have begun our walk in the one light that Paul perceives as necessary to our human journey. As the Dali Lama might say love is our raft across the river of suffering and pain. But however we got there, whatever we believe about the rest of existence - whether we are Buddhist, Christian, Humanist, or Atheist - however we identify ourselves love has now become our guiding star. Nor at this point can we beg off by asking for more information on love and the nature of our journey. We have all the information we need. We are not to be arrogant, or rude; we're to be patient and kind, not resentful, not seeking our own way. We're to be open-hearted and generous to others. This is not an impossible task. Within the next hour or two we will meet a face in need of such a response on our part. We don't have to finish the book to begin. It is open to us to begin, or for many simply to continue on. We've been given an understandable direction well within our power to pursue. Undeterred by obstacles we are free to give our lives to the radiant energizing power within us that seeks to benefit the other person rather than ourselves.

That's it. As long as we are able to love no other wisdom is required. Our curiosity about the other questions of existence - where do we come from? Where are we going? What does it all mean? What is the nature of reality? Is there a God? - may lead us to consider the answers given by philosophy, science or religion but the essential direction of our life has been set. Whether we are ultimately proved to be right or wrong in our assessment of the nature of the universe, the elusive spiritual realities, or the course of historical events will not matter so much - if we have loved. Our theology, psychology, cosmology, our methodology, our epistemology, our hermeneutics will all be altered, revised or discarded by later generations. All these are time-worn, historically conditioned. Only Paul's Love will endure; unscathed, unaltered. Ever fresh, ever new.

Chapter

IV

Closing the Gap

A pragmatist turns away from abstraction, from verbal solutions, fixed principles and pretended absolutes and origins. He [or she] turns toward facts, toward action… At the same time he [or she] does not stand for special results. It is a method only."

William James (*Pragmatism*, p.31)

"The scientifically skeptical position says: No beliefs, [these are] only hopes, desires, yearnings and the like. The quasi-Jamesian position says: Do not worry too much about whether what you have is a belief, desire or mood…. You need not worry about whether you have a right to have… such states as hope, love, and faith."

Richard Rorty (*Philosophy & Social Hope*, p. 155)

I

How do we bridge the gap between our two Descartes? Descartes the isolated self- doubting, self-affirming mind trapped in a body who thinks in order to exist, and Descartes the human being who interacts with others in a loving way? What is that allows Descartes to move beyond his knowing self to respond to the love he's received from family, friends, and fellow philosophers? For however much or little love Descartes may have received at some point early on Descartes is invited by the significant others in his life to choose to return or not to return their love. An essential aspect therefore of Paul's Love is choice. Without choice one cannot be kind to others; cannot refrain from arrogant behavior. Choice bridges the gap between the knowing self and the Other.

Perceptive continental thinkers who explore the role of choice in human life include Kierkegaard, Nietzsche, and Sartre, but since Kierkegaard's choices occur in the context of his religious concerns, and Nietzsche and Sartre resolutely make their choices in world without God, I would have us turn to a more neutral source unencumbered by religious or non-religious presuppositions.

Pragmatic philosophers: William James, John Dewey, and contemporary pragmatists like Richard Rorty are less constrained by strong cosmic views, though as we'll see they do have their own presuppositions apart from the pragmatic methodology they champion. Most philosophy is frankly not congenial to choice. After all philosophy is about knowing, or more recently analyzing, not doing and choice is about doing. Most philosophy is about knowing reality, or at least knowing the limits to knowing, but even the most radical skeptic knows something. There's always something left in the cookie jar. A few equations, linguistic bits and pieces, scientific probabilities. To doubt everything would take us back to Descartes' doubting self and no one wants to go down that twisty path a second time.

Most traditional philosophy, from the pre-Socratics to the end of German Idealism with Kant, Schopenhauer, Hegel and debatably Nietzsche[1], has been about knowing reality including epistemology (knowing the limits of knowing), getting at the essence of things which means articulating first principles, illuminating eternal realities, reducing complexities to their simple component parts, tracing phenomenon back to its origins. Recently philosophy has taken a less comprehensive, more specialized approach acting as a sounding board and support system for other areas of human expertise. Science, psychology, language and linguistics, popular culture, feminism, racism, sociology and political science, among other areas of interest have replaced the broader vision of previous philosophers. Analysis rather than knowledge (already well mined by the specialized disciplines above) has become the postmodern *modus operandi*, while wisdom the original goal of philosophy is an archaic embarrassment for most analytical and many continental philosophers. Exceptions who view contemporary society like a wise Gandalf might view a troubled Middle Earth include: Habermas the reigning European voice of liberal (quasi-Marxist?) reason, Luce Irgray the perceptive French feminist, Cornel West the philosophic voice for Dr. King and radical social change, and Charles Taylor the Canadian Catholic sociologist-philosopher who opens the window onto Paul's Love still hard at work in the secular world. Alain Badiou, a remarkable Platonic Mao-Marxist - a what? Who places Truth and Justice in certain historical... *John?*... Yes Lord?[2]... *Move on...* Yes Lord... Actually not a bad group and there are more that come to mind as I write: the later Derrida, Hannah Arendt,

---

[1]   Despite Nietzsche's scathing critique of previous philosophies his monolithic principle of the Will-to-Power would replace previous comprehensive philosophies, and open the way for the European Existentialists Kierkegaard, Heidegger, and Sartre, and the American Pragmatists.

[2]   The occasional interruptions by what I've called the inner Voice of love (Jesus for me) have been a distraction for some, while others religious and non-religious appreciate the conversational ambiance they create.

bell hooks another feisty black voice with Cornell West, but that's enough. Once again I apologize to lay readers for the references to obscure thinkers, and to philosophers for the sketchy treatment of some of the seminal figures in modern thought. However since none of the traditional and postmodern thinkers we've mentioned dwell on choice as the critical gateway to Paul's Love we'll continue our journey with James.

As I was saying choice is restless with too much knowing, too much analysis, too much speculation. Pragmatism wants philosophy to get on with life leaving its mistakes in the past. Pragmatism looks for new challenges; looks to the future not the past. Pragmatism is wedded to choice, to change, for better or worse. As James writes, "No particular results then... only the attitude of looking away from first things, principles, 'categories,' supposed necessities; and of looking to the last things, fruits, consequences, facts." (*Pragmatism*, p.32).

Ah but consequences for what? To whose benefit? Whose loss? It's not that pragmatists were unmindful of the goals towards which their methods tended. James' concern is to change the world in ways which John Stuart Mill ("our leader"), the utilitarian who preached the Enlightenment gospel of the "greatest good for the greatest number", would have approved. Rorty spells out the common pragmatic goal, "The most distinctive and praiseworthy human capacity is our ability to trust and to cooperate with other people, and in particular to work together to improve the future." (*Philosophy and Social Hope*; P. xiii) Rorty like James and Dewey proposed working in piecemeal practical ways within a democratic framework toward a more just and humane society. This pragmatic goal would seem at first glance to be consistent with Paul's Love and the Dali Lama's compassion. Pragmatism's piecemeal approach, which resolves problems as they arise, rather than imposing an ideal order as Plato's *Republic*, or Marx's Communist state, or even a particular paradigm of the kingdom of heaven does, seems well suited to the gentle, personal tone of Paul's Love.

But can the goal of a just and humane democratic society be reconciled with a pragmatic methodology? If practical results are posited as the essential criterion for truth, who is to say which consequences are desirable and which are not? As Marx, Nietzsche, Foucalt and a variety of tough-minded post-modern thinkers maintain, the question of who defines workability or usefulness is critical. And while I agree with tender-minded humanists like Habermas, Gadamer and feisty anti-Platonic liberal Popper, in their more hopeful view of human communication's ability to promote emancipatory goals that American pragmatists would applaud, the question remains; is the open-ended, value-free methodology Pragmatism endorses compromised by having goals *per se?* In other words haven't James, Dewey and Rorty already defined practical consequences – workability - as that which promotes pre-established goals? Would Nietzschean goals of the rights of the leader, the superman, the genius, over the resentful mob be acceptable? And if not why not? It worked for the great empire builders of history. Are comparatively short lived modern democracies to be judged as more workable than the millennium long Egyptian and Chinese dynasties? Was child labor unworkable? Or colonialism?

My concern is not that the pragmatic methodology of workability is open to interpretation by various power factions in society (a major post-modern concern) but that the proposed goals (a more just and loving democratic society) involve value-judgments made prior to, and apart from, the problem-solving process. Value-judgments (rejecting child labor and colonialism) reflect absolutes of some sort, that remind us of the enduring realities of Plato (Justice and Truth), and the pre-sensate principles of Kant which notably include treating each human being as an end in him or herself. Rather than a means in the service of society or even a holy church the absolute values or principles that Pragmatism, and most other contemporary philosophies have rejected still roam the corridors of western thought like the ghost of God-future that haunted dedicated humanists like Nietzsche and Heidegger. Though barren corridors still unobtrusively connect the various bustling laboratories and classrooms of academia the ancient absolutes - "the metaphysics of presence," "the ghost in the machine" - still silently partner the academic endeavors of modern philosophers.

Let us wrestle for bit with James' example that if he is lost in the forest truth means finding a path to an inhabited house for directions, rather than contemplating the essence or nature of the woods. If what I've referred to as absolutes are not to be found in the woods perhaps they may be found in James. Why we would bother to solve what we perceive to be problems, in one way and not another, depends again not only on who is doing the evaluating and solving, but on the importance we place on the various elements in what we perceive to be problematic. Is it the woods having the problem or is it James? The woods seem not to have a problem with James's being lost; in fact it might flourish without his and others continuing presence. And while it is true, as James implies, that truth - a path to safety - leaves us free to pursue our lives and make more pragmatic choices the first order of business is to make a choice that will preserve James' life. At crunch time it is human life that is at stake, not the possibility of making more creative choices farther on. If a forest ranger should attempt to find James in the woods, he or she might risk their own well-being to preserve James's life, not only as a problem-solving organism adapting to its environment (Dewey), but as a organism, - a person? - of importance for whom they might, if pressed, be willing to risk their own life! Which we might note would seem to privilege Paul's Love above concern for one's own much valued life. Conceptually it can be argued that such a rescue effort fits with any of several problem-solving scenarios, but practically - pragmatically - it is hard to avoid the conclusion that transient choices have been made to serve something - someone - of enduring even of absolute value? In this case Jame's life.

Without attempting to place absolutes in a more systematic philosophic setting I would suggest that absolutes, however vague the allusion, still linger in our consciousness. Despite a relativistic post-modernism which reflects many significant aspects of our culture, people still act in their personal, political and religious commitments as if absolutes existed; absolutes for which they are in certain circumstances willing to sacrifice life itself. I'm not suggesting all absolutes are worthy of such sacrifices. More often than not they are used to inflict sacrifice on the other person or cause. The rhetoric of collective sacrifice (of "redemptive violence" in Walter Wink's telling phrase) stresses the laudable intentions of ones' own group but the reality of collective absolutes is that generally they seek to preserve their own existence by sacrificing their opponents. Successful soldiers, as general Patton noted aren't on the battlefield to die for their country, but to make damn sure the other guy dies for his. Suspect nationalistic, ethnic, racial, and religious absolutes are one of the major curses of our troubled planet. On the other hand leaders like Dr. King, Mikhail Gorbachev, Senator Ted Kennedy, Gandhi, the Dalai Lama, Dorothy Day and Mother Teresa adhered to absolutes that included human dignity, justice, and the peaceful resolution of national conflicts. Absolutes cut both ways but they cannot be ignored even in our changing pragmatic world.

II

While our concern lies mainly with Paul's Love, which is of course the absolute with which we are primarily concerned I can't resist a side trip to briefly explore the puzzling search for an intellectual absolute. Intellectual here meaning concerned with knowing and analysis, rather than making the right choices in life. Those who would keep their focus on our main concern, Paul's ethical absolute, love, may rejoin the discussion a few pages along in section IV.

Most post-modern thinkers reject even a whiff of absolutism i.e. the now archaic conflicting monolithic truth claims and grand narratives, which would lure us back to the earlier distracting appearance-reality, relative-absolute, conundrums. A few however like Paul Riceour (the preeminent French hermeneutic reconciler of opposing views), and theologians of course, accept some form of dualism that recognizes a two-story, or two-dimensional, reality in which the ultimate absolute, God, exists apart from (but involved in) human consciousness and the measurable universe. And while most contemporary philosophers lament the lingering linguistic influence of concepts such as "eternal", "absolute", "unlimited" preferring more earthy concepts: "timeworn", "partial", "relative", and "limited", each concept needs the opposing other to convey its own meaning. Timeworn, transitional, or some such phrase points to that which is not timeworn and transitional. Partial speaks of the whole, imperfect of the perfect, relative of the absolute. Limited leans toward the unlimited. Dismissing these differences, these counter concepts, as linguistic relics from a less enlightened era, doesn't answer the question why a creature that sees itself as limited, transitory and timeworn - all of which are partially true - can even make this distinction? How can we say there is no perfection, no absolutes, unless there is a suspicion that these terms have some meaning? Some reference, some reality toward which they point, however dimly and obliquely. We are limited beings - who think in terms of the whole! When Paul says, "Now I know only in part; then I will know fully," he has a sense even in his partial state of knowing that knowing fully is possible. He trusts that his present limited condition will lead to a fullness of knowledge later on. But even in this limited imperfect state he thinks in terms of completeness, of perfection. What the most balanced of Existentialists, Carl Jaspers, calls the "Comprehensive" or the "Encompassing." (*R. and Existence*, P.10) Otherwise Paul could not speak of knowing in part and knowing fully. Riceour and other believers see these apparent counter concepts (partial/ whole, imperfect/ perfect etc.) as accurately reflecting our search for the elusive realities toward which we tend.

Think of it! A speck in time our finite intellect can embrace the entire thirteen billion years of creation, from the Big Bang to whatever End Times scenario, scientific or religious, seems credible to each individual. The mind is able to grapple with the vast mysteries of infinitesimal quarks exploding through atoms and organisms, solar systems and galaxies into expanding space. Limited and fragmentary our consciousness is structured to organize experience as a totality, a comprehensive understanding of all the fragments, all the elements present at any given time. Ever changing yes, but ever comprehensive. Always we seek for the wider view, the whole truth. And always we fall short. Ah, but of what? Puzzling when you think about it. The content of thinking is partial, fragmentary, but the frame of our thinking is wholistic. And so we live in the confusing tension between the particulars of our perceptions and thoughts and the comprehensive context which is continually gathering parts into an ever expanding, or sometimes receding, whole. Imperfections hint at perfection. The timeworn tilts toward the eternal. On the receding horizon distant absolutes (Truth, Justice, Beauty and for many the Creator, God) draw our attention. Like clay ducks at a shooting gallery the proposed absolutes are continually being shot down - and continually reappear!

III

The most we can say so far is that absolutes (James's life is one) serve as a silent partner to the more visible pragmatic choices we make on behalf of Paul's Love. Absolutes are seen as a contributing, perhaps even a determining, factor, in directing our energies toward workable solutions to one problematic situation after another. And if the choices are workable i.e. if they are not just about getting our own way, but are patient, kind, and attentive to the other person's need, then we simply pursue our lives moving from one problematic situation to the next. We grow up at home loving our parents, siblings, and friends; go to schools to increase our capacities to understand and peacefully interact with, even care for, the widening world around us. Perhaps we marry and raise children whom we treat with patience and kindness. Or we take a partner whom we love and care for, work at a living which we judge to be beneficial to others. We become engaged in communal activities we judge to be consistent with Paul's Love. Religious, political, educational etc. We grow old loving those around us, and eventually we die. Our attempts to act lovingly may not have produced the results we'd intended, but if we have not been arrogant, or resentful, Paul says our love will outlast all knowledge, all mysteries, and all prophetic powers.

Paul does not insist our love should be well received or effective, only that we "have love." Three times he uses the expression to "have love" emphasizing that the love he speaks of is accessible, is something that we may in some sense possess as our own i.e. our free choice. "If I speak in… but do not have love, I am a noisy gong", "if I have all faith... but do not have love, I am nothing," "If I give away all my possessions... but do not have love, I gain nothing." Then he goes on to treat love as a separate entity, with a life of its own. "Love is patient, love is kind, love is not envious... It does not insist on its own way; it is not irritable or resentful." In the first instance love would seem to be an attitude that in some sense resides within us, something within our control. At the same time it has a life of its own, it exists apart from the individual or any individuals who "have love." The first usage would seem more easily associated with choice. We "have love" that we may use at our discretion to benefit others. Or not as we choose. The second usage points to that which comes to us apart from our will, choice, or control. These two aspects of Paul's love leave us much to ponder but the pieces are not yet ready to be put together. We are feeling our way slowly, testing the various elements of love against one another - and against our conceptual understanding and life experiences - before drawing further inferences.

IV

If the initial rock of Paul's Love launched us out into the turbulent river of life to the first stone - Levinas's Other, Buber's Thou - we have now stepped gingerly onto the stone of pragmatic choice balanced awkwardly by vaguely defined absolutes. Here we may rest momentarily to stabilize our footing by reference to the ordinary realities of life.

If Paul's Love is, at least, a matter of choosing to act in ways that are patient and kind to others, then we must assume that love is grounded in everyday reality. Paul does not talk of love in an abstract or purely spiritual sense. He mentions handing over one's body to be burned and giving up one's possessions, as if love were in direct contact with the surrounding sociopolitical environment where Christians were occasionally martyred in the great Roman amphitheaters and coliseums, and where there was already a tradition among believers of giving their possessions to the poor. For Paul love occurs in a particular historical context, but since he says love will endure, that love never ends, we must assume he meant for love to be relevant at other times and places. Today the Roman Coliseum is filled with tourists, and only a select few are called on to give up their possessions (which Paul says wasn't the point anyway). But love is still an option, a choice.

Since each person is thrown-into, in Heidegger's terminology, a unique set of worldly circumstances the choices made on love's behalf will vary. A stock broker for example like our son Steve, who is aware of the moral restrains on investing in tobacco or arms manufacture works hard to provide for our old age, coaches John's and Emily's basketball teams, and keeps in close touch with his twin brothers, two sisters and their growing families will make one set of choices. Our daughters Chris and Wendy, who work with Hispanic immigrants and the mentally and physically disabilitied respectively, and have demonstrated on behalf of peace, women's rights, and gay rights have made their choices. Occasionally as a family we discuss our differences, sometimes sharply, but because we respect each other's choices, and the varied talents and interests that went into those choices, even the differences seem to enhance our family unity. Amazing when I think of it; three strong free enterprise capitalists who value Ayn Rand for stressing excellence and responsibility, and who usually vote Democratic; two bleeding heart liberal social workers; a Swiss peacenik "Raging Granny" mother, and a left leaning charismatic Catholic-Quaker dad. All living peacefully under one roof when we get together. Like other grandparents Betty and I are grateful that Paul's Love has increasingly found its way into our family life. Not perfect, still struggling, but still present, still valued above being arrogant, resentful or getting one's own way.

At this point my thought forks in two directions. First while Betty and I are grateful for our close-knit middle – upper middle - class family what of the great sea of poverty and injustice that surrounds these islands of well-intentioned loving family life? Didn't Jesus speak sharply of such self-contained islands of harmony and love, saying even the heathen love those who love them? Didn't he say one must hate one's closest relatives? What of poverty, suffering, and war? How does Paul's Love cope with that? Before grappling, in parts II and III, with institutional evil however we must pursue the wisdom and logic of love in its more restricted individual setting.

The second fork in my thinking takes us back to our ongoing argument where I take it as established that an essential aspect of Paul's Love is choice and that choice is never made abstractly i.e. never made apart from a particular individual acting in a particular set of circumstances. Whether it is Paul himself acting in a first century Roman Judeo-Christian setting; or one of our five children acting in their middle-class American early third millennium milieu; shaped, as Paul was, by their family background, socio-economic status, prior choices, individual natures and interests, etc. As long as all goes well, given the commitment to Paul's Love, each individual's life will unfold as a series of pragmatic choices made to resolve problematic situations. No other decisive factors need be involved in the basic thrust of a life that is able to continue to act with kindness and patience in all circumstances.

Despite loud calls from zealous believers that all the others need to get on board; that no one can survive without God, without Jesus as their personal savior, there are people today who survive quite well without a religious faith. Certainly many humanists with varied political agendas have consistently responded to the prodding of love's elusive logic. Michail Gorbachev, the last and greatest Russian Communist leader; the gentle Scotch skeptic David Hume; Albert Camus; Thoreau and John Stuart Mill; John Dewey; Carl Sagan and Rosa Luxenberg, the Communist martyr who said if she couldn't dance she wasn't joining the Revolution, are only a few names that spring to immediate mind. Many of our friends like Kitty Clark, who worked as a social worker in south Boston for most of her adult life; Drs. W.T.M. and Elizabeth Johnson, who've picketed and protested for over forty years on behalf of civil rights and environmental causes, have each lived loving productive lives. Each has chosen in one situation after another to adhere to Paul's Love. Though they would not use those terms and certainly reject the rest of his theology.

But what if choice breaks down and even with the best intentions one is not able to be patient and kind? Ah! Now things get interesting.

Here the argument quickens. Here another aspect of Paul's Love that exists in itself beyond our reach emerges, and we must examine another facet of the glittering gem that is Paul's Love as we reach out toward the next tippy stone – gift.

Chapter

V

Paul's Love as Gift

"If everything which appears has come as given - given only in consciousness if you want, but always given - it implies the phenomena cannot appear without appearing to be given to me."

Jean-Luc Marion, French Philosopher

"I want to focus my interest on the phenomenological dimension of giveness, first of all and in general... Later we could ask why some phenomenon appear as more given, or given in higher degree that others, and we may call them paradoxical or saturated phenomena."

Jean-Luc Marion,
(*God, the Gift, and Postmoderism*; p. 57)

I

One reason Paul honors love above faith and hope is because while faith is rooted in sacred events in the past, and hope waits on the future, love like a common garden tool is at hand this very day. While past and future are beyond our reach love is available in the present moment as a tool, as a choice we may exercise or not as we wish. And yet for some of us in an ongoing way, and all of us at times, the tool becomes rusty, broken - unusable. Despite our best efforts to be patient and kind we are in fact impatient and arrogant. When those around us respond in kind we grow frustrated by the tool's ineffectiveness and we turn away from Paul's Love. Envy, resentment, and anger crowd out our good intentions. The inner landscape darkens; the night is cold; but eventually on the dark horizon, on the margins of awareness there are signs of hope. The air grows warm, once again the world comes into focus, and we're able to pick up the garden tool to nurture the struggling life around us. This elusive element – sunlight – that revives our ability to adhere to Paul's Love comes to us not as tool easily accessible but from a distance as gift. Both of course, tool and sunlight, contribute to the growth of the growing plant.

Sunlight as gift is not meant as a metaphor for God since any theocentric premise might well funnel us into a constricted theology where faith and love are in danger of being equated, and the tension between the two established by *Corinthians 13* is diminished. Equating faith in God with love as Paul noted does not necessarily strengthen love. Even the faith to move mountains may fall short. Paul's Love it would appear is quite capable of standing on its own.

Rather than run the risk of having Paul's practical love (patience and kindness) being co-opted into a wider world view, I prefer to view our metaphorical sunlight- as-gift as independent of any particular theology. Astute and devout theologians such as, have after all variously justified the imprisonment and execution of heretics, the ravages of war, capital punishment (Augustine, Aquinas, Luther and Reinhold Niebuhr, nuclear deterrence (Reinhold Niebuhr) and the demonization of contending religious communities. Even Paul writing on the role of slaves, women, homosexuals is open to criticism. The dangers of identifying love with any individual's or any faith community's interpretation of God's will are well documented. Which is not to dismiss the claims of religion, which are yet to be considered, but simply to be wary of any theology or church teaching which would modify Paul's stringent requirements for a simple pragmatic love. How far this practical faith in love extends into public life will be our concern in the final two sections of the book.

By gift I would indicate, following Jean-Luc Marion the contemplative French Catholic philosopher, everything that comes to us apart from our own consciousness and the choices that flow from our consciousness i.e. everything that comes to us either from the surrounding world, or from the secluded psyche that is inaccessible to our immediate awareness. The love we receive from others is of course beyond our control. It comes to us as gift. A secondary factor in our own loving the gift of love we receive from others invites, but does not compel, our response. As Machiavelli recognized one may chose to love others; one cannot control whether others will love us. Which is why the wise ruler depends on force which he can control, rather than the good will of his subjects, which he cannot. Which explains why force, rather than Paul's Love is so often the decisive factor in political affairs. Our immediate concern however is not with the thorny issue of power, law, and love, but with Paul's Love which comes to us as gift.

The routine events of everyday living often bring us the gift of love. A chance meeting, a common task, and a shared tragedy, all may bring us face to face with the gift of the Other, which may lead to friendship, romance, or help in time of need. As we become sensitive to the random events of ordinary life we come upon unforeseen opportunities for Paul's Love to blossom.

While our primary focus remains on Paul's Love as it relates to our interaction with other human beings, I might briefly mention a few of the gifts we receive apart from our contact with our fellow human beings that are supportive of our efforts to be patient and kind to others. By expanding our self-absorbed territorial boundaries these varied gifts introduce us to a wider world; a world apart from our particular woes and worries. A clear night sky, Sandhill cranes rising from a meadow under the Sandia mountains in Albuquerque, and the endless ocean off the Jersey shore, all renew our spirits, reminding me of Hildegaard of Bingen's vision of the fiery arms of love embracing the whole creation. A favorite piece of music or work of art may also help dispel the negative feelings that keep us from attending to those we're meant to care for. Dreams, visions, and meditative practices like Yoga, deep breathing, and letting the geese of fleeting thoughts squawk and flap their way across our concentrated gaze on the wide sky behind, have been a special gift for many.

While Freud explored the basement of our unconscious lives others like Jung, Joseph Campbell, the scholar of the cultural unconscious, and Tibetan Buddhists delighted in the wonders stored in the attic unconscious. Mandalas, symbolic images, and a variety of spiritual companions (archetypes, spirit guides and angels) visit the consciousness of those receptive to their elusive presence. Without these auxiliary gifts from the natural world, from the creative world of art and music, and from the spooky world of visions and dreams, many of us would be unable to respond to the high calling of Paul's Love. We too need love to love. Love from others, but also love and comfort from Hildegaard of Bingen's fiery arms of love holding the whole creation in a warm embrace. For believers, like myself, in dark times we're like wounded lambs crying to be lifted up and held against the shepherd's breast. Creation's fiery arms of love, the good shepherd's embrace; two images that come as gift to keep us faithful to the intent of *Corinthians 13*.

Perhaps a few brief examples may help clarify the odd notion of Paul's Love as gift. Let us assume Mother Teresa becomes ill in her work for the poor in Calcutta. First she must see a doctor; then she can return to her work. A second example; at age forty after twenty years of teaching elementary children, and helping raise our five children, my old neurotic patterns surface in mid-life burn out and I seek help from a Jungian counselor once again. When I complete the therapy I return to my work and family life with renewed vigor. One last example. When Dorothy Day, a 1930's Depression era far left journalist with a dissolute Bohemian life-style, becomes depressed she turns to a higher power to give new meaning and direction to her life. In the first example no major change of inner attitude is required. Mother Teresa simply lends the experts her body to be healed, follows their guidance and hopefully returns to good health. Mother Teresa, I'm sure as a devout Christian, also prayed during her illness, but no basic attitudinal changes were required for her recovery. Atheists and agnostics also lend their bodies to the healing experts hoping to return to good health, using the resources of friendship and their own belief systems as auxiliary aids to recovery. In my case I had to give over more than my body into the care of others. I had to entrust my impaired mental and emotional faculties to their expertise, that I might be rescued from the neurotic fears and resentments that were working against Paul's Love. These destructive tendencies were making me arrogant, envious, and resentful of others on whom I projected the unloving figures and forces within my own nature. Without therapy I was unable to recognize, let alone counter these negative tendencies to act in more loving ways. Not only was I entrusting my body into the healing hands of others, I entrusted my mind and emotions, to the companioning influence of Jung and David Hart, my insightful, caring counselor. Though I could be not be healed by others directly their guidance and influence provided the support I needed to recognize the negative tendencies within my own nature and utilize new insights and images to find a way back to normal living. Their support allowed me to cooperate with God's healing power to become a more loving father, teacher and friend.

The case of Miss Day is even more critical. Not only did she trust her body, mind, and emotions into another person's care, she risked her world-view, and inner aspirations which had provided her with her identity. Admitting that her previous understanding of existence had been limited she opened herself to God's comfort and guidance. The power from within-above that as George Fox, the first Quaker said, spoke to her condition, had become the organizing agent around whom she might build her life. But hers' is a different case than the first two examples. Here the very core of the person's life has shifted. One is no longer the person one had been. Even though one's physical appearance, and many habits and personality traits remain familiar to others, something at the center of one's life has changed. Even in counseling with Dr. Hart I did not lose my identity as a Christian with which I'd entered therapy. Even in therapy I was still a child of God; I was still a follower and friend of Jesus. The therapeutic experience only deepened my faith as I realized that God loved me at all levels of my being, unconscious as well as conscious. But Dorothy Day's conversion (or any conversion experience, Christian or otherwise) is an identity altering experience. The free-thinking radical reformer and dissolute Bohemian had become a beloved daughter of what Francis of Assisi called the Most High, she'd become a new creation in Christ. Her relationship with the higher power was not a blind surrender of her own powers of choice, as if she had become a automaton, a mere instrument, for God's will, but was a cooperative effort. Miss Day was being invited into a friendship with God in order to join God's efforts that God's will be done through Dorothy's transformed love for the poor whom she served the rest of her days on earth.

The only point I wish to draw out of our three representative examples is that when a person fails to act in accord with Paul's Love one is impelled by the nature of love itself to seek assistance. One cannot say I love God but I won't accept the gifts God sends to help me follow the path God intends for my life. Mother Teresa cannot avoid seeking healing if she wishes to continue to comfort those dying on the streets of Calcutta. I cannot claim to be a loving father unless I seek counseling that enables me to return to my accustomed role. Miss Day cannot keep faith with the poor unless she's willing to risk even her radically left wing political views, even her own identity, in an effort to become the kind and patient champion of the oppressed that she longs to be. That much of Miss Day's radical politics was preserved in her new role as a Catholic (not Communist) worker reminds me of the Jesuit mantra that God is above all, through all, and in all.

We seek cures for our physical ills and mental hang-ups not just to become well, but to serve the power of Paul's Love which connects us to those around us.

All three of our examples suggest that in order to follow Paul's Love we must allow ourselves to be cared for and loved by others. To love others, we must depend on others! Doctors, counselors, friends and family; we must humble ourselves to seek assistance from something outside the fascinating thoughts and aspirations circulating in our boney skulls. To give love we must first receive love. We must chose to give up for a time our own powers of choice. Mother Teresa listens to her doctor, I listen to Jung and Dr. Hart, and Dorothy Day listens to the inner voice of love who quickly emerges as Jesus, the Messiah, the saving triune God of Christian faith. Seeking to remain faithful, even given her many failures and weaknesses, Dorothy Day's cry for help has brought her into the presence of God, who becomes the new cornerstone of her life; the stepping stone on which believers depend as they pursue their way across the troubled waters of daily life.

Chapter
VI

Turning to a Higher Power

"The sun that shows itself is not the real sun."

Popol Vuh, Mayan sacred text

"There is a witness of and from God, in every conscience… [which] anchors it on the eternal rock; the meekness, patience, gentleness, humility, &c. which is not nature, but the gift of God, and the nature of the heavenly Giver."

Isaac Pennington, Quaker Theologian,1617-1679
(*Light Within and Selected Essays*, P. 12)

I

If one can walk in the light of Paul's Love without the assistance of the unseen Other, God, one has fulfilled the requirements of *Corinthians 13*. Energized by the power of Paul's Love one "delights to do no evil" to other human beings, either those near at hand or those at a distance in the wider world. But for some of us addictions, compulsions, and oppressive life situations, have impaired our ability to adhere to Paul's Love. The people around us have become sources of irritation and resentment. The faces for which Levinas insists we bear an ultimate responsibility have become tiresome, devious, and vindictive. We grow depressed, as Miss Day did, and frustrated by our inability to live up to the goals we have set for ourselves. The physical and therapeutic healing resources no longer work. As a last resort many have turned to an unseen authoritative source, a personal deity, force or principle beyond oneself for comfort and guidance. Like an alcoholic at her first A.A. meeting pressed to admit our failure to adhere to Paul's Love, we have cast our hope on a higher power. We have invited that power into our decision-making process and a partnership has begun which has sustained us over a lifetime.

It's important to note that a higher power that is founded on anything other than Paul's Love is not consistent with Paul's clearly stated opinion that without love everything else, even faith and hope, is as nothing. A God of glory and power, all knowing, righteous and just, and the final judge of human behavior, who is without love, who is not patient and kind, would not be consistent with the one value that Paul prizes above all others. Such a God, Paul implies, would be as nothing. Those of us who have appealed to a higher power to enable us to love, welcome God's presence in our lives in ways that are consistent with Paul's Love. To become arrogant, or boastful, or seek our own will on behalf of the newly acknowledged higher power would break faith with Paul's Love. On the other hand we must not restrict God's movement in our lives, but must trust that God will act through us in ways that though they may seem strange at times are consistent with Paul's Love.

Otherwise we limit the higher power's ability to effect real change in our lives, and end up replaying our old ethical CDs under a new label.

The dilemma between the ethical demands of Paul's Love and the theological demands of obedience to God's will, is one believers have wrestled with since Job. The difference between believing philosophers, such as Plato, Descartes, Kant who "denied knowledge to make room for faith", Kierkegaard, James, Levinas, and Buber, and humanistic thinkers is that for those who trust in a higher power the issue is a real issue. There is a real unseen Other being addressed or related to. The humanist may consider the various options available to Abraham as he wrestles with the decision whether to preserve his son's life or obey God's command, but for the humanist there is no real wrestling, no real choice, because for the humanist there is no real higher power. Since there is no God there can be no serious discussion of God's will. What had been for Abraham a riveting dilemma becomes an intellectual exercise if God is viewed as a cultural concept which one may evaluate at second hand.

II

The initial act of turning to God, trusting God to be more than a concept, is a very special moment. It reminds me of the later Heidegger's "clearing" in the tangled forest of our flawed and shallow ordinary existence where we wait on that which answers our thirst for authenticity; for Non-Being in the midst of a multitude of particular beings. It is a time of giving over of one's existence, one's self, into the unseen hands of what so many have called the living God, master of the universe, spirit of love, the lord of life. Up to now God has been presented as an option available to those seeking to walk in the ways of Paul's pragmatic practical love. A conceptual possibility much like my understanding of romantic love before I fell in love with Betty Jean., after which the love poems of Shelly and Keats no longer seemed stilted and extravagant. But God comes to us as so much more than an intellectual option or a quasi-ethical supporting agent in our struggles to lead a good and decent life.

Placing myself at God's disposal I find the quiet eyes of God looking, speaking metaphorically, not past me to those I would care for, enlisting me in the divine plan to renew the creation in love, but looking at me! John. Just John. "Beloved of God." And I am overwhelmed that the Creator, the Spirit behind all life, who spoke to Abraham, Sarah, and Hagar; to the prophets Amos and Jeremiah; through, and in, Jesus of Nazareth, should look upon so insignificant and unworthy a creature. Every day since I first encountered this loving God, over forty years ago, I have been in awe of the Most High God (St. Francis of Assisi's term) who has bent so low to address God's lowly subject. And I know I am loved and cared for, cherished and valued. I turned to God as a possibility, an option, and over time I found God to be love and more love, and more love, till there is no end to the love I sense coming from the One who is love.

III

A few days later, reflecting on the last paragraph, I sense the ongoing argument has been interrupted – shattered - by the intrusive intensity of the unseen Thou, and I worry that the intrusive Other may reorient our discussion around a theocentric worldview. I worry that the living God may become an "It", a symbol, an abstraction, a movable concept placed in various unsuitable settings. Aquinas' "Supreme Being", Barth's "Wholly Other", and Plotinus's Neo-Platonic "The One" have a visceral reality that lies beyond the arguments and words themselves. If we have been in a similar relationship to the Compassionate Mystery they honor we will be moved as well; not by their arguments but because their primary experience matches in some way our own.

To the worshipping believer the thought of God as an object of knowledge, a primary concept, will seem limiting. Necessary at times, but limiting. And if God is indeed a higher power how could one not relate to that power with some expression of thanksgiving, praise, and worship? If we have been moved by shimmering pink charcoal gray sunsets, towering snow-tipped peaks, and star- sprinkled darkness how could we not be moved by the one we believe to be the creator of all these wonders? How could we *not* adore the one who has brought the universe into being? Every blossom every galaxy.

The mystical theologians; Dionysius the Areopagite, Meister Eckhart, John of the Cross, and currently Jean-Luc Marion, the French religious phenomenologist, tell us God is beyond God; that every reference to God, as omnipotent, holy, righteous, merciful, even loving, can only suggest the plenitude of what lies beyond our limiting conceptions of God. Not because God is elusive but because God is ever present, overwhelming, pervasive. God's plenitude overflows as the gifts of life, breath, and a wondrous universe distant as the far sky, close at hand as a lover's embrace, a friendly smile, simply overwhelms our conceptual capacities. The wonder is as Heidegegger exclaimed that *anything* should exist. Existence itself is the mystery that leads many to seek the sovereign source. Our limited minds thirst for but cannot comprehend the "fullness," the "completeness", of God's plenty, of which Paul's speaks. "Above all, through all, in all," creating, sustaining and redeeming the entire creation!

Seven billion human beings – each one created individually and cared for lovingly! Who can grasp it? God, for many like Marion and David Tracy, an insightful American Catholic hermeneutic thinker, is a "saturated phenomenon" who permeates existence, like sunlight against which we must constantly shade our eyes. And yet this Compassionate Mystery, this blazing love, the creator of heaven and earth, is the same inner voice of love who speaks to each of us in our times of need. However awesome this blazing love may be when I see God "face to face," when I "know fully even as I have been fully known," still God will be patient and kind, not boastful, rude or arrogant. A thin thread in a troubled world, beset by systematic violence, greed, lust, and sporadic horrors, Paul's Love leads us home at last into the care of the one who made and sustains us. Who is as patient and kind to each of us as a mother or father delighting in their only child. We are each one of us the joy of God's desire! Treasured and loved beyond measure.

Chapter
VII

Glimpses of a Wider World

"One must avoid… the drive to systematize… To render any totality system present is to efface the fragment, the distinct and potentially explosive image in favor of some larger architectonic of which the fragment is now made a part… Let go of the hope for any totality system whatever. Focus instead on the explosive, marginal, saturated… fragments of our heritages… Remove them from their seemingly coherent place in the grand narratives we have imposed upon them. Learn to live joyfully… in the great fragments we do indeed possess."

David Tracy, American Catholic Theologian
(*God, Gift..*p.178-9)

"The Master of the Universe gives us glimpses, and only glimpses. It is for us to open our eyes wide."

Chaim Potok, *My Name is Asher Lev*

I

Pondering the mystery of God as creator of heaven and earth, of all that is seen *and* unseen, and the still small voice of love that speaks to each human soul on earth I become aware of the spooky interactions that have shaped my life. The oceans of darkness and light in the ER, my first encounter with Jesus, the inner vision during the guided imagery of a Dream Walk among Native Americans and others dancing at Acoma of a cosmic Circle-Without-End, the inner voice of love saying "I want you to become a Catholic" and years later, "I give you the whole world to fill your heart". Early Friends called these peak experiences "Openings;" glimpses of a wider world, an unseen reality, that lies beyond our ordinary understanding.

How are we to treat these blessed moments philosophically? Are they windows onto reality? Or illusions? Can they be utilized in a reasoned and comprehensive worldview? If so how? On the one hand openings may be viewed as intuitive, personal, and irrelevant to the common body of reliable knowledge. Interesting, but unverifiable. Mystical and vaporous. Anecdotal. Such a view would, I believe, unduly dismiss compelling evidence for non-sensate spiritual reality. The religious experience of billions including Moses, Jesus, Mary Magdalene, Paul, the Buddha, and Muhammad would be reduced to fantasy.

At the other extreme such openings may be transcribed into theological systems that presume to explain every facet of reality. A riveting religious experience does not however, provide an unerring comprehensive map of reality. My encounter with Jesus in my mid twenties radically altered my understanding of reality but I still wrestle with the common dilemma of God's justice in an unjust world; the problem of evil and innocence. Like a significant minority of Christian thinkers – like Kierkegaard, and the T.S. Eliot of the *Wastelands* and *Four Quartets* I resist a systematic theocentric interpretation of reality. As Kierkegaard cautioned, "System and finality are pretty much one and the same, so much so that if the system is not finished there is no system... A system which is not quite finished is an hypothesis... A persistent striving to realize a system on the other hand, is still a striving... not for nothing... but for truth." (*Unscientific Postscript*, Hong and Hong?, p.195-6). Eliot concurs, referring at the end of the *Wastelands* to, "These fragments I have shored against my ruin" concluding *East Coker* with the same note of fragmented persistent striving:

> Old men ought to be explorers
> Here and there does not matter
> We must be still and still moving
> Into another intensity
> For a further union, a deeper communion
> Through the dark cold and the empty desolation,
> The wave cry, the wind cry, the vast waters
> Of the petrel and the porpoise. In my end is my beginning.

Similar fragments of ultimate reality, what Quakers call Openings, anchor the faith, not only for Christians, but for all the major religions. The voice of YHWH speaking to Moses, the female disciples' encounter with the risen Jesus, the Enlightenment of Buddha, Allah dictating the *Koran* to Muhammed in the cave; all when articulated in faith statements focus the lives of millions of believers. The creed I recite as a Catholic during Mass reminding me of my own encounter with Jesus gathers me with those who have a similar commitment to Jesus as truly human, truly divine. For us Jesus is Christ, the Messiah, one in being with the creator. It's a statement of faith in the primary truth claim, the saving narrative, adhered to by most Christians, but it does not bind me to any particular theology. Accepted by theologians as diverse as Aquinas, Luther, and Leonardo Boff, the noted Liberation theologian, the Trinitarian Apostles' Creed reflects the foundational Openings – revelations – of Christianity. It's by such primal assumptions that the world religions distinguish themselves from one another, while theologies tend to identify the various elements within a particular faith community. Liberal Catholics may gravitate toward Karl Rahner, Gutierrez, or Mary Radford Ruether; conservative Catholics take solace in von Balthasar, Allen Drury, or Cardinal Ratzinger. Doctrinal statements present the core beliefs of any faith community. They are the defining truth claims of a particular tradition. Theologies, are individual interpretations of these primal claims presenting a more detailed comprehensive view of reality.

Theology faces two ways. First of course it faces the intended object of its interest – the unseen Other, our sovereign source - God. Second, theology faces its audience, the faith community and the world at large. Facing its audience theology must communicate its understanding of the divine through language: words, arguments, and style. As a reasoned articulation of faith theology does not automatically evoke its subject – God – but allows us "to conceive its formal possibility." The word God, stands in for the reality it intends, just as the word "tree" signifies a physical tree. God as a concept, a word, is, in Buber's terms, an "It" rather than the Thou that evokes worship, praise, and obedience. Though Buber has referred to God as the ultimate Thou; the only Thou who cannot become an it, once in place the word "God" does take on a life of its own. Conceptual systems that grow up around the key words - Jesus, Christ, God, sin, peace, discipleship, Spirit etc. - are subject to the limitations of language, human reasoning and human bias. Once written they become text, presenting themselves for the varied interpretations of whoever reads them. Still in the "clearings" of our tangled individual forests where Openings occur words are spoken that come from what a New York poet whose name escapes me called an "inarticulate source". For some the source is a figure who may be addressed but not seen - well, except for that one time, and even then, at the most real moment of my life, I would not say this is the way Jesus must appear to others, but only this is the way Jesus appeared to me. To Teresa of Avila Jesus appeared a child coming down to meet her as she was walking – really, not in a dream – up the staircase in her convent. To another believer I know Jesus appeared as a companion who sits beside her at the piano as they play duets together.

It's frustrating, of course, that these riveting glimpses of the divine milieu do not lend themselves more easily to our language forms; that they are so difficult to capture in our webs of reason; our theologies. But if they *were* more easily conveyed in words, in a definitive worldview, there would be no need to seek the reality of the divine nature apart from language. The words and ideas would be enough. One could worship a particular theology or scripture itself rather than the One of whom scripture speaks.

II

But if Openings, those riveting experiences on which doctrinal statements and theologies are based, are considered apart from their psychological and theological implications what have we left? Fleeting glimpses of a wider spiritual realm? Exactly! My varied personal Openings - some more vertical, more God centered, others more horizontal, more relational as in the ER - as well as the foundational Openings of Moses, Mary Magdalene, Paul, Buddha, and Mohammed - may well be, not comprehensive revelations of ultimate reality, but glimpses of the vast unseen unmeasured universe which impinges from time to time on our constricted consciousness. If we know, as science tells us, only five percent of the measurable physical universe, why not assume that even after all the revelations the world religions bring us, more remains to be known? Given the wealth of Openings humanity has already experienced, a portion, perhaps even the greater portion of the spiritual riches eventually available, remains unrevealed? Paul speaks of our present understanding as "partial," saying that "now we see in a mirror dimly, then we will see face to face." Here in *Corinthians 13* - unlike another celebrated passage where he equates adulthood with Christian maturity – Paul depicts our mature understanding as childish in the face of the completeness to come. That our present understanding is partial, childish, and dim does not make it wrong. Only incomplete.

Paul lived in obedience to the Openings he did receive. Throughout his long ministry Paul depended, not on a comprehensive theology, but on these ongoing Openings (that Jesus was the risen Messiah come to initiate God's kingdom on earth, that Jesus was alive in every believer, that God's other world... *John?*... Yes Lord?... *Move on*..... Yes Lord... Paul's Openings shaped by the needs of the faith communities he was addressing became his theology.

Paul's Openings initiated by the Holy Spirit guided him in planning his missionary travels to Antioch, Corinth, and Rome. Henry Nouwen called these Openings "the inner Voice of love", while Paul himself spoke of "Spirit of Jesus" as his guide and comfort during his strenuous ministry. Whatever it's called the Holy Spirit is still the elusive problematic factor in any Christian theology; the factor that enlivens the other two components of the Trinity. It's the Holy Spirit who invites believers into communion with God the Father (and Mother for some) and Christ the Son of God.

Later in the fullness of knowledge we may see the connections that reconcile the revelations of Moses, the Enlightenment of Buddha, Christ's Resurrection, and the Oneness of Allah. *Corinthians 13* allows for such a hope, but it does not prevent us, as it did not prevent Paul, from announcing the good news that we do know. Nor from continuing to celebrate the varied specifics of our particular tradition. Nor from sharing with others the particular truth claims associated with our faith. I have been touched by God through the presence and companionship of the man who lived in Galilee who remarkably talked and ate with his followers three days after his death. How could I not want to witness to the love of my life? The everlasting joy of my heart? My friend, Rick McKinney, long time Buddhist and president of the Greater Philadelphia Buddhist Society is enamored of the eternal truths that flow from his Enlightenment. Rick is animated by the compassionate Buddha within his own nature to share his faith with others. How could he not be? Must our different glimpses of the eternal realm around us, be a source of dissension? Rather than tolerance, even appreciation? Are the spiritual skies not vast beyond our imagining?

In any event however we access the state of our present spiritual knowledge, are we not impelled by the teachings of our own traditions to be patient and kind to those with who we disagree?

III

Of course if truth claims are assumed to be, not glimpses of the eternal, but *the* definitive vision of reality, then I must press my claims more vigorously. If I know what the whole truth is then my view of reality diminishes contending views, and I must correct, like a good scientist or historian would, the erroneous views that others hold. Paul however, in agreement with Kierkegaard and T.S. Eliot, speaks of his knowledge as partial and incomplete; staking his life not on comprehensive knowledge but on faith in the sufficiency of the knowledge he does possess.

Let us look briefly at Paul's faith, which centers on the presumed return to life of a crucified Jew just outside Jerusalem in first century. Neither vague nor uncertain Paul does not preach a symbolic, or metaphorical, resurrection, but speaks unambiguously of the resurrection as a historical fact. Not merely a restitution of Christ's physical body but his physical body risen and transformed. Able to appear at will among his disciples, and yet physical enough to convince a doubting disciple of his return to life. Most main stream Christian thinkers, like the systematic German theologian Pannenberg and the English biblical scholar T. M. Wright who have argued at length for a historical resurrection, would agree. As I would. If Jesus did not return to life as more than a vision, a purely spiritual presence, then Christians are as deluded as Nietzsche, Bishop Sprong, and Robert Funk's Jesus Seminar, believe us to be. Our faith is not in faith itself as a purely internal event, but is in an outer historical event attested to by scripture and church tradition; confirmed by the experience of countless individual Christians. While I hold these quite orthodox views I would not, like some Christians, insist that only those with such views are Christians.

Marcus Borg and John Dominic Crossan, leading biblical scholars from the non-orthodox Jesus Seminar, for example, have insights into Jesus' radical concern for social justice, that are sorely needed by most main line and evangelical churches today.

Jesus appears to our diverse contemporary consciousness in various guises as prophet, role model, teacher, symbol of transformation, spirit guide, one of many divine incarnations, friend and companion as well as savior, Son of God, and second person of the Trinity. I would not wish to deny anyone access to the figure I revere above all others. When I'm tempted to press my witness to the risen Christ who interrupted my life over forty years ago beyond the limit set by Paul's patience and kindness, I'm reminded of a shy woman I met at a Catholic workshop on Jesus. Defending her unorthodox interpretation of Christ from my passionate evangelism, she gently protested, "Please - don't step on my journey." Her words ended the argument. What did I know of her struggles, her inner life, of how God was working in her soul? What did I know of the books, teachings, and images, which I find objectionable that were being used to bring her closer to the person she was created to be? Having made my witness to the Jesus I treasured how should I presume to judge her response?

IV

There are four, at least, advantages of depicting Openings as glimpses of a wider spiritual realm, rather than the defining centerpiece for a theocentric representation of reality. First, it's consistent with Paul's understanding of our present knowledge as partial, childish, and dim; as prelude to the completeness that lies ahead.

Second it encourages dialogue with other religious traditions. A dialogue in which we may come to appreciate the gnarly particulars of other faiths as well as the ethical and religious truths we hold in common. Nor should our varied religious expectations (in universal Enlightenment, the return – or coming - of the messiah, Allah's Paradise and Judgment etc.) become a matter of contention. Since we all wait for the resolution of our eschatological hopes we may, in the meantime, be kind and patient with each other's efforts to make sense of our common human destiny and not allow one's own religious hypothesis to become an occasion for coercing others to our expectation. Since none of us knows what the future will bring, each tradition is at liberty to pursue its own hypothesis; it's own particular hope for creation's culminating event.

The third advantage of not insisting that our truth, our way is the only way to the please God, is that it allows Paul's Love a life of its own free from the constraints of a constricting worldview, whether scientific, political, or religious. It allows the power working in us by whatever name to fulfill the ancient commandments to love God and our neighbor as ourselves. As Paul did it puts love not faith, works, or hope at the very center of our lives.

Finally, for the Christian, seeing Openings as glimpses of reality preserves the faith and hope that Paul spoke of as abiding (as coeternal) with love. Leaving others to their particular worldviews to promote Paul's Love as they see fit, the interpretation of Openings as glimpses of reality, rather than the defining premise for competing theocentric systems, Christians are free to vigorously pursue their own lives, buttressed by the traditional truth claims of faith and hope.

The integrity of love's two eternal companions is preserved, by insisting that faith and hope involve risk and uncertainty. Which, after all, is the point isn't it? To have faith in the resurrection and to hope for the impending cosmic springtime, the Kingdom of God on earth? If I knew all this, had certain knowledge, I wouldn't need faith, or hope. As it is I face each day together with my sisters and brothers all over the earth, often uncertain, fearful and anxious, but also hopeful that the particular wonders of my Christian faith will encourage me on the long slope of existence toward the unseen sun at the summit up ahead. Where the blazing presence of God lightens the path and warms the hearts of the children of light. A presence who dwells in the unapproachable splendor that is mirrored in the smallest act of mercy done on earth. AMEN.

Chapter

VIII

Paul's Love 101 in the Postmodern Classroom

"If philosophy is love of wisdom, it is also, and primarily, the wisdom of love.

Emmanuel Levinas

I

If I were introducing a university philosophy course on Paul's Love I might assume that students had come to absorb a common body of knowledge. That was certainly how students gathered in my college days. We took notes, pondered and argued among ourselves and with our professors the salient points being advanced, and carried into our later lives the main features of the knowledge we'd absorbed. Allowing for individual responses to the common teaching we'd received it was assumed philosophy majors especially would be receptive and eager for the wisdom being dispensed. Certainly the notable philosophers of the past make this assumption, i.e. they write in a general way to illuminate the truth they see in the realities around and within us. Plato unveils the elusive world of ideal forms that exists apart from the common sense world of appearances. Descartes, Hume and Kant examine knowable reality as it's perceived by the limitations peculiar to human nature, i.e. they focus not on what we perceive (ontology), but on how we perceive (epistemology). They focus on subjective rather than objective truth.

Later German idealists identify Kant's enigmatic ultimate truth, the unknowable content of perception – the thing-in-itself apart from its attributes of weight, shape, color etc. – as the blind striving will (Shopenhauer), the transcendent intellect or Spirit (Hegel), or the will to power (Nietzsche). But from the Pre-Socratics to Nietzsche, philosophers have not been shy about addressing receptive students who it is assumed have come to them for wisdom. One truth fits all, or else it isn't universal, isn't comprehensive, isn't true.

Recently however philosophers have become reticent about speaking in such a general way. Truth is seen to be partial and fragmented. Our human understanding of reality is limited by certain critical factors: language perhaps or scientific probabilities, hermeneutics and the politics of power, but in any case Introduction to Paul's Love 101 has been canceled this semester, while seminar courses in linguistics, trends in technology, popular culture, and art history, fill the vacuum. Nor would I challenge this decentralization of thought in the name of order, consistency or an archaic theocentric worldview. I'm at home in the pluralism of our postmodern era. It reminds me of the public debates in Athens to which Socrates, Plato, Aristotle and later, Paul, contributed their insights. To complain that the ancient and noble search for truth has been lost in the complexities and crassness of the times, is to assume that truth has outlived its usefulness; that modern minds do not relish, as Socrates, Plato, and Paul did, the contentious interaction of defending the truth that burned in their consciousness. Socrates and Paul we may recall chose martyrdom rather than relinquish their pursuit of wisdom.

Wittgenstein, in our era, gives away a huge family fortune in order to court truth unfettered by the demands of managing wealth. Kierkegaard forgoes the joys of marriage, and later on risks, even baits, public humiliation in pursue of truth.

Sartre, active in the French resistance, later becomes a quasi-Marxist to support his sympathies for the oppressed and marginalized poor. Women intellectuals including Simone Weil, Simone de Beauvoir, Virginia Wolfe, bell hooks (a special friend), and Luce Irigaray, are demeaned and trivialized for challenging the patriarchal intellectual tradition. Religious thinkers like Bonhoffer, the Dalai Lama, Gandhi, Simone Weil, and Dr. King risk their careers and lives to proclaim spiritual truths they hold to be more than local and partisan.

Not all philosophers were as admirable as Socrates and Simone Weil, who's worth Googling if she's new name. Heidegger, perhaps the most insightful philosopher of our century refused to explain his support of the Nazi regime even after the war. And yet his two excursions into the nature of Being - as Dasein (human existence, early Heidegger), and Being *per se*, aka non-Being - revitalized philosophic issues that thinking humans will wrestle with for decades. Jean Paul Sartre, whose personal courage I admire, emphasizing a few select aspects of Heidegger's far broader and more nuanced vision, seems restricted to a particularly intense period in post-war European intellectual history.

Though I trust a zeal for truth exists in our time, no less than it did among the Greeks, we can't assume an eager university audience is waiting to base their lives on a treatise on *Corinthians 13*. But if love is as privileged as Paul claims neither should it be presented as merely an ethical option, or an inspirational ideal reserved for special occasions like weddings and funerals. Having put to one side the first principles (self, science, Being and God) which were obstructing our understanding of Paul's Love, perhaps it's time for the philosophic splendor of Paul's Love to stand forth from its secluded presence in religious and domestic life.

And if an audience cannot be gathered collectively to ponder Paul's words of love freshly, Paul's Love must go in search of those who will listen to his Corinthian call to action.

II

Searching for my intended audience I realize that none of the people with whom I've shared the text, or was mindful of as I wrote, are students. Our five children are working at various jobs in either business or social services. One friend is a recently retired third grade teacher, another a psychotherapist in Boston, another a professional artist who paints by the Tanguy pond on a three-legged stool wearing a straw hat. Our immediate neighbors include a prison warden, a music teacher at a Friend's school, and a carpenter and construction worker. The devout lesbian couple on the far side of the ball field though ostracized by their Christian churches, still revere Jesus and maintain regular periods of meditation. Barbara works for *Women Against Rape* initiating conflict resolution programs in schools and community organizations. Diane is the contact person in West Philly for Penn State, providing scholarship opportunities for teenagers from the black and Latino ghetto. They live next door to Anne and Peter, Quaker pacifists, who are teachers and professional folk singers who've just returned from giving a month's worth of concerts in New Zealand. Joe from Middletown Friends Meeting is a part time farmer and works for a large agricultural supply company. This Sunday at our Quaker meeting we'll celebrate Dan Frysinger's 85th birthday. For decades Dan ran his own business, which made industrial belts for the shoe industry. Steve Trimble, another meeting friend is a retired banker. Kathy recently remarried, a psychologist, works for a local Norbetine parish coordinating adult catechism, Pre- Cana marriage preparation programs and retreats. My brother-in-law, in Champaign Illinois, taught public health, and psychiatry, at Northwestern and Harvard. An ex-roommate and fellow philosophy major from Haverford, Norris and I still argue the pros and cons of Christian love and compassionate self- interest. I will call him next week to resume our conversation on his response to the book I am writing, and that you - hopefully - are reading. The point of this rambling litany of neighbors and old friends is that none of them are waiting on a treatise on *Corinthian's 13* to give direction to their lives. All are already well immersed in the flow of life, yet Paul's Love I believe is critically relevant to each of their lives.

I envisage my intended readers, likewise, as having already made the commitments that shape their adult lives. The major components of their lives — background, education, vocation etc. are securely in place. As is the particular mix of Choice and Gift that determines the trajectory of each of their lives. Some rely primarily on a higher power to sustain their intended life-direction; others rely solely on their own resources, while most perhaps, find themselves somewhere between the two. To sit them down as a group to discuss Paul's Love assuming that one lesson, one sermon, fits all, would be unthinkable in our restless intellectual environment. Among postmodern philosophers I would be quickly taken to task for ignoring the varied perspectives and power positions assumed in our diverse, contentious culture. Nor, in fact, does *Corinthian's 13* insist on a common vision toward which we are all encouraged to strive. We cannot look to Paul's Love for a list of worthy objectives such as might be found in the UN charter, or the mission statements of most benevolent organizations. Paul does not insist that world hunger be eliminated; that crime, overpopulation, the excesses of global Capitalism, or ethnic wars, be alleviated. There is no vision of what love in the future will look like. All Paul says is that wherever we are, whatever we are doing, whatever we believe, whatever our analysis of, and solutions to, the problems in our individual lives and the wider world around us may be, that we will be patient and kind. Paul's Love, is about means not ends. It's not about reaching our goals; it's about how we work toward our goals which beckon to us from the future. Paul focuses on the present, the partial, on what is dimly seen. If we get that right the rest will follow.

III

Webster's defines a patient person as one "bearing misfortune, provocation, annoyance, delay, hardship, pain, etc. with fortitude and calm without complaint, anger, or the like." A kind person is one who is, "of a good and benevolent nature… considerate, or helpful… mild, gentle… 5.*Archaic*. loving." Rather vague. Bit circular. But sufficient, perhaps, to suggest the level of abstraction appropriate to our discussion. First patience, then kindness. Interesting order. First the ground is prepared in a general way: one is to be patient with other's annoying habits, but also with circumstances: unforeseen accidents, flight delays, health problems, job frustration, pain, one's own spiritual development, even death. With anything. Paul does not say one never gets frustrated, or angry, but that when one does love, almost as an independent inner attitude, an entity separate from one's own conscious, willing self, will be patient. Paul doesn't deny the full range of human emotions and attitudes. He simply says that love is the preeminent and enduring element in human existence. *Corinthians 13* doesn't confront or deny other human tendencies; in fact Paul's Love supports where possible, and works with a variety of feelings and intentions. Like a golden thread woven into the fabric of our lives Paul's Love brightens the emerging patterns, whatever shape they may take.

Paul does not say "I" will be patient and kind, but that love will be patient and kind. If I find this energizing love that allows me to bear misfortune, etc. within myself, under my conscious control, well and good. If not I must turn to other resources in the immediate environment, or to a higher power. In any case I am first to be patient, or rather to allow love in me to be patient. To "Lean on Love" as an old 1960's bumper sticker puts it. Having become patient in my surrounding lifeworld and my convoluted interior landscape Paul says I am to be kind to other people. I am to reach out to others, being considerate and helpful. Patience prepares the way, sets the stage, for the active reaching out to the other person that is to follow.

These last words are the heart of what Paul has to say to each one of us whatever our situation might be. We are simply to be patient with

James' "blooming, buzzing, confusion" around us, and second we are to be helpful, considerate and gentle to the people with whom we are in contact. That's basically it. Not very exciting is it? We are probably doing that most of the time anyway. Except for the occasional lapse and then we try to get back on track.

Let's look at Paul's words more closely. Let us image ourselves in a social setting talking among friends. Someone brings up an old slander against an absent member of the group, a person we know fairly well. We aren't sure whether the allegation is true or not. We let it pass. Later the person confronts us. "How could you allow people to talk behind my back? I thought you were my friend." We apologize and promise to do better next time. The next time the slighting reference is to a person we barely know. Do we defend their reputation? Or someone we don't know at all. Or a public figure. Or perhaps a group of people. An ethnic, occupational, age or racial group? Does Paul's injunction that we be considerate to others require that we interrupt slighting references to absent friends - but not to public figures? To groups? Or only to certain groups and not others? Where does one draw the line?... One doesn't? One *doesn't* draw the line!? Why not?…

Because Paul's Love is not an injunction, a principle, a rule for living. Against Kiekegaard who in *Works of Love* insists that love, seen in the light of the Eternal, is a divine commandment "Thou Shalt Love," I would argue that to make love a command, a law even from God, distorts the nature of Paul's Love. To be guided by fear of divine retribution - however gently nuanced - for not loving negates the very generousness of Paul's Love. Huck Finn's willingness to risk damnation to help his black friend Jim escape slavery, is an extreme but legitimate example of the possible tension between Paul's Love and cultural religious norms. I would therefore read *Corinthians 13* as a descriptive rather than a prescriptive text i.e. it describes that nature of love, but does not threaten those who choose not to love. It does not insist on its own way.

There are of course consequences that flow from adhering or not adhering to Paul's Love, but that is another matter. One that would lead us into the thorny issue of ultimate accountability (the Day of Judgment for many believers), distracting us from the task at hand. And which does not, in any case, effect the thrust of Paul's Love as we observe it at work in this world.

Justice and law, operating in this world, do set standards for behavior, do insist on their own way. Love's only concern is to be kind, considerate and helpful to the people with whom one has contact. Not to access blame, or exact retribution. As we read *Corinthians 13* we sense we are not reading a contract that spells out the responsibilities one human owes to another. There is no odor of obligation about the words that pour from Paul's heart as he writes in jerky, bursting phrases that tumble over themselves. 'Without love I am a noisy gong; if I have this or that or the other without love I am nothing. Moving mountains, giving up my life, my possessions, without love I am nothing.' Don't be fooled by the mild words "patient" and "kind" that seem so ordinary, so mundane after 2000 years, but listen for the furious energy Paul's words unleash. A lava flow of love pours over the world! Love does not insist on it's own way? Get real! Come on. Our whole society is built on people insisting on their own way! No system on earth can survive without insisting on its own way. 'But Love rejoices!' In this troubled world? After the injustice, the horrors of...? 'Love bears all things! Believes all, hopes all, endures all!' On and on it goes. 'Love never ends! Prophecies will falter, tongues and knowledge will end' libraries and data banks will end, computer screens will go blank, 'for now we know in part but then...'

I find it hard to continue. The power of Paul's words leaves me trembling.

A completed text is like a garment, seamless and delivered whole. Writing, the process of writing, is of course done in stages, bit by bits, which are seamlessly woven into a completed text, unless - occasionally - a metaphor, a burst of inner insight, breaks through the slowly forming text. At the end of yesterday's writing the furious energy of Paul's words that I've been pondering for months broke through, instantly creating a whole new range of insights and questions. How is energy - Blake's energy – Jakob Boehme's primal energy - the blazing energy of Unseen Love at the heart of creation - related to the routine courtesies of patience and kindness? If Paul's Love can be furious, volcanic, primal, how will it play out in ordinary life? How do we adjust to this deeply disruptive dimension of Paul's Love as it erupts in our unloving world? How will it effect our political thinking? Our art? Our law? So far we have suggested its presence in individual lives where each person must read Paul and assess for herself the impact of his words in her life. But my mind is racing ahead now to the impact of Paul's words on the groups and institutions of which we are a part, for we exist not only as Kieergaard's solitary individual, but we also do our thinking, live our lives, among others in a social and institutional environment. But whatever our communal commitments, our worldviews, Paul's Love stands waiting – as handy as a garden tool, as warm as sunshine – to nurture our thinking and our lives. Paul's Love is ever available as an animating inner energy that we may begin to renew our lives, and that portion of creation around us we are drawn to care for.

The burst of volcanic energy I sensed last evening, and that permeated my experience in the ER, is the unseen sun of our earth-bound existence; the sustaining source of our efforts to live good and decent lives. How this applies to individuals and collective entities (political parties, religious communities, schools of thought etc.) is not spelled out in *Corinthians 13*. Thirteen verses long *Corinthians 13* ignites a fire that may light up many lives, renew many organizations. Thirteen verses that can transform the whole worn and wary warring world.

IV

When I listen to a challenging sermon or lecture I am especially careful as we approach the appeal to conscience, the altar call when I'm called on to respond in a tangible way. As I ease back in my seat leery of the persuasive manner being employed to lure me into life-altering decisions I sense the speaker's arguments being spoken within myself and I weigh carefully the consequences of taking the action proposed. Eventually as a believer of course I invite Christ, the inner teacher, to support, or not, the direction being suggested. But in any case I become uneasy, tentative, counting the cost of taking on a new project. What am I being asked to give up? How will my life change? How does the challenge the sermon, lecture or text presents effect my current commitments and lifestyle? How will it effect those I care about?

We are quite right to be uneasy when we turn our full attention to Paul's Love, and yet the challenge Paul presents is not, at first glance, very demanding. Paul's Love sets no lofty goals, nor is it very different than what we're already doing. Our possessions remain in tact; we maintain our lifestyle; we are not required to sacrifice our bodily well-being for a noble cause. We're not asked to be more generous in our giving to the poor, or the homeless, or the disabled; to make a career change; to reconsider our value systems, or join a more enlightened faith community. Or take a stronger stand against racial or gender intolerance; to vote for this party instead of that party. All we are invited to do - for Paul does not ask, let alone insist - is to be patient and kind in whatever we are already doing. We are not to insist on our own way; we are somehow - he doesn't say how - to overcome our inclination to slip our achievements into the conversation; are not to be rude to others even when they are rude to us, or to resent their accomplishments. On reflection fears that Paul is asking the impossible melt away. We begin to relax realizing Paul's Love is doable. Not a perfect fit perhaps, but like a slightly uncomfortable new garment that may require a bit of exercise and dieting on our part, Paul's Love offers itself to our use.

V

And it's true. Paul's Love is doable within the worldview each of us now holds. Opportunities to love other human beings are available to moderates, liberals, conservatives, believers and humanists alike. But if compassion and love are readily available there is a relentless logic to Paul's Love that once adhered to will irrevocably alter the direction of one's life. This wisdom of love, this seed of caring for the common species begins to take on a life of its own within the particular circumstances of each individual life. A consistency emerges between love's premise and the various choices and actions which flow from the premise.

The wisdom of love can be seen unfolding in individual lives as we trace its first small beginnings in self-absorbed adolescent neurotics like Florence Nightingale founder of modern nursing, and Thomas Merton the archetypal 20th century monk, to adult lives increasingly at the service of Paul's Love. Just as we observe the effect of sunlight on a spacious garden teeming with a variety of flowering plants so Paul's Love is evident in the rich diversity of human nature.

Philip Neri was a sociable fun-loving saint, an extrovert like Francis of Assisi, who enjoyed the company of others: singing, laughter and parties. Clare of Assisi, like Charles de Foucauld who befriended the Bedouin nomads in the Sahara desert, was a shy, intense introvert. Dorothy Day was a Christian anarchist who often challenged her church's policies on war and justice for the poor. Mother Teresa of Calcutta, a traditional Catholic, was supportive of the policies of the Vatican authorities. Both were determined, passionate women who unstintingly cared for the poorest of the poor. Despite their different political perspectives Miss Day, I'm told by a nun who worked with them both, was the only outsider to receive the symbolic black rose, signifying membership in Mother Teresa's order. Gandhi was a small-boned, cheerful saint whose appeal to the average Indian citizen is reminiscent of amiable John Wesley at 5' 2", who preached a theologically inclusive social gospel to working class and wealthy citizens alike that challenged the injustices of early industrial England.

Albert Camus, modern myth maker, atheist, and French resistance patriot explored the role of compassion in a world without God. A world of brutal absurdities. Fridjof Nansen humanitarian, biologist, and polar explorer was awarded the Nobel Peace Prize for rallying world support for those starving in Russia after World War I. Albert Schweitzer was a tall imposing liberal German biblical scholar who later served as a doctor to those in central Africa who had no medical services. His authoritative patriarchal manner contrasted with the common touch of the 14th Dalai Lama, or Princes Diana a naïve, shy, sometimes troubled woman, whose concern for the disadvantaged was evident to all who knew her. Different personality types, different roles in life, different religious and political commitments, but each adhering to the wisdom of love as it developed in their own lives. It is this wisdom, the relentless logic of love that provides the elusive structure, the hard bones, we have been seeking, in order that our well-intentioned weak flesh might stand up and begin to walk in the light of Paul's Love. And we might become the children of light the gospel calls us to become.

Chapter

IX

Seed and Subjectivity

"Don't be surprised that we have to make a long detour; it is because the goal is glorious, though not the goal you think of."

Socrates in Plato's *Phaedrus* (#273, P.519)

"Direct communication requires certainty, but certainty is impossible for a person in the process of becoming."

Kierkegaard

"Philosophy must always be concerned with non-philosophy, because it has no object of its own... It must still receive its sources from outside... What makes Kierkegaard awkward is that he belongs both inside philosophy and outside it at one and the same time."

Paul Ricoeur

I

Buttressed by three critical insights: Other, Choice, and Gift, we've begun to see Paul's Love rise as the cathedral-like centerpiece of human existence. Buber and Levinas refocused attention from Descartes' thinking self to the other faces around us and the unseen Other – God. The pragmatists, James, Dewey and Rorty, guided our thinking on Paul's Love in its practical mode as Choice, as tool. The contemporary French philosopher Jean-Luc Marion, echoing the mystical tradition of Eckhart, Teresa of Avila, and Dionysius the Areopagite, reminded us that love also comes as Gift from beyond our rational consciousness, i.e. from nature, the unconscious, or for many from God, which enables us to make the hard choices for Paul's Love that we're unable to sustain over time. Now I would suggest that somewhere between Choice and Gift, between the tool at hand and the distant sun, a critical third element has emerged. The wisdom of Paul's Love, cultivated by tool and nurtured by sunlight is also evident in the growing seed. Along with tool and sunlight perhaps seed may serve as useful metaphor for Paul's Love as it manifests itself in the individual human being.

Speaking of Paul's Love as Choice and Gift it seemed appropriate to maintain an objective tone. Mother Teresa, Gandhi and other saintly individuals were judged by their peers, and history, to have clearly reflected Paul's Love. When hard soil and dark skies frustrated their worthy intentions they clearly had turned to Paul's Love not as a choice they were capable of sustaining but to Paul's Love as a gift from the Divine Nature, from God.

II

Considering the wisdom of love as seed developing slowly in an individual's life the case is a bit different. There the relative certainties of Choice and Gift give way to a vagueness of concept, a confusion, which is difficult to trace. Seed is about growth, change, becoming what one was not, or with Plato becoming more of what one already is. Choice and Gift are enduring universal features of Paul's Love i.e. they may be considered apart from any particular individual. A tool is available to any hand that cares to utilize it; the sun shines on everyone. Though choices vary, the formal elements of Choice and Gift remain the same. Each maintains its essential nature over time; neither is critically affected by the presence or absence of a particular person. But a seed is unique for unless it grows and blossoms creation has lost one irreplaceable element. Seeds may be said to be specific, unique and individual in a way that tool and sun are not. That there are many, even billions of seeds, does not diminish the uniqueness, the otherness of each individual seed. And while a tool maintains its own nature as it waits to be utilized and the sun radiates steadily day after day the seed is always changing, always growing one way or another. It lives and dies. Whether it survives beyond death to any further purpose is still not clear. In any event unlike tools and sunlight seeds are fleeting, fragile, and problematic.

Unlike Choice and Gift, which remain constant, the individual alters its perception of truth over time. T. S. Eliot suggests we've "had the experience but missed the meaning." In reflection, Eliot claims, it is possible to uncover new meanings to past experiences where the shame of "motives late revealed" may still be rectified. On the other hand undeserved early guilt may later be relieved. Ethical accountability and therapeutic healing both survive in consciousness. While the observable act is complete, over and done with, the interior intent which lives on in consciousness, is still fluid, still open to change.

Another challenge the philosopher faces, apart from than the ambiguity associated with fluid intentions, is how language can meaningfully refer to nonlinguistic realities, which includes at least the entire physical world and a debatable but sizable portion of the inner world of thoughts and feelings. If we would distinguish, for example, a particular human being from the abstractions of language we must use words and ideas to refer to what are not words and ideas. "Real", "particular" and "existing" are all words. Existentialists contrast "essence" (ideas, especially philosophic ideas) and "existence" (real living), Buber distinguishes between the "I-It" and "I-Thou", and Heidegger between "inauthentic" and "authentic" existence. All these are insightful distinctions I find useful in illuminating the elusive self - a real person - but a distinction is not a person. A person is not an idea – or a complex of ideas. Unlike certain linguistic philosophers I would not deny that language *does* refer to a nonlinguistic reality, but still the dilemma of the relation between the two remains. If we give a person a name and a biography we have presented only an image of the person. Even a photograph does not produce the person herself. Yet what else have we? We must use words and ideas to evoke the individual human being but not – and this is Kiekegaard's great insight – objectively, not directly. How we're to use language to probe the mysteries of the conceptually elusive individual human being is our next challenge, our next stepping stone across the river-like uncertainties of existence.

As we grope our way toward a conceptual framework for dealing with this most elusive phenomenon, i.e. – of a seed-like finite human allowing Paul's Love to grow in her life, let us return for a moment to *Corinthians 13*. On one hand Paul writes of love in a clear and direct way. Love is patient and kind, enduring and concerned for the other person. But Paul does not supply us with criterion that might be used to determine which acts are patient and kind, and which are not. He seems to be saying 'Yes we all recognize what love is, we all can acknowledge love is patient, kind, long lasting etc. But, no, we can't be certain if any particular action is done in love or not." Even the most seemingly unambiguous act, martyrdom for example, is open to question when performed by an individual human being. Paul protests vigorously against any attempt to identify love as an interior attitude with the actions (works) that flow from Choice (martyrdom, giving away one's possessions etc.). He refuses to identify kindness or patience with any observable act. Paul values the intention over the act itself because it allows for future rectification; i.e. for future repentance and what follows. The act is forever frozen in the past, the intention preserved in memory, is open to change; to sorrow, regret and a desire to act in a more loving way. Privileging intention over act, the subjective over the objective, Paul's Love emerges as the one critical factor in a person's existence. And yet this decisive relationship to Paul's Love is an intangible reality. A mystery, not mysterious, but tentative, uncertain, hard to describe within the normal parameters of philosophic thought.

Glimpsed in drama, literature and art Paul's Love embodied in individual characters is fixed in another time and place. There, in the work of art it's as if we were peering into another solar system where a sun similar to our own sustains the encircling planetary life; a parallel universe spawned from the artist's imagination which resembles our own and is lit by a similar light.

III

To illustrate Paul's oddly elusive love as seed, as becoming, we turn once again to our philosophic road map. This time the subtle logic of Kierkegaard will be our guide. Distinguishing between objective and subjective truth Kierkegaard writes, "objective truth invests everything in the result... subjective thinking invests everything in the process of becoming and omits the result." (*Concluding Unscientific Postscript*. Hong and Hong editors. P.73) And again, "the truth is not the truth but... the way is the truth, that is, the truth is only in the becoming." (*Concluding Unscientific Postscript*, P. 78) Subjective truth, truth for the finite individual rather than the objective truths of science, history and even the assumed unseen realities probed by philosophy and theology, is about the process of becoming. It's about change and growth, but not an objective growth and change which might be evaluated and measured like a change in the weather, or the growth of a flowering plant. Nor is subjective truth concerned with reaching a goal, because the goal for Kierkegaard is the infinity of being loved by God. In relation to the eternal the individual always falls short; is always becoming. Not, on the way to God, as if life were a journey to a distant God – though God for Kierkegaard is infinitely distant, the "Wholly Other" but in relation to God at the only moment available to the existing individual – the present moment, now. It's not the nature of God or of the individual that is of concern for Kierkegaard, but how much does the individual yearn to be in relation to God? How much does the finite human being desire, long, sacrifice, to be in relationship with the infinite, eternal God – now? This subjective passion – and for Kierkegaard there is no other kind - is critical for Kierkegaard, not an objective understanding of truth, of God, or of God's plan.

Two final reflections on Kierkegaard's subjective truth. First it cannot be communicated directly – i.e. objectively. "Ordinary communication, objective thinking, has no secrets; only… subjective thinking has secrets; that is, all its essential content is essentially a secret, because it cannot be communicated directly… cannot be stated directly." (*Concluding Unscientific Postscript*, P.79) Equally puzzling is the seeming lack of certitude and clarity associated with subjective truth. "Direct communication requires certainty, but certainty is impossible for a person in the process of becoming." (*Concluding Unscientific Postscript*, P.74).

So – if we're going take Plato's long detour and speak meaningfully of the seed of Paul's Love that Kierkegaard cherishes we'll need to radically alter our approach.

If truth is not truth – but only the way to the truth, which is not a reachable goal, but rather an impossible (Kierkegaard's word) relationship between the finite human being and the infinite higher power, built not on objective knowledge, but on the flimsy inner passion for becoming rather than certainty, and if this subjective thinking cannot be shared directly in language, how *can* we explore the critical notion of love as seed?

IV

Let us reflect on an example. A week ago Friday a friend spent four to five hours helping me look for my first computer. The Brother word processor I've used for years had finally frozen on me and I was delighted to have Tom guide me to a very serviceable second hand Toshiba. Tom had been away all summer and it was good to catch up and renew our long standing friendship as we drove from one computer outlet store to another. Enlivened by lots of pent-up laughter one can enjoy only with a close friend, and some serious sharing of our private failures and struggles. Last night driving to the men's group at Middletown Friend's Meeting I'd invited Tom out for dinner on Saturday. His choice - Chinese, French-Italian or a sport's bar with homemade brew and fresh salmon. Paul's Love? Caring for a friend? Or repaying a debt? Something to compensate Tom for his help in selecting the Toshiba — and an encouragement to put him in my debt when I ask for assistance in setting up the new computer? Hard to say. Mixed motives! But what is a mixed motive? Is it Paul's Love or isn't it? Paul's Love unfortunately doesn't leave room for anything else. Existing human beings may not be able to sort out their motives, but Paul is quite clear that love is one thing — being more concerned about the other person than one's own self. Reading *Corinthians 13* I sense my arrangement with Tom (if that's what it was) of enlightened self interest — having my computer attended to in exchange for a meal and listening to Tom's problems and opinions for an hour or so, is not what Paul meant by love. Nothing short of a genuine concern for Tom as the Other who took precedent over my own needs, would seem to satisfy Paul. But how can I be sure that my offer for dinner is free from ulterior motives? I think it is. But I can't be sure. And I certainly can't prove it in a discussion or in writing. Deconstructionists, like the wily Derrida would ferret out the meaner motives in a moment. After a brief pause I drop the introspective examination of my mixed motives and we move on to planning for the upcoming meal together. Whatever my assessment was, or may be on reflection later on, my main task is to focus on my friend Tom rather than my own interior motives.

Whether we speak of mixed motives or subjective truth it would appear we've entered murky waters. As long as Paul's Love might be matched to actions that flow from Choice we were on relatively firm ground. Mother Teresa's work among the poorest of the poor in Calcutta would seem to the outside observer a clear example of Paul's Love. But from Mother Teresa's perspective the situation is not so clear. Saints do not see themselves as saints; and they certainly don't echo the generous sentiments of their admirers. Tom's offer to help me find a new computer seems to me a generous act. But from Tom's point of view – from the subjective perspective of the existing individual – the whole question of whether or not he is acting in accord with Paul's Love is confusing, awkward, and embarrassing. Even to the reader perhaps, and myself, the issue seems tiresome and vaguely unpleasant. Like analyzing love in the midst of lovemaking. Why this uneasiness? Perhaps because Paul's Love is focused ultimately not on the purity of one's own motivation, but on the welfare of the other person. On the "you" rather than the "I" in "I love you." For Tom to express his motives, even to himself, would detract from the spontaneous desire to help out an old friend. If he finds himself becoming impatient or arrogant he may wish to examine his motives and redirect his behavior. Even for Tom to credit his generosity to a divine source, attempting to deflect attention away from himself, would only draw attention to *his* humility, *his* religious beliefs, obstructing his primary intent which was to help an old friend select a computer.

Not only is Tom focusing on my welfare; he is doing so over time, as we drive to tax-free Delaware, browse the giant discount stores, talk together, and discuss the pros and cons of a particularly attractive second hand Toshiba. But not – or not only – in clock time. Four hours. Five? Does it matter how long we spent together? Henri Bergson, the French philosopher esteemed by both American pragmatists and 20th century European existentialists, spoke of non-clock time, as "duration", emotion-laden, dynamic rather than static; as what Kierkegaard might have called subjective time, or felt-time. Time which, unique to the existing individual, is not conceptual, quantitative and measurable. Tom and I finished our trip together within a measurable amount of clock time, but the subjective – the intersubjective - quality of our travel and conversation cannot be captured by clock time. Subjective time unique to each individual (or shared as intersubjectivity) is central to the thinking of Kiergegaard, Bergson, and Heidegegger, and novelists such as Proust, Joyce, or any writer who portrays the human individual acting, feeling, remembering, struggling, in her everyday life.

That painters, like Rembrandt, and writers more easily evoke the subjective dimension than philosophers would suggest that conceptual language has difficulties depicting the existing individual. But artists and writers, who have created a rich assortment of memorable individuals, have their own parameters. The limitation of a narrative depiction of the existing individual, of Proust's narrator in *Remembrance of Things Past* or Mr. Bloom from Joyce's Ulysses, is that there is only one Bloom and he lived only one day, June 16, 1904 in Dublin, Ireland. An intriguing blend of personal, cultural, and imaginative elements literature's memorable figures do not directly address our concerns. Like conversation overheard on the subway they remain within their own time and place, addressing concerns of their own era. Concerns which we may empathize with, learn from, and critique, but not engage. I may speak to Bloom on any issue I wish; he will not answer me being in conversation with others.

Philosophy, less reticent, welcomes the reader's response. The arguments advanced by Plato continue to engage readers even today. Puzzling questions once posed on appearance and reality, truth or justice, restlessly seek the reader's response. What's your opinion Plato asks? Do you agree with Socrates or not? If not why not? Give us your reasons. Philosophy's invitation to dialogue with the truth claims presented greatly enhance our understanding of what being human means. That's part of what we do. We present our views and listen to other views. We argue, agree and disagree, and revise our thinking. But sharing ideas – on justice, on the conflict between Truth and truth, on the limitations of human understanding - is only part of being human.

Philosophy does a credible job of depicting human nature in a general way but whether one paints with an optimistic brush like Kant or Bergson, or with a more pessimistic palate like Schopenhauer,

Hobbes, and Foucault philosophy's varied portraits of human nature fail to capture the essence of any one existing individual. Except of course in an awkward way the main features of the presenting philosopher. Yet even Kierkegaard, hiding behind a plenitude of pseudonyms fails to produce even one existing individual – certainly not as he tells us Kierkegaard himself. Art and literature leave us with an unconnected scattering of well-defined individual characters who speak only for themselves within the confines of a particular quasi-imaginative world, while many philosophers provide insightful generalizations about human nature without ever presenting a authentic portrait of any one human being. Except Plato's Socrates and his dialogue partners. Neither, art nor philosophy, by itself provides decisive insight into the subjectivity of an existing individual wrestling with the demands of Paul's Love.

Having entered murky waters – subjective truth, subjective time, Paul's Love in the existing individual – we must become accustomed to a new conceptual environment. We must find an alternate way of thinking and expressing ourselves if we wish to explore the more nuanced subjective aspect of Paul's Love. The relative clarity with which we identified pragmatic Choice and the illuminating Gift of a Higher Power recedes as we focus on the existing individual persisting through time.

Conceptual thought, which utilizes ideas and arguments pursued from premise to conclusion is the natural environment for philosophy. Yet, as William James noted, philosophy is as much about temperament as it is about truth. The genial skeptic Hume, the intensely introverted believer Kierkegaard, and the robust revolutionary Marx all utilized reason to advance their philosophic concerns. That they reached different conclusions; presented differing worldviews, only enhances the ongoing search for truth. Just as great paintings inspire new artists to join the continuing effort to portray beauty, to express the human condition, or to reflect the underlying cultural themes of their time, so philosophers utilize reason and temperament, to elucidate the elusive realities of existence.

Given the breadth of existence alluded to earlier it would seem unreasonable to expect any one philosophy to present the final, definitive truth about reality. Yet if our concepts point to reality; if the word "chair" or "God" for example indicates a particular object or entity (the "signified" referred to by the "signifier" in contemporary philosophic terms) then we can refer to Paul's Love in a conceptual way as well. And Tom should be able to talk about his patience and kindness to me as easily as he might refer to the computer and printer we eventually ended up buying or his religious beliefs. But of course he can't. Paul's Love of which we spoke so freely before has become problematic. To repeat myself in blunt non- philosophic terms I can talk about Tom's choice to delay his plans to prepare for the opening day of a new school year to help me find a computer as evidence of Paul's Love. I can if I wish credit Tom's kindness to a higher power, but I cannot expect Tom to mention this kindness – to me or even to himself – without diminishing the love implicit in his act. One just doesn't do that. Even to himself Tom must put aside the insidious thought "Ah a good deed! Now I am loving my old friend, John." I cringe even to think of such a thing. Not that I – we – don't wrestle with this insidious thought from time to time. All we can do is trust our intent to love the other person is genuine; not tainted by any other considerations which will somehow reflect to our own advantage.

How then can I or Tom or anybody know if their actions and attitudes are kind and patient rather than self-serving? I don't think we can know; for when we identify our own motives as loving we alter the motive itself to include the possibility of wanting to be viewed by others and ourselves and even God, as a worthy and superior person. We end up – perhaps, for one is never certain of these subjective assessments – subtly enhancing our own image, advancing our own cause. In any case Kierkegaard's non-objective truth, truth for the existing individual, acts like a smudge on our blueprint of reality. Truth has become personal, puzzling and intensely compelling. The dilemma we face between objective and subjective truth is not just conceptual, nor is it non-conceptual i.e. beyond language, but only awkwardly, less conceptual – quasi-conceptual. As we explore the ambiguous fourth component of Paul's Love, the individual as seed, we will need to go beyond the visceral imagery of literature and the abstractions of philosophy to the evocative language of analogy and personal experience.

Chapter

X

The Swimmer-Observer

I

Perhaps a parable may help. Standing on shore the swimmer's view is wide and unobstructed. Once under water, let us assume in a coral reef off Australia, the swimmer's vision becomes clouded and her movements constricted as she adjusts to the opaque watery environment. The fellow creatures in the water around her intrude upon the awkward rhythm of her motion. Some are appealing and seem friendly; others are more ominous. As reflective beings, as thinkers, on shore we live in a broad and airy environment; as bodies underwater our faculties, primarily sight, speech and movement, must adjust to the more constricted environment.

Human consciousness faces a constantly receding horizon, a broad vista, which spreads around it from one end of creation to the other. The beginning? My mind leaps at once to the initial creative burst some 13 billion years ago. Then quickly to amino acids randomly interacting in the limpid cooling oceans to form microscopic life, 2 perhaps or 3 billion years ago and on to the plains of Olduvai, a mere two million years past, as the lumbering primates evolve rather briskly into the first definable human beings. The end of creation? In a flash my mind envisages several of the various scientific and religious scenarios available that bring history and nature, as we know it, to a catastrophic or transforming close. Whatever direction I look my mind is there ahead of me, ahead of the rest of me. Able to project myself in thought to any place in the universe, at a moment's notice I'm limited in my body to the confines of the immediate environment around me. If I would move my body to New York, a mere hundred and twenty miles away for my cousin's wedding next month, I must consult railroad schedules, arrange for a ride to the station, wait in the ticket line, sit in the train several hours, walk up through Grand Central station, discuss with Betty whether to take a bus, subway - or spurge on a cab - to take us to our hotel. In my mind we are there now sipping champagne and savoring the weekend ahead in New York. As an existing human being – the lived body, the body as subject, as Merleau-Ponty the imminent French phenomenologist describes it – I am constricted in my vision, speech and movements to a particular time and space.

Turning to our parable we find our heroine awkwardly swimming underwater trying to decide which of the creatures around her are friendly and which are not. Some seem to wish her well, drawing her into a world that is mutually supportive. Other creatures while not noticeably unfriendly remain at a distance. Slow in her movements, restricted in her vision that cannot see far ahead in the dim waters the swimmer-observer treats each creature, known or unknown, as if they were all one family. She feels safe and is fascinated with the wonders around her. From time to time our heroine reemerges from the ocean and surveys the wider world. After standing on the beach reflecting on her experience underwater she looks out at the distant ships, the changing weather patterns, and the calm, but increasingly turbulent waters, in the seascape wrapped around her. Finally she reenters the murky waters.

This time the creatures are not so friendly. They lunge and tear at one another and the swimmer-observer is fearful she will be drawn into the developing confrontation between the warring factions. Afraid of the sharp teeth and poisonous tentacles that threaten her vulnerable flesh she backs away to consider her options. Instinctively she reaches for a sunken branch on the bottom to ward off her adversaries. The creatures circle and lunge at one another. Blood is drawn; the waters darken, and the conflict escalates into a frenzy of attack and counter-attack. The ocean of love that had delighted the swimmer-observer has become an ocean of darkness where all life seems bent on a furious orgy of mutual destruction. Yet some creatures move apart from the slaughter, swimming alone or darting in and out to offer assistance to the wounded. At times they glimmer among the dark shapes of the frenzied adversaries. At other times they seem lost to view to our troubled swimmer-observer who is torn between joining the contending creatures and wandering with the vulnerable ones who occasionally gleam in the dark and bloody waters. In her dilemma our swimmer-observer swims away from the conflict and moves back up on shore.

Standing on the beach she looks out over the turbulent waters that churn and peak, faintly reminiscent of the savage struggle beneath the surface. The swimmer inhales deeply savoring the spacious vista. Momentarily freed from the harrowing underwater experience, she begins to process her varied responses to life underwater and life on land. From her impressions of the two realms the swimmer- observer uses language to articulate a comprehensive view of her experience. Subject to change as life around her changes her working world view seems to her to be an accurate account of the two realms. Then she notices there are others on the beach. She wonders what their working world views are like. Do they agree with hers? Those nearby she assumes will have seen things in a similar way; those farther off may have a different perspective. Some will have seen savage conflicts in the coral reef; others will have visited the reef during a comparatively peaceful time. As the swimmer-observers on shore (living and deceased) gather to discuss their different perspectives, their different world views, of the reality they've all experienced, there will be disagreements, and closely reasoned arguments presented in support of one view or another. But since the horizon of even the most far sighted of swimmers-observers is limited, compared to the vast unseen world that lies beyond the horizon no one worldview of reality will prevail. The discussion will continue as a new generation of swimmers gazes out over the wide waters from varied perspectives, recording their own impressions of what lies before them. New ships, new weather patterns, new developments on land; new intensities of conflict and conflict resolution in the coral reef, will alter the discussion as the generations rise and pass. Thus do reason and philosophy view the wide expanse of our dual reality; life on land and life in the constricted but dangerous and radiant coral reef. Philosophic discussions that would resolve the various perspectives to a single worldview contribute to the evolving but ever unfinished search for truth.

At the risk of repeating myself let's look more closely at the swimmer's journey. Entering the dim waters the swimmer-observer's movements and vision are far more constricted. Here she enters the grim and joyous realities of the oceans of darkness and light. Her flesh is exposed to the sharp teeth of predators, and also to the kindness of her fellow creatures. Seeking allies to defend herself against the contending forms of life she may choose to align herself with one contending group or another; or she may turn from the mounting frenzy to pursue a path consistent with Paul's Love. She may act alone or join others who are responding with patient and kindness to their fierce enemies. And risk being devoured in the ongoing contentiousness. Thus each of us as individuals experiences existence, in contrast to reason's broad impartial gaze, as constricted and precarious.

II

The real home of the swimmer-observer is under water. There she, and each of us, exist not only as recording eyes and articulate analytic minds surveying and wrestling with the contradictions presented by our wider world, but as swimmers who must fend off or embrace the creatures around us. If we make a misjudgment on land – misidentify an ocean craft or a certain species of wildlife - it is no great matter. We may confer with other observers, revise our judgment and accumulate a body of reliable information about the world around us. But if we misjudge the situation close at hand under water we effect our own and the lives of others around us.

The contrast, however, between the swimmer's life on shore and underwater must not be overstated. If we stress the distinction between our conceptual faculties and the underwater life of the swimmer – between essence (thought) and existence - we may unduly separate what are two interwoven aspects of one nature. The two realms, conceptual and subjective are not entirely dissimilar, and while the parable assumes I move, and am vulnerable, under water in a way the functioning intellect on shore is not, I can still see and think under the water. I can still communicate with the fellow beings around me, but if the two realms interact with one another they are not interchangeable. They resemble one another as the later Wittgenstein might have phrased it; but they do not correspond to one another, as the early Wittgenstein assumed. Knowledge acquired in the airy realm on shore resembles, but does not correspond to, the reality underwater which it would portray.

On shore one may discuss pain, for example, but underwater it is felt pain, rather than medical or religious explanations of pain, that evokes the ideas and words expressing that experience. On the other hand the swimmer-observer under water must utilize the concepts formed as an observer on shore to convey in some fashion the altered realm under the water in which she swims. There are no other words to use. "Pain" is still "pain". There is only one language to deal with both dimensions of her existence. Which is why Kierkegaard is careful to separate objective truth (the view from the shore) from subjective truth which can only be experienced in the constricted ocean of our bodily existence.

III

An example that is very much with me may illustrate the point. A few pages back discussing Paul's Love in relation to Tom's generosity I wrote, "Paul's Love is focused ultimately, not on the purity of one's own motivation, but on the welfare of the other person." Standing on the shore trying to organize the scene before me – in this case the implications of Paul's Love on philosophy – the statement was not particularly compelling. If challenged I would have defended the statement with references to Buber and Levinas, but it would not have been a matter of life and death to me. As I reread the statement four days later it has become vital. Last Friday I learned that my wife, Betty, has a cancerous growth on her back that may require "drastic measures." I had seen the discolored spot months earlier but had not brought it to her attention. I was consumed with feelings of loss and guilt for not having acted sooner. The inner pain is intense. Yet if I pursue these thoughts however persistently they surface in wave after wave of fresh self-incriminations and feelings of possible loss I am ultimately choosing to focus on my own motivations rather than on the welfare of my wife.

Yesterday, Sunday morning, when the inner turmoil had become unbearably intense I turned to the resources that had worked in the past. I allowed the troubling doubts and recriminations, that seemed to have a life of their own, to surface as I journaled and prayed and looked for patterns in similar past experiences to suggest a way out of my dilemma. As I wrestled with the process of relating Paul's Love not to more abstract examples but to my own situation I found myself reading Kierkegaard. Two sentences riveted my interest. "You do not have a right to love despairingly." And its' corollary, "You shall preserve yourself and by and in preserving yourself preserve love." Aha! At the root of my confusion Paul's Love and Kierkegaard's despair lay snarled and intertwined. One or the other – love or despair - that was the clear choice before me. Though I could not dismiss the turmoil, the regrets, the nagging uncertainties, that had taken on a life of their own, I could turn toward the best light available, which is for me, God's love through Jesus. It was Jesus whose presence I'd sensed since the first day upholding me with words of encouragement who could not, and perhaps and did not want! to shield me from the ongoing agony of living with the awareness of Betty's growth and my inattention to her condition. Why? Because it's in the process of living – confronting the wrenching dilemmas of subjective existence – that God becomes more than a concept, a belief, but becomes the saving companion in my constricted subjective life. The doubles partner who must play the critical shots.

What I would draw from this example – for it is only an example after all to the reader who has his own subjective dilemmas to wrestle with – is that Paul's Love considered conceptually does not change but deepens as it is integrated into the life of the existing individual. Just as my concept of romantic love was not redefined but enlivened when I met Betty Jean.

Looking back one might comment on my agonizing experience in a variety of ways. Could you tell us more about the therapeutic element in resolving your dilemma? Did you ever think of turning to scripture rather than Kierkegaard? Would a small circle of friends, or talking with a trusted minister or therapist have helped? All friendly and perhaps useful suggestions, but what I would emphasize is that this dilemma is not over. We still wait on the results of the lab test on the growth removed from Betty's back. Every day the same wrenching feelings and regrets still surface. That's the way life is under water. It's not the same as standing on shore looking out over a problem that needs solving. And yet it's not that the observer on shore represents reason contrasted with the surges of emotions encountered under water. It's not just mind above water and body swimming under water; Descartes' mind-body dichotomy. It's mixed. I think under water, I can mouth words under water, I try to explain myself to others under water – it just goes slower. On shore my eyes fly. Under water problems arise and persist past the indicated solutions. I knew, before learning of the discolored spot on Betty's back that Paul's Love was more important than my own reaction but living through it is a whole different experience. I can't focus only on the Other, as Levinas might encourage me to do, but I must relate to Betty through my own troubled and flawed nature. I too must be preserved. I need healing, and prayer, and friends, and who knows what to cope with compulsive despair. Once that became clear to me I'm able to trust the loving realities in my life (my gracious savior, my wonderful God). I am able to enlist those realities to support my efforts to resist the despair, the fear, the guilt which shuts out a forgiving love which would turn me from following Paul's elusive path of patient kindness.

Let me sum up. This is the way life is. Not just for me, for my example is only that, one example well removed from those not immediately involved, but that's the way our world works. We are all observers and thinkers, all philosophers, drawing from the culture around us the axioms, concepts and guidelines that enable us to make our way through the underwater world. And we are all conscious observing swimmers in this unseen world of the individual's subjectivity in her physical surroundings. This common subjectivity, the human condition, is the realm of regrets and delays, and unfinished business, and interruption of plans and making choices without having all the information, and being wrong, and trying again and praying to some higher power for help if one needs to, and doing the best one can if one doesn't have that Gift. It's so hard being human. For every single one of us.

And all we can do is put our hands out and hope someone is there to grasp them and say it's OK you'll get through it, or God cares, or whatever it is that turns us from despair to the odd journey we're all making together into the unknown. Please God, heal Betty's cancer! Amen.

Part II

Paul's Love and Capitalism

Chapter

XI

Search for the Missing Stone

'You must show me the way.'

Here is no path," I said, "and the wood is dark and perplexing; still we
must push on."

'Let us push on.'

Plato's *The Republic*

"Something in us hungers to offer up our specks of life as
fragile tesserae toward the vast mosaic... to be embedded
in its fabric as if, once, it was from that we were broken off."

Denise Levertov

I

Moving lightly into the river of life from the initial rock of Paul's Love to the stones of Levinas's Other, pragmatic Choice, the Gift of truth and beauty apart from our conscious ego, and finally to Kierkegaard's subjective truth, seed, we find ourselves facing a seemingly unbridgeable gap to the next stone. Paul's Love made visible in political and social institutions. As the river rushes on we seem to be stranded midstream. Behind us lie the stones of Paul's Love as it relates to the individual human being; ahead lies Paul's Love in its more challenging role in the in the wider society.

No one I think can seriously quarrel with the main lines of our argument so far. Paul's Love is generally conceded to be the essential element in individual relationships in the family, among friends; even with associates and strangers with whom we interact on a daily basis. The challenge will be to pursue the implications of Paul's Love into the wider economic and political arena. That we are to be patient and kind with those around us is not in dispute. What is in dispute is how we act in our roles as employers or employees, as voters and citizens to deal with the ongoing tragic events around us: pervasive poverty, discrimination, and violence. If Paul's Love has no real answer to these dilemmas it might as well return to the cozy confines of family life and periodic religious services, where telling people to love one another is not likely to meet much opposition.

Once one moves outside friendship and romantic relationships: the home, faith communities, and voluntary organizations the language of Paul's Love no longer focuses the conversation. In the business world it's money, not Paul's Love, that does the talking. "Market share," "the bottom line" and "staying ahead of the competition" are key concepts in the market place. In the legal realm the talk is of rights and justice, of evidence and accountability. Crime and punishment. Law and order. In the political world campaign issues, shifting demographics, taxes, the will of the people, and national security, focus the conversation. The military speaks of discipline and loyalty, of outdated weapons and new technology, of being prepared to respond effectively to any contingency. Artists, writers and musicians talk of creativity, honing one's craft, finding one's voice, and occasionally, the role of the artist in a materialistic society. In popular culture the talk is outrageous, sexy, rebellious, and youth oriented. For the older generation the talk is of travel, the classic sitcoms of yesteryear, and staying young at heart. And on billboards, the Internet and TV the message is about buying, bargains, offers and opportunities, value and quality and no money down. The subliminal message is all about enhancing the ego, and feeding the libido.

However we might evaluate the various language games – Wittgenstein's term for the ways different subsections of society express themselves – in play concurrently around us I think we might agree that Paul's Love is not a predominate theme. Alasdair MacIntyre the contemporary British-American neo-Aristotelian philosopher argues the complexities of modern society create an "exceptional degree of compartmentalization" in which "the norms governing activities in any one area are specific to that area" casting the individual in "differing roles" that require on occasion "incompatible attitudes." (*Alasdair MacIntyre Reader*, 235-6)

While no one can doubt that the individual in modern society is called upon to play many conflicting roles, if ethical compartmentalization is the last word my thesis that Paul's Love is the most pervasive element in creation falls apart. If social institutions may be perceived as interacting but largely autonomous language games then each institution is entitled to create its own set of rules with limited interference from any other institution. Chess is played by one set of rules, baseball by another. And while football and hockey allow for tackling and body checking other sports do not. So also may the state use force outlawed in other institutions. Different nations and ethnic groups, different classes and interest groups are free to develop the criterion that best suit their needs. Business, art and academia may develop their own language games, their own ethical norms and customs. Certain very general guidelines of course apply to all games: no cheating and no physical violence beyond the rules of the game. In institutional matters similar guidelines are implemented by laws and public opinion, yet for the most part organization and other social groups are free to devise their own norms and customs, without outside interference.

If this is an accurate description of the way things are then the idea that any cross- institutional set of common standards is clearly ruled out. Values and practices appropriate to a religious or family setting may be seen as inappropriate in political or business settings. Truth telling and keeping one's promise, for example, may be modified in certain circumstances by the state or a large organization in order to preserve the vital interests of a nation, corporation, political party or faith community. Every organization has an image of its own worth which it may feel at times is impaired by telling the truth or keeping a promise made in earlier circumstances. What one does at home may not carry over in one's public life.

My task will be to show that common norms do exist; and second that Paul's Love is the preeminent norm which supersedes other proposed norms such as, justice, freedom, fairness and happiness – "the greatest good for the greatest number."

Rather than norms Alasdair MacIntyre speaks of virtues notably justice, courage and truthfulness as the foundation of any moral society. If I wanted to introduce Paul's Love as a virtue, as in fact the preeminent virtue, I need not insist that other virtues have no role, but only that other virtues must play a supportive role to Paul's Love. My contention is of course that Paul's Love is the linchpin that holds the various ethical systems and social organizations together. I'll be arguing that kindness and patience are the bedrock foundation of our social institutions; tough-minded, to use William James' terminology, as well as tender-minded. Tough- minded institutions can be characterized, borrowing a selective sampling of adjectives from James, as "materialist", "pessimistic", and "skeptical." Tender- minded institutions may be described as "idealistic" and "optimistic. Both tender and tough-minded organizations generally encourage positive bonding within the organization. "We're all family here. Welcome to the team. Sometimes sacrifices must be made for the good of the organization. We're all working for the same goals; you'll like it here." Relating to those outside the organization however tough-minded business organizations tend toward an us-against-them mentality which is suspicious of competing organizations; law and order and the military are suspicious of those who'd threaten social stability: law breakers and hostile foreign powers. Tender-minded organizations which exist to serve rather than protect or profit from their fellow citizens tend to be less suspicious of the surrounding world. While schools, hospitals, social agencies, and religious communities may sometimes speak ill of other organizations their commitment to kind and patient service to others does not condone such behavior. Tough-minded organizations tend to ignore or discourage positive bonding with surrounding organizations. Being willing to drive a competitor out of business to increase market share and defeating a hostile enemy in times of war are engrained in the ethos of most companies and nations. Except for the Dalai Lama's Tibet, Switzerland, Sweden, and Costa Rica which have a long tradition of peacefully co-existence. And maybe Ben and Jerry's Vermont run ice cream enterprise.

Whether the dichotomy between tender-minded institutions (the family, schools etc.) and tough-minded institutions (capitalism, the police and judicial system, and the industrial-military complex) is as sharp as Reinhold Neihbur postulates in *Moral Man and Immoral Society*, or whether it's simply a matter of diverse ethical attitudes suited to different institutional situations is irrelevant from the viewpoint of Paul's Love. In either case love, the generous caring of one individual for another, has been relegated to a domestic role apart from the "real world" of public affairs.

The task before us will be to bridge the gap between tender-minded institutions and what are often taken to be – mistakenly in my view – impersonal economic and political institutions. I hope to illuminate Paul's Love glowing in the tough-minded public institutions as well as in the more intimate domestic settings in the home and faith communities.

II

Traditionally philosophy has had a two-fold approach to ethics. Either the "ought" leads to the "is", or what "is" precedes what "ought" to be. On the one hand it can be argued that the world of economics and politics ought to be based on Paul's Love, rather than on competitive and materialistic attitudes. Plato in *The Republic* argues that the dim illusion-haunted cave we take to be the real world ought to be transformed by the eternal forms of the good and the just. Plato argues that those who have turned toward the light and see the real world outside the cave ought to teach those who still live in the darkness of the cave. This real world of light, of truth and justice among human beings, is reflected in the ideal society he presents in The Republic, which ought to replace our present passion ridden, ego-centric social order. Christianity likewise offers an alternative to our present unhappy condition – the Kingdom of God - which ought to supersede the present society in which darkness, sin and injustice seem to prevail. The neo-Kantian John Rawls in *A Theory of Justice* argues in a similar manner, basing his vision of a more equitable and humane society on rational principles of what ought to be.

Aristotle and his modern interpreter in political philosophy Alasdair MacIntyre take the second approach arguing that only what already is has the potential to develop into what ought to be. In other words if I want to show that Paul's Love is relevant to business and political life I have to show that Love is already present in those institutions. I can't just argue that Paul's Love ought to be a decisive factor without showing that it already *is* a significant factor, which has the potential to successfully replace or reform the corrupted institution in the future. Like a seed that contains the potential to become a tree, or an architect's plan that prefigures the completed building, I must show that Paul's Love is at least a viable seed, a promising plan, in the present institutional environment capable of further development. I do not have to prove that Paul's Love will prevail – for who can be certain of the future - but if I can show that Paul's Love is already present in our institutions and has the potential for growth, I have made my case.

While I admire Aristotle's practical wisdom which moves from the is to the ought I would not discount the first approach, for without a vision of the ought to balance the discouraging present reality of what in large measure already is: gross inequality, poverty, war, discrimination, etc., who would venture the hardships of trying to alter the status quo? Both approaches, one historically and structurally based on Aristotle's is, the other based on the energizing vision of what ought to be, may prove useful in advancing our argument for the decisive presence of Paul's Love in institutional life.

Presenting the ought first, a vision of what should be, it's understood that I use the word ought not its restrictive sense; such as one ought to act in a certain way because of fear of punishment, or respect for authority. As, for example, when it is said one ought to obey the laws to avoid going to jail; or one ought to follow the advice of one's doctor, pastor, priest, or rabbi. Lawrence Kohlberg, the American psychologist and ethical philosopher, found after extensive testing that that there are six stages of moral development in which the oughts at each stage culminate in a final stage in which the individual and the laws and social agreements arrived at are based on "universal principals of justice: the equality of human rights and respect for the dignity of human beings as individuals." (Habermas, *Moral Consciousness*.. P. 124-5). While I find Kohlberg's formulation far too rationalistic to do justice to Paul's Love, I do appreciate his careful analysis of the six stages that all human beings go through in their moral development. Stages that take the individual from one understanding of ought to the next until freed of the lower forms of social influence one is solely motivated by a universal ought which carries its own authority. One ought to tell the truth, or act justly to others not for fear of the consequences but simply because honesty and justice are valuable *per se*. Like beautiful art or music the ought at this level is savored for its own sake.

Moving from personal to public ethics whether one appeals to humanity's better nature as Plato, Kant, Kohlberg, and Rawls do, or is content to build on humanity's lesser motives as Machiavelli, Darwin, Marx, and Adam Smith do, each political thinker has some primal ought which they propose as the rectifying vision to the ills that beset our worn and weary world. No one is writing political philosophy to say, "Don't change a thing. The world is fine just as it is." All are proposing some alternative, some ought, some corrective and healing vision which will shepherd humanity through troubled times.

Many doctors are prescribing many different cures and while skeptical philosophers, deconstructionists like Derrida, deny any such lofty intent as they interject the odd comment, the insightful aside into a heated conversation all contributors make some claim to truth, if only to discredit somebody's else ought. Making truth claims is not a relic from our philosophic past, but the unavoidable result of using language. Philosophers in today's postmodern environment often hesitate to make such claims but by discounting other truth claims one is in effect making a claim of one's own. Analysis is never neutral. Not just because we are all individuals who have a particular package of interests and needs which leak through into our objective analysis, but because as Habermas, the current voice of European reason, recognizes language itself cannot avoid representing the statements it presents as being true statements.

If for example I say Plato's theory of ideal forms is irrelevant or patriarchal I am saying that my statement – that Plato's theory is irrelevant – is true. Otherwise Plato's original statement remains unchallenged. In presenting reasons for Plato's being wrong I am claiming that my reasons are true, and valid if only in a particular historical setting, and that therefore Plato's claims are not true whether *per se,* or even if limited to a particular historical setting. In short one truth claim can not be challenged by anything other than another truth claim. Whether one objects to Plato's claim for political reasons like Popper who sees Plato as a threat to our democratic open society, or as the Anglo-American scientific analytic thinkers do for venturing beyond our cave bound sensate world, or even by Derrida's merely coughing at the critical moment when Plato is summing up his line of thought is immaterial. Whatever the objection may be it claims to be true, thus refuting Plato's original claim. That's the way the language works.

At this point the general reader may well have nodded off but I must pursue the discussion a bit further because I need to establish the philosophic grounds for the next stage in my argument. If not my line of thought can be easily be dismissed as anecdotal, and irrelevant. By mentioning Habermas and Kohlberg's moral development theory, with faint references to Plato, Aristotle, Descartes, and Kant, thrown in, I would remind the reader there's a tradition that values human rationality, disputes moral relativism, and cares passionately about the state of our suffering world. This tradition believes that comprehensive human thought – philosophy – has historically and will continue to effect real changes in the way society operates. Certainly the six philosophers I've just referred to fit this pattern. They are part of the tradition that I draw from to buttress my contention that Paul's Love is critical to social and political affairs.

So far we have established that moral political theory may be based either on what ought to be; in Kohlberg's culminating universalistic meaning, which allows for various options (Platonic, Christian, Kantian etc.), or on an Aristotelian model which begins with what is and leads to what ought to be.

III

Reflecting on my own ethical wrestling I find that first I am stirred by a vision of what ought to be, and then I look for signs of that vision already present in the situation. First I am shaken by a compelling ought which lifts me from my everyday existence to consider a radical change in my life style, then I look for evidence of this radical ought in the world around me to see who else has had this transforming insight.

When I became a conscientious objector in an *American Friends Service Committee* work camp in rural Mexico six months after being discharged from the Army, I had a visceral sense that people ought not to kill their fellow human beings. I was sitting alone on an adobe roof in a poor village reading Tolstoy and the Sermon on the Mount, looking across to the twin mountains Popocatepetl and Ixtaccihuatl when I had the riveting sense of being part of the entire human family.

I knew at once I could no longer entertain the possibility of taking the life of one of my sisters or brothers. I was exhilarated to know that despite any unresolved questions and personal failings I might have "At least I won't have to kill anybody!" I knew at that moment sitting on the flat clay roof in the warm sunlight, that I was a vital member of the human family. I knew that every person on earth was as close to me as my wife, Betty, or my parents and close friends.

We are family! All of us! How can we even think of killing each other? I may get angry at an infuriating sibling. But kill? Take his life with a bayonet clipped to the end of a rifle as I'd been trained to do – thrusting upward after impact? I could do that to an enemy, and would have while I was in the Army for my two years, but now? Now that I knew – knew in my bones, my brain, my gut – that we were one family, how could I have even considered taking a sister's or brother's life?

It's not a matter of knowing that we are all related biologically or metaphorically. Or saying that world wide brotherhood or sisterhood is a worthy ideal. It's as if that person I am being asked to kill – to defend the nation or to protect society from criminals – were related to me. Were a distant cousin – no not a cousin but were a brother or sister. Even though I haven't seen most of them. If we're one species, one family, then we don't kill each other. You don't kill Mary, or Harry or whatever siblings you have. You just don't do it. You might quarrel or even hit one another but you try and work out the differences somehow. Brothers and sisters don't kill each other. Or rather they shouldn't kill each other. They ought not to kill each other.

After four decades this ought still burns in my gut. It's the place where what I should do merges with what I most deeply want to do. The deepest desire of my heart becomes what I am impelled to do. It certainly isn't a chore, or a fear of what somebody else will think. It isn't one of the lesser oughts on the ought ladder of moral development. Another example would be my relation with Betty. I do love Betty and therefore I know I ought to love Betty. Loving Betty is not a chore, but it is a responsibility. It's more than just a good desire. Something I want to do. Something I like and choose to do. But what I want to do has become a passion, a duty, something that takes sacrifice – like writing – but that I can't imagine not doing. Artists and writers and anybody interested in their work will understand this beloved ought.

And my beloved ought is to care about other human beings knowing we are all one family.

IV

I will argue in the following chapters that this opening, this beloved ought, this glimpse of a far wider reality, is more than a personal experience. I'm not concerned to explore the personal implications of my experience but with sharing this experience as a truth claim with others. I don't know, as I said before, what reality looks like in its totality. But if this glimpse of reality is valid for others it will transform every person, every institution on earth. I hope it raises questions for the reader. I don't know what questions these will be, but if every human being on earth is your blood brother or sister it will change the way you think and your thinking will change the way you act.

I don't know how my dear son Steve ought to act as a stock broker, or Wendy who's a advocate for the handicapped, or Tom who works for AT & T. They know the obstacles and opportunities in their own situations far better than I do. But I know that if we treat other people - individually and in our organizational roles - as we would our family members it will transform our lives. And more importantly, if we privilege Levinas' and Buber's concern for other people over ourselves, it will change the lives of those around us.

In the following chapters we will examine the obstacles that prevent us from being the fully functional family we were created to be, so that in our institutional as well as our more personal relationships we can begin to live in the light that permeates our dim cave calling us out of darkness into the fellowship of being one human family. Calling us to be patient and kind to our sisters and brothers in practical ways in our everyday lives.

Chapter
XII

Paul's Love as Family

"We are family"

Willie Stargell, beloved slugger who
led the Pittsburgh Pirates to the
world championship in 1979

I

At the end of the last chapter the submerged stone that bridges the
gap between the individual and the wider society finally surfaced as

the human family. It's there in the immediate and the wider, inclusive family, that Paul's Love finds its most enduring social expression. But is the family a valid social manifestation of Paul's Love? Is it the preeminent institutional model of Paul's Love? The claim that the family is the most compelling social manifestation of Paul's Love rests on two lines of thought. First there is the historical reality that people are born into families, raised by other family members, and remain bonded to their families throughout their lives. Once a daughter or son, parent or sibling, always a daughter or son. One may change one's citizenship, one's religion, but family relationships, for good or ill, endure. The second reason the family may be considered the social equivalent of Paul's Love is that, as Aristotle, Rousseau, and a host of political thinkers recognized, the family is the original social institution; the institution from which tribes, villages and nations developed and whose norms and virtues still influence the ethically diverse compartmentalized institutions of modern society.

The family however is not the only model available. Friendship among two or more closely bonded individuals is another worthy model of Paul's Love. Faith communities also serve as social manifestations of Paul's Love. But since friendships are often restricted to one-on-one relationships and faith communities draw on the family as the model for their own communal life we may use the family as our primary model. Both friendship and religious fellowship I might add draw strength from being associated with the inclusive family I experienced on the slopes of Popocatepetl. To limit Paul's Love to a restricted circle of friends or to a particular faith community apart from one's relationship to the inclusive human family would seem a clear denial of Paul's Love which seeks in all its contactswith other people to be patient and kind. If Paul's Love is, as *Corinthians 13* clearly implies, the most compelling force in creation it must make its presence felt in all areas of creation.

Another reason for using the inclusive family as the preeminent manifestation of Paul's Love is that *Corinthians 13* by focusing on the other person rather than the self implies a social setting of some sort. *Corinthians 13* as we learned from Levinas and Buber is about being kind to the Other, not being resentful of others, etc. Paul's Love *needs* other people to be operative. It is a social virtue or norm. The family both in its restrictive sense and its inclusive sense is the implied social setting for Paul's Love. Not the only setting, but I believe the one most deeply grounded in our institutional life. As the neo-Aristotelians might say, the family is grounded not only in what "ought" to be but is grounded in what already "is".

Since we are using the family as the critical model or metaphor to trace Paul's Love in the wider society it's essential to establish that the human family, in both its restrictive and inclusive sense, is grounded in Paul's Love. Not that every family is loving and kind, but that the family as a functional institution is the best model of Paul's Love we have. While all this may seem obvious to the general reader philosophers are sometimes more obtuse, and if I am about to use the family as a model, or stand-in for Paul's Love as we examine the wider economic and political institutions some would insist I give my reasons for this shift. Switching terms without establishing the connection between the two terms can be misleading and I trust we may now use the human family as a critical metaphor for Paul's Love as it manifests itself in the institutional complexities of modern society.

As an institution the family, of course, can't love anyone. Only people can be patient and kind to one another. What the family can do is establish roles and guidelines that encourage parents and children and other relatives to care for one another. Like other institutions the family provides the opportunity for Paul's Love to flourish but it's up to flesh and blood human beings to utilize this opportunity. No family, hospital, school, business, church or nation can create the animated energy of Paul's Love that bonds one human being to another, but institutions do provide a structural opportunity for humans to relate to one another in loving ways.

In a certain sense institutions can be viewed as ethically neutral social structures which may be used for either benevolent or malevolent purposes, and while some institutions like the family and religious communities, have built in mission statements to promote Paul's Love, and others like law and order, the military, and business have other goals, its quite possible these tough minded institutions may adhere more closely to Paul's Love than families, churches, synagogues, and temples.

However, since certain institutions seem to nurture Paul's Love better than others we'll begin with those which most clearly manifest Paul's Love. Or more precisely, those that most clearly provide an opportunity for individuals to be patient and kind with one another. The three major traditional tender-minded institutions, (four if friendship is viewed as an institution) which are inconceivable without Paul's Love, are marriage (including a committed relationship between homosexual couples), the family, and faith communities. While spouses, or partners, are not always patient and kind with one another, and divorce rates hovers at 50%, marriage as an institution encourages individual citizens to be loving and caring toward one another. It's written into the original contract. Marriage does not guarantee Paul's Love but it does provide an opportunity for Paul's Love to develop. It provides the legal and ceremonial supports that are designed to protect the fragile seeds of human affection.

Even in the exotic realm of sexual relations Paul's Love has a decisive role to play. The cooperative dance of sexual passion requires that lovers be concerned, not only for their own pleasure, but also for the pleasure and well-being of their partners. Sexual activity without mutual love is soon tainted with resentment, coercion and ill will, which will eventually undermine the whole relationship. And the shy delicate dance of erotic passion itself becomes labored and awkward.

Leaving aside for the moment the inclusive human family let us look at the family in its more familiar institutional role. Devoted to raising children who are the fruit of sexual passion, the family is likewise workable only as it adheres to the animating energy of Paul's Love. Without Paul's Love given in large daily doses children grow up emotionally stunted, spouses bicker and fight, and the early promise of happiness and bliss becomes a nightmare for everyone. Over the centuries in a variety of historical settings the family, grounded in Paul's Love, has survived basically intact. Just as our cave dwelling ancestors did we too fall in love with one another and raise the offspring of our passion as tenderly as our primate ancestors the apes and chimpanzees.

Homosexuality, which has a long and more troubled history, has also been nurtured by Paul's Love. Visiting our daughter Wendy and her spouse Myrna, Betty and I find the same animating energy of Paul's Love that sustains our other four married children bubbling up between those two lovebirds.

Religious communities have a long history of providing its members with security and purpose. A security and purpose which is unthinkable apart from Paul's Love, whatever their other theological beliefs may be. Churches, synagogues, Quaker Meetings, Pow-Wow's, temples, and mosques still gather the faithful into one body to renew their commitment to Paul's Love as it comes to them from the higher power they worship together. Which they are encouraged to share among themselves and with the wider world. These three – marriage and committed relationships, the family, and religious communities - are generally conceded to be grounded in Paul's Love. That they so often fail to adhere to their high calling does not negate the nature of their effort.

III

As we move outward from these three intimate institutions Paul's Love is less evident. Political parties, corporations, small businesses, and large nations do not seem to operate from a primary commitment to Paul's Love. But even here, if we will take the time to listen closely, we may hear beneath the strident goal focused voices gentler voices reminiscent of those in the ER. To attune our ears to the enduring sounds of the great ocean of love I sensed around us in the ER takes patience and time. It takes hard thinking, and imagination. Arguments and analogies. And most importantly a heart that is willing to personalize its relationship to social institutions. It will take an inquisitive heart open to feeling its way through the abstractions of social organizations; companies, churches, and nations, into the unity that pervades the inclusive human family, in all its varied institutional activities.

Perhaps an analogy may help. Watching the weather report the news is often discouraging. Dark clouds, ice, freezing sleet, wind chill below zero, hurricanes moving up the coast. But without the ever glowing sun behind these seasonal changes why would we bother to worry about the approaching storms? It's the sun to which I would direct our attention; the radiance of Paul's Love glowing in our families and religious communities that sustains us in our economic and political lives as well.

When I first mentioned my experience in the ER at Chester County Hospital I concentrated on the animating power of love that bonded one human being to another as relatives and hospital staff cared for the patient, but as an institution the hospital is meant to cure our physical ills in as loving and caring a manner as possible. A nurse, doctor or paramedic is *meant* to be patient and kind to patients. Relatives and friends are also nurtured in social institutions – the family, schools, teams, and clubs – to foster a caring attitude to a sick mother or child, or one's friend. The ER provided an opportunity – not guaranteed – for individuals to interact in loving ways with one another.

I was an elementary school teacher for twenty-five years. Part of my job was to be patient and kind to my pupils. I did this by my manner and also by the things I taught them – how to read, how to add and subtract, how the three branches of government work, how to wait your turn, raise your hand, and get along with kids who bug you. How to work together to put on a medieval pageant for the parents with country dancing, story telling and juggling. How to study for tests. How to write creatively. "Five minutes non-stop. No using the same word over and over. Ready? Get set. GO!... STOP! OK, now count the number of words. Who wants to share? Do you want any comments on your writing Karl? No? Fine. Mary what about you?" So it went for twenty five years. A large part of a teacher's job is to prepare students to live in society in kind and loving ways. That was the role created for us by the educational system.

There were, of course, drawbacks to teaching. Issues that troubled my conscience and my understanding of Paul's Love. As an enthusiastic new pacifist, who'd given my allegiance to a loving Creator, I worried my first year about having to insist that every student participate in the pledge of allegiance. I was uneasy when I first moved from an inner city school to teach in a wealthy suburban district, which I felt perpetuated many of the materialistic and elitist values I deplored. Was I merely helping wealthy kids adjust to their future role as leaders of an insensitive materialistic society? Was I more a part of the problem than my idealist intent would admit? But on balance teaching was a wonderful opportunity to care for kids in a positive way. I was able in the course of teaching the prescribed curriculum to point out the inequities and challenges our society faced. I trusted that the questioning and cooperative attitudes the classroom community fostered would lead my students to loving and productive lives.

For twenty five years the institutional structure of the public school system gave me an opportunity to be patient and kind to my students and to encourage them in turn to be patient and kind to others. As a Quaker and child of the radical 1960's concerned for Civil Rights, the Vietnam War, and later women and gay rights I questioned the institutional evils of the time. As a public school teacher I came to appreciate the value of institutions.

What my experience in the ER and during twenty-five years of teaching suggests is, of course, that the possibility of Paul's Love is built into a great many of our social institutions. Hospitals, schools, social agencies, mental and physical health facilities, and many other social organizations clearly manifest the two intentions of Paul's Love. First they are designed to provide opportunities for one human being to act in loving ways to another within the confines of the social organization. Second, their attitudes and actions toward those outside their own community are also to be patient and kind. Those two criterion: adhering to Paul's Love within the organization and those they may serve, and adhering to Paul's Love in their relations with organizations and individuals outside their own organization will become critical as we continue to view the wider social world through the eyes of Paul's Love. It is not enough for a school system, for example, to adhere to Paul's Love among its own teachers and students, it must teach attitudes consistent with Paul's Love to all segments of the human family.

Since the educational system reflects other societal concerns – nationalism and support for the economic and cultural values of the society, for example – Paul's Love is not the only factor involved in educating children. Still, overall I think our case is strong that families, churches, schools and the other helping institutions do – or at least can - adhere to Paul's Love. Not always of course in practice but that they were designed to do so. These are institutions which no matter how badly they have failed to carry out their mandate to encourage Paul's Love – internally and to the outside world – may be reformed. Dysfunctional families, corrupt and arrogant religious communities, schools and hospitals may be revived by returning to the particular form of Paul's Love which lies at the heart of their reason to exist in the first place. Even should every individual family and faith community act in ways contrary to Paul's Love still as an institution the family and the religious communities are grounded on Paul's Love. Even when a generation of German school children in the 1930's entrust their developing lives to the Third Reich the institution of the school survives to act as a generally caring and loving institution in other times and places.

But what of the economic and political institutions? What of our capitalist system, and the state, which at times seem to cast individuals in less loving roles that require attitudes incompatible with those fostered by Paul's Love? But before giving these two tough-minded institutions the extended attention they deserve, we must prepare ourselves by considering the classic and current thinking on justice and Paul's Love in their institutional setting. To which we now turn to political philosophy.

A Condensed Overview
of Political Philosophy

"How should the relationship of philosophy to politics and
politics to philosophy be understood? Every complex form
of social life embodies some answer to this question and
the societies of Western modernity are no exception."

Alasdair MacIntyre

I

At the risk of losing the momentum established by working our way out from the tender-minded institutions grounded in Paul's Love to the more problematic economic and political institutions I feel I must summarize, in an interim chapter, some of the thinking that has already been done on the subject. Unlike science which updates its information on an almost daily basis political philosophy has been wrestling with the issue Plato first raised in *The Republic*, "What is Justice?" ever since. Comprehensive responses to the question first raised by Plato and Aristotle of how human beings may best live together in numbers larger than the extended family and tribe, still circulate today. The pros and cons of democracy and the autocratic alternatives are still being debated. Whether justice is to be grounded in "goodness" and "truth," i.e. on the shared values of a common culture as the Greeks proposed; rather than on notions of "fairness" and "natural rights", championed by Enlightenment thinkers such as Kant, Locke and Rousseau - which seem to some more suited to a pluralistic society like own - is still a very live issue.

For readers who wish to be reminded how philosophy has shaped our public institutions this interim chapter may prove useful. A great piece of literature nourishes countless individual lives, but the ideas of Plato and Aristotle, Locke and Rousseau, Adam Smith and Marx have shaped our economic and political institutions. Whether we live under a capitalist, socialist, democratic, or totalitarian system depends on which philosophy – which ideas – are favored over the other options. Ideas are an essential component of any social institution. Just as a play depends on a script as well as actors and scenery, ideas provide the script for our social institutions. No script no play. No ideas no institutions. Our past institutions from the Greek city state to the modern struggle between various forms of democracy, free market and state influenced economies, come from certain ideas that prevailed over other ideas. Without ideas the various fluctuating forces of society (the constitution, laws, customs and accepted practices) the competing interest groups and social classes, have no focus; nothing to protect or promote, nothing to rally around. Philosophy– comprehensive thinking about issues of vital concern to a culture – still has a critical role to play in shaping our future.

Two examples. Immanuel Kant the towering Enlightenment thinker was the first to clearly state, in non-religious terms, that morality required that we, "Treat every man (person) as an end in himself and never as a means only." (*Philosophy and Religion* (Dictionary) P.375, check *Critique of Judgement*.) This principle articulated the revolutionary spirit of the time that each human being had innate value and could not be used only as an instrument to serve the interest of a ruler or any other outside authority. The interests of the individual were – for good and ill – placed ahead of the interests of the community. Kant's articulation of the dignity and rights of the individual is a critical part of the rationale for our present legal and political institutions. It is part of the global consciousness written into our constitution, the UN charter and the ethos of rock bands and protest movements around the globe.

A second example of the power of a well articulated idea is Kant's proposal, in 1795 just as the constitutional democracies were getting under way in Europe and North America, that nations in order to avoid the ravages of war, relinquish a portion of their sovereignty to a "permanent congress of nations." The "universal union of states" envisaged by Kant was later, of course, to be embodied in the old League of Nations and the current United Nations, which exists to promote the "perpetual peace" that Kant treasured. By perpetual peace Kant meant a peace among nations based on enduring rational principles, rather than a merely political peace which served as a truce until fresh wars broke out. Whether his congress of nations is viable in our volatile world is still being tested.

Beyond these two examples a brief overview of the major themes in political philosophy may be useful as I prepare to present my thesis that Paul's Love has a far larger role in shaping our economic and political institutions than has generally been acknowledged.

II

Some political philosophers, notably Machiavelli, Hobbes, and Edmund Burke, would justify the rights of the ruling elite over common citizens arguing that only an autocratic covenant provides the social stability necessary for any workable society. Others like the Anglo-continental European thinkers: John Locke and Jean-Jacques Rousseau, view the implied social contract among unruly individuals in their natural state, first voiced by Plato's Glaucon in *The Republic* c. 375 almost four hundred years before Christianity, as *supporting* the rights of the common citizens. These democratic philosophies, which have evolved in the thought of John Rawls, the neo-Kantian American political philosopher, and Jurgen Habermas, the preeminent European social scientist and philosopher, advocate forms of economic justice which occupy a middle ground between the presumed stability of autocratic forms of government, which honor the rights of property and accumulated wealth over the demands of the poor, and socialism which many claim courts social instability by advocating economic parity at the cost of individual freedoms. All these efforts - autocratic, democratic, and socialistic – represent thoughtful attempts to control the self-seeking unruly nature of individuals. They all seek to prevent by social agreement and law Hobbes' "war of all against all." They all seek to hold back the destructive instincts, the "will to kill" that Freud uncovered in the unconscious. As Glaucon in *The Republic* states, "when men have both done and suffered injustice and… not being able to avoid the one and obtain the other, they think they had better agree among themselves to have neither; hence there arise laws and covenant." (*Republic,* p. 624).

Many political philosophers follow Glaucon in postulating some form of an original social contract that lays down the ground rules for society. Thinkers like Hobbes, the 17th century English monarchist, Locke, Rousseau, and the great French essayist Montesquieu, laid the groundwork for the constitutional governments that prevail today. Hobbes took the first step by advocating adherence to the social agreement in which the people gave their power to the king in exchange for law and social order. Having relinquished their powers the people, Hobbes said, had no right to demand it back again no matter how badly the king acted. Locke and Rousseau said no, the people had only *lent* their God-given natural freedoms to the government and were free to reclaim their freedom to form a state more to their liking. The real social contract, they claimed, was among the people themselves who agreed to limit their natural and unruly freedom for the sake of a constitutional government which they ran themselves, through free elections and the balance of powers; Montesquieu's executive, legislative and judicial branches of government.

Others like Marx and modern fascists reject the social contract theory arguing that the state evolved from conflicting historical forces (Marxism) or directly from the spirit of the people (the Volk in German). In fascist governments the spirit of the nation is viewed as embodied in a supreme leader – the father of the country – who acts to fulfill the national destiny. Utilizing the German idealist Hegel who had argued that abstract thought, Spirit, works its way through history in a dialectic fashion the fascists equated Hegel's Spirit with their own particular state. In Italy Mussolini argued that "Against individualism, the Fascist conception is for the State; and it is for the individual in so far as the individual coincides with the State which is the conscience and universal will of man in his historical existence." Mussolini claims that, "Fascism reaffirms the State as the true reality of the individual;" that the "State as the universal will is the true creator of right." (Doctrine of Fascism, 1939, P626-7, *Great Political Thinkers*, Ebenstein.) Those sentiments derive from Hegel who himself equated the near ideal state with his own Prussian constitutional monarchy. Which is not to say Hegel would have approved of modern fascism, any more than he would of Marxism, which also utilizes certain aspects of his philosophy.

Despite Nietzsche's opposition to anti-Semitism and German nationalism the fascists in Germany drew on the great German philosopher's exaltation of the *ubermensch*, the strong noble leader who is not subject to the petty morality of the resentful democratic mob. I find it disturbing that such an anti-democratic ruthless thinker as Nietzsche should be so honored and emulated today. While I appreciate his insightful exposure of the *resentment* that lies behind the often hypocritical policies and practices of the Judeo-Christian love ethic, I'm troubled by his failure to provide a viable alternative that would allow for a more authentic human bonding. Instead we are left with a rationale for the will-to-power which pits one group, one individual against another. An ancient theme in the thinking of Glaucon, Machiavelli, and others which not only explained but justified the political violence that has brought so much suffering into the world. While Schopenhauer, the quintessential philosophic pessimist, grieved over the suffering caused by the ego-absorbed ruthless will Nietzsche exalted in the will's ability to flaunt conventional moral norms. Whether Nietzsche's impassioned prose style was serious as some commentators believe, or merely ironic and metaphorical as others contend does not alter the dangers of installing the will-to-power as the primary thrust of a political philosophy.

While Nietzsche may well have deplored the anti-Semitic jingoism of Hitler's Third Reich his central thesis does lend credence to autocratic institutions. Though many of Nietzshce's modern admirers (Andre Gide, Foucault and Derrida, and Walter Kaufman who resurrected Nietzsche's reputation after W.W. II) argue for a non-political aesthetic, psychological, or linguistic reading of Nietzsche others including Heidegger, Karl Jaspers, Thomas Mann and Alan Bloom are troubled by the cultural and political implications of his writings. In an exhaustive treatment Heidegger finds Nietzsche is "not an overcoming of nihilism… [but] the ultimate entanglement in nihilism." (*Cambridge Companion*, P. 312) While I agree my own concern is more narrowly focused; to expose Nietzsche as a significant contributor to Hitler's regime which Heidegger supported. Nietzsche's master/ slave motif, for example lends itself more easily to a political than a purely aesthetic or linguistic interpretation. Equally disturbing is the pungent violence of Nietzsche's historical examples and metaphors, which must await further mention until we consider the state and war later on. Metaphors which sympathetic commentators in any case – except for the French libido-driven irrationalist Georges Bataille – fail to echo in their thoughtful analysis. Theirs is a muted analysis which fails, in my mind, to wrestle with the implications of Nietzsche's ethical obscenities. By dismantling conventional morality without providing a more humane alternative Nietzsche opens the way for institutionalizing humankind's most ruthless instincts.

At the opposite end of the power spectrum Utopian visionaries like the 19th century French communally minded anarchist Proudhon, also forgo the legalism of a social contract, which they feel justifies the state's suppression of the individual's innate natural freedom. These peaceful visionaries – though some anarchists of course were not peaceful at all - advocate a society where the state is gradually abolished ("withers away") as smaller more democratic and flexible social groups arise to solve common problems (feeding the population, manufacturing goods, providing public services, controlling crime, etc.). Cooperation, voluntary mutualism, in their view allows intermediate social organizations (farms, factories, social agencies etc.) to grow to their full potential, protecting atomistic individuals from an impersonal despotic state. Peter Maurin's and Dorothy Day's *Catholic Worker*, with its mix of urban houses of hospitality and rural farms designed to provide a model of productive communal life, building the new society within the shell of the old, drew heavily on Proudhon and the peaceful anarchists. Before infusing the communities with their own faith-based Christianity.

The contemporary English philosopher Alasdair MacIntyre, in a less radical way than the Utopian visionaries, would revive the role of communally shared values – virtues - in shaping our political life. Drawing on Aristotelian ethics MacIntyre grounds morality not on abstract principles as Kant and Rawls do, but on the virtues, practices and institutions of particular historical communities. Irish fishing and farming communities for example. Later we shall relate MacIntyre's insightful work to our own concern for illuminating Paul's Love in the institutions in which we live.

III

I mention these works to remind readers that a great deal of careful thought over the centuries has gone into what constitutes a good society. From Plato on it can be seen that political philosophy in each era wrestled with the historical dilemmas peculiar to its own situation. Time and again philosophy has provided the conceptual solutions embodied in new forms of social and political life.

Machiavelli writes for aspiring rulers in the pervasively corrupt late Renaissance Italian city-states, Plato for the more idealistic classical Greek city-states. Hobbes is concerned to hold back the rising rebelliousness of the early industrial lower classes; Rousseau – a marvelous stylist and thinker – *wants* to encourage the rising rebelliousness of the common people. Prelude, with Locke and Thomas Jefferson, to the American and French Revolutions. Marx has a passion to guide the restlessness of oppressed industrial workers into viable political channels.

John Rawls and Jurgen Habermas in our own time seek – in two distinct ways - to promote a more equitable distribution of goods and powers. Balancing their zeal for social justice against the realities of political possibilities they respect the stability of society and the rights of all contending social and political factions. Unlike Marxism, for example, as it was practiced and distorted in the old Soviet Union and in China under Mao. In a pluralistic society, without shared moral and religious values which shape the entire society's view of what is good and just Rawls and Habermas aim at a society that is workable and fair to the various contending groups. They aim, not as Plato, Marx and the Utopian Socialists did, at a unified good and just society but at a fair and feasible society. MacIntyre, on the other hand advocates a good and just society based on historically tested virtues: justice, courage and truthfulness. Recognizing the problematic nature of each group's collective history MacIntyre advocates not, as some critics contend, a conservative return to the past, but a respect for historical communal traditions which continue to reform themselves from within to adhere to the virtues and practices which inspired them in the first place.

Reflecting on the major contemporary political philosophers one notices at once the great debt each owes to philosophers from the past. Rawls is unthinkable without Kant. MacIntrye draws heavily from Aristotle and Aquinas. Habermas continues the liberal Enlightenment tradition of Locke and Rousseau, and later Marx and Engels. Postmodern anti-Enlightenment philosophers like Foucalt, Derrida, Luce Irigaray the insightful French feminist philosopher, and Ayn Rand, were, in various ways, deeply influenced by Nietzsche. These left leaning disciples of the autocratic Nietzsche, except for Ayn Rand, utilize the Nietzschean analysis of power to expose the mechanics of oppression suppressing emancipatory movements favoring the poor, women, and other marginalized groups. Groups which Nietzsche despised.

Unlike science where the rug of past achievements rolls up behind the forward facing ongoing truth in philosophy – and particularly in political philosophy – each generation of thinkers utilizes truth-claims from the broad and textured past in the light of contemporary social needs. The political truth-claims society holds today will likewise impact on our political and economic life. Whether we hold worldviews that draw from Locke or Marx, Adam Smith or Nietzsche, or contemporary thinkers like Rawls, MacIntyre and the yet to be mentioned nonviolence of Gandhi and Dr. King political truth-claims will continue to shape our institutional life. Philosophy in one form or another will continue to play a major role in clarifying and shaping our economic and political institutions.

IV

Reflecting on the major themes of political philosophy I do not find Paul's Love featured as a significant element in the formation of our social institutions. At least not overtly. No one except a few non-violent saints like Gandhi and the Dalai Lama, and the rather scattered peace movement is advocating Paul's Love as an appropriate response to terrorism and war. Speaking of terrorism I'm reminded not only of 9/11 but of the US's use of drones and systematic torture, and the T-shirt that sells well in New Mexico with four Indian warriors under the words, "Fighting for Homeland Security against Terrorism since 1492". In our complex and compartmentalized society Paul's Love as a distinct language game is rarely heard beyond the domestic borders of private life. In public affairs the talk, at its best has turned to human rights, justice, and peaceful social change. But if we look more closely I believe we'll find our impersonal, sometimes repressive social institutions, glowing with possibilities for human bonding. I believe we'll find evidence for Paul's Love permeating our social institutions in ways that allow room for the transformation of the entire social order.

No one I think would deny that the political ideas of Plato, Hobbes, Rousseau, and Marx have had a profound effect on history. Take out Chaucer, Skakespeare, and Emily Dickinson from world literature and life goes on. Take out Adam Smith, Rousseau and Locke, Karl Marx and Nietzsche, and history has a different texture. Ideas matter. For good or evil. One way or another ideas – philosophy – shape our social and political lives. Which is why I am forced to put my case for Paul's Love in philosophic terms. Frankly I'm more comfortable speaking from my own experience; giving my insights in a narrative manner, but the gut feelings that drive my writing are far more pervasive than the personal examples, and images I've used to illustrate my points. My concern to illuminate Paul's Love in philosophic ways is driven to effect change in the viewpoints from which all of us view the world around us. Not to insist on change – Paul's Love does not insist, but to present an option, an alternative possibility to our accustomed response to public affairs.

To present Paul's Love as a viable political option I will have to challenge our current compartmentalized ethics. Only then can I make the case that Paul's Love provides a workable hypothesis for alleviating the ills that plague our fevered world.

Chapter
XIV

Justice or Paul's Love?

"The ontology of love… shows the primacy of love in relation to power and justice." (p.22, *Love, Justice and Power*)

Paul Tillich, Theologian

"It would be a serious mistake to contrast the bronze face of justice with the merciful face of charity. Because it is the only measure of ethics, compassion will need to be present just as much in the legal world as in international and domestic relations… Thus its function is to guarantee the cohesion of a world which is irrevocably plural. The permeation of this measure [compassion] through all structures is obviously a process that cannot be finished."

Jean Greisch, Dean of the Faculty of Philosophy
at Institut Catholique de Paris

"Some friends have told me that truth and nonviolence have
no place in politics and worldly affairs. I do not agree."

Gandhi

I

Chapters eleven and twelve argued that Paul's Love manifest in the inclusive human family was central to the tender-minded institutions. Drawing on a riveting experience in the local ER and twenty-five years of teaching elementary age children, I maintained that religious communities, schools, hospitals, etc. were established specifically to provide opportunities for individual human beings to relate to one another in a caring and loving manner. But what of the tough-minded institutions? Of capitalism and the state at war, twin guardians of public life, at least in the non-Islam western world, which serve as the ultimate organizations, i.e. the two bodies of public power which when push comes to shove can exercise their will over lesser institutions? A religious body or scientific community, for example, though it has its own area of influence cannot seriously challenge the power of capitalism or the state. How does Paul's Love effect these dominant guardians of the public welfare?

There are of course other social organizations besides the family and faith community and the two ultimate tough-minded institutions. The academic, scientific, the creative and performing arts, and the pervasive mass media, for example. But if we wrestle with the compartmentalized ethics and "incompatible attitudes" between the tender-minded family and the seemingly tough-minded norms of capitalism and the state at war, we may gain insights into the other significant institutions as well. In any case our task seems daunting enough as it is.

II

If Paul's Love is the preeminent domestic norm then justice, according to conventional wisdom, is the preeminent civic norm. When we speak of what we "ought" to do among our family, friends and associates Paul's Love is the primary premise. When we would rectify the problems that plague society we speak of equal opportunity, fairness and justice. Unlike marriage vows there are no strictures written into our laws that insist people care for one another. That is left as a private matter.

But is this shift in terminology from Paul's Love to justice justified? Most political philosophy ever since Plato asked, "What is Justice?" as the fundamental political question have said yes. Even Levinas who champions the Other, the human face for whose well-being I am responsible, questions the relevance of Paul's Love in public affairs. Seeing the I-Thou relationship as an *amorous dialogue* and love without justice as "a pious intention oblivious to real evil" Levinas clearly states that "Law takes precedence over charity." (*Entre Nous*, P.21) I would suggest, however, a more nuanced relationship between justice, law and Paul's Love than Levinas and most political philosophers allow for. Paul's Love, as we shall see, plays a decisive unacknowledged role under girding the commonly accepted views of justice. Without Paul's Love, without the inclusive human family, there is no real justice. Justice, I shall argue, is possible only in an assumed family setting.

III

But can even justice, as championed in Plato's *Republic* and by Enlightenment- minded philosophers from Descartes to Habermas and Rawls effectively influence public affairs? Perhaps Rousseau and

Reinhold Niebuhr, the Cold War neo- orthodox theologian, were right to isolate the moral individual apart from "immoral society". Perhaps a compartmentalized ethics, adapted to the conflicting purposes of tender and tough minded institutions, is the best we can do. Three of our most astute political philosophers, Rawls, Habermas and MacIntyre have said no. They suggest that justice, if not Paul's Love, *is* possible in our pluralistic society. We will consider their arguments, before suggesting not that Paul's Love replace justice and law, but that Paul's Love under girds and enhances their efforts. But first we turn to the three proposals.

Rawls argues that in a democracy "justice and fairness" dictate that individual rights of conscience must be protected and that secondly, "Social and economic inequalities are to be arranged... to the greatest benefit to the least advantaged." (*Theory of Justice*, P.302, or *Rawls,* P43) In essence Rawls contends that a multicultural society like ours can preserve the individual freedoms of its advantaged citizens and also enhance the rights and well-being of its least advantaged citizens. One senses at once, the generous intent of Rawls' formulation that a free market democratic society provide economic justice to the poor and marginalized. Rawls' thoughtfully crafted proposal while it echoes Liberation theology's radical "option for the poor" is careful to preserve the individual freedoms inherent in the democratic tradition. Balancing the demands of individual freedom and economic justice in a pluralistic society Rawls' proposal has revived political philosophy in the late twentieth century.

Habermas, the liberal European humanist, takes a more procedural approach. Rather than, in effect, legislating justice on the basis of principles fair to all as Rawls does, Habermas argues that justice arises from rational dialogue between contending parties in any social dispute. His "discourse ethics" postulates that, "Only those norms can claim to be valid that meet (or could meet) with the approval of all affected in their capacity as participants in a practical discourse." (*Habermas,* by Howe, P36 or *Discourse Ethics* by Habermas) Providing a Socratic setting for contending parties to search together for workable just solutions to social problems, "discourse ethics" hopes to avoid the precarious compromises that emerge from purely power driven negotiations. Compromises that often serve the interests of the stronger party, and that dissolve under pressure. As with Rawls I sense a truly generous spirit behind Habermas' intent which allows the emancipatory movements, which champion the poor and other marginalized segments of society, to discuss their grievances on a level playing field with their powerful economic and political adversaries.

The third approach, advocated by MacIntyre, bases justice on the virtues, practices and institutions that have a proven record of providing society with a commonly accepted morality from which to wrestle with the challenges of a complex, relativistic modern world. Grounding justice in "moral traditions" by which religious, ethnic, and rural communities have preserved a core of beliefs and practices over time, MacIntyre challenges the philosophically abstract approach of Rawls and the ethically pragmatic approach of "discourse ethics." Rawls and Habermas in turn view MacIntyre's views as hopelessly out of date in our multicultural world where there is no commonly agreed upon set of moral values. To insist on one universal set of moral principles, they claim, ignores the cultural diversity which is the central challenge of the post-modern era.

Each of these approaches is currently being hotly debated; attacked and defended from various points of view. Each as I've suggested are astute and generously intentioned attempts to ameliorate the effects of ethical compartmentalization. My contention will be that while all three wrestle with the inequities and injustices of modern society they all overlook Paul's Love as the dominant factor behind their efforts.

IV

By focusing on justice Rawls, Habermas and MacIntyre have neglected the animating reality of Paul's Love on which all justice is based. For unless we cared about people in a visceral way as our brothers and sisters why would we care whether they were treated fairly or justly? We don't agonize over providing justice to rocks or other inanimate objects. Why should we agonize so over the oppressive conditions and inequities so many of our fellow human beings face on a daily basis? When I get an appeal in the mail from Jimmy Carter or the American Friends Service Committee asking for money to help what Rawls calls the least advantaged I don't need to see a hungry face to personalize the appeal. I know immediately what is being asked of me. One of my kin needs help. One of my sisters and brothers needs my support. It's not about justice in an abstract sense, being sure everybody has a fair chance in life. Unless I cared about the person or persons being deprived or oppressed why would I bother to go out of my way to help? Unless justice is about bonding with real people why spend my time and money on their behalf? Justice ultimately is about relating to the other members of the inclusive human family (and for Buddhists and many others to all living creatures) in a loving way. Without the assumption that justice involves the animated bonding of the human family – even at a distance – justice remains abstract and impersonal.

It's a matter not of proximity but of kinship. Our two daughters live in South Carolina some six hundred miles away. Would they become less our daughters if they moved to San Francisco, some three thousand miles away? Or Japan? If one of them had a new baby girl in Japan would we not still care about her as a beloved grandchild even before we had seen her in person? Kinship, not distance or a face to face relationship, is what creates family unity. Even an absent or long lost sibling may be accorded the privileges of family membership. In the inclusive human family the ties between members are binding whether one lives with or personally knows every member.

Going back to justice let us assume I am wrong. Let's assume that justice *can* stand on its own apart from Paul's Love. In order to fulfill Rawls' requirement that all citizens have their rights protected and that society privilege the least advantaged we could sit at our computers and order out to have all our needs met. We could be educated, fed, clothed, housed, and entertained in complete isolation from one another. As long as no one went hungry or had their other rights violated we could have perfect justice without ever leaving the comfort of our own homes. The race could even continue to propagate itself without there being physical contact between one human and another. Perfect justice perpetuates itself perpetually.

If we follow justice utilizing Habermas's model of discourse ethics we might use the Internet to have group discussions in which each adversarial party expresses its own needs, listens to the other party's needs and work together to find solutions acceptable to both parties. Or the talks might be held face to face. It wouldn't matter as long as justice is arrived at without *necessarily* considering how the participants relate to one another. Paul's Love in other words is, in Habermas's formulation, an optional element. As long as the disputed issues are resolved in a manner agreed upon by all participants justice is served. Habermas might well argue that in our contentious world this is quite enough. That after discourse ethics has engaged the participants (Palestinians and Israelis, multinational corporations and the Third world, etc.) in resolving common problems better human relations might well have a chance to develop. Justice come first - then possibly Paul's Love.

I would argue that the way the two parties relate to each other is part of the mix from the start. To expect intellectual moral discourse to resolve volatile issues without resolving the emotional conflict between the parties is unrealistic. The need is to transform hostility and suspicion into positive attitudes that promote an ongoing familial relationship. If both sides treat each other with patience and kindness future disputes can be dealt with in the context of the positive relationship already existing between the two parties. Just as attitudes may change between individuals so individuals as members of a group may also change their attitudes to their one-time adversaries.

Habermas himself by emphasizing empathy for the other side's point of view and "mutual understanding" has introduced elements consistent with Paul's Love. The extent to which this leads to the animated bonding between human beings of Paul's Love rather than merely a temporary agreement or truce is I believe the real value of Habermas's discourse ethics. In brief, discourse ethics becomes ethics rather than merely an intellectual agreement when Paul's Love is utilized as an essential element in building the trust between contending parties necessary to sustain the agreements reached.

The third approach to justice, which leaves open the possibility that Paul's Love might be among the primary virtues, comes closest to acknowledging the critical presence of Paul's Love. By speaking of justice as a primary virtue along with courage and truthfulness MacIntyre centers ethics on what he calls "internal goods." Unlike external secondary goods – fame, money, and power - a virtue "is an acquired human quality" that is intrinsic to a given practice. Chess, physics and medicine are practices which have no external goals but "the goals themselves are transmuted by the history of the activity." (*The MacIntyre Reader*, P.86 *After Virtue*) In other words one plays chess for the challenge and enjoyment of playing chess, not for the sake of prizes, fame or money which are external to the practice itself. Medicine is a practice, which perpetuates itself in research and healing. Not in the financial rewards and prestige accorded health care professionals. These rewards are incidental to the practice of medicine. Morality likewise is viewed as an acquired human quality that is nurtured in a social setting – often by an ethnic, religious or rural community - where one practices justice or truthfulness as a self- validating activity. One learns to be honest, just or courageous in a social environment which views these virtues as inherently valuable and necessary to the life of the community.

Institutions play a more sinister role in MacIntyre's thinking. While schools, hospitals and religious communities make possible the virtues and practices MacIntyre values they also undermine the internal goods they were intended to promote. Institutions, tender and tough minded alike, get caught up in the demands of a free market economy for example and hospitals and health care agencies must become financially profitable as well as medically effective, which can lead to cutting corners in caring for patients' needs and even corruption. As MacIntyre writes, "the essential function of the virtues is clear. Without them, without justice, courage and truthfulness, practices could not resist the corrupting power of institutions." (*After Virtue* in *Readings..* P. 87)

Frankly I was surprised not to find Paul's Love more strongly emphasized in MacIntyre's analysis of the foundational social virtues. The discussion of "cooperative friendship", for example, might have more sharply engaged his three featured virtues. Justice, courage and truthfulness are certainly historically tested human attributes, which have sustained, or at least challenged, a wide range of institutions from families to corporations and nations. Certainly no institution would present itself to the public as anything less than just, brave and truthful. But where is Paul's Love?

Looking closely at MacIntyre's featured virtues I find they can not stand alone. Without Paul's Love, each of his primal virtues fails to sustain the "moral traditions" he values as the proper philosophic response to a relativistic and ethically compartmentalized world. Justice without Paul's Love, as we've seen, becomes either an abstract intellectual exercise or an impersonal procedure for people who simply coexist without affection, bonding or real responsibility for one another. Certainly the "moral traditions" – the historical communities that MacIntyre champions are *not* grounded in justice, courage and truthfulness *per se*. They *are* grounded in the affection and kindness the members of the community feel for one another. The successful communal life envisaged by MacIntyre, without Paul's Love is unthinkable. Being just, brave and truthful in a communal setting makes sense because it strengthens the bonding among the members. One doesn't treat a brother or sister unjustly, or tell them lies. One is brave in defense of the community. Virtues in moral traditions make sense only in the context of Paul's Love, or to speak in social terms, make sense in the context of community as a family.

Like distant stars belonging to the same constellation an impersonal justice makes us aware of each other across space but there is no animating energy that bonds us together. We are not family. We are separate human entities that share a common historical space in time. That we are all fed, housed and allowed to develop our talents in a just and fair manner is small consolation for the loss of Paul's Love – for the animated bonding that sustains us all.

Courage while a virtue necessary at times to support communal life, without compassion can easily slide into arrogance and, at the political level, Machaivellian ruthlessness. Necessary, because without courage Paul's Love is not able "to endure all things… to bear all things." In order to love my sister or brother I must act fearlessly in their defense. The form this fearless courage must take in order to adhere to Paul's Love will concern us when we consider Paul's Love and the state.

Truthfulness, MacIntyre's third featured virtue, which means to tell the truth in all situations, also cannot stand alone. For truth-telling quickly brings us into conflict with Paul's Love. Should one, for example, always tell the truth to one's friends and family? About their looks, their health their personal shortcomings? Should one tell the Nazi where the Jews are hidden in one's house? In these instances MacIntyre's truth-telling would seem to defer to the higher value of Paul's Love. A thorny issue at the theoretical level truth-telling at the practical level seems constricted by Paul's Love which is, so I am arguing, to be given primary consideration. All three of MacIntyre's featured virtues, justice, courage and truthfulness, would seem unable to stand on their own - especially in the communal setting of MacIntyre's moral traditions. Viewed as supportive of and emanating from Paul's Love justice, courage and truth-telling become essential elements in the creation of a moral tradition.

V

If my argument is convincing that Paul's Love under girds justice in the thinking of philosophers as diverse as Rawls, Habermas and MacIntyre why have political philosophers so often privileged justice at the institutional level? Without unduly interrupting our main argument a few brief comments might be useful.

It's not I think that no one has related Paul's Love to political affairs. Many thinkers active in the political arena speak quite openly of compassion and the unity of the human family. Gandhi, Dr. King, Bishop Tutu and Nelson Mandala in South Africa and the Dali Lama speak of justice as infused with the radiant fellow feeling Paul champions. Paul Tillich, *the* religious philosopher for the 1960's in America, clearly places Paul's Love in its philosophical setting. His *Love, Power and Justice* especially is a primer on Paul's Love and its relation to power and justice - the two supporting and subsidiary components of existence. "Life is being in actuality and love is the moving power of life. In these two [ideas] the ontological nature of love is expressed. Being (existence, reality) is not actual without the love that drives everything that is towards everything else that is… Love is the ultimate principle of justice. Love reunites; justice preserves what is to be united. It is the form in which and through which love performs its work." (*Love, Power and Justice.* P 25, 71) The contemporary German moral philosopher Werner Marx in *Ethics and Lifeworld,* also is eloquent in defense of "compassion" and "being able to sympathize." Speaking of the overlapping compartmentalized institutions as worlds Werner Marx says, "All that happens in the numerous worlds turns on the question of knowing whether and how the measure of being able to sympathize is active there… it is compassion that measures all behavior. Thus when all is said and done it is [compassion, being able to sympathize] which governs the numerous worlds." (*Ethics,* P. 58)

Philosophers however do not generally mention sympathy and compassion; especially in public affairs. Perhaps as thinkers, especially as academic thinkers, they are temperamentally uncomfortable around feelings. Always probing for the essential or structural truth behind the smoke screen of T. S. Eliot's unsettling "squads of emotion". And Paul's Love is about feelings, as well as reason and the will. Caring about the other person, being kind and patient, involve fluid and to the philosophic mind untidy emotions. As a mix of emotion, reason and will love is often labeled a secular passion best left to poets and psychologists; though there is an intriguing line of thought running from Plato and Aristotle through Heidegger to Buber and Levinas, that focuses on friendship. While Tillich clearly presents Paul's Love as the basis for ontology (the study of being or existence) pointing to love (and occasionally eros) in Plato and Aristotle, Augustine, Hegel, and the modern Existentialists as evidence that "love has played a major ontological role" in philosophy and human existence, I find this claim less than compelling. Its not that love in the sense implied by *Corinthians 13* is totally absent from classical and more recent philosophy, but rather that its presence is muted and often obscured by the other concerns. Speaking from within

Plato's ideal Forms of goodness, justice etc. Paul's simple love has lost its own clear and distinct voice. By the time one has glimpsed Eros, or will, or Hegel's Spirit, or Aristotle's Unmoved Mover at the heart of the philosopher's vision one has lost touch with Paul's animated bonding between two human beings. The focus has shifted from Paul's Love to the system, which enshrines and utilizes love, especially in theology as many contemporary humanists have been quick to point out. Despite Tillich's concern - and mine - that love which is at the heart of existence have its own voice in our philosophic and public life other concerns and concepts have obscured its primal authority. Despite the perceptive work on friendship and the muted ontological interest on love, Paul's Love has clearly been philosophically slighted.

Another reason sympathy and compassion are so often ignored in political philosophy relates to the possible gender bias of our mostly male sources. Since most of the political thinkers I've referred to have been male I wonder to what extent this has reinforced my own gender based predilection to view life as a confusing puzzle to be best understood by uncovering the secluded principles and underlying truths of reality. Which is, according to many feminists, a typical but limiting masculine perspective, which marginalizes emotions, relationships and the elusive interwoven web of life. Concerns common to Paul's Love and to many feminists.

Carol Gilligan's groundbreaking study, *In A Different Voice*, on the moral development of young men and women, found that Kohlberg had badly misinterpreted his own study on the six stages of moral development. Kohlberg's study showed many young men reaching the higher levels (five and perhaps six) while young women peaked at the third level. Kohlberg had assumed that moral development was about discovering ethical principles: a series of ever more autonomous and universal "oughts". His study failed to identify moral development as the ability to empathize with others, establish intimate relationships and relate to the wider interconnectedness between all human beings and even the rest of creation. How far my own thinking has been restricted by a similar bias is hard to say, but it does seem clear that Paul's Love is based more on the web of animated bonding which enhances the inclusive human family, than on universal principles or rational procedures for resolving disputes. How this moral sensitivity relates to the first of our tough-minded institutions, capitalism, takes us to our next stepping stone in chapter XV.

Chapter
XV

Capitalism, Self-interest and the Inclusive Family

"Virtue is the center without excuse. I have above all admitted it is my duty to do the most good through the whole course of life."

Josiah White, Early American Capitalist
Pioneer & a distant relative

"At the heart of capitalism's inhumanity – and no sensible person will deny that the market is an amoral and often cruelly capricious master – is the fact that it treats labor as a commodity… an unsold commodity is a nuisance, an unemployed worker a tragedy."

The Accidental Theorist, Paul Krugman

I

To prove that Paul's Love plays a significant role in our economic lives I will need to show that as an institution capitalism encourages one human being to treat another human being in a patient and kind manner. I will need to demonstrate that capitalism is *not* an inhuman and cruelly capricious master, but rather an eccentric well intentioned servant who has the best interests of the family it serves at heart. Since we are concerned with Paul's Love rather than justice I must not stop short with talk of fairness and equal opportunity but must uncover a visceral and positive relationship between human beings in their economic lives. Unless capitalism provides opportunities for positive bonding, as the tender-minded institutions do, Paul's Love will have failed to demonstrate the pervasive claims made in *Corinthians 13*. Before pressing these challenging claims some background on capitalism, its various political settings and its relationship to the more amorphous "mood of the people" may prove useful.

Webster defines capitalism as the economic system in which investment, ownership of the means of production, distribution, and the exchange of wealth in carried out by "… private individuals or corporations, esp. as contrasted to cooperatively or state-owned means of wealth." For the definitive statement explaining why capitalism works we turn to a few familiar pungent thoughts from Adam Smith's foundational *Wealth of Nations,* published just as the industrial revolution was getting under way in 1776.

> "It is not from the benevolence of the butcher, the brewer, or the baker that we expect our dinner, but from their regard to their own interest. We address

ourselves, not to their humanity but to their self-love, and never talk to them of our own necessities but of their advantages."

With this introduction to capitalism we seem to have moved from Paul's Love, so evident in the tender-minded institutions, to self-love and personal gain as the primary motivation supporting our economic system. The result of this narrow focus on one's own interest is, in Adam Smith's view, of great benefit to the whole society.

> "The employer... neither intends to promote the public interest, nor knows how much he is promoting it... he intends only his own gain, and is in this led by an invisible hand to promote an end which was no part of his intention... By pursuing his own interest he frequently promotes that of the society more effectively than when he really intends to promote it..."

> *Wealth of Nations,* (Princeton.. .P 318, 326-7)

Here, clearly stated, is the commonly accepted rationale for the economic system under which we live. The point of conflict with Paul's Love as expressed in our families and MacIntyre's "moral traditions" seems clear cut and obvious. Paul's Love is about caring for the other person. Capitalism is about caring for oneself and trusting the invisible hand of the free market economy to work for the benefit of the entire society. Selfishness leads to economic productivity and social harmony. Greed is good. In religious terms Smith is saying the economic gods write straight with crooked lines; that the invisible hand moves in mysterious ways to the benefit of all.

Whether or not capitalism necessarily leads to social harmony; domestically and around the globe is open to serious debate, but it does provide jobs, income, and a better standard of living for billions of people. It has survived the challenge of both democratic and totalitarian socialism, two major world wars, and a variety of governmental regulations and social welfare programs, which modified but did not alter the basic thrust of Smith's free market economy. While capitalism has been challenged by many thinkers on the Left including Cornell West and bell hooks (rare American socialists), Norm Chomsky (noted linguist and libertarian communal anarchist), and Alain Badiou, a French Maoist Marxist who focuses on economic inequality as the *bete noire* of capitalism, others notably Rawls, Habermas, and MacIntyre, propose modifications to make the system more just to all segments of society.

Historically, of course, Adam Smith's *Laissez-faire* capitalism has already been modified over time. Since its beginnings, in industrial England in the 1760's, modern capitalism has been most seriously challenged by socialism and trade unionism. Forced by these labor oriented movements to address the critical issues of low wages and oppressive working conditions capitalism has been significantly modified to be more responsive to the needs of employees and society at large.

Laissez-faire capitalism has long since given way to a variety of capitalist economies. The turn of the millennium post-communist gangster-tinged economy in Russia, the repressive Chinese managed economy, the welfare economies of Scandinavia and other European countries and the rugged individualism of American capitalism, still in tension with F.D.R.'s New Deal legacy of a compassionate free enterprise system that protects the rights of labor, and provides safety nets for those in most need, all participate in the global capitalist economy.

The shape that capitalism takes in various settings is largely determined by the interaction between the economy, the political environment and occasionally the elusive "mood of the people". In a post-communist Russian state with a depressed economy and uncertain leadership capitalism emerges in one way. In smaller Scandinavian nations with stable democratic political leadership capitalism takes another form. Capitalism functions somewhat differently in communist China than it does in Japan, or Germany or the United States.

While the more amorphous mood of the people seldom operates in a decisive manner to disrupt the back and forth play between the economy and the state, when it does seismic shifts in the economic landscape occur. Political philosophers and economists articulate these seismic shifts and introduce new ways of approaching the altered landscape. A depression, for example, in the U.S. in the late twenties and early nineteen thirties spawns the economic theories of the liberal economists John Maynard Keynes and later, Gunnar Myrdal and J. Kenneth Galbraith. Advocating a larger role for government in the economy the liberal economists helped create a state structurally concerned for the welfare of its marginalized, unemployed, and aging citizens. In the late 18th and early 20th centuries the mood of the people effected revolutionary changes first in America and France and later in Russia, as the economic and political status quo was challenged to give the underclass greater opportunities to share in the narrowly focused benefits of early capitalism. During the early stages of the industrial revolution in England pessimistic economists like Thomas Malthus and David Ricardo predicted a grim future. Their idealistic opponents, thinkers like Robert Owen the utopian socialist and John Stuart Mill, the utilitarian reformer, articulated a rosy future. While neither prediction was fully justified by events both lines of thought continue to influence political thinking today.

Too nebulous to be clearly identified with what Rousseau called "the will of the people", historically these public moods surge and recede, activating seismic shifts in the more visible institutions. Surfacing initially in the cultural and artistic life of the society, the "mood of the people" creates the great traumatic revolutions of history. And also those mythic communal events, when Paul's Love in one form or another brings us closer to being the inclusive and caring human family we all long for. Hopeful events in our time would include the creation of the United Nations, the successful nonviolent struggle for Indian independence, and the ecumenical efforts of the World Council of Churches and Vatican II. Other events include the Marshall Plan that helped European recovery after W.W. II., the labor movement of the 1930's, Civil Rights movement of the 1960's, Women's and Gay Liberation toward the end of the century. With this sketchy background in place we turn now to Paul's Love as it engages modern capitalism.

II

Capitalism, according to many economists and business people is built on self- interest and greed. There is an in-your-face quality to their defense of the way business people make their living. "Yes I'm a son-of-bitch at the office. I'm hard- nosed, ruthless. Would cheat my own mother to close a deal." Things the capitalist would never say in his role as a parent or friend or in his faith community. Who would take pride in being a ruthless parent? Or crafty friend? A selfish believer? Why this need to identify with the immoral selfish and ruthless greed espoused by some capitalists? To become the economic Nietzschean superman exalted by a particularly aggressive brand of capitalist rhetoric? Notably Ayn Rand, and her many devotees on the Right. Is it a psychological escape valve from the mushy ethics men learn at home? From women? A way to be the wild man untamed by the moralistic restraints of society? Is the work place viewed as the last arena where a man may relish the challenge of competition? Establish his identity as an adventurous entrepreneur? A real man? Or today, a real person as more and more women join the competitive struggle of all-against-all? To risk our most prized possession – our money – in hopes of making a killing? Is there an inner urge in all of us to lose oneself in the only real jungle left where one is forced by the hostile environment to defend oneself in order to survive in a dog-eat-dog world? Where no matter how badly one acts one can always say, "the market made me do it!"

Perhaps capitalism as it has developed in a largely male world *has* become imbued with the male ethos that seeks separation, self-identity, and being alone at the top rather than the relationship and interconnectedness Carol Gilligan records in her studies of female psychological development. But is this a balanced picture? Is capitalism as it operates today the savage arena of kill or be killed often portrayed? And secondly, even if it is, which I will suggest is only partially true, does this necessarily have to be so? Does the economic theory of capitalism, aside from some of its present practice, allow for capitalism to ameliorate the global inequalities associated with capitalism as it functions today? In short is and must capitalism be driven by greed?

Some capitalists drawing on the hard-edged Adam Smith I've quoted, as opposed to the Adam Smith who valued work as a moral sentiment that promoted creativity and a striving for excellence, seem to have overstated their case. Here's how the hard-edged Adam Smith characterizes the motives behind work. "Avarice and ambition in the rich, in the poor the hatred of labor and the love of present ease and enjoyment... Passions which are universal in their influence." (Princeton, P.328-9) Pretty clearly put. The rich are greedy and ambitious; the poor are lazy and slothful. And Karl Marx writing from the worker's side seems to agree, speaking of worker resentment, boredom, and hostility to repetitive factory work as alienation. Alienated not by sinful or flawed human nature, but by capitalism itself. Since Marx identifies the human being with the work she performs, to be alienated from one's work is to be deprived of one's humanity. Both Adam Smith and Marx however agree that capitalists are motivated primarily by greed and self-interest and workers whether lazy or alienated do as little work as possible. But is this characterization accurate?

Certainly individuals may utilize the system under which we all make our living to satisfy their personal avarice and ambition but there are other reasons to work as well. My Quaker ancestor Josiah White in the early post-revolutionary period made a sizable fortune as an inventor and business man whose Leigh Valley Coal and Navigation Company became the largest company of its kind in America. Initiating the system of canals that brought anthracite coal from the mines of central Pennsylvania to Philadelphia and New York Josiah White's company was able to supply the energy necessary to run the fledgling industries of the new nation. Later in life Josiah White campaigned vigorously for public funds to support a canal system reaching from the east coast to the Mississippi River. A project wisely aborted as railroads replaced canals as our primary means of transportation. When the Pennsylvania legislature was considering the Grand Canal System in 1832 to link Pittsburgh with Philadelphia Josiah White presented a plan for how this might be accomplished and "offered his own services without fee to build this navigation." (*Josiah White, Prince of Pioneers*, P.147) The year before he died in 1850 he took up a cause long in his heart and founded schools in Indiana and Iowa for the children of ex-slaves, Native Americans and "deserted children" – orphans as he had been. The schools continue in operation today as the oldest and largest residential schools in those states. While it is impossible to know what mix of motivations guided Josiah White's work it is possible to question the supposition that he was driven primarily by greed and self-interest.

Since everyone receives financial recompense for working it is possible to assume that everyone is working solely for the almighty dollar, but breathing is also essential to human life and no one - except perhaps certain Buddhists - claims a full life is limited to breathing. It would be a mistake to suppose that while money is essential to the capitalist system money is the only or even the primary reason for working. While everyone works for the external goods (money and power) that result from one's work, virtues intrinsic to the work itself and other factors as well, may be a more significant factor for many. Beneath the prevailing mythology of capitalist self-interest there are other factors at work. The desire to care for one's own needs without being a burden to others is a major concern for many as is the challenge and creativity of the work itself, just as it was for Josiah White. Self-interest read as self-fulfillment and caring for one's own needs presents a feasible alternative to the conventional view, which views an avaricious and ambitious self- interest as the primary motivation for capitalism.

Another motive for working either as employee or employer is to enjoy the company of others sharing in a common and valued task. Belonging to a team or family of coworkers in what is perceived to be a worthwhile project, can be a strong inducement to give of one's best for the sake of others. As a teacher I drew strength from knowing I was part of a community of dedicated educators. We became friends as well as colleagues. People I could count on for help in my work and who understood, as no other group did, the struggle to bring productive order to a classroom full of restless nine and ten year olds. Caring for one's own family is another not unkind motive for working. One may even, as my Quaker ancestor did, have a genuine concern for the wider society. Even the inclusive global family. In short there are a variety of reasons for working other than the ones highlighted by certain hard-edged passages from the Adam Smith and Marx.

But even if one assumes – as I would not - that avarice and ambition – the craving for money and power – are the driving forces of our present economic system this does not prove purely selfish motives must *necessarily* drive capitalism. The desire to make a profit? Yes. Josiah White made a large profit from his labor, innovative ideas, and accumulated capital. Everyone in business wants to make a profit but not everyone is driven by the same motives. Many workers, employees as well as employers, hide their tender-minded motivations behind the tough-minded rhetoric of business. Behind the persona of the contemporary business person one often hears the longing for a fuller, more creative work life for themselves and their family and often a better society, a decent world for everyone. Yet whether their motives and rhetoric are tough or tender minded all would acknowledge the need to make a profit.

Consider a parallel institution: sports. Just as in business everyone wants to make a profit so in any competitive sport everyone wants to win. But there are various ways to win. By any means necessary? At all costs? Or enjoying the game itself? Or the skills one develops in playing the game? Being part of a team effort? The challenge of competition? Savoring victory and learning from defeat? Sustaining one's identity through striving for a common goal as one plays one's part within a larger drama? Building memories to savor later on? Gaining the approval of a parent or loved one - even the source of one's faith? To whom some athletics express public gratefulness for their victory. Not to my mind entirely appropriate - as if God's plans revolve around the outcome of athletic contests, but still a heartfelt gesture of thanks for surviving the hardships of competition. All are possible motives for striving for victory. Profit as the goal of business, like winning in sports, would seem to elicit a similar range of motivation. Aging athletes often continue to play past their prime because, "I just love the game." and "What I miss most is being with the guys in the locker room." Some reasons for playing sports are not in conflict with Paul's Love; others are. To assume that only narrowly focused selfish interests are involved in seeking a profit is to ignore the strong probability that Paul's Love in various forms plays a significant role in our working lives.

It can be argued that the avowed goal of any activity system: sports, business, government, or a faith community does not in itself explain the various possible motivations that impel individuals to participate in the activity. The traditional Thanksgiving Day football game may be a life-giving friendly competition. Or it may lead to mean-spirited hostilities. Even a public riot. Worshippers attend churches, mosques, and synagogues for a variety of often conflicting motivations.

Capitalism likewise may be utilized to promote oppressive inequalities or to increase the wellbeing and capabilities of the general population.

But does Paul's Love play a significant role in the market place? A few years ago Betty and I were traveling in western Ireland. It was early in May and we noticed the houses, pubs and shops were being repainted in bright cheerful reds, yellows, blues, and greens. Signs and doorways and the flaked walls were receiving the blessings of spring. On Sunday we stopped for Mass where the priest was exhorting his flock to express their Christian love to the travelers who would soon be arriving. He reminded them of the affection many of the visitors had for Ireland as their ancestral homeland. Of the sacrifices they had made to come. The visitors were to be welcomed with the same attentive affection that Jesus welcomed the hungry crowds that came to him for food. When he'd finished I felt a surge of hospitality sweep over the congregation. Not the perfect analogy for caring for Christ's hungry crowd, but not perhaps out of place. As we continued our trip and were welcomed by those who had something to gain by their friendliness, and those who did not, Betty and I felt taken into the life of our sisters and brothers who lived in such a rare and green land. We felt ourselves treated not only as tourists, but also as visitors, pilgrims and family.

Of course it might be pointed out that the town's economic well being depended on how the visitors were treated. One might assume that other priests and public officials all over Ireland might be making similar appeals in early May. Purely to boost the economy. Purely to make a buck. But why bother to make that assumption? Why miss the opportunity to be welcomed into a country where we were among family and friends? If I was wrong and misinterpreted acquisitiveness for friendliness, self-interest for Paul's Love, perhaps my foolish response might serve to remind my sister or brother of our primary relationship. As Dorothy Day often said – roughly - "You put in love and you'll take out love." You look for sisters and brothers around you you'll find them. You look for deviousness and greed you'll find deviousness and greed.

That the animated bonding with our Irish kinfolk occurred in an economic setting should not mask the generous motivation we sensed behind the welcome we received. In fact the profit motive rather than distracting from the friendliness might be credited with helping to promote the friendliness we received. Could this be Adam Smith's invisible hand introducing me to my brothers and sisters in their working lives? After all I'd received a good salary for teaching children for twenty-five years. Wanting to truly earn my salary I was motivated to do a more loving job as a teacher. If one feels one being rewarded fairly financially, won't one be motivated to do a better job? As a teacher, employee, or employer? If my salary, my profit, my reward, was a sign of the institution's appreciation of my labor why wouldn't I want to return the favor? Seen in this light, profits become an inducement to promoting the virtues and practices consistent with Paul's Love. Rather than being seen as a visible sign of avarice as it was in the medieval church and is among many liberals today. Or as the Protestant Reformation had it, a sign of God's favor (which clearly removed God's blessing from the poor who were deemed incompetent and lazy). Capitalism, including profit and money, can become a catalyst, a medium, for the exchange of good will between human beings. I cannot claim that profits and money are always utilized in this benevolent way to bring more of Paul's Love into the world, but I would claim profits and money can, and often do, facilitate a positive relationship between people. When I credit the goods and services that nurture my life to my Master Card, I am receiving in exchange the fruits of the well-intentioned labor of the people who produced those goods and services. When Josiah White reinvests his profits in research to build better canals those profits become of benefit eventually to the wider community. When a banker lends money, or a stock broker handles the exchange of stocks for his clients, he also is utilizing money and profits as a catalyst for the increase of wealth. An increase which may well promote a more animated and friendly relationship between members of the inclusive human family.

So far the argument has been made that capitalism has acted as a good and faithful servant, providing the global family it serves the goods and services it needs to live and thrive. Behind the focusing goals of capitalism we discerned a variety of probable motivations; some consistent with Paul's Love, some not. It was pointed out that entrepreneurs like Josiah White and community leaders like the Irish priest have encouraged employers and employees alike to value their labor as individually satisfying and an act of kindness to their fellow citizens. I even viewed the suspect profit motive as a catalyst for the exchange of goods, services and goodwill between members of the inclusive human family. I implied that rather than viewing our economic lives as dictated by impersonal laws of the market place, or the manipulations of avaricious and ambitious capitalists, our economic system, like the family and non-profit organizations, provides another institutional outlet for the manifestation of Paul's Love. Another channel for Paul's pervasive Love to permeate and support our increasingly interconnected inclusive human family.

When the clerk at the ACME counter rings up my weekly grocery bill and packs the bags for me to carry to my car I sense she is performing a kindness, an act of mercy, to me. Without her and thousands of farmers, fishermen, factory workers, truck drivers, managers, executives, stock-holders, and even C.E.O.s, I don't eat. When we lived in caves and someone brought in the precious bear that would supply us with food for a month we were grateful and perhaps we etched animal and hunting figures on the walls of the cave. Or danced. Or prayed. We gave thanks to the bear who had given up her life for us. When we raised our own food and one spouse tilled the field and the other cooked and the children were fed this was considered caring for one's family – being a loving father or mother. Later when we sold our surplus crops to our neighbors in exchange for goods and services that we needed to live this was considered being a good neighbor. Today, though life is more complicated, we can still be grateful to our fellow human beings whose intelligence and hard work bring us the goods and services we need to live a fully human life.

III

It is also true that profits and wages have created inequalities between workers and management. C.E.O.s and high level executives make ten, fifty, sometimes a hundred times the income of their own employees. Since profits are made in conjunction with the labor of the employees there is much debate as to who is actually making the profits possible. Is it the employers who provide leadership and creative ideas in a competitive market? Are they, as the managers, innovators, and risk takers, the critical factor in a competitive market? The hub on which all else turns that drives the capitalist economy? Or is it the surplus value of the employees' labor, which is being siphoned off into excessive profits, which is the essential element? Is it the workers, who pick the fruit and design and assemble the products we use, who are the driving force in our free market system?

In any case, though there are telling arguments on both sides of the labor- management conflict, if employer and employees are members of one inclusive family, how can we justly reward a few siblings' efforts so richly, while other members are in need? However we decide where the profits come from. Even if a brilliant C.E.O. works twice as long, presumably twice as hard, and is ten times as smart, is she being unfairly rewarded for her efforts in relation to her employees and perhaps the wider society as well? Political philosophers like Rawls, Habermas and MacIntyre, and economic philosophers like Adam Smith, Marx, and more recently the British Keynesian scholar Joan Robinson and Amartya Sen the Indian Nobel Prize winner, wrestle constantly with the issue of economic inequality.

Adam Smith writes that "No society can surely be flourishing and happy, of which by far the greater part of the numbers are poor and miserable." The advantage of a capitalist system for Smith is "... that the

universal opulence… extends itself to the lowest ranks of the people."
Rather than viewing capitalism as establishing the rights of property
and business over the working class Smith saw capitalism as the faithful
servant that attends to the needs of poor as well as the higher ranks of
society.

While I am grateful for the hard working sisters and brothers I
sense behind the economic institution that supports my well being, I
am also aware I am part of a deeply flawed family. Though I benefit
from their labor, intelligence and generous efforts to meet my varied
needs I also share in their shortsightedness, their greed, and their self-
serving ambition.

If I personalize capitalism i.e. view it as an institution created and
maintained by the wider human family, rather than dwelling on its
particular laws and patterns I cannot avoid picturing the inequalities
and injustices that are also part of our common economic life. Just
as the specifics of medical knowledge or the techniques and theory
of teaching take place in a wider concern for human welfare, so too
do the much debated economic laws and patterns. Seen in this wider
context the owners, stockholders, and managers at ACME are also my
sisters and brothers. To picture them reaping excessive profits from the
labor of banana workers in Central America and the migrant workers
of California is painful. Not only because I grieve for the injustices to
the children of the parents who work in the tropical forests, fields, and
sweatshops of our underdeveloped areas, but because a wealthy brother
or sister has seemingly ignored the needs of their own flesh and blood.

To me it's a family matter. Complicated and complex though it may
be the basic fact sticks out that if my vision in Mexico is valid – if we
are one inclusive family – then many of us have enjoyed the fruits of
our underpaid kin's labor. While their children grow up in poverty and
fear our own children are well fed and attend prestigious universities.
That is the other reality that burns in my mind when I ease my way
into being part of the human family.

The majority of my sisters and brothers are trapped in a global
economic system which allows me to live in relative comfort, while it
deprives two thirds of my family of the basic components of a fruitful

life. Forget for a moment the problem and the possible solutions. Why it isn't a problem – or isn't my problem. Or why it doesn't matter, or no one can do anything about it anyway. Or if they just tried my solution or my church's solution, things would be better. Or it's all God's will. Or spiritual values are more important that material values. Or I earned my fair share by hard work. Or what can one person do anyway. Put all that aside for now and let the mind move away from problems and solutions, comments and analysis.

The only question that burns in my gut is are we related to the poor people in the world? Not justice but kinship drives my concern. If we are related *then* we begin to think about problems and solutions. If those aren't my family members working in the tropical forests and fields then I don't have a problem. I do my work and make my salary. They do their work and we work out an exchange that fits the current customs of economic interactions. But if it were my daughter – left over perhaps from my duty overseas - working in the sweatshop making Nike sneakers I'd find a way to get her out. If I knew my daughter was ill-fed, living in a slum, working ten hours a day at a machine making sneakers I'd raise hell. Boycott. Picket. Write letters. Vote differently. I'd damn well be activated to care what happened to my daughter or my sons and the kids they worked with. I'd read books. I'd check the Internet. To start with I wouldn't wear Nike sneakers. I'd want to meet with people who had kids in the sweatshops. We'd talk; we'd organize. And no talk about the difficulties, and economic complexities, no graphs about optimistic long term trends, would prevent me from working to improve conditions – if it were my daughter, my son, my sister or brother involved. Who knows if it would work? If I, and perhaps a few people with the same concern, could make a difference? But that wouldn't be the point would it? Once I cared, once we cared, then we'd think about what could be done. Not whether it was feasible or not.

It wouldn't be about justice, or fairness, or equality or a perfect world. It wouldn't be about my political views, whatever they were. It would be about not letting my daughter live in deplorable conditions that I have power to try to change. It would be about being family.

Caring for each other. Being patient and kind to each other. It would be about Paul's garden variety love.

IV

Even as I grieve the tragic inequalities created by the way capitalism has evolved over time I'm also grateful for the meaningful employment and physical necessities it provides for billions of my fellow human beings. Those two images create the dilemma which should encourage and trouble any thoughtful person. First the wonderfully complex interconnected inclusive human family that cares for our needs with patience and kindness linking us to the global family every time we use a computer or ask a brother or sister in India for help, eat a meal, or make a phone call or leave a text message.

In the economic realm, in today's capitalism, Paul's Love is the gentle influence that bonds us one to another in gratefulness for all the hard work that goes into exchanging goods and services. Here we celebrate the capitalism that has been a good and faithful servant in providing for the family's needs. And then I see that same inclusive influence at work in efforts to rectify the injustices and inequalities around the world, not primarily for the sake of justice, but for the sake of not allowing a sister to be in need while we had the will and the means to alleviate her suffering. That too is Paul's Love.

That's the main point for me. Those two images. First the wonderfully complex interconnected inclusive human family that cares for my needs with patience and kindness. Second there's the troubling reality of knowing that there are family members who still live in deplorable conditions which I have the power in some small way to alleviate. If we focus excessively on the first image we may become complacent. We may assume all is basically well; that the problems will work themselves out in time. If we focus on the second image we may become disheartened and bitter at the impossible challenge of bringing our family together so there is real caring and love between all its members. Beginning with compassion for the poor and those facing discrimination we may end with resentment, hatred, and violence to those in power. It is in the tension between these two images of my wonderful, my broken family I am given the strength and will to play my role as a part of the human enterprise.

An odd thought intrudes now. When I die, when anybody dies, we won't die alone. That same hour thousands of other human beings will also die all over the globe. And what ever happens then, at least we will face it together. Wherever we go – or don't go - at least we'll be together.

O Lord, grant us the wisdom and love to be the family you made us to be. Give us hearts of flesh to care about those around us who have not the advantages that we have. Be with us God as we make the decisions that affect the other members of your family. Teach us to love one another in our economic lives. To be the inclusive family you created us to be. Not because we have to, but because we want to.

Amen.

Reflections on Capitalism, Justice and the Inclusive Family

"We must not listen to those who urge us to think human thoughts since we are human, and mortal thoughts since we are mortal; rather we should... do all we can to live by the finest element in us – for if in bulk it is small, in power and worth it is far greater than anything else."

Aristotle

I

The basic line of thought so far runs as follows: Paul's Love established in Part I as the critical component of the individual's existence is manifest in Part II as the inclusive global family. Chapter XI reminded us that both Plato's ethical "ought" and Aristotle's "is" support the thesis that the human family is the social equivalent of Paul's Love. Chapter XII argued that the human family was the best conceptual image available for grasping the underlying nature of our benevolent institutions: schools, hospitals, faith communities etc. Chapter XIII was an aside, an interlude summarizing political philosophy since Plato. In chapter XIV the inclusive human family is seen to both enhance and supersede the three major contemporary responses to Plato's question "What is justice?" Rawl's social contract theory that justice is fairness was viewed as abstract and legalistic because it ignored the implied familial relationship between human beings. Habermas's discourse ethics was viewed as dialogue among family members. If siblings disagree on the rules and customs governing family life then it makes sense to try and work out those disagreements in a peaceful and fair manner. MacIntyre's virtue based social ethics grounded on justice, truthfulness, and courage, as they are sustained in historical "moral traditions", was seen to have undervalued the critical virtue – Paul's Love – which unified and energized the others. In short justice driven social ethics were viewed in the context of the inclusive human family. Paul's Love was seen as the critical missing factor behind all three theories of justice.

Chapter XV argued that capitalism was not, and need not be, limited by a profits above people *laissez-faire* mentality but that cultural differences, a broad spectrum of motivations - many consistent with Paul's Love - energizing individual human beings who made capitalism work, and government restrictions protecting the rights of workers and the general public had to a limited extent, and definitively should rectify the gross inequality that left millions in poverty to support the life style of their wealthy brothers and sisters.

The second half of the chapter viewed capitalism as a remarkable creative and productive economic expression of the human family's desire to produce goods and services for the benefit of all. Capitalism was also viewed as a dysfunctional family in which inequality between the "haves" and the "have lots less" was an ongoing challenge to any followers of Paul's Love whatever their political views might be. Holding these two views of the economic global family as wonderfully productive and sadly dysfunctional in tension was seen as a hedge against unwarranted optimism that the market would solve all the problems or the pessimism that stunted creative responses on behalf of Paul's Love acting through justice. The visceral sense of kinship to other human beings is our strongest asset as we confront the violence and poverty around us.

II

Moving on to pick up on the lines of thought of our liberal reformers in the light of Paul's Love, if we are family *then* Rawl's suggestion that "social and economic inequalities are to be arranged… [to work] to the greatest benefit of the least advantaged" seems a generous and humane approach to dealing with the global family problems of poverty, lack of educational opportunity and inadequate health care. If we are family *then* Habermas's discourse ethics can be viewed as a useful tool for having family members discuss their social and economic differences. If we are family *then* MacIntyre's virtues are seen as elements essential for the building up of our common human family. All three approaches would, in the context of the inclusive human family, seem relevant to providing the theoretic framework for wrestling with the economic and social problems we face.

But why should we bother to reframe political economic issues in terms of Paul's Love – or its social equivalent the inclusive human family? Why not pursue relevant forms of contemporary justice as political philosophers from Plato to Rawls have done? Why refocus attention from what has been a closely argued concept – justice – to a fuzzy platitude borrowed from Sunday sermons and a reassuring wall plaque? What advantages has Paul's Love over competing concepts such as justice, happiness, or social stability?

First Paul's Love provides us with a commonly accepted foundational concept that however ambiguously interpreted, does reflect the reality that human beings are related to one another, biologically, historically and viscerally. If I leave a court room where I'm involved in a lawsuit with a man who has grievously wronged me, and see him wander into on-coming traffic I may risk my life to save his. Humans have a species affinity humans have for one another that is, *in general*, more intense than the affinity we have for other forms of life. We are one kind of being whatever our physical and social differences may be. If we meet a stranger, someone from Thailand or Zaire, someone from another social class, we will greet each other in some fashion. Every day strangers give way to each other on the highway, exchange friendly conversation, offer assistance to one another. If a natural disaster threatens other humans in another part of the country or overseas we'll send money and offer prayers for their safety. This we do for complete strangers, people we know we will never meet, or from whom we can expect no response whatever. What operates here is not primarily justice but a sense of being in some vaguely defined relationship with the other people in the world. Naming this reality, saying we are family, has a power that touches the deepest part of our being. Imprecise, fuzzy, ambiguous or not Paul's Love is the deepest thing we know. It is certainly the deepest thing we can all agree on. And if Paul's Love is philosophically vague isn't the role of philosophy to clarify the elusive truths of reality?

A second advantage to naming Paul's Love as a major component of our economic and political lives is that it is non-theological, and therefore to many, non- threatening. If God is a concept that inspires conflict and bloodshed at times no one is fighting over being kind and patient to other people. Paul's Love slips into any dispute quietly, unobtrusively. Positions may not change in a heated discussion.

Israelis and Arabs, Irish Catholics and Protestants, may *not* reach agreement in the dispute under discussion but the voices are lower. There is something new in the atmosphere, a subtle shift of inner intent as one realizes one's adversaries are sincere in their desire to resolve differences. If one is truly patient and kind the polite forms of diplomacy which so often mask devious intentions begin to give way to renewed efforts to resolve the differences. One begins to sympathize with one's opponents. It's not that Paul's Love is smarter, can analyze complex issues better than the razor sharp intellect – it can't – it's because love is more persistent, because love, "bears all things, hopes all things, endures all things." Love simply outlasts all the other motives and faculties we bring to the table; not as a separate imperial faculty but as faculty and virtue that is willing to work with other virtues like justice, truthfulness, and courage, and other faculties including intelligence, emotions, even unconscious desires. Paul's Love utilizes the other virtues and faculties to serve not itself but others.

One short paragraph to digress for a moment. A day trip from the main argument to suggest that if Paul's Love is a faculty associated with, but distinct from, the commonly acknowledged human faculties: will, reason, emotions and memory, there is an element of love that is unaccounted for. Something that is not the will, reason, etc. Something which animates the other faculties, but which remains apart. For the religious person, of course this elusive element, this secret ingredient, has a sacred source. Since this critical element is beyond one's reason and will one must petition the sovereign source for the love one needs to respond in patient and kind ways to those around one. Not my will – my love – be done, Lord, but your will – your love – be done, becomes the believer's inner intent. Drawing on a trusted resource beyond herself the believer leaves the tough points to her unseen doubles partner. The humanist who shares equally in the elusive element that is Paul's Love, credits this love to human nature, but in either case, for believer and humanist alike, Paul's Love comes as an elusive element. Something to be courted and cherished. Something that comes to us as a gift as well as a choice.

Even when acknowledged as the preeminent virtue Paul's Love does not negate the role of other virtues. It's not a matter of taking out justice and putting Paul's Love in its place. Unlike justice Paul's Love does not have a final goal or a plan to reach those goals. Paul's Love is not wedded to a particular institutional solution to our economic and social problems. Paul's Love does not threaten other proposed foundational premises – justice, freedom and practicality. Or their institutional equivalents – capitalism, democracy etc. because Paul's Love is not about goals, plans, structure, and the future, but about means, methods and the present, she is able to coexist with various economic and political structures. Even when she disagrees with contending proposals, which sometimes can't be avoided, Paul's Love does not label and demean her ideological opponents, but utilizes what she can, and politely rejects what she must. By not insisting on its own way, and being respectful of other views, Paul's Love is less argumentative, less threatening than other proposals. Just as a warm spring sun coaxes the traveler to remove her winter coat, so Paul's Love may quietly alter our ingrained economic patterns. Because Paul's Love is gentle and non-threatening she welcomes diverse political factions. Justice is often divisive, pitting one side against another. Paul's Love is inclusive. Theoretically as well as practically Paul's Love provides a broad-based premise for political thinkers as well as ordinary citizens to find common ground.

A third advantage that Paul's Love holds over justice is that it engages the full range of human faculties rather than focusing on the rational; as justice does in formulating principles and procedures for establishing fairness, equal opportunity and lawfulness. Emotions and the more reticent subconscious and spiritual intuitions, as well as one's rationality, are energized by Paul's Love. A person or community, becomes fully engaged in the attitudes and actions pursued. If institutional life is a family concern then reason is no longer the sole factor in resolving social problems. The process of seeking what the Nobel Prize winning Indian economist Amartya Sen has called "instrumental freedoms" to expand the "human capabilities" of even the most disadvantaged person, involves emotional, and spiritual, capabilities as well as economic and financial capabilities. The heart as well the mind and will is an intrinsic component of Paul's Love.

A fourth advantage is that Paul's Love works at all intellectual and social levels. Paul's Love engages philosophers such as Kierkegaard, Tillich, and Levinas at the theoretical level. As well as nonviolent practical visionaries like Gandhi and Dr. King whose world views are grounded in the divine love that permeates the creation. And yet Paul's Love is equally at home in the routine courtesies, intentions and actions of ordinary citizens.

When Habermas considered by many the most erudite and rational philosopher of our time first debated with the Derrida, the reigning French deconstructionist, his initial premise was "Nevertheless I am your friend." Again and again Habermas came back to this statement trying to establish common ground, a friendly relationship, with his philosophic adversary. Nor was this intended as a distracting embarrassment, for many philosophers including Buber, Heidegger, Cicero (marvelous essay on friendship), Aristotle and Plato had already established the animated bonding of friendship as a significant philosophical category. Utilizing Paul's Love as our focusing concept allows us to draw on the wisdom of the human race's finest intellects, as well as tap into the everyday experience of the rest of us. While the humbly endowed citizen may not follow the intricate reasoning of political philosophers and economists they can understand talk of Paul's Love and its social equivalent the inclusive human family.

One final advantage that might be mentioned is that Paul's Love has not, to my knowledge, been explicitly named as the central reality behind our economic and political life. There is aura of freshness, a sense of newness, about Paul's Love. As a new idea Paul's Love does not carry the baggage of older dead end conflicts where traditional adversaries – liberal / conservative, religious / humanistic - are already locked in mortal combat. No one and no ideology, is excluded or demeaned or judged – first because a fresh start is open to everyone and second because Paul's Love is charitable to opposing views.

It's as if a shy stranger had slipped into the board rooms and staff meetings around the country - into the factories, farms, shops and workplaces where people spend their working days. A vaguely familiar figure, almost at times an embarrassing friend whom one had known in another setting whom one is afraid to acknowledge, Paul's Love is a fresh presence. One that may take some getting used to. At first the stranger is attentive, listens carefully to the ongoing conversation. The back and forth – or the top down directives and rambling stories.

And then the magic moment of decision opens up when one is asked to acknowledge that one knows the stranger. Unless of course Paul's Love has already become an accepted part of group and has a history of partaking in the discussion and decision-making that goes on. But let us assume that Paul's Love is a stranger to the work environment and one risks one's standing in the group by associating oneself with her open-hearted suggestion, her generous option. Which may well be passed over. But the stranger is patient. She does not insist on her own way. She waits for the situation to turn in her direction, and in the meantime treats her coworkers with patience and kindness, listening to their frustrations after the meetings. She commiserates and sympathizes with others, without losing touch with her own nature which is cheerful, optimistic, and animated.

There is one drawback. The stranger is truly shy. She does not draw attention to herself but remains in the background. She will not say, "Yes, I am creation's finest treasure. I am the chief virtue. I will outlast all lesser motivations." Others may say that for Paul's Love. Paul, himself, may exalt love. She will not in the boardrooms and work places say that of herself. She will work for a productive and unified work environment that others - her offspring, her kin, may become closer to one another and to the wider world that their goods and services benefit. Like a good mother or father Paul's Love remains in the background delighting in the growth and achievements of her cherished children.

III

Having noted the advantages of Paul's Love in relation to Plato's justice, I must also admit that there are philosophic objections to utilizing Paul's Love as the centerpiece of a social ethics. The first objection comes from those who would follow Levinas in insisting that Paul's Love, the energizing *between* Buber's I and Thou, is not capable of sustaining social order without the tough-minded state in its law enforcement and legal role. Somewhat sadly I'd have to agree. I'm not suggesting Paul's Love replace law and order, or even in certain circumstances the military; although as a pacifist it pains me to say this. Later in Part III we'll wrestle with the conflict between Paul's Love and these tough minded institutions. In any case we may say Paul's Love has no plan; no favored institution to leave its imprint on history. If we read *Corinthians 13* carefully we will see she has more modest goals. Paul's Love does not insist on its own way. She has no overall plan, or vision of what a peaceful loving society will look like. What Paul's Love does have is a method, a way, to approach social problems. Which is to be patient and kind to those family members with whom one disagrees. At bottom that's it. We have already suggested in a general way how this primal image – the family – might modify our free market capitalism. Later, on a future stepping stone, we will reflect on how Paul's Love intersects with the other ultimate institution – the state.

For now I would simply note that Paul's Love wishes to work within the institutions and ideologies already in place. She is older and more enduring than our present economic and political systems. She has already outlasted the top heavy dynasties of Egypt, the Near East and China, Mesoamerica and the great Roman empire, medieval feudalism, and the rise of urban centers and modern nation-states across Europe. Like the blinding sun which illuminated the hillside caves of Neolithic Spain, the Gothic cathedrals of France, and the bombed out cities of Hitler's war Paul's Love is part of our enduring human consciousness. Unlike our socioeconomic systems and our technology Paul's Love remains constant. Part of our sociopolitical life from the beginning she sustains us still and reminds us of our failure to be become the fully functional human family we long to be.

Though Paul's Love has an illustrious history, I would emphasize again, that she does not have a discernible plan, or a particular social structure. There is no worker's paradise that Marx envisioned, no capitalistic promised land where the free market will resolve all our ills. Not even the vision of a theo-centric society favored by some of the more fundamentalist believers present in every major religion. Paul's Love is not about getting somewhere; it's about how we get there.

It trusts the now dim and incomplete future to come to fruition in its own time, while Paul's Love concentrates all its attention on being patient and kind in the only time in which it has any influence – the present. The fragmented, partial, frustrating, inconclusive present time. Where we don't know how things will turn out. Which trends will ripen and which will wither away.

Paul's Love, in *Corinthian 13*, never claimed to have certain knowledge of the future, which remains dim, partial and incomplete. Paul's Love never claimed to have a socioeconomic blueprint, plan or vision, which would embody her values. That she left to the family members to work out for themselves in different historical settings. Trusting her children to talk among themselves and care for one another in ways that seemed appropriate to each era Paul's Love adapted herself to various institutional and ideological environments. All she said was start with love. Be patient and kind and put the other person, the other side, first, and you will begin a journey that will sustain you the rest of your life. It will provide the animating energy to sustain you in all circumstances. It will sustain you in your daily routine, as you become increasingly aware that your individual journey is only a small part of the common journey that the whole family is taking into an unknown future. If you choose to receive the welcome offered you as an Irish visitor you will enrich the economy there and enter into a real relationship with your kinfolk in Ireland. If you work hard to make a profit building things people need like my great uncle Josiah White, you will become increasingly aware that you are part of a wide and wondrous community whom you will come to appreciate and love more and more deeply as the years go by. Just how each individual, or each economic entity – company or corporation – may adhere to Paul's Love in our present capitalist environment takes us to the stepping stone just ahead.

Chapter

XVII

Capitalism for Swimmer-Observers — I

"The stage is set for a quantum leap in world wealth and that leap is already underway… To put the world wealth figures into per capita terms, the potential is $166,666 of assets for each of the 6 billion people on earth, compared to the approximately $20,000 that has been achieved until now… The steep rise in wealth can be made to continue."

The Wealthy World – the Growth and Implications of Global Prosperity (2000) John C. Edmunds

"The political and strategic impact of surging populations, spreading disease, deforestation and soil erosion, water depletion, air pollution, [etc.] will promote mass migrations and, in turn, incite group conflicts."

The Coming Anarchy (2000) Robert D. Kaplan

I

Earlier I spoke of *The Prince* as a rare example of a political text written not from the broad perspective of Adam Smith's impartial observer, but from the vantage point of one of the key players in the political drama. But while Machiavelli counseled the aspiring prince on ways – devious and otherwise – to advance his career in politics I would suggest ways an advocate of Paul's Love might conduct herself in her economic life. Returning to an earlier image, we might equate the advocate of Paul's Love with the swimmer-observer who finds her underwater existence more constricted than the spacious view she enjoyed from the shore.

Immersed in a vulnerable and uncertain environment the swimmer-observer is faced with specific life challenges, rather than the general reflections she pursued on shore. If she is wrong about her ideas of justice, Paul's Love, and capitalism on shore she must adjust to new arguments and insights. If she makes the wrong move as a swimmer she may lose her job, or take the wrong job, or act in ways she regrets later on. Her economic choices in the tangible world are an integral part of her life. Her identity as a human being is significantly shaped by the role she plays in the economic drama. Whether she pursues one career rather than another, or invests in the market in one way rather than another are choices that shape her character as it is perceived by others and by herself. The products she buys, the work she does and the way she invests her capital shape the economic woman (or man) who interacts, for good and ill, with the other members of the human family.

In this chapter and the next we shall focus attention on the economic woman as she interacts with capitalism. If her concern is solely to maximize her assets, i.e. to have as much power and money as possible without regard for other factors, she won't find much wisdom here. Here we are concerned only with the individual (female or male) who has already made a commitment to Paul's Love; i.e. the individual who chooses to act in her or his economic life so as to nurture the freedom and capabilities Nobel Prize winner economics professor Amartya Sen identifies as vital to all members of the inclusive human family. For others as well as herself. It is also assumed that the economic individual is concerned not primarily for justice but is acting out of a genuine affection for other human beings.

As we reflect on the consequences of walking in Paul's Love as economic men and women three guiding insights may prove useful; before going on to discuss the individual paths that seem right for each person.

II

The first and essential insight is that each swimmer-observer moves in her underwater environment in her own unique manner. Thrown into the world in a particular set of socioeconomic circumstances: her immediate family setting, ethnic background, income level etc., the economic woman is guided by a mind set shaped by surrounding circumstances and her response to those circumstances. Her mind set, comprised of thoughts and principles abstracted from her experiences and her own reflections, determines the way she interacts with her economic environment. If she is a strong environmentalist she won't work for, or buy stock in oil or lumber companies. If she is a conservative Republican she will *support* oil and lumber companies, which keep unemployment down and the economy humming. If she's a Muslim from Pakistan she may welcome the Internet and foreign trade as a means of building up a strong Islamic state, able to resist corrosive Western influences. She will not buy alcohol or tobacco, wear Western dress, or watch Hollywood sitcoms. Interacting with the shopping mall, workplace and stock market, the economic woman will be guided by the insights and values that comprise her mind set.

The phrase "in her own unique manner," is intended to protect the individual from the dismissive tendency to view human beings as generalized individuals defined by their ethnic background, nationality or income level etc. Seen in this way individuals soon become statistics, abstractions in economic graphs and predictive studies, who may be moved like pieces on a chess board at the will of experts who understand the rules and strategies of the game. Unless each person is viewed as a unique human being there is no possibility of Paul's Love animating a relationship with other human beings. Generalized individuals, defined by their cultural characteristics cannot interact in a loving way, or any other way, with other humans. A certain kind of justice theory can operate with a generalized individual: the legal and moral category of the impersonal citizen, defendant, party of the first part, or Levinas' universal "you" that supersedes Buber's dialogical "Thou", but the affectionate bonding of human beings presupposes we have flesh and blood human beings who interact with one another. Certainly the individual's cultural, economic, and ideological background influences the range of ethical options he or she faces, but it should not obscure the fact we are dealing with unique individual human beings, who often act in unpredictable ways.

III

The second guiding insight is that each individual views the world within a wider cultural world-view, which both illuminates and distorts his or her understanding of Paul's Love. In economic matters an individual's mind-set may well be shaped by the authoritative wisdom of one school of thinking or even one author; that is by the one big idea which purports to encapsulate the climate of the times. Since the one big idea involves political as well as economic factors we may broaden our discussion to include sociopolitical events, such as the Civil Rights movement in the 1960's and world wars I and II, rather than focusing solely on the economic aspects of what are in fact interrelated realities. Already in the previous chapter we noted how the political setting in chaotic post-communist Russia, authoritarian China, and democratic Scandinavia and the United States affected the kind of capitalism present in any one economy. The one big idea that dominates the world view of a significant number of people in any one generation often embraces a variety of cultural, economic and political factors.

When I was in my mid-twenties walking from Philadelphia to the UN in New York on a peace march to protest the testing of nuclear weapons, we met with local groups in New Jersey along the way. At one meeting I remember an anxious young mother with an infant in her arms asking me what I thought the future held. I replied that in twenty years we wouldn't have a future, that we would have destroyed all life on earth. The woman's face fell, but she did not argue with me. I was the expert. I'd read the right books; I had information she didn't have. The climate of the times gave credence to my harsh prediction. I cringe whenever I recall my insensitivity. Not because I was wrong – thank God – but because I had no right to limit her future by my dire prediction. Big ideas can do that, can limit the individual's ability to respond out of her own inner urgency.

Because of the presumed necessity of responding to the crisis of the era in a particular way individuals may forgo the virtues – truth telling, justice and compassion – that have anchored their lives. Enchanted by the one big idea - the prevailing religious, economic or political world-view - individuals may no longer practice the virtues they cherish.

As we look for the one big idea in the climate of the times over the last hundred years the scenes change, historically speaking, quite rapidly. At the turn of the century Progress, Science, Teddy Roosevelt, competitive colonialism and the expansion of world markets. In 1914 the international best seller, *The Grand Illusion*, announces that world trade will make wars a thing of the past. The business interests and political leaders will never allow national conflicts to disrupt the rising tide of prosperity and profit sweeping the world. Endless progress is the wave of the future. After W.W.I despair: loss of faith in western civilization, religion and science. The decline and fall of the West. The world is a wastelands. In the roaring twenties it's peace and prosperity; let the good times roll. The thirties – world depression, the Grapes of Wrath, decadent capitalism gives way to the inevitable triumph of socialism. The Age of Anxiety. After W.W.II a bipolar world is threatened by nuclear annihilation. Vietnam. Civil Rights. Political assassinations and riots. Protecting the free world from Communism. The Age of Anxiety rides again. In the eighties and nineties Communism falls, western market values prevail. Capitalism and democracy win!

Early into the second millennium the big idea, the next inevitable trend, seems to be continuing globalization, capitalism, the Internet, and democracy. Major wars again are ruled out. The flood of rising global prosperity will; so Francis Fukuyama, the eminent social scientist from George Mason University, Thomas Friedman the Pulitzer prize-winning foreign affairs commentator for the New York Times, and others argue, negate cultural conflicts and world poverty. Democratic capitalism offers the only real hope for developing countries to develop.

Fukuyama, proclaims in the ironically titled, *The End of History and the Last Man* (1992), "The end of history as such: that is, the end point of mankind's ideological evolution and the universalization of Western liberal democracy as the final form of human government." Noted economist and investment consultant Harry S. Dent is also optimistic. In *The Great Boom Ahead*, Dent approaches the iffy future head on. "The economy is highly predictable. New forecasting tools tell of a coming era of prosperity with the Dow reaching as high as 8500 by 2007... the taming of inflation, and the resurgence of America as the premier global economic superpower... We are on the verge of the greatest boom in history." These cheerful prophetic words uttered in 1993 were reiterated in 1998 in Dent's paean to the new millennium, *The Roaring 2000's*. Again we hear echoes of Hegel's and Marx's apocalyptic golden era. The final stage of human historical development has found a new home, not in a constitutional monarchy, or a classless humane society, but in global democratic capitalism. Local conflicts will be isolated or resolved by peacekeeping actions initiated by the UN or alliances of the powerful free market democratic countries. Western technology and democratic values sweep the globe. Capitalism and democracy prevail worldwide. Or maybe not. There is another option. Another big idea.

The dissenting view predicts a coming clash of cultures - or civilizations - as old tribal animosities erupt in the aftermath of the Cold War. Samuel P. Huntington, Harvard professor of international studies and director of security planning to the National Security Council during the Carter administration, articulates this dissenting position and summarizes the concern of the less optimistic commentators. "The breakdown of governmental authority; the breakup of states; the intensification of tribal, ethnic and religious conflict; the emergence of international criminal mafias; refugees multiplying into the tens of millions; the proliferation of nuclear and other weapons of mass destruction; the spread of terrorism; the prevalence of massacres and ethnic cleansing... [all contribute to] a world in anarchy, a world in chaos." (*Clash of Civilizations*, 1996, P. 35,) Fueled by Western technology, but hostile to Western values, China and Islamic fundamentalism, according to Huntington, emerge to challenge the gradually declining West. Asian and Islamic traditional authoritarianism reject Western democracy in favor of indigenous religious and cultural values. The West declines as other great civilizations rise to power. Or a more terrifying subplot. Lonely terrorists on the Internet plot acts of biological and nuclear violence. Famines, war and chaos. The fall of the West – again.

The point of looking at the two big ideas current in the spring of 2001 of what the future holds is not to debate their relative merits, or suggest an intriguing synthesis of the contending views but to examine their relationship – or any big idea's relationship – to Paul's Love.

The key point for the swimmer-observer who would adhere to Paul's Love is that she not be bound by either of these big ideas, or by any future big ideas which will arise to account for our uncertain future, but that she utilize the big ideas for her own purposes. Just as Machiavelli's astute prince utilizes his sociopolitical analysis – his world view - for his own, rather different, purposes. We need to embrace the opportunities big ideas provide for adhering to Paul's Love, but not allow them to distort our core beliefs. There was nothing wrong with the peace movements' protesting the arms race and the Vietnam War in the Sixties. When the global family was threatened Betty and I and many others were impelled from motives of Paul's Love to make our witness public. To have allowed the human family to be destroyed by war without protesting would have been to abandon our brothers and sisters in a time of need. That many of us acted passionately, patiently, and persistently over several decades, from the mid-fifties to the mid-seventies, on behalf of millions of people we had not met face to face, is strong evidence of the vitality of Paul's Love, and its social manifestation, the inclusive human family. We utilized the one big idea – that peaceful nonviolence might bring an end to the arms race, racial injustice and the Vietnam War - to act patiently and courageously for the wellbeing of the whole human family.

When we became enamored of the one big idea - the liberal world view of the time - as a goal in itself, rather than as an instrument that served to bond one human being to another in promoting a more peaceful world we opened ourselves to the enemies of Paul's Love. A youth oriented hedonistic life style, soul sapping cynicism, and hostility to our political enemies. In the name of peace we sometimes acted in ways that were not peaceful. "Hey, hey, L.B.J. how many kids did you kill today?" is not a nonviolent slogan. Treating returning Vietnam veterans with public contempt is not a nonviolent act. These actions rightly brought shame to a movement dedicated to peace and love.

Despite these deplorable incidents however, I found most of my fellow citizens over these difficult decades to be patient, kind and level headed in pursuit of a more functional human family. Many of those who demonstrated for Civil Rights in the South or marched peacefully to protest nuclear testing and the Vietnam war were well aware of their responsibility to be nonviolent in both their personal and their public lives. Paul's Love glimpsed in one area reinforced a growing sense of the persuasiveness of this oddly animating energy that drove us to sacrifice our own interests for the sake of our sisters and brothers, in the political struggles of the time. That so many diverse individuals, age-wise, religiously, ethnically, and politically, were able to unite in promoting the wellbeing of the human family, is strong evidence of Paul's Love acting in a wider social environment. Why else, except to promote the assumed familial relationship would so many act on behalf of millions of people they would never see, or who were not even alive yet?

IV

The main reason Paul's Love is not deterred by the big idea is that while big ideas are rooted, optimistically or pessimistically, in predictions of the future, i.e. in historical judgments about what will happen, while Paul's Love is *not* rooted in history or in historical judgments. If we return to *Corinthians 13* we discover that Love is not restricted to historical reality. Paul's Love is in history but is not exhausted by the transient flow of passing events. Because love never ends! While history of course does. Love abides... forever! It is part of our ordinary daily life – patient and kind, not arrogant and so on – and it lasts forever. That's the truth claim *Corinthians 13* makes. The claim may be false, but it can't be proved false by historical events because Paul's Love resides – in part - outside history. However often Paul's Love may seem to fail in the flow of history, its ultimate justification lies outside history. The apparent defeat of an advocate of Paul's Love like Dr. King, Gandhi, Jesus, or Paul himself is an enigma - whatever the historical consequences of the defeat may seem to be - because Paul's Love by outlasting history is beyond the judgment of history. Only in the completeness at the end of time that Paul mentions toward the end of the passage, can the success or failure of love be accessed. Until then our understanding of Paul's Love is dim and incomplete. As Kierkegaard pointed out there is a subjective, a hidden, side to Paul's Love that waits on the future for its uncovering. In the meantime as the old Bruderhof hymn has it we would "grow green and strong beneath the snow, in this winter world of ours."

When ordinary people went on peace marches or worked for racial harmony and justice in the Sixties, or today are involved in political action to make our world a safer, more humane, place for the wider human family they too share in the trans- historical aspects of Paul's Love. Even if one does not accept Paul's trans- historical grounding of Love in the coming completeness at the end of time, and the abiding presence of a transpersonal love – God - even now in history, they do share fully in the animating energy that bonds one human to another. Paul's Love is Paul's Love wherever, and however it occurs. No religious tradition or historical movement owns Paul's Love, which is available to diverse communities, religious and political. While the religious virtues, faith and hope, are necessary for millions like myself love is greater than our religious belief. Open to all, humanists and believers, in all cultures, in all civilizations Paul's Love is the ultimate criterion by which human action and attitudes may be accessed. Either roughly within history or definitively, for those with a religious orientation beyond history.

V

Another critical actor affecting the interaction between the economic woman and capitalism is technology. As many thoughtful commentators (meaning of course those who agree with me) including Heidegger, MacIntyre, Karl Jaspers, Einstein, and Norm Chomsky have argued technology influences but does not alter the essential components of human life. When human beings first lived on the African plains near Olduvai gorge nearly two million years ago, we were born as we are today between our mothers' sweaty thighs, we were suckled as infants, cared for as children and as we grew older we learned the ways of our elders. We struggled to make a living, we mated with other humans and we raised our young in a caring way. We cooperated with others for purposes of survival and defense; we created art and cultural events that fed our spirits. We got sick, we grew old; we died and were mourned in some fashion by our fellow human beings. As the eons passed and large scale farming and urban centers developed two basic groups emerged: the "haves" and the "have lots less". Pharaohs and farmers, nobles and serfs, management and labor, rich and poor. Those with power who ruled and those with little power who were ruled. Which is not to deny that other groups played a significant role as well; meaning the middle class groups between the two extremes, but always the extremes persisted. This basic disparity has survived in various forms throughout our history. Though our economic and political systems have changed many times the disparities between the "haves" and the "have lots less" has remained about the same. Most people in early Egypt, or Mesopotamia, or China or tropical Latin America had small homes, lived in crowded conditions, and had little power to improve their options in life. A few people lived in big homes and had a far wider range of options for education, entertainment and political power. Worldwide the same disparities still plague our human family. While status quo optimists stress the worldwide rising standard of living, and more pessimistic reformers point to the immorality of world poverty and the entrenched patterns of political injustice, the gap between rich and poor grows ever wider.

The enduring components of human life however remain the same: birth, death, love, hate, work, beauty, suffering, injustice and mystery. My point is that technology however fresh and innovative does not, in itself, resolve the ongoing dilemmas of suffering, injustice and meaning. How technology is utilized is still a human decision, i.e. an ethical decision. Slavery and child labor, or laws against slavery and child labor do not arise spontaneously purely as the result of technology but arise from the will of human beings who sanction the use of technology for certain agreed upon purposes.

The reason I felt it necessary to point out this rather obvious relationship between technology and Choice is that many commentators neglect this critical distinction. There is an assumption that new technology: pills both healthy and harmful, industrial innovations, weapons, communicative devises, special effects in entertainment, etc. shape our lives apart from human choices. You can't stop progress, is a postmodern mantra, but how we respond to technology as individuals and as a society is always a choice. Smoking once common is on the wane. People eat healthier and exercise to live longer. Many citizens are protesting our governments use of drones and the electronic devices that give the NSA - and potentially others as well? - a wealth of personal information on every citizen. While we play as children with our dazzling new toys, and quarrel and fight perhaps for a larger share than we have, we forget that toys are just toys. Things that we use for various purposes, can share or not as we choose, but which will rust, break, and be superseded, while the quality of our lives – our choices, our friendships, our bonded lives together - will outlive all the marvels of technology.

To repeat myself, technology from the wheel to the worldwide web has modified the way we live; it has not altered the basic components of life. Birth, death and the meaning of existence are as enigmatic as ever. The need for work, protection, sex, companionship, beauty, and loyalty to the community have remained constants no less significant today than when we gathered together on the plains of Africa almost two million years ago near Olduvai and began to spread northward toward Europe, the Near East and Asia. The challenge for those who would adhere to Paul's Love is not to collect as many toys as possible but to share the toys in ways that bring delight to others and bond us to our sisters and brother in the inclusive human family. From the point of view of Paul's Love technology is to be valued, modified or rejected to the degree that it promotes the animated bonding between human beings.

Having distinguished Paul's Love between unique, non-statistical, individuals from the encroaching influence of the one big idea and the mesmerizing wonders of technology, we are positioned to focus, in the following chapter, on the relation between capitalism and the economic individual. The swimmer-observer plunges into the great ocean of ordinary existence.

Chapter

XVIII

Capitalism for Swimmers — II

"There is no such thing as 'Labor.' The working force is made up of a number of individuals each having a personality different from the rest... One may deal with things without love; but you cannot deal with men without it."

Leading member of the Roundtree family of eminent British Quaker industrialists

"My art of midwifery is not with the body but with the soul that is in travail of birth. The highest point of my art is the power to prove whether the offspring of a person's thought is a false phantom or instinct with life and truth... You take me for a sort of bag full of arguments and image I can easily pull out a proof to show that our conclusion is

182

wrong [or right]. You don't see what is happening. The arguments never come out of me; they always come from the person I am talking with... The many admirable truths they bring to life have been discovered by themselves from within."

Socrates in Plato's *Theatetu*

I

Ignoring the lure of the major trend, the one big idea that shapes our future, and the alluring sparkle of our technological toys, we turn to the individual in her specific economic environment. We move from the lecture hall of the past few chapters, where the human family was celebrated as the primal paradigm under girding capitalism and justice, to a more informal conversation between classes, where Paul's Love engages the reader one on one. In the lecture hall I as author, presented Paul's Love in a very general way. If I'd been asked for specifics I would have defended Paul's Love with the conceptual tools at my disposal. Presenting my left-leaning Christian world-view, my big idea, as representative of Paul's Love I would have immediately been challenged by others with conflicting world-views. A conservative Christian or liberal humanist, an ardent feminist, a devout Muslim, or a committed environmentalist would each have promoted his or her own world-view as a worthy, perhaps a definitive, expression of Paul's Love. Or perhaps would have reframed the debate in a way that diminished the role of Paul's Love.

While debate between contending viewpoints is critical to a workable consensus for resolving pressing public problems, it alone cannot elicit the animating energy of Paul's Love in each human mind and heart. For that the individual must engage Paul's Love in more personal conversation; a conversation which serves as a Socratic midwife to the impulses of love pressing for birth within each individual. My intent in this and the following chapter will be to uncover Paul's Love, not within my own world-view, but within the world-view of others, i.e. to present my argument for Paul's Love from the reader's own view of reality, rather than trying to convince others of the rightness of the author's world-view. To facilitate the transition from public lecture to the interior dialogue that each economic individual engages in with Paul's Love, it may be useful to embellish our image of the observers on shore, and the swimmer-observers who move under water.

I can picture John Rawls, MacIntyre and Habermas standing together on the beach, energetically exchanging views on justice and fairness in today's society. Close by John Stuart Mill, Barbara Bergmann, and Amartya Sen, - all liberal economists - and David Ricardo, Frederich Hayek, and Milton Friedman - all conservatives - engage Adam Smith in lively conversation while the red bearded Marx listens impatiently unable to break into the ongoing discourse. By the water's edge a dour Samuel Huntington huddles with historian Paul Kennedy and an animated reporter Robert Kaplan, while nearby Francis Fukuyama flanked by Thomas Friedman from the *New York Times*, Harry Dent, and Bill Gates of *Microsoft* gesture wildly in opposite directions. Huntington and Kaplan to the dark clouds on the left, Fukuyama and Gates to the sunlit rainbow glittering on the right. Occasionally the scattered groups turn and look back higher up on the beach to the encircling body of figures who talk among themselves and patiently wait to be drawn into the spirited conversations of those groups closer to the water's edge. One hears from time to time the revered names of Plato, Aristotle, Rousseau, Locke, Jefferson, and many others. I picture myself listening to, then walking through the groups clustered on the shore before plunging into the ocean itself. Eager to stretch my limbs in the cool water I am ready to test my will as an observing swimmer against the invigorating environment of the dim and treacherous waters of the great wide ocean.

This little scene I submit is an accurate image of the human condition in which we ponder the wisdom of others, past and present, and then take the plunge into the great ocean of ordinary existence. There we must swim on our own, through the beautiful and deadly reefs of daily life, occasionally returning to shore for conversation with the revered figures still conversing among themselves, who offer us insight and encouragement before we plunge back into the dark and swirling waters. Back and forth we move between the shore and the depths gaining strength and wisdom for navigating the treacherous underwater terrain. Alternating between thought and action, reflection and ingrained attitude, we learn to swim ever more skillfully. We learn to move spontaneously among the reefs and the crowded waters which are filled with other observant swimmers, awkward and graceful, as we journey together like a school of glittering fish, or a family of turtles slowly swimming farther and farther into the depths of the great ocean.

II

As we move toward the final stages of the argument as it relates to the economic individual we face two seemingly contentious tendencies. First Paul's Love must speak to the condition of each individual offering comfort, hope and guidance. It must adapt itself to the unique set of circumstances each swimmer-observer faces in the ocean of ordinary life. On the other hand Paul's Love must retain its own integrity, which cannot be twisted to suit the needs of any individual. Unlike religious and political truth claims Paul's Love does not insist the individual adhere to particular world view, but Paul's Love is not an amorphous ink blot to be interpreted to the advantage of a diverse variety of observant swimmers. Paul's Love has its own logic, its own requirements. It is not arrogant, does not seek it own way, and is patient and kind. Any intention, attitude, feeling, or action that can meet those requirements is a valid expression of Paul's Love. Any intent or action that does not meet those requirements is not Paul's Love.

But who is to say which intentions or actions are patient and kind? Won't each individual and each group claim its own intentions and actions are benevolent? And if, speaking as an assumed adversary might, there are no objective standards, no actions *per se* indicative of Paul's Love – even martyrdom and voluntary poverty have been ruled out – how can Paul's Love be distinguished from what is not Paul's Love? If Paul himself ruled out any objective standards, relying solely on patience and kindness as the defining characteristics of love, doesn't this leave the evaluation of what's Paul's Love and what's not up in the air? Vague and undefined? I think not.

Just as Aristotle and Kant drew on the moral wisdom of their culture to help establish ethical norms so we may utilize the wisdom of our culture to help identify which attitudes and actions adhere to Paul's Love and which do not. Studies similar to those by Kohlberg and Gilligan on the stages of moral development would I believe demonstrate that Paul's Love is a recognizable and to some extent at least, measurable component of human existence. Even postmodern relativists are hard pressed to deny that the animated compassion of a Mother Teresa or the savage cruelty of a Hitler cross cultural boundaries. Some events still illuminate – still stain – the varied epochs and cultures of our common history. Auden's wry comment that some things can't be seen with a microscope reminds us there are pervasive cross-cultural notions of justice, equality, and in our case Paul's Love. A history that mislabeled slavery, child labor, or the sixteen hour working day, as acts of kindness would hardly be credible. Even those underdeveloped nations where such practices persist evoke necessity, rather than justice as the justifying rationale. Yet while Aristotle and Kant found validity in the ethical axioms of their time they did not rely decisively on the culture which they realized could be parochial and self-serving. Likewise, in discerning which intentions and which actions adhere to Paul's Love, we too must respect communal norms; without neglecting the individual conscience which interprets and enlivens those norms.

Without launching into an extended discussion on the complex relationship between communal norms and the individual conscience, it may be said that each individual is responsible for interpreting the moral axioms of their culture.

Especially the particular religious and political teachings they adhere to, before they decide how Paul's Love is best served in their own attitudes and actions.

III

Finally, we're ready to wrestle with the insight I've been waiting to share since the beginning; which is that each individual, whatever his or her political or religious beliefs may be, is able to follow Paul's Love within the framework of their own world view. In other words Paul's Love is not dependent on any ideology - Christian or otherwise — but may enliven a variety of worldviews. An obvious observation perhaps but one that has unsettling consequences for traditional justice-based political philosophy and society at large.

Perhaps my own experience, shared not as an interesting anecdotal event but as a paradigm or model of Paul's Love as seed growing in fertile soil, might be helpful. Seed not as previously the Kierkegaardian subjective self, featured at the end of Part I, but seed which resembles the gospel seed which grows within each believer. My contention is that this energizing inner seed (which is of course not divine for humanists) enlightens individuals holding diverse and conflicting political and religious world views.

Raising our five children, three boys and two girls, Betty and I tried to convey the liberal counter-cultural values associated with our socially active Quakerism and the anti-war, civil rights ethos of the 1960's. As they grew into adults taking up their own political and religious positions and varied occupations, I especially was disappointed there was not more enthusiasm for the values that had enlivened my life. No one became a practicing Quaker, four took a somewhat distant stance to the Christian God I cherished, and Wendy swung too far the other way and became, in her twenties at least, a fiery fundamentalist who rejected the thin soup of Quaker liberalism on which she'd been raised. I felt my values had failed to find a real home in our kids; that somehow I had not been an effective role model for the religious nonviolence I felt was the one hope of our troubled planet. If our own children were not convinced by my compelling worldview what hope was there for the wider world? Christian nonviolence on which I'd based my life suddenly seemed suspect. Was it merely a personal preference? A devotional hobby? Which even I'd failed to adhere to in any consistent way, with my middle class life style and bursts of moodiness, anger and selfishness?

My life, as I saw my children move in other directions, seemed an idealistic option without significant impact on the real world. In the 1960's many of us had felt "the time's they were a changin'"; that at last the world *was* capable of real and radical change. Now like millions of my generation I saw it all slipping away as the world returned to its old ways. History produced a few noble exceptions; saints like Gandhi, Martin Buber, Dorothy Day, the Dalai Lama, Thomas Merton and Dr. King – who had their own weaknesses. But exceptions do not make the rule. Or the rules. No wonder the hopeful surges of life I'd studied and admired among the Hebrew Testament prophetic communities and early Christians, Franciscans and Quakers. had so soon died away. Leaving institutional corruption, human cruelty and avarice as the dominant forces in history.

Such were my gloomy reflections, until over time and shaken by circumstances that would distract us from our main argument, I began to look to the margins of life around me rather than the focusing on the riveting public events. I stopped evaluating our children's progress in terms of my own world-view and began to see their choices and development from the view point of what after the ER experience I'd come to call Paul's Love. I no longer scrutinized others for the critical convictions I'd assumed were essential to any worthwhile life - especially our children. I put aside my own experiences and beliefs in order to catch a glimpse of their evolving views of the world. And what a range of options these presented! Over the years our offspring embraced Christian fundamentalism (pro- life, Reagan, placing herself – unsuccessfully - in "submission" to the father of the family), Ayn Rand Milton Friedman capitalism (individual freedom and self-interest), radical feminism (Women Against Rape, demonstrating for gays and lesbians), and nonviolent pacifism (chaperoning mothers of the "Missing" in Guatemala during the death squad era, civil disobedience in Georgia, New Mexico and West Germany). Our family's belief systems have included non-theistic humanism, vegetarianism, covenanted fundamentalism, Unitarian universalism, main stream Protestantism and Vatican II charismatic Catholicism. One is a social worker, one a market analyst, another is a stock broker, the fourth an advocate for the handicapped, and the fifth is an office manager for A.T. & T.

The insight that Paul's Love might be at work within each of these world-views and occupations did not come easily to me. Betty who understood almost at once simply appreciated our children's efforts to utilize their various abilities and inclinations to make a living and provide for their families. My conversion took longer. As a Christian philosopher I was puzzled the core values associated with Paul's Love should have found expression within diverse even conflicting worldviews. Watching Paul's Love at work in our five children I was confronted with the awkward implication that Christianity's greatest treasure, Paul's Love, was so often to be found outside Christianity. Reflecting on the life choices of believers, humanists and our five wonderful children who had surprisingly retained the essence of the worldview in which they been raised, and I began to take a broader view of public life.

As I considered the secular institutions and the allegedly divinely inspired religious traditions they seemed, like my own religious community, to be a patchy mix of light and darkness, good and evil. Some of the great collective acts of mercy in our century: the civil rights movement in Montgomery Alabama, Solidarity in Poland, the base communities of Latin America and the lives of saints like Dorothy Day and Bishop Romero had Christian roots. "We do it all for Jesus. Everything we do is for Jesus," Mother Teresa has said, explaining her order's motivation to help the destitute in Calcutta. Yet many of our most savage conflicts: in Ireland, the Balkans, South Africa and the segregated American south also invoked the name of Jesus. The conflict between good and evil, Paul's Love and its various enemies, has permeated the traditional faith communities as well as the warring political and cultural factions. Unable to make sense of the confusing world around me; I began to explore the way Paul's Love had permeated worldviews other than my own. I began to rethink my strong opposition to the free market capitalism our three sons espoused.

IV

In energetic exchanges with Steve - our oldest child, a stock broker and an ardent capitalist - on whether selfishness and/or a striving for excellence lay at the root of our economic system I came to realize there was an intense concern for the civic welfare — for the human family — at the heart of Steve's thinking. One night after the kids had gone to bed we talked for several hours. Recognizing that no truly wealthy person needs more than a small proportion of their income to live well, and not wanting to have the excess capital absorbed by an incompetent government bureaucracy Steve proposed that the wealthiest 1% of Americans not be required to pay taxes. Since, Steve claimed, they, not the government had earned the money fair and square. However, Steve went on, since there were unsolved social problems — urban blight, crime, poor schools, racial tensions, unaffordable health care, old highways, substance abuse, chronic pockets of poverty, etc. — he would require — by law — that Bill Gates and the financial elite spend a portion — 80% was the figure he suggested — of their income on meeting those social needs — in whatever way they saw fit. Since the wealthiest 1% were smart and knowledgeable about running corporations, effecting real change, managing budgets etc. they were better suited than politicians or academic experts to provide leadership in resolving our social problems. If their initiative and wisdom were called upon in a more systematic way Steve felt that society's recognition of their achievements in the private sector would encourage the wealthy entrepreneurs to turn their talents to resolving our chronic social ills. By honoring rather than shaming the capitalist innovators we would encourage them to work for a more just and humane society.

My response was to propose a larger role for the democratically elected government. Since I didn't trust big business any more than Steve trusted big government I would have allowed the state to use 40% of Bill Gates' annual earning to continue to perform its basic functions; leaving Gates 40% to alleviate pressing public problems. We also discussed strategies to educate the public and the wealthy elite to their new roles, so that the rich and powerful, the general public — especially the poor - and the government might all work together to repair the social fabric.

It was an exhilarating evening sharing ideas back and forth with Steve after the grandchildren had gone to bed, and gave me a new appreciation of Paul's Love operating at the theoretical level within a world-view that differed in significant respects from my own. This fruitful exchange was repeated, in various ways, with the other children till I began to glimpse the seed of Paul's Love pressing upward into their economic and political views, as well as permeating their domestic lives as parents and spouses. Like a gardener who'd cultivated only one species of flowering plant I was beginning to appreciate the wider garden.

Steve's final proposal was more personal. He was considering – and is still considering several months later - leaving his present job as a stock broker and formally requesting that Bill Gates fund him for two years to pursue practical ways to allow excess capital, without government interference, to alleviate pressing social problems. Steve's willingness to even consider leaving a profitable career with a wife and three children to support for such a Quixotic venture provides fresh evidence that a sense of kinship with others beyond our immediate family is a strong component of the human psyche.

The talk with Steve reminds me that comprehensive ideas – philosophic ideas – are essential to shaping a more humane society. I don't know if Steve's ideas are viable or not. To me they seem a reasonable and loving approach to alleviating the ills that plague the inclusive family. In any event the process of discussion and dialogue around public issues allows Paul's Love to operate at the social and political level. It reminds us that democracy, socialism, and capitalism are not mindless, inevitable, historical events but depend significantly on the epoch altering ideas of individual human beings. Locke, Rousseau, Marx, and Adam Smith also pondered and discussed the ideas that were to shape, for good and for ill, the public institutions of their time. Like Steve they were, each in their own way, obsessed with formulating ideas they assumed would be of benefit to a worn and wary world. Each assumed their ideas would help create a social order where as Peter Maurin, the Christian anarchist and cofounder with Dorothy Day of the *Catholic Worker,* said "it is easier for human beings to be good."

Chapter

XIX

Interior Conversation

"You [must] embrace a world without once caring to set it in order."

James Merrill, American Poet

"Let us wake with a wing'ed heart;
And give thanks for another day of loving."

David Richie, founder of the *Philadelphia Weekend Work Camps,* a Quaker saint, and my first boss, began his day with this prayer from Gilbran.

I

If we were to meet you and I, reader and author, face to face to consider the role of Paul's Love in your economic life you might first share your particular situation: your background, your values and convictions, your compelling interests and future plans. There would be time to ponder the intellectual dilemmas and personal struggles associated with adhering to Paul's Love in today's world. There'd be time for reflection and, for some, prayer, as we moved from options and possibilities to choices, commitment and action. If we could speak face to face, or more significantly, if Paul's Love itself might speak directly to each reader's condition the conversation might run as follows.

Where is Paul's Love in your economic life? How is this animating energy active in the way you earn your living and spend your money?

Do you spend your money in ways that are mindful of the needs of your brothers and sisters in the wider family? Are you willing to sacrifice your own wants for the sake of another's need? Not in a rigid or principled way but as one might share toys with a sibling – not evenly perhaps but to the degree one is generously motivated. Do you cling to your present lifestyle for dear life? Or at the other extreme are you seeking a formula of fairness to relieve the tension of guilt? As Gandhi's nonviolent concern for all God's children would have it. Or can you live with the tension of being in an ongoing relationship with one's wider family, sharing when moved by compassion rather by a concern to embellish your self image? Entering into the sorrowful mystery of human division and suffering to the degree you feel led by the spirit of Paul's Love?

Are you patient and kind to those around you at work? If not what needs to be done to repair relationships? Mend fences? Create a more carefree and caring environment? Do you offer encouragement and praise to your fellow workers?… Are you willing to follow the spontaneous impulse that may seem sentimental or awkward or out of keeping with the sometimes cynical tenor of the work environment? Do you trust the power of Paul's Love supported by your own intention however weak and feeble to grow stronger as you face the challenges of everyday living?… If religious do you offer up your sisters and brothers at work to the mercies of the higher power you depend on in your own life? Do you utilize your religious resources, or your humanistic resources, to mobilize yourself for the great work of serving Paul's Love in difficult situations?... And finally are you fed by the little victories of mercy and kindness that break through every day around you? Or do you gravitate to the negative, the unresolved, the worrisome, without reminding yourself as the psalmist says, "That surely goodness and mercy shall follow me all the days of my life." Every day! Every day there is goodness; everyday there is Paul's Love. Like a rain soaked dog coming in from the storm we can shake off the damp wetness and lie down at the end of the day before the warm fire of goodness and mercy in front of us. And rest for tomorrow.

Does your investment portfolio reflect your commitment to the inclusive human family? Do you limit your investments to stocks and bonds that promote the welfare of the human family? Forgoing the financial rewards of supporting ventures you find morally objectionable? Are you willing to discuss borderline investments with others? Recognizing the human predilection to favor oneself over others are you open to allowing your faith tradition, value system and respected friends to critique your financial patterns? To point out your blind spots, and financial fears, which may be obstructing the growth of Paul's Love in your life? Is Paul's Love, as you understand it, the decisive factor in your economic life? Or have the auxiliary pursuits of status and money diminished your commitment to the inclusive family?

Do you respond generously to those appeals that you feel promote the welfare of the wider human family? Do you contribute in a systematic way to the economic and political freedom of our suffering and oppressed wider human family – just as you would for the needs of your immediate family?

II

Having been addressed by the inner voice of love each reader must ponder an appropriate response. An elusive concept – appropriateness – formed in part from the western rationalism that goes back to Aristotle's practical ethics. An ethic that seeks a reason based appropriate response - for Aristotle the golden mean - between extreme alternatives. An ethic that has evolved over time to reflect MacIntyre's "moral tradition", the highest attainable ideals for one's conduct in the culture in which one lives. The more intuitive Buddhist tradition speaks of appropriateness as "skillful means" - the ability to spontaneously make the right decision, like a master butcher hitting the pivotal joint in an ox leg in one decisive blow. Or a Zen artist sketching a tree branch with one quick stroke. Taking appropriate action (or non-action) for the economic individual means not being unduly swayed by past practice or by future concerns, but responding to the present need with patience and kindness.

In the early developing decades of rural American life it was appropriate to know and care about everybody in town. One was able to express Paul's Love through the relatively uncomplicated social structure of the time. Today it is not appropriate to demand the same neighborliness of an urban population who encounter hundreds, perhaps thousands more people in one day than our ancestors did. Going to work on the subway it is not appropriate to engage every person one meets in conversation. In the workplace another level of social interaction is called for. At home and among close friends a more intimate relationship is assumed. What is appropriate is to act at each level of interaction in a neighborly manner. Rather than pine for the golden age of neighborliness or yearn for a brave new world where one's cherished values prevail one acts appropriately in one's everyday world to allow the seed of Paul's Love to flourish. Not that one gives up one's hopes and plans for a more humane world, but one allows Paul's Love to temper those hopes and plans. Recognizing that without patience and kindness all our hopes are as nothing – all our plans worthless.

Appropriateness relates not only to the individual's cultural environs – her lifeworld – but also to the kind of person she is. If she is boisterous and hearty, opinionated and direct her commitment to Paul's Love will take one form. If she is shy and introverted another. There is no pattern for what Paul's Love looks like. Dr. King was forceful and full throated, his compassion rolled down like a mighty river. Mother Teresa was practical, thoughtful, intense. Thomas Merton a gregarious hermit was impulsive at times, a scholar at home with intellectuals, poets and rebels. Einstein was brilliant, quirky, and good-naturedly naïve. Carl Sagan the genial cosmologist, a staunch atheist, was even-tempered, intellectually curious, a man who thoroughly enjoyed his role as a cultural teacher. All, despite their flaws, radiated Paul's Love expressed in an abiding concern for the welfare of the human family.

Personality types like those identified by the Enneagram (a Sufi based personality test) or the Jungian based Myers-Briggs another insightful personality test, will respond in different ways to Paul's Love, just as different flowers do to sunlight. What is appropriate for one person may not be suited to another. Over time one learns to make peace with one's given nature so that whatever its limitations it too has a part in promoting the welfare of the human family. One learns when to hold back and when to go forward, when to speak and when to be silent. Working within various institutional settings and historical epochs; activating a bewildering array of individual natures Paul's gentle love continues to nurture the human family. Never coming to a completeness that overcomes all obstacles but always present, always hopeful.

III

Having assessed one's responses to the queries (an old Quaker tradition) posed by Paul's Love in the light of their appropriateness to one's direct relationship to others, one confronts another series of questions. These questions focus on the effect of one's choices as a member of a working community, especially in the working community's relation to other social organizations and the wider human community. **Do the goods and services your company, or work community, provide promote the welfare of the wider human family?** Have you considered the effect for good or ill that these goods and services have on others? Do they benefit only one segment of the human family, one economic class or nation, at the expense of the wider community?... If the inclusive family is your primary commitment would you consider leaving a job that in your judgment, violates this commitment? Such as the tobacco or arms industry... Recognizing that all work communities – like all other institutions – have ethical ambiguities and that working for reform within a company is often a valid and loving response, do you trust your conscience and intellectual awareness to guide you in discerning the particular path Paul's Love would have you take?... Have you the desire and the courage to follow Paul's Love wherever it leads? Even if it runs counter to certain aspects of your world-view? Do you understand that like any institution capitalism at times requires one to sacrifice their own interests for the interests of others? That just as lovers at times forgo the chief physical satisfaction of marriage (sexual pleasure) so also capitalists at times must forgo the chief physical satisfaction of capitalism (financial rewards) to promote the welfare of the human family. Are you aware that like any institution an economic system involves responsibilities and sacrifices, as well as personal benefits?

IV

Some individuals nurture fresh initiatives by responding to queries such as those above. Some make pro and con lists, little diagrams, or symbolic drawings that reflect the possibilities being considered. As I do they relish the intellectual foreplay that proceeds decisive action. Other ease into the new commitment by talking with friends, keeping a diary, or reading scripture. Some begin at once with a small step that breaks an older pattern. Others prefer to weigh and sift a range of probable consequences before moving into action. These are individual matters. Once one has made a secure connection with Paul's Love one's intellectual faculties begin to orient themselves around one's new commitment. Arguments that had seemed irrelevant suddenly begin to make sense. Ingrained assumptions weaken and give way to alternative approaches. A fresh complex of ideas and habits gather around the impetuous to live one's economic life in relationship to one's sisters and brothers.

Buttressed by the gentle, inclusive side of one's moral tradition and one's own inner wisdom the individual suddenly realizes she is part of a cosmic enterprise that would transform the harsh realities of economic injustice.

Part III

Paul's Love and War

Holy Mother the State Goes to War

"A prince should have no other aim or thought, nor take up any other thing for his study, but war and its organization and discipline, for that is the only art necessary to one who commands."

Machiavelli, 1531

"I discovered in the earliest stages that pursuit of truth did not admit of violence being inflicted on one's opponent, but that he must be weaned from error by patience and sympathy."

Gandhi, 1919

I

I'd like to view the other ultimate social organization, the state, as an institution like capitalism, that can and often does act as a medium of human bonding, but I can't seem to shake the images of Texas prisons, men strapped to electric chairs, and savage wars. The first two, prisons and the death penalty, are dealt with more easily. Prison reform is possible. Criminals though confined can be rehabilitated, rather than merely punished. The death penalty, as in almost all civilized countries, can be abolished without undermining social order. As an advocate of Paul's Love I recognize the seeds of reform are already at work in the state's peacetime pursuits.

But war is another story. The most horrific recurring event in history, war flatly contradicts Paul's Love and humanity's most deeply held values. Truth-telling, democratic process, freedom and compassion all give way — enthusiastically or reluctantly — to deep impulses to impose one nation's will on another by any means necessary. The unpublicized torture of prisoners, systematic demonization of the enemy, and the intentional bombing of civilian populations (London, Dresden, Hiroshima, and New York), even threatening to destroy whole nations with nuclear weapons (or else why does one have them?), are rationalized as necessary acts of waging modern war. Augustine's medieval argument that it is possible to love the enemy's soul in accord with Christian teachings while killing their body, in accord with the demands of justice, is not an argument many would pursue today, and woe to the advocate of Paul's Love, or anyone else, who dares question the unified nation's right to defend itself during times of national emergency.

Has Paul's Love finally met its match? Has the fragile human family we've so carefully nurtured in the intermediate institutions and capitalism finally been unmasked as an illusion? A sham behind which the dark forces of hatred and violence operate at will? Unchecked by reason, law, or kinship? Is the jungle of crimson tooth and claw our ultimate social model? At this moment — a week after the terrorist attack on the World Trade Center and the Pentagon, as I sense the war clouds gathering again for the military response favored by 88% of our citizens, I'm not clear where the truth lies. Jack Nicklson playing a ruthless marine captain in *A Few Good Men* on the front lines against Communism in Cuba snarls to the civilian world "You can't handle the truth." The truth that civilians don't want to know how freedom is defended by the state. Has Nickleson's harsh truth on the necessity of state violence exposed the limits of Paul's Love? Is there in fact a limit to the extent to which Paul's Love in its social aspect as nonviolent defense of justice through loving one's enemies is effective? As I think my way into this dilemma, the most daunting the advocate of Paul's Love faces, two lines of thought emerge. One personal, one public.

II

First the personal. Since Paul's Love is a matter of individual choice each citizen must decide for him (or her) self to what extent he or she can participate in war. When captain William Penn of His Majesty's royal navy asked George Fox, the pacifist founder of the Quaker movement, whether he should resign his commission and turn in his sword to become a Quaker Fox advised Penn "to wear it as long as thou canst." When I asked Douglas Steere, my mentor at Haverford College, another Christian pacifist, if I should refuse to serve in the Army during the Korean War I was encouraged to not absent myself from military duty. Because, Douglas said, though I had intellectual qualms about fighting, I did not have the inner conviction, the gut instinct, necessary to sustain a viable pacifist position. In both cases the individual conscience was honored over the convictions of a religious body or a trusted mentor. I would take the same position. Utilizing an earlier image; each swimmer-observer ultimately must navigate the uncertainties of ordinary life in accord with his or her own conscience. Which does not excuse one from the obligation to reflect on the broader discussions taking place on shore before plunging back in the turbulent water of one's tangible existence.

The second line of thought relates to public matters. Moving back on shore to learn from the political philosophers I do not find much that challenges my contention that the state - in its internal affairs - often is, and can become, an institutional advocate of Paul's Love. By this I mean our democratic state provides opportunities for the animated human bonding already uncovered in capitalism.

During peacetime the state has proved to be a necessary and useful institution. Post offices, FDA regulations, progressive environmental and labor laws, international agreements; even the police, courts and prisons dedicated to rehabilitation rather than punishment, are not beyond the reach of Paul's Love. In the give and take of political forces the potential for positive change are present. During times of peace, in its internal and international affairs I would argue that Paul's Love is far more evident than is often assumed. Citizens are protected on the streets, the sick and needy are cared for at public expense, highways, parks and libraries provide access to recreational and aesthetic treasures. A ring of safety is drawn around society's varied institutions which are, for the most part, left free to pursue their own concerns. The competing interests of this assortment of largely autonomous social organizations are sorted out and regulated by the state, which acts as the final arbitrator of internal disputes.

Acting as peacemaker, educator, protector of the poor and powerless, maintainer of public safety and essential services the nation is accorded the heart-felt loyalty of her grateful children. Often challenged by her unruly children in peaceful times, in times of stress, citizens turn to the state for comfort and leadership. And then at the critical moment the wise and peaceful parent shows another face. Outraged at being threatened or demeaned, the state, in the name of justice, unleashes a fury which washes away all justice. War is justified always and everywhere as just, but where is the justice of taking innocent life? Bombing civilians? Torturing other humans – for whatever reason? Mounting massive public campaigns based on vengeance and hatred? Stifling all opposition to the war effort – until the world is safe for freedom again?

How did the state, acting as a wise and benevolent parent nurturing her children become an instrument of terror? The knife that tears the social fabric to shreds? How could I as a young man in the Army read the gospels at night while during the day I learned the art of plunging a bayonet into a human stomach? Thrusting upward after impact? Why would I and my fellow soldiers, do for Dorothy Day's "holy mother the state" what none of us would condone in any other area of our lives? That which we held to be the most heinous of crimes – killing other human beings – we now embraced as a sacred duty. Why?

One feels of course a strong sense of obligation for the mothering state, that to turn one's back on her in her hour of need when everyone else is willing to sacrifice their lives in her defense, puts tremendous pressure on the grateful citizen. A few lies, a few curtailed freedoms, a brief period of carnage, and all will be well again. Your fellow citizens need you. The flags are out, the songs and media images fill the heart with love for the motherland. Come – a few brief hours, a small sacrifice, and mother will be placated. Your countrymen and women support you. We're all in it together. All you have to do is your part. Others will do the dirty work. Others will release the bombs that inflict the inevitable collateral damage. Others will tell the lies that boost morale and torture the bodies presumed to bring us vital information. Others will plan the strategies that lead to victory. Just do your small part. Join the great effort. Look who's supporting the war effort! Celebrities, professors, scientists. All, or most, of the advocates of Paul's Love – the ministers, priests and rabbis are urging you onward; urging you to make an exception during the national emergency. Turn the wall hanging of Paul's hymn to love over for a few weeks. Put the Sermon on the Mount aside for another time. Leave the savior, the prince of peace, to hang on the cross alone. Just for now. Come - join your fellow citizens in defense of the beloved motherland. Fatherland. Homeland.

III

In these turbulent days a few weeks after the terrorist attack on the World Trade Center and the Pentagon – of whose consequences you as reader will know better than I – I find my private film of unfolding events has suddenly gone haywire. Grieving, dismay at the anger of others, frustration at what I take to be the ominous direction of the national will, are condensed – or oddly elongated in time. Certain images linger, others race by chasing kaleidoscopic late breaking developments. While most of America is drawn into a swirl of emotional responses – grief, shock, anger, impatience, and vengeance - advocates of the inclusive human family alternate between the isolation of being shut out of the national mood and riding the mood with one's fellow citizens, sharing their grief and outrage if not their thirst for vengeance that has usurped the national agenda pushing for better schools, health care and affordable prescription drugs.

My own plans to shed light on Paul's Love's influence on the state have been disrupted. I am no longer enthusiastic about taking time to make a convincing case for the peacetime state as a benevolent parent, as I did for capitalism. That case seems obvious to me. If not in universal practice at least in theory the peacetime state is open to reform. But how does one reform modern warfare which grows ever more deadly? It is the state in its critical mode at war with other states, that presents the greatest challenge to the thesis that Paul's Love permeates our social institutions. And frankly the political philosophers we've drawn on do not give us much help. Extolling the virtues of a state that nurtures "the obligation to mutual love amongst men on which [is built] the duties they owe to one another" John Locke (Locke, *Social and Political Philosophy,* P 169) allows for the armed defense of the nation from her external enemies and from internal "criminals…who may be destroyed as a lion or a tiger, one of those savage beasts with whom men can have no society or security." (P.173d) Rousseau whose heart wept for the suffering citizens, born free but everywhere in chains likewise advocates an eye for an eye, "It is expedient for the State that he [the criminal] ought to die… because his life is not to be considered simply as the boon of nature, but as a conditional gift from the State." (*Social and Political Philosophy*, P229) Ominous words, "conditional gift from the State." In order to preserve social stability Rousseau claims, "It is the right of war [against criminals] to kill the vanquished." (P. 229) In war against other nations Rousseau also breaks no new ground. "All, it is true, must fight for their country when their service is requisite." (P. 228). His efforts bore fruit in the French Revolution of which Jefferson in America in

1793 writes, "was ever such a prize won with so little innocent blood? My own affections have been deeply wounded by some of the martyrs to this cause [the innocent slain by the Revolution without trial], but rather than it should have failed, I would have seen half the earth desolated... My sentiments are those of 99 in a hundred of my countrymen.... What signify a few lives lost in a century or two? The tree of liberty must be refreshed from time to time, with the blood of patriots and tyrants. It is its natural manure." (P. 260-1)

Rawls, Habermas and MacIntrye suggest modifications in our present democratic state, but none decisively addresses the conflict between Paul's Love and the state at war There are suggestive lines of thinking in Kant's short essay on *Perpetual Peace*. And in Plato's *Republic* which highlights the goodness and justice that permeates the rightly ordered state, but when I am faced with the rush to war around me I do not turn instinctively to the philosophers. No one now has time to ponder a theory of justice with Rawls or engage in "discourse ethics" with Habermas. Or reflect on the social virtues of truth-telling, courage and justice with MacIntrye. These are optional peacetime pursuits. Truth-telling is whatever the government says it is. Courage is steeling oneself to kill or help kill other human beings. Justice is defeating the enemy.

Sitting in prayer after President Bush's nation gathering call to arms for a crusade to fight terrorism muffled outrage and helplessness flooded over me. I was not afraid for my own life for I'd been in Israel and Rome during times of terrorism and had already gone through the fear and confusion associated with war: in Vietnam, Central America and the Gulf war. At seventy my own time on earth is winding down. I felt so sad for the victims and for my fellow Americans who were struggling to understand this affront to normalcy. "Why did they do it?" I heard people ask. "How could anyone feel such hatred for Americans? What did we ever do to them?" I knew why. One day in Jericho at the Palestinian refugee camps told me why a few intense people might give up their own lives to destroy the hated oppressor. Poverty, despair, the un-honored Oslo treaty, all tacitly supported by the pro-Israeli US foreign policy. Justice delayed was truly justice denied.

For almost exactly seventy years. I was frustrated by the president's threats to get terrorists in any nation that harbored them. In sixty different countries? How could Bush stir up and mobilize the nation's vulnerable and dark emotions for such precarious aims? Isolated and hostile to the impending insanity around me I found myself speculating on possible peaceful responses to the terrorism and rising militarism we faced. Actions I might take and communal responses to the horrors of inflicting harm on other innocent victims to make up for the suffering we'd endured. Sardonically I thought 6,433 people died on September 11. Couldn't we just kill 6,433 of them – the faceless terrorist supporters we felt surrounded by – and call it even? Alan Herkowitz the noted civil rights advocate from Harvard, a voice of liberal sanity, suggested surgical assassinations as a prudent measure to insure justice. "To prevent random violence to the wider Arab population." Liberals advocated government sponsored assassinations; conservatives advocated decisive military actions – including the risk of collateral damage – the killing of innocent civilians. Wasn't that what got us started in the first place? Killing innocent civilians? I could barely concentrate on God. Or God's will for my life.

Overwhelmed by turmoil, sitting in prayer, I tried to listen for God's leading, until finally the words came; *"Love Bush… You must love Bush and everything else will fall into place."* Gradually my frustration lifted and once more I was at home with my beloved inclusive family again; in touch with the peaceful Spirit that sustains us all. The family was still one. A most puzzling and amazing word, but when I listened; when I could not love, but could at least choose to want to love the focal point of my fear and hostility; when I could want to love my worst enemy either as a person, group, or ideology the anxiety lifted. I was no longer alone and fearful, surrounded by angry predators. I was simply part of the family again, able to share their sorrows, anger, and frustration, without judging. Love Bush and I could love the rest of my enemies. I might present and argue my position, but I was not to insist. It wasn't my love, I was advocating; it was God's Love. I was only a small part of the suffering human family. Even Bush and the militarists were my siblings. Even the dedicated Islamic terrorists. I didn't have the answers, or at least they aren't clear to me now, but the frustration lifted when my anger at Bush gave way to an inner intent of friendliness. Which must be sustained or each new development will inspire fresh hatred for *my* particular set of enemies. I'm not ready to advocate my response in a public way. I'm just sharing an experience that lights me one step along the way as I try and make sense of these still unfolding horrific events.

IV

Standing on the shore I leave the political philosophers for now and turn to my religious wisdom figures. Gandhi comes to immediate mind. How can we, I ask him, champion Paul's Love as politically relevant when violence - and hatred - seem so essential to the state's existence? Gandhi says he isn't an expert in nonviolence; just an experimenter with truth, a seeker of nonviolence. When he started in India in 1931 he was told force was necessary to repel force. Independence would not come cheap with diplomacy, friendly smiles and a few prayers. The American, French and Russian Revolutions had, his patriotic Indian compatriots argued, all been violent. No nation had ever won its freedom without violence. Well, Gandhi said, let's be the first. And in 1948, seventeen years later, 400,000,000 poor and unarmed Indians gained their independence from the mighty British Empire. Peacefully. No acts of vengeance afterwards to the former oppressors. My time is over he says. Then he smiles, shrugs his shoulders and turns back to his conversation with Thoreau, Jesus and the ancient Indian sages. Leaving me to my own reflections.

V

To restate my dilemma; to which I must return again and again until the issue is resolved one way or the other, I'm challenged as a philosopher by the fact of recurring wars to abandon my thesis that Paul's Love is the primary truth. I can of course maintain my personal witness against war, but the experiences in the ER and rural Mexico then become merely personal. Anecdotal evidence with no real application to the overlapping realms of political thought and national conflicts.

Let me state my present fears. On the one hand it is unthinkable to me that *Corinthians 13* has only a limited application, that compartmentalized ethics with its different roles and incompatible attitudes should encourage behavior in one area it forbids in another. On the other hand though I've suggested, to my own satisfaction at least, that the inclusive human family is the primal model underlying hospitals, schools, businesses *and* the state in its internal and peacetime functions, it would appear that these opportunities for animated human bonding owe their continued existence to legalized deception, torture, and killing. And I can't handle that truth. If the primary ultimate institution responsible for the nurturing of the human family in its various organizational forms must ultimately depend on killing human beings to survive, then *Corinthians 13* is problematic. This is the dilemma the advocate of Paul's Love faces in wrestling with war.

Another set of fears I have relates not to the disappointment of being wrong in my philosophic judgments, but in being right. I fear that by winning the argument, enthroning Paul's Love and the human family as the true basis of political as well as family life, I may be endangering other lives. Am I another Neville Chamberlin advocating peace in our time as Hitler's tanks prepare to invade Czechoslovakia?

Is force, whatever the reasoning behind it, sometimes necessary to defend innocent civilians? Willing to sacrifice my own life rather than take another life, have I the right to insist children go undefended?

Chapter

XXI

The Other-as-Enemy

"War antedates the state, diplomacy and strategy by many millennia. Warfare is almost as old as man himself, and reaches into the most secret places of the human heart, places where self dissolves rational purpose, where pride reigns, where emotion is paramount, where instinct is king... [Yet] History reminds us that the states in which we live, their institutions, even their laws, have come to us through conflict, often of the most bloodthirsty sort."

John Keegan, British Military Historian

"You have heard that it was said, 'An eye for an eye and a tooth for a tooth.' But I say to you Do not resist an evil-doer... You have heard it said, 'You shall love your neighbor and hate your enemy.' But I say to you, Love your enemies."

Jesus in Matthew 5

I

After wrestling for weeks with the devastating effect of war on any philosophy of Paul's Love I find the way clear to resume writing. Inwardly at peace – not that I've resolved the issue – I've gone as far as my poor brain and the grace of God can take me at this time. I am energized that Paul's Love continues to hold the central place accorded it in *Corinthians 13* not only at the personal level, but also in the wider institutional arena. Even in the midst of war.

In order to trace Paul's Love's golden thread woven into the blood stained fabric of war we must proceed in a systematic and dispassionate manner. We begin with a look back to what philosophy might tell us. At first glance there isn't much. The definitive *Cambridge Dictionary of Philosophy*, second edition 1999, devotes five and a half columns to modal logic ("the study of the logic of the operators 'it is possible that' and 'it is necessary that'"). Nothing under war; not quite a full column under violence; nothing under peace; and a column under nonviolence. Wittgenstein and Heidegger, to many the 20th century's two outstanding philosophers, rarely mention the subject, though both lived through World War II and the horrors of Hitler's rise and fall. Wittgenstein as a public humanist and Jew, with secluded religious leanings, who felt deeply the horrors of his era; and Heidegger as an enigmatic wartime Nazi supporter. If anyone had asked them why the thorny issue of war merited only slight attention they might well have replied that the philosophers around them were discussing other issues. Wittgenstein at Cambridge debated with Bertram Russell and G.E. Moore the issues of logic, language and meaning. Heidegger, in Germany pondered the relationship between ontology, the classical philosophic study of Being, and contemporary Existentialism and Phenomenology.

If we probe a bit further however we discover certain thinkers do gravitate to the fault line between Paul's Love and war. Hobbes, Schopenhauer, and Freud expose but regret the dark motivations: aggressive self-will, greed, and lust for power, that fuels war's furious activity. Others like Machiavelli, Marx and Nietzsche, depict not only the necessity, but champion the rightness of armed conflict. Nietzsche especially seems to revel in, ironically intended or not, violence including war as the noblest expression of human nature. In our search for the elusive contributing causes for war these iconic figures remind us that we are accompanied by thoughtful minds. Minds often untuned to the nuanced conflict between love and its enemies, but always insightful and challenging.

II

Exploring the tension between Paul's Love and war, we're confronted with two dangers. First we must not minimize the effect of war by emphasizing the positive more hopeful elements in life: reason, human creativity, God (for some), and Paul's Love. War has invaded the peaceful realms of public life far too often to be dismissed so easily. Universities, cities, churches and temples lie in ruin as the dogs of war ever strain against their frayed and fragile leashes. On the other hand we would not give war the last word. We must not stress its physical – or its metaphysical – powers beyond the limits history provides. Nations continue to survive wars, the human family remains torn but in tact. Cities and temples are rebuilt from rubble. The positive forces of intellect, creativity, religion and Paul's Love still work against war to hold together the fragile family. As we explore the nature of war we must weigh evenly the varied factors involved without unduly stressing the importance of any one factor. We will allow each factor – justice as well as violence, heroism as well as blood-lust, sacrifice as well as greed, to have its voice. Any theory of war which emphasizes only one factor, or one set of factors, ignores the complexities of this ominous "paradoxical and saturated phenomenon." A phenomenon which defies conceptual clarification, and is perhaps the main reason war so often goes unmentioned in philosophy. War does emerge as a subliminal element in many philosophic works, under the guise of evil, will, or power. yet without the philosophically slighted war I would suggest these enigmatic concepts lose much of their power. Evil and power without the visceral reality of war seem somehow less intense, less threatening. A world without war is a toothless tiger, still dangerous but manageable. Our focus remains however not on the vague and controversial terms, evil and power, but on the catastrophic disruption of communal life - war.

III

It seems obvious that since war is, as defined by Webster's Unabridged "a conflict carried on by force of arms between nations or between parties within nation" that war from the perspective of any one party is about the Other. Not Buber's beloved Thou. Not the Other in its role as the vulnerable face Levinas' portrays for whom I am responsible, but the Other as adversary who must be defeated. The Other-as- Enemy. "The face is what forbids us to kill," Levinas had said. "The face is what one cannot kill." (*Ethics and Infinity* p.86-87) Yet when Levinas is asked about the Other at the institutional level he reluctantly concedes that the collective face of a national enemy may be resisted, even killed.

An interviewer puts the question directly to Levinas. "Emannuel Levinas, you are the philosopher of the 'other'. Isn't history, isn't politics the very site of the encounter with the 'other', and for the Israeli, isn't the 'other' above all the Palestinian?" Levinas disagrees. "My definition of the other is completely different. The other is the neighbor, who is not necessarily kin, but who can be. And in that sense you're for the neighbor... "(*Levinas Reader*, P294). Here he seems to privilege the Other as Jewish compatriot over the Palestinian adversary and ends up, while sympathetic to the Palestinian plight, supporting his Jewish Other in its struggle with the Palestinians. In the interest of justice, and the defense of the homeland Levinas reluctantly viewed war as a viable option. "In society such as it functions one cannot live without killing, or at least without taking the preliminary steps for the death of someone." (*Ethics and Infinity*, P.120).

In times of political unrest and outright war the Other-as-Enemy wears many masks. The economic enemy threatens to deny the state resources held to be vital to its interests. Oil, foreign markets, cheap labor, etc. Our political enemy threatens to encroach on our territorial interests, including those of our allies. As North Korea did in the Korean War of the 1950's. Religious animosity fuels long- standing tribal-like feuds in Ireland, the Middle East and central Africa. Behind these more easily identified war-triggering conflicts of interest: economic, political, and religious lie elusive suppressed emotions, which psychologists and cultural commentators tell us energize our responses to the more obvious reason to go to war. We think and say we are fighting over vital political or religious interests, but less conscious, more primitive, factors may be involved as well.

Freud, Jung and more recently the biblical theologian Walter Wink, and a Frenchman whose name escapes me who exposed the sacrificial scapegoat involved in violence, all view the projection of inner demons, personal and public, onto an external enemy as a major factor in war. Unacknowledged fears and frustration within millions of individual citizens are gathered into a national consciousness and hurled, vomited, spat out onto an outer enemy. The collective face of another nation has become the object of patriotic aggression. Siblings in the common human family are prepared in war to put aside the injunction forbidding killing. The other state composed of the faces of countless sisters and brothers has become the enemy. No longer the individual face of naked vulnerability that enlists our care and love the Other has become a menacing collective visage, hateful and devious, which must be destroyed. We are right; they are wrong. We are good; they are bad. Not entirely and not for all members of the warring states but unless a sizable majority in each state frames the conflict in terms of good and evil, often religious evil, the will to commit war will be lacking.

Politically, as well as psychologically, the Other has become the enemy; the authorized legal enemy; the *only* group of other human beings who may be legitimately killed. Killing, the most heinous of domestic crimes, the most heavily punished, has become almost a sacred duty. Capital punishment as the vast majority of nations have discovered is not necessary to maintain law and order; even in the United States one may hope for reform that prevents the state from taking the lives of its citizens. But war remains another matter. It's the unresolved issue for any political philosophy of Paul's Love.

Not that Paul's Love is to be identified with what actually exists today. Violence, greed, and various forms of self-interest still permeate our society, but at least Paul's Love has been shown to be a viable option. Something that has been done and ought to be done. The case for Paul's Love as an alternative to violence, greed, etc. has been made. In families, hospitals, and schools. Even in our present economic system, capitalism, Paul's Love has been presented as an undergirding influence that allows for animated bonding between sisters and brothers. An influence that despite ongoing inequities and injustices between family members allows for future corrections.

But can we view war as a similar undergirding influence? Or is war as Levinas and Keegan reluctantly argue a necessary stabilizing factor in social life? If it is our – well mine at least - efforts to enshrine Paul's Love as the reconciling agent between the compartmentalized areas of life is brought into question, and "differing roles" in different institutional settings still lead to "incompatible attitudes." Especially between the values held by the family and those of the state during times of war. Not because violence has often prevails over Paul's Love in ordinary life, but because war is accepted *in theory* as well as practice, as a *legitimate* way of protecting the interests of all the other more peaceful human institutions that compose the whole society. It's the intention, not only the act that negates Paul's Love and ruptures the inclusive human family. The problem for the advocate of Paul's Love is that the animated bonding encouraged by tender- minded institutions, as well as capitalism and the state in its internal and peacetime functions, is made possible *only* by killing large numbers of human beings! A circle of violence, or threatened violence, surrounds with few exceptions every nation on earth. As the contemporary French ethical philosopher, Andre Comte- Sponville, claims war narrows the focus of kinship, and one member becomes disconnected from other members of the human family. Who are then targeted in war as the enemy.

From the perspective of social stability, justice and international law war can survive this dichotomy between the peaceful state and the Other-as-Enemy. If the main concern is to rectify injustice, maintain the rule of law, and establish social stability, taking the life of those who act unjustly and abuse their neighbors, or who are criminals in the eyes of the law, is not a major issue. Social stability, justice and law come first. The offending nation should have considered the consequences before taking aggressive action against their neighbors, but from the perspective of Paul's Love if one treats one's neighbor as a Thou, a face for whom one bears infinite responsibility, taking human life is not permitted. Killing other human beings – one's kin, one's siblings - is not consistent with adhering to Paul's Love. That is the dilemma the advocate of Paul's Love faces.

However, as we discovered in examining the harsh features of capitalism a more nuanced approach may uncover the power of Paul's Love glowing – dimly but steadily – even in the midst of war. Our task will be to illuminate that small but vibrant flame that may yet unite the entire human family - without having to kill our brothers and sisters in the process.

Chapter
XXII

National Choice, Personal Choice

"Once to every man and nation comes the moment to decide..."

My memory is the hymn referenced above
was one of Dr. King's favorites.

I

Most citizens do not choose war. That is left to our elected representatives. What most citizens choose is how to respond to the choices the state provides. In a broader sense individuals choose from among the options made available by the groups and institutions in which they find themselves. I would like to have been an exiled poet monk living in the hushed mountainous regions of interior China during the T'ang dynasty. Chanting and mediating as part of a community of peaceful artists in the dew-laden sloping forests. But that choice is not open. My choices are restricted to ones that support, ignore or resist the social organizations around me. Most important of which is my response to the state's call to arms.

War does not occur without a decision being made by a few empowered individuals on behalf of a whole society to kill the armed citizens of another state. War, whatever the provocation, does not occur without choice. And not every nation faced with a conflict situation has resolved it by war. Later we will explore alternate options for resolving conflict. Conflict, of course, among states given the competing interests of states for resources, land, spheres of influence etc. is inevitable. Just as conflict among brothers and sisters with individual interests and natures is inevitable. No family, no set of nations have ever lived without conflict. Disagreements, arguments, bursts of anger, hurt feelings, etc. But violence and war are not inevitable. They are choices made to resolve the conflict in one way rather than another.

First states make their choices: to go to war or not to go to war, and then the individual citizens respond with their own choices. One by one. As Jean Paul Sartre and the pragmatists, remind us no one can avoid responsibility for the choices they make. The Nazis on trial at Nuremberg who justified their actions by saying they were only obeying orders were not excused. Thoreau called for citizens who opposed the Mexican war and slavery, to "serve the State with their consciences [even if] they are treated by it as enemies. [They] are the heroes, martyrs, reformers in the great sense." (Civil Disobedience, *Social. & Political Philosophy* P 284). Claiming holy mother the state made me do it is no more convincing than the plaintive plea that the market made me do it. Choice remains as Sartre insisted the ultimate human burden and last hope, however constricting the circumstances may seem to be.

II

At every level, in every institution except the state taking human life is unacceptable. Why then should the state be given this unique privilege? Political philosophers from Plato to Marx, have condoned war, either, for some, on the part of the state or, for others, a revolution which would install a new and improved state. Arguments on behalf of social stability, justice, defense of the weak, international law, common sense, cultural wisdom, and God's plan have all been advanced to justify war. Many of the arguments revolve around social contract theories which, articulated by Plato's Glaucon in the *Republic* and elaborated by Hobbes in the *Leviathan*, depict unruly individuals agreeing among themselves to forgo violence, and stablish a collective institution – the state – to punish internal wrongdoers and protect its citizens from the violence of other states. Other lines of thought explore a free flowing theory of competing forces of society: rich versus poor, the noble few versus the sheepish masses, owners against workers. And lately with Foucault, the French institutional genealogist, the mircro-mechanisms of power – the specific procedures of faceless bureaucracies – are seen to undergird the conventional macro-mechanisms of power wielded by a dominating class or social elite. A nuanced and unconventional view of power Foucault focuses on the way the individual's freedom is constricted not by a ruling elite but by the faceless procedures of the various institutions and modes of thinking; in mental health, clinical medicine, the social sciences, and the broader areas of human knowledge and sexuality. Without featuring the army as such Foucault often views the mindless obedience of military discipline as operative in the managed control exerted by modern institutions. His findings, while a perceptive view of the way regimes of power operates to enlist the cooperation of citizens in time of war, obscure the fact that someone, or some group, does make conscious decisions to utilize postmodern technology and bureaucracy in certain ways and not in other ways. Guns do not fire themselves; bombs and drones are not activated unless a human finger presses the right button. For every citizen at every stage from voting to paying war taxes, from induction to combat, war is a choice.

Theologians like Augustine, Luther, and in my lifetime Reinhold Niebhur, postulate a compartmentalized sacred / secular, church / state, morality where family ties binding among believers are rescinded in the secular realm. While Paul's Love rules the church, violence is viewed as the ultimate peacemaker in the wider society. A peacemaker that insures that churches, temples and mosques remain open.

Perhaps if we trace the development of choice in the citizen's institutional life it may clarify why we seem to move so easily from the loving choices of childhood to the horrific choices of the adult citizen engaged in the frenzy of war. Initially the child is bonded to its family, but as the child grows she (or he) bonds with other social institutions and eventually is bonded to the state. As the child develops she bestows her allegiance on ever larger, more inclusive groups. She identifies with a faith community, a school, a neighborhood, a city and state, and later perhaps to a political or cultural movement or a generation. Each of these groups in turn might at be called "the circle of the relevant family" - i.e. a particular section of the inclusive human family which has become imbued with the same ethos as one's immediate family. Coming in contact with ever more inclusive groups the circle perceived as the ultimate relevant family changes over time. The child becomes aware of other groups; sometimes hostile, sometimes cooperative and friendly. In school, and hopefully her faith community, the child learns to respect the rights of people from other backgrounds, other religions. But always she is held securely in her particular circle of the relevant family, to whom she offers the same loyalty and love she shares in her immediate family. None of these proto-families demand she take part in killing other humans; though they do instill attitudes the state may later utilize in support of war. But only at the national level are these attitudes overly sanctioned to permit the taking of human life.

A child does basically what her parents or caregivers suggest, but eventually as her range of choices increases and she becomes an adult citizen, she is asked to freely pledge her allegiance to the ultimate relevant family, the nation. This ultimate family for most citizens the beloved homeland that has nurtured and cared for the growing child through the medium of all the other nurturing institutions: schools, churches, etc. now calls her to support the war effort. When the state is threatened the loyal citizen is obligated, even eager, to play her small role in defending her family and friends; her whole way of life. Supporting holy mother the state in her time of greatest need – national preservation – is one major reason citizens agree to commit war.

Another major reason is national self-interest. Competing for raw materials, world markets and a larger voice in world affairs the interests of one nation, or one civilization, are bound to clash with those of another. If one nation, America, representing 6% of the human family utilizes approximately 50% of the resources and wealth of the world, it is bound to create resentment among the poorer family members. The 2/3's world, as they are referred to by Elise Boulding, a Quaker peace activist and sociologist at Dartmouth, seeks to relieve its poverty and improve its relatively powerless position in world affairs. The 1/3 world, including significantly America, pushes back to preserve its political power and economic well-being. Economic inequity has certainly been a major contributing factor in many of the wars of the last century, notably in Latin and South America, Israel, and Ireland. Tension between competing ideologies, including democracy, fascism and dictatorship, Chinese socialism, the Scandinavian well-fare state, and Islamic fundamentalism is another significant factor, as are the long standing ethnic and religious animosities in Ireland, Bosnia and Serbia, central Africa, and the middle east. In short economic, religious, and political factors, often obscured by the patriotic public persona war wears, play a substantial role in determining which conflicts the state chooses to resolve by war and which it does not.

Whatever reservations citizens may have in the name of morality or religion, most will support the call to war based solely on national self-preservation and national self-interest. The British public during the several centuries of English imperialism that dominated large portions of North America, Africa, and Asia did not decisively challenge the government to forgo the material benefits of those conquests; despite British support for the Enlightenment values of self- government, individual freedom and fair play, which England herself had pioneered. Most Germans in 1939 applauded Hitler's liberation of Czechoslovakia and Poland. Iraqis, by and large, rallied behind Sudan Hussein in the Gulf War. Americans for many years followed president Johnson's "light at the end of the tunnel" in the decade long Vietnam War. In short most citizens in time of war will support the state no matter what it does. Animated by fear of defeat; eager for the benefits of victory, motivated solely by self-preservation and self-interest most citizens support their country in time of war. A rogue nation like Hitler's Germany, or Stalin's post World War II Soviet Union, however, cannot plead self-preservation, to an unbiased audience when it invades its neighbors. Self- preservation and self-interest without just cause attested to by disinterested third parties are in themselves pre-ethical. Which is to say the fatal commitment to my country right or wrong is made prior to any other ethical or religious considerations.

Even in the already mentioned religious community citizen-believers on both warring sides almost always overwhelmingly supports the nation's call to arms. Theologians following Augustine and Luther argue for a compartmentalized chuch / state morality where family values among believers may on occasion be ignored in the secular realm. While Paul's Love is viewed as critical to family and church life violence is seen as the legitimate ultimate authority in the law and order, and military institutions. Nor has religious support for war abated, even in our enlightened era, where Christians, Jews, and Muslims, routinely evoke the divine will in support of the nation's war effort. From the perspective of Paul's Love citizen-believers in every faith tradition choose to forgo their commitment to the creator's inclusive human family. For the sake of one segment of the human family they are prepared to kill other members of God's inclusive family. In substantial numbers, by whatever means seem necessary. But before we examine more closely that horrific decision from the viewpoint of Paul's Love there are other factors to be considered.

Some citizens are not satisfied with self-preservation and national self-interest as the sole rationale for war. They demand that wars involve justice as well. During World War II most of the world believed Hitler's Third Reich to be a cruel and immoral regime. The Allied response was widely viewed as an act of justice, seeking to restrain the bully from usurping the rights of his fellow national states. Hitler's regime had violated the fundamental laws of justice that governed the community of nations, and so regrettable though war was held to be, Germany must be resisted. In fact it seems clear that justice – real and imagined - has been a significant component of all wars. Revolutionary wars for national independence like our own are generally viewed as justified responses to political and social oppression. Civil wars in our own country, Latin America, Ireland and Palestine have again been rightly seen as efforts to emancipate citizens from oppressive conditions. Even ethnic wars in central Africa and southeastern Europe are fueled by long standing claims and counter claims of injustices perpetrated and redressed.

Where there is war there will be claims, open to varied interpretations, of injustice resisted. Of justice defended. Self-preservation, economic religious and political self-interest and finally justice would all seem to be valid responses to the question "Why do nations go to war?"

IV

To sum up; states, not individuals, choose – or not – to engage in war. Individuals either choose to serve the state with their pre-ethical allegiances or with their conscience as well. Considering the matter ethically allows for the alternate option of not going to war, and many citizens after considering the alternatives decide in good conscience to join the state's war effort. Most citizens however in every nation I would suggest face the issue of war as one of patriotic allegiance rather than ethical discernment.

Citizens must choose to support the wars which are presented to them by the state. Children grow toward citizenship by participating in a series of proto-family social organizations – schools, faith communities, etc. The ultimate circle of the relevant family in our world is at present the state, which unlike intermediate institutions invites its citizens to participate in war. An awkward phrase perhaps, the "circle of the relevant family" would indicate by circle that a segment of the inclusive human family has been marked off as the individual's ultimate community. In Neolithic times the tribe or clan served as the circle of the relevant family. In classical Greece and the late middle ages city-states were the communities of ultimate allegiance. The group one calls, "my people", for whom one would die - or preferably kill. As the American general George Patton told his troops in World War II their role was not to die for their country, but rather to make damn sure the other guy died for his country.

Since political philosophers who have insightfully analyzed the nature of the state have devoted less attention to explaining why states go to war, we will turn in the next chapter to the wisdom of others: psychologists, social scientists, military historians and two allegedly non-political philosophers, Schopenhauer and Nietzsche, to help us understand this puzzling but critical issue.

So far we've identified self-preservation, national self-interest, and justice as the three most obvious factors motivating war. Self-preservation would protect the state and its citizens from the hostile actions of other states. Justice sanctions war to protect the innocent and resist oppression, as discerned by third party nations and the general judgment of history. Self-interest would advance the state's economic, religious and political concerns, apart from, but not necessarily in opposition to, justice and self-preservation. Quite a complex of interwoven motivational factors, with plenty of room for discussion and disagreement, depending on how heavily one weighs one factor or set of factors against another. But not, it seems me, enough to explain the awesome vitality of war; nor the ethical compartmentalization that dictates such radically contrasting behavior. It doesn't account for the fury and dedication with which good and often religious citizens devote themselves to the defeat of the hated enemy. The next line of thought leads us to consider a more elusive factor; one beyond the borders of our current historical and psychological understanding; yet one that plays a major role in generating war's awesome vitality.

Chapter
XXIII

War is Hell

"Everyone wants everything for himself, wants to possess, or at least control, everything, and would like to destroy whatever opposes him... This disposition is *egoism*... We see this from its dreadful side in the lives of great tyrants and evil- doers, and in world-devasting wars."

Schopenhauer, *The World as Will and Representation*

"The famine became more intense. The roofs were covered with women and babes, the streets full of old men already dead. Young men and boys, swollen with hunger, haunted the squares like ghosts... Bandits broke like tomb-robbers into the houses of the dead and stripped the bodies and came out laughing... [soldiers] cut open the refugees and ransacked their bellies [for gold coins]... At first the dead were buried at public expense; as they could not bear the stench; later, when this proved impossible, they threw them from the walls into the valleys... The Romans were exuberant... The soldiers delighted to stand near the walls and display their own ample supplies of food, by their own abundance inflaming the hunger of the enemy."

Josephus, Roman governor of Galilee and Jewish historian describing the fall of Jerusalem in 70 CE.

"In two nations such tensions, and such a mass of hostile feelings, may exist that a motive for war, very trifling in itself, still can produce a wholly disproportionate effect – a positive explosion."

Karl von Clausewitz, *On War*

"The tendency to collect human trophies escalated during the conflicts in Korea and Vietnam when the body parts most favored were ears, teeth, and fingers, but the collection of heads, penises, hands and toes were all reported... In the words of [one Marine] 'We used to cut their ears off. If a guy would have a necklace of ears, he was a good killer, a good trooper. It was encouraged to cut ears off, to cut the nose off, to cut the guy's penis off. A female you cut her breasts off. It was encouraged to do these things. The officers expected you to do it or something was wrong with you."

Joanna Bourke, *An Intimate History of Killing – Face to Face Killing in 20th Century Warfare*

I

John Keegan, the acclaimed British military historian, who chronicled the major wars of the 20th century and analyzed warfare from Neolithic times onward, has said, "I do not know why men fight wars, though I make an attempt to sketch an answer in the pages that follow." (*War and our World*, Keegan, Page *IX*) No one I believe can go beyond his cautious words. The answers provided by Keegan and other informed commentators on war are suggestive and partial at best. They are certainly diverse.

Some scientists find the causes of war in the central lower region of the human brain, the limbic system – "the seat of aggression" – which fortunately is controllable to some extent by the higher brain located in the frontal lobes. The rare XYY gene and the energizing male hormone testosterone have also been linked to male aggressiveness, which fuels war. How the two parts of the brain interact and why common generic hard-wiring does not play out more evenly in different cultures is not clear. If genes, brain development, and aggressive hormones were the primary factors in war one would expect to see war, like sex or child-raising, more commonly pervasive in all cultures and historical periods. Which is not the case. Europe for example was free of armed conflict for most of the 19th and the early part of the 20th century. Switzerland, Sweden, Costa Rica and Tibet have not engaged in war for the greater part of their history.

In 1986 UNESCO's Statement on Race, at Seville, disavowed five tenets of a social Darwinism, which claimed that given the innate aggressions of human nature and the socioeconomic jungle in which only the strongest survived, war is inevitable. "It is scientifically incorrect," the statement claimed to believe, "we have inherited a tendency to make war from our animal ancestors" or that "war or any other violent behavior is genetically programmed." It is also scientifically incorrect to believe that humans have a "violent brain" or that war is caused by" 'instinct' or any other single motivation". (*War and World,* Keegan P. 19-20) The American Anthropological Association has embraced the Seville statement as its own. Basing their position on studies by Margaret Mead and others on the peaceful conflict resolution strategies utilized by many primal peoples, the rise of international cooperativeness evident in the U.N. and the emergence of nonviolent movements around the world, many social scientists argue against the inevitability of war.

Others disagree. Freud states as a "general principle that conflicts of interest between men are settled by the use of violence. This is true of the whole animal kingdom, from which men have no business to exclude themselves." Konrad Lorenz, the Nobel prizewinning anthropologist, explaining not justifying war, following Freud saw the aggressive instinct in Neolithic man seeking satisfaction – being 'discharged' – by the act of killing animals. Later on human interlopers on their territorial rights suffered the same fate as the animals. Hunters had become killers and later as social organization expanded wars between contending states followed a similar pattern. Freud's destructive instinct, Lorenz argues, still seeking satisfaction by killing the releasing agent, the individual in murder or an opposing state in war, plays itself out in relationships between nations today.

Military historians and theorists while they generally eschew the thorny philosophic question of what causes war see things from yet another perspective. Content with chronicling the various stages in military strategy and technology from Neolithic tribal ritual battles, to the huge conscripted armies of the 20th century utilizing weapons of widespread even mass destruction, military scholars generally avoid sweeping proclamations on the causes of war. They do point out, from Sun-Tzu the Chinese military sage (c. 453-221 B.C.E.) to Clausewitz the battle tested Prussian officer of the Napoleonic Wars and advocate of 'true' or 'total war', that the soldier's role is to devise strategies to win battles and wars; not to ponder the murky realms of motivation, but to use their special expertise to defend the state in time of need. While all stress the need for an *esprit de corps*, hierarchical discipline, and loyalty to the military way of life, some like Clausewitz would have a society's military elite galvanize its civilian population for 'true' or 'total' war. As opposed to the 'real' half-hearted wars fought by a society Clausewitz viewed as conflicted about its reliance on violence. "In affairs so dangerous as war, false ideas proceeding from kindness of heart are precisely the worst... He who uses this force [war] ruthlessly, shrinking from no amount of bloodshed, must gain an advantage." (*On War*, P265) Clausewitz's philosophy of war as "The Use of Force Theoretically Without Limits", according to Keegan was the rationale behind the two global hot wars, and one nuclear cold war of the past century. Known as the 'architect of World War I' and revered by Hitler Clausewitz's philosophy and specific strategies became the bible for hard-line militarists in the 20th century. Keegan's own views similar to Sun Tze's, the first military philosopher, who said "the higher excellence is to subdue the enemy's army without fighting at all", (*Book of War*, P.79) would utilize the non-military factors of diplomacy, rules of humanitarian restraint in warfare, humane treatment of prisoners and civilians, and appealing to the peaceful inclinations present in the opposing states, as tools to resolve international conflicts peacefully. Even among military scholars and professional warriors there is significant disagreement over the origins, goals and methods of war.

II

What of the philosophers? Two, Schopenhauer and Nietzsche, have been in my mind since I began the chapter. Schopenhauer because no one presents the dark underside of the human condition so pungently. Nietzsche because no one exalts this dark underside of conventional morality more perceptively. Schopenhauer's contentious egoistic will and Nietzsche's will-to-power while philosophically vague at times lead us to the next stage in our investigation of war by directing attention to several of the essential elements of war. "Every individual," writes Schopenhauer, "makes himself the center of the world, and considers his own existence and well-being before everything else; he is ready to annihilate the world in order to maintain his own self... This disposition is egoism, which is essential to everything in nature... Real wickedness that seeks, quite disinterestedly, the pain and injury of others without any advantage to itself...[is manifest] in the lives of great tyrants and evil-doers, and in world-devasting wars." (*World as Will and Representation*. P.332-3) Where, Schopenhauer asks, did Dante get his images of hell but from the world around him? And where is hell more explicitly depicted than in the brutalities of an Aztec culture, which made war on its neighbors primarily to take prisoners to be offered in daily ritual sacrifices to a demanding and merciless sun god? Human sacrifices that ran into the tens of thousands. Where is hell more evident than in the terrorism of the great horse conquests that periodically swept over China, the Near East and eastern Europe from the steppes of central Asia? Ruthless nomadic armies of Huns, Mongols and Turks led by Attila, Genghis Khan, Tamerlane and other great warriors. Where is hell manifest on earth if not in the rape, pillage and slaughter of innocents perpetrated by war from the Assyrians to the Serbs? Or in the sirens blaring over London, Dresden and Toyko screaming warning to the citizens below – too aged, infirm or weak to resist the ominous drone of approaching aircraft. Buildings falling, bones splintered, dust and smoke choking the lungs, fires raging, screams of those trapped in debris, blood running from torn bodies groaning with terror, limbs and internal organs scattered mindlessly like a pile of autumn leaves blown by the wind. Do I exaggerate? Think back to Jerusalem where Crusaders waded in Islamic blood up to their shins. To Constantinople, capital of Orthodox Christianity, sacked and desiccated by Catholic Christians from the West. Think back to the horrors of London, Dresden, Hiroshima, New York's Twin Towers. Did I miss anybody's favorite atrocity? Fill it in. Call to mind the war that still hides in your brain – unseen, un-mourned, un-repented.

O Lord what have we done? O God of all nations how have we treated our brothers and sisters? What have we unleashed in our incessant search for self- serving justice? For retribution? What have we unleashed by giving way to the enlivening human energies – genes, hormones and tendencies – that were meant to build, to explore, to invent and to love those we cherish? What forces have we set in motion by our national myths that script our contentious neighbors as implacable enemies? How have our bloodless plans evolved into the tactics and responses that at a distance bring a reign of terror on those whose faces we will never see? The thousands of Iraqui civilians sacrificed as collateral damage, in president George Bush's war on Iraq, and the civil war that followed. Refugees streaming for the borders of Afghanistan to flee the cluster bombings that release several hundred deadly offspring from each mother bomb; expunged from our T.V. screens by a vigilant government that our resolve not weaken as we stand up to, make a statement to, our distant enemy. If self-preservation, self-interest, and justice comprise three enduring components of war, the specifics of war - the horrific component of war - must also be taken into account.

III

Let us pursue this horrific component of war before we ponder a broader view of war in the context of justice, and Paul's Love, bearing in mind that hell, the grim specifics of war, is not the only, though the most disturbing, aspect of war.

Schopenhauer, one of the most astute available guides, leads us to the crater's edge of the inner horror that spews forth the outer ravages of war. After meticulously recording the suffering, violence and illusion of the universal blind striving will at work in the individual Schopenhauer sees the state as "the common egoism of all." "Eris" the Greek goddess of discord, "happily banished from within, at last turns outwards; as the conflict of individuals, she is banished by the institution of the State, but she enters again from without as war between nations, and demands in bulk and all at once, as an accumulated debt, the bloody sacrifices that singly have been withheld from her by wise precaution." (*Will and Representation*. P. 345, 350) Here I would suggest we are looking at an unimaginable horror – the collective ill-will, simmering resentments, and boiling repressed rage of two nations pitted against each other over a sustained period utilizing the deadliest weapons available. It is here I sense that the "radical evil" associated with wars has created chaos. And chaos doesn't make sense! It's off the scale, it's beyond our conceptual radar screen. Like the other paradoxical and saturated phenomenon God, war can't be grasped solely by reason.

There are of course military scholars and warriors who sit in classrooms at West Point, Annapolis, and Sandhurst to study war, just as seminarians sit in other classrooms to learn about God but the reality of both topics of concern is ultimately beyond the reach of reason. I don't mean that war is wholly irrational. War is quite rational – up to a point. Clerks in the death camps across Germany and Poland kept meticulous records of progress in Hitler's war against Communists, radicals, deviants, and Jews. Plans were made and revised, orders given, strategies altered to accommodate changing circumstances. Before every war options are debated and finalized, citizens mobilized and trained, supplies gathered and weapons are tested and made ready. During the conflict itself intelligent responses to the changing fortunes of war are rewarded. Astute informed military and political decisions are made to enhance the chances of victory. After the conflict memoirs and histories reflect on the major trends and lessons to be learned and passed on to the following generations who will be asked to fight new wars.

But though the obvious economic, political, and military factors in war, and the psychological and culturally religious aspects can be analyzed the horrific component eludes conceptualization. When general Sherman said "War is hell!", he wasn't saying war was difficult, or grueling, or people died in gruesome ways. He was saying it was a chaos that was beyond the understanding of even those who'd given their lives to waging war. Just as a saint or mystic may stare into the raw radiance of God's unseen love, so a warrior in war looks into the darkness of forces beyond his understanding. And like the mystic is both awestruck and often exhilarated.

Like the saint the warrior encounters a reality which is beyond the range of ordinary understanding. Like the saint he is utilized by influences he fails to fully understand. He commits himself to an allegiance on one side of a conflict, which he understands only dimly. Like an actor thrust on stage unprepared he must play his role as best he can, and stumble off at the end of his scene as the play continues towards its as yet unknown climax. There is no guarantee of a successful resolution of the conflict of which he has chosen to become a part. All he can do is his best and hope that victory in war, or in the case of the believer the full springtime God's kingdom will validate his puny efforts.

Chaos, (*Eris* the Greed goddess of discord), the uncivilized dimension to reality that warriors experience in warfare has been hinted at by several philosophers, notably: Hobbes, Machiavelli, Clausewitz, Schopenhauer and Nietzsche. Schopenhauer as we've seen, viewed social chaos as the blind universal will forever dividing against itself from which pour forth the violence, illusion and mindless suffering so evident in the visible world. Nietzsche saw Schopenhauer's tragic will-to-live as bursting with possibilities for the individual resolutely willing to utilize it for his own purposes. Schopenhauer's restless universal will becomes for Nietzsche the more focused, more intentional, will-to-power which is, as we'll soon see, even closer to my own experience. And to scripture.

While Schopenhauer grumbles and grieves over man's inhumanity to man Nietzsche exalts in the destructive human impulses. The noble warrior nations (Roman, Arabian, Germanic etc.) "in their relations with one another show themselves resourceful in consideration, self-control, loyalty, pride and friendship [but] – once they go outside, where the strange, the *stranger* is found [they become] not much better than beasts of prey [engaging in] murder, arson, rape, and torture. One cannot fail to see at the bottom of all these noble races the splendid *blond beast*... exhilarated and undisturbed of soul, as if it were no more than a student's prank" (*Genealogy.of Morals, Basic Writings of Nietzsche.* P476) Again, almost at random. "To see others suffer does one good, to make them suffer even more: this is a hard saying but ... without cruelty there is no festival!... Mankind in the mass sacrificed to the prosperity of a single *stronger* species of man – that would be an advance... The essence of life [is] the will to power." (*Basic Writings*, P. 503, 514, 515). The real threat to humanity, for Nietzsche, is not cruelty and violence but the fact that the victims, "slaves" dare to band together to resist their noble "masters." "The sick are man's greatest danger, not the evil, not the 'beasts of prey.' Those who are failures from the start, downtrodden, crushed; it is they, the weakest who must undermine life among men, who call into question and poison most dangerously our trust in life." (*Basic Writing*, P. 558)

The noted Nietzschean advocate Arthur Danto distinguishes between commentators who portray a hard Nietzsche – as I would – and a soft Nietzsche. Yet Danto writes that even the soft commentators, for whom he often speaks, are challenged by Nietzsche's ruthless rhetoric. "How precisely is one to forget what he writes about Jews, slaves, justice; about barbarians, morality, torture, cruelty and war, women and the will... even if the book also provides passages enabling him to say, soothingly, that he did not exactly mean what he said?... A man cannot write this way and then stand back in mock innocence and point to the fine print, to the footnote, to the subtle conciliatory phrase." (*Reading Nietzsche.*, P. 18)

Whether I read Nietzsche rightly or not, and many scholars prefer a gentler reading that see rebellious creativity and irony where I see a hard Nietzsche promoting a dangerous rationale for violence, Nietzshe does focus us on the secluded motivations, the invisible dark depths of human nature that stir nations to war.

IV

From my own experience as a Christian I must part company from both Schopenhauer and Nietzsche. Neither the hungry striving self-divided will nor the exalted will-to-power fully explain the elusive influence I sense at work within the chaos of war. Several critical events shape my thinking. First when I was in the early stages of Jungian therapy in my mid-twenties, alone in an empty house, I found myself groveling on the floor groaning in the presence of an oppressive influence I had previously encountered only in dreams. Over the years I have traced the rigid features of this dark figure among others more benign in action pictures; a series of quickly drawn scribblings that allow my suppressed feelings and the inner figures (terrifying and comforting) to find their varied voices in the harsh jagged lines and in the soft willowy lines. And in black and the darker colors, while the sky blues and God-like golden yellows signal more positive aspects of the unconscious. These action pictures, ten to fifteen done at a time, often lead to one or two culminating mandalas, which depict the four featured influences in my life at any given time, encircled in a controlled, more integrated imaginative setting.

I put the mandalas up on the wall as a mirror, a portrait that reflects my unseen self. Several gaze back at me now as I write. The grim figure has been a constant companion in those pictures; and in the harsh voice which he uses to express himself through my own voice at times. I've integrated the figure I called KA — taken from the Egyptian double soul — into my life many, many times. He lends me a strength and gritty realism I need to balance the idealistic, gentler aspects of my nature. And yet the awesome reality of evil I experienced as I lay groveling on the floor has not left me. Certain aspects of KA, of Jung's Shadown, do not wish me well — ever! The repetitive threats to my life and all life have not abated. Aside from any knowledge of historical or theological evil I've acquired over the years I know I am capable of terrible deeds. The secluded interior chaos that Shopenhauer called the will, and Nietzsche the will-to-power, seems more evident, more focused for me, as the decades pass.

Most religions including Christianity have acknowledged and named this unsettling figure, but though I find the gospels insightful in depicting the destructive figure, the darkest aspect of the already dark Shadow — the Shadow within the Shadow - I do not approach the figure as many Evangelical Christians do. The dangers of mislabeling one's enemies as evil or satanic, in order to justify one's own violence are too well known to bear repeating. My rule of thumb is that only 5% of the Shadow tinged events I encounter derive from a truly evil source. The perception for many — probably most - citizens on either side of an impending war, on where evil lies is misdirected zeal projected onto the Other from their own inner store of unresolved conflicts. Writ large in the national consciousness such projections wreak havoc in conflict resolving encounters between contending states.

The second event that shapes my thinking on war is the Holocaust; Hitler's total war against the Jews and other enemies of the state. Ever since my late teens when I first learned of Dachau, and later of Buchenwald, Treblinka, Austwitz and literally hundreds of other death camps and their subsidiaries scattered across central Europe, beginning in Dachau in 1933 and ending in 1945, I've had a visceral connection to that event. The Holocaust writ large what I'd seen in my own soul. I also realized that what had interrupted the continuity of my civilized consciousness had other expressions as well. War seen from this perspective did not surprise me. Having experienced the self-righteous rage spewing from this inner evil, the violence that visits humankind from time to time is understandable. No one as Keegan suggests has decisively traced the causes of war, but I can understand that given this destructive "Radical Evil" in Hannah Arnedt's telling phrase, as a major component of human existence, wars will occur. It's not that war is inevitable. I wouldn't deny that states freely choose war over peace, in fact I would insist on it, but I also understand that the option for war is influenced by the presence of a transpersonal radical evil. Just as I do not comprehend the nature of God, but do glimpse the numinous reality of God so, like Keegan, though the inner nature of evil remains murky for me, I do glimpse the reality of Radical Evil in war and other horrific acts of violence.

Aware of the dangers of evoking images of hell and evil which are already at work in projecting unresolved hostilities onto the Other, I still find I cannot avoid the conclusion that real evil – the destructive intent uncovered by Schopenhauer, Nietzsche and Freud – impinges on human conflicts. Especially in war. Let us go gingerly then as we seek to unravel the elusive mysteries of war.

V

Repeating myself, conflict is understandable. National conflict is understandable. States compete for raw materials, markets, political influence, and to defend the national honor. What is not understandable is the chaos of war, the inevitable excesses of war. The vicious lies, the demonization of the enemy, the enthusiastic, intentional acts of brutality directed at military and civilians alike. Associated with understandable responses to the threat to national self-preservation, self-interest and justice there is a destructive craziness that exceeds the rational, sometimes legitimate, military actions between contentious states. A nation is attacked or abused by another nation and righteously goes to war. But somewhere along the line warriors find themselves cheering the sight of starving civilians, cutting off fingers or ears, or dropping tons of deadly explosives on, or near, defenseless civilians, while citizens at home ignore or condone the actions taken by their brave defenders, and support in general whatever action is taken on their behalf.

Some may see this destructive craziness as evidence for Schopenhauer's egoistic universal will, eternally divided against itself; or Freud's death wish directed outwardly to the Other; or to a genetic or hormonal predisposition to violence. I wouldn't dismiss these suggestive insights for they take us beyond the bloodless rationalism that sees war as largely an economic and political matter; regarding war, as Clausewitz did, as "Nothing but the continuation of state policy with other means." But even the probing hypotheses that search below the surface of events do not illuminate the elusive presence that left me groveling on the floor or that methodically pursued its campaign against Communists (early victims), Jews, homosexuals and other internal enemies of Hitler's state.

Two examples. In my senior year at Westtown, a Quaker boarding school near Philadelphia, I was subtly ridiculed for weeks by a lanky red-haired fellow student. Finally, we had words in the stone stairwell that served as the fire escape in our dorm, and when he shoved me I swung back. We grappled on the steps and after turning him on his back I took his head and began banging it on the steps. Fortunately others were present and pulled me away. Later as a senior at Haverford college, during a beer party well after midnight through the boozy fog - grinning at me in a way I found offensive. I swung again. When I woke up the next morning I found I'd knocked out John's four front teeth. No need one might say for a murky theological hypothesis here. Simply late adolescent frustrations and too much beer, but I've never shaken the belief, even after four extended periods of therapy that those incidents were my first conscious awareness of the destructive insanity that later focused itself as the dark energy behind the Holocaust and war.

KA, the Shadow-within-the-Shadow, as I've come to know him over the years, in his unadulterated form, has a very simple agenda. He wants to kill. To destroy first me – John Corry, beloved of God. And he wants to kill others as well. Any others, all others, by name. He delights to kill. That as I encounter him is all he wants to do. He delights in weapons, especially atomic weapons; he used foul language; he is ritualistic and repetitive. His voice is harsh and guttural. His eyes gleam blood- red from a midnight face. But the Shadow figure is not pure evil; often he lends me his strength, his sturdy realism, his straightforwardness. He is someone I need in my psychic life. Jung was right in all that. But part of Jung's Shadow overlaps with the figure in John's gospel who "was a murderer from the beginning." This is the figure I see utilizing the opportunities provided by human conflict and the meaner emotions. The Shadow within the Shadow, like Hopkin's Holy Ghost, also broods over the bent world, waiting on the opportunity to inspire one human being to kill another; inciting the nation to unleash the murderous anger held in check by the law-abiding, law enforcing state against an opposing state or states. Unable to take life directly the malevolent spirit must depend, like the Greek gods above the killing fields of Troy, on the affairs of men and women to implement his intent.

Kept in check by the bonds of fellow feeling that hold together the human family, the Shadow within the Shadow is unable to achieve his stated purpose in the normal course of history. Citizens build, argue about, and create institutions and art and occasionally the truly dark secluded KA is able to inspire a brother or sister to embody his intent. As I did in inflicting injury on the red-haired boy or my friend Kit'ridge, but in general the bonds of Paul's Love, acting through the restrains of family related justice and rational self-interest, hold the human family in its institutional aspects together. Food is raised and distributed, disputes are settled by private agreement or law. Hospitals, schools and faith communities enhance life. Poetry, music, and art feed the aesthetic soul. Technology and social reorganization improve the quality of life for a rising population. Until war breaks out. Now Eris, now Freud's will-to-kill, now the Shadow-within-the-Shadow, the one who was a murderer from the beginning seizes the opportunity. Political disputes, pent-up resentment, un-rectified injustice, and the unresolved hopes of a nation are raw material for his intent. From KA's point of view it does not matter what caused the war. All that matters is that human beings should kill as many human beings as possible.

I'm not saying Radical Evil is the only significant factor associated with war. National self-preservation, national self-interest, and justice also play a major role, as does Paul's Love whose role will become clear in time. But the bloodthirsty secluded KA is not deterred by the human desire for justice, nor the kinship that bonds the inclusive family. He works behind the scenes urging on the combatants to ever escalating levels of conflict until the – ah! – the satisfaction of taking human life! It is this satisfaction that many warriors and citizens come to share that creates the aggressive insanity at the heart of all wars. But however enthusiastically or reluctantly war is pursued the KA rejoices. And hungers for the next opportunity; for the final feast.

VI

From my experience in therapy, reading scripture and pondering the grim mysteries of the Holocaust I would argue that general Sherman's dictum that "War is hell," and Hannah Arendt's depiction of the Holocaust as "Hell… not allegorically… but literally", are, as they stand, incomplete and ultimately misleading, because they fail to mention, however tentatively, the force or figure who rules hell. A hell without an evil one, a Satan, is needlessly vague and implausible. It is this central figure who goes by many names in the major religious traditions, who confirms the pervasive influence of this ominous companion to war. Not limited to one culture, one theology or one religion, this elusive figure has a special relevance to the horrific events of the past century. During the period of enlightenment from about 1815 for a hundred years to the start of the first world war, when science and reason spoke with unassailable authority, it was possible in international affairs to ignore the chaotic frenzy of war that interrupted civilized progress. After the horrific events of the 20th century the ominous forces associated with war must be acknowledged and explored. To leave the metaphor of hell hanging, as if there no conscious intent behind this reality only increases the intensity with which one pursues one's own previous understanding. If one is peace minded the knowledge that war is hell seems a clear reason to abandon it at once. If one is a warrior one is inspired to greater efforts. No dedicated warrior ever says, "O dear me, war is hell, we'll have to stop." Rather they are inspired by the challenge itself to pursue their role as warriors with greater zeal than before. Until after the war perhaps, when they may reflect on the problematic realities behind the glib phrase "War is hell."

The notion that war is hell unsupported by a force or presence who inhabits the hell of war on earth is untenable. A hell without an evil one, is vague and allows for conflicting responses. Only by acknowledging the possibility that something, someone perhaps, has the intent of utilizing war for purposes that lie beyond the understandable concerns for self-preservation, self-interest and justice can we begin to dimly perceive the wider conflict around us. And avoid the risk of inflicting violence on our sisters and brothers seeking Radical Evil not in the transpersonal realm where it resides, but in other human beings, who compose the hostile state which threatens us. Only as we acknowledge our own inner evil, our shadow side, can we be freed of the compulsion to label others – individuals, groups and nations – as evil, deserving of violence and death.

We must, however, be patient and not allow this explosive knowledge of Radical Evil to dictate our reasoning and actions until we've considered two other critical factors at work in the deadly insanity of war. First a deeper look at human justice, and second Paul's Love, which remains the main subject of our concern. With these three factors, radical evil, human justice, and Paul's Love, in place we can then explore the nature, as far as human understanding permits, of the pervasive conflict involved in war. Having presented the horrors of war it's time to look at war from the perspective of the dedicated warrior, the champion of justice in the state's armed conflict with its enemies.

Chapter

XXIV

The Lawful Bearer of Arms and the Inclusive Family

"You chose a vague heroism [war], and having chosen it for yourself, chose it for everybody else and for us. We were forced to imitate you in order not to die. For a long time that was your great advantage since you kill more easily than we do... We who do not resemble you, bear witness that mankind, despite its worst errors, may have its justification and its proof of innocence. This is why at the end of this combat, from the heart of this city [Paris] that has come to resemble hell, despite all the tortures inflicted on our people, despite our disfigured dead and our villages peopled with orphans, I can tell you that at the very moment when we are going to destroy you without pity, we still feel no hatred for you. We want to destroy you in your power without mutilating you in your soul... [Now] we can say as victory returns, without any spirit of revenge or of spite: 'We did what was necessary.'"

French Resistance fighter, Albert Camus, writing to a friend in Germany in July 1944 (*Resistance, Rebellion and Death*, P.30,31, 40)

"War is wholly unlike diplomacy or politics because it must be fought by men whose values and skills are not those of politicians and diplomats. They are those of a world apart, a very ancient world, which exists in parallel with the everyday world but does not belong to it... The culture of the warrior can never be that of civilization itself. All civilizations owe their origins to the warrior; their cultures nurture the warriors who defend them."

John Keegan (*History of War*. P.xvi)

I

While the immediate causes of war are accessible to reasoned analysis the secluded contributing causes that reside in the collective human psyche, - the collective soul of a people, the dark angel of the state – are less accessible. Quasi-conceptual; and open to varied and conflicting interpretations. Social scientists and military historians examine the evidence for the economic, political and cultural – often religious – factors involved in war. Some tough-minded philosophers like Schopenhauer, Freud and Nietzsche going beyond a purely historical perspective see an aggressive primordial will permeating the socioeconomic and cultural institutions that fight wars; while some Christians like myself sense a broader spiritual conflict between Radical Evil and Paul's Love. Utilizing insights into the nature of evil - as unseen, cosmic, conscious and intentional - does not, in itself, however require that we embrace any particular religious world-view. Dachau, Dresden, and Hiroshima are horrific events in any faith tradition; in any humanistic worldview. That said its time to look at war from the prespective of those who fight not only to defend their state but, wittingly or unwittingly, to preserve justice among the family of nations.

II

In this chapter I want to pay homage to the warriors who fight the wars peace minded people like myself deplore. Without choosing my words carefully to fit previously established positions I want my gratitude to these brave defenders of my country and my life style to lead us to reflect on the heroic components of war. I've said we would allow each major element in war: justice as well as violence, heroism as well as blood-lust, sacrifice as well as greed, to have a voice at the table. Now it's time to speak of justice, heroism and military sacrifice. Later our primary voice Paul's Love will respond to the widening discussion.

We begin with heroism and military sacrifice. Though war partakes of the chaos engendered by killing members of the human family every nation is well served by its brave young men and women who respond to the call to arms. Every nation, victorious or defeated, justified or vilified after the conflict rightly honors those who bore the brunt of the struggle. The code of military honor, which is written into the training and discipline of every professional warrior is one that promotes the attributes of courage, loyalty, self-sacrifice, intelligence and love of comrade in arms and of country. That some warriors in the heat of battle fail to adhere to the code of military honor, does not detract from the faithful service of those who do, nor from the code itself which expresses the nation's moral constraints on how it will defend itself militarily. That different nations at different times have adhered to varied codes of honor – some we might judge more brutal, others less so – again does not negate the intent of military discipline. Keegan has identified three distinct warrior traditions; two, allow for either disciplined ruthless military action: von Clauswitz's "total war", and the slash and burn pillaging of Attila the Hun. The third tradition, exemplified by the early Greeks, utilizing values from the wider culture: no killing civilians, humane treatment of prisoners, negotiated peace treaties etc., Keegan deems legitimate for democratic nations. The other two models he rejects as unworthy of a civilized nation. It is this third tradition embodied in men like my uncle, Fisher White, who served in the Navy W.W. II and Duke Schneider, enthusiastic West Point graduate, Army captain and our son's Tom father-in-law which I would honor, and which challenges my understanding of Paul's Love as the dominate component of human existence.

It has been clear to me ever since I became a pacifist that my stance did not absolve me from the moral dilemma posed by war. If I would not fight others must. A few wars seemed to me unavoidable if the nation was to exist free and functional. The American Revolution and World War II. Many wars seemed unnecessary and unjust; serving narrow national interests rather than justice or national self-preservation. The Mexican War, the Spanish American war, the Vietnam and Gulf wars. The Civil War, with its horrific modern weaponry and tactics seemed to me debatably avoidable. Might we not have divided peacefully into two nations, until the withering away of slavery and a calmer mood brought us together again? Or not? Was it worth 650, 000 lives, and a hundred years of segregation, lynching and civil strife to preserve the union? To insist southern legislators meet in the same building with northern and western legislators? That one postal service rather than two deliver our mail? Perhaps as times changed slavery would not have been seen as an economic necessity, while had the anti- slavery movement remained strong, and the implications of Thoreau's civil disobedience taken hold other possibilities than the horrific Civil War might have emerged. England, largely due to crusading efforts of religious anti-slavery advocates, was able to abolish slavery in the 1830's, thirty years before the American Civil war. On the other hand, the case for abolishing slavery by violence is not easily dismissed, especially since the nonviolent option was not widely seen as a viable alternative to war. In any event, though many of our national conflicts seemed resolvable by means other than war armed conflict with the colonial British, Hitler's Germany and the Japanese warlords seemed to me historically unavoidable, if we were to preserve ourselves as a nation by challenging the aggression of a ruthless invader. Some wars do seem just.

III

Any argument supporting war that appeals to the advocate of Paul's Love cannot be one dependent solely on justice since as Gandhi, Dr. King, and other peacemakers insist nonviolent social action takes us beyond the legalistic limits of justice to embrace the enemy as sisters and brothers in the inclusive human family. Nor can war be sanctioned by separating the spiritual realm from the worldly realm as if Jesus taught that one might kill enemies on earth and love them in heaven.

The only argument open to an advocate of Paul's Love is one that reconciles, or at least shows some relationship between justice, war and the inclusive family. Those, like Camus and Keegan, who reluctantly advocate doing what is necessary militarily to resist aggression, draw on an assumed common human kinship. When Camus refuses to hate the German invader he implicitly includes his friend as still a member of the human family. When the Marshall Plan, after W.W. II provides the defeated Germans with material aid to help rebuild their devastated cities Germany is implicitly welcomed back into the family of nations. When Keegan acknowledges the pacifist as an essential spokesperson for civilized values even during wartime and the "lawful bearer of arms", the warrior, acting within a strict code of honor as "a practical necessity" he tacitly implies that the unity of the whole human family must be maintained by both camps, war-makers and peacemakers. And there is a distinction between the two. When Jesus blessed the peacemakers he was not supporting the industrial-military complex or the use of drones. The pacifist articulates the ideal of human solidarity and Paul's Love between all humans, while the warrior protects a portion of the family – and in principle the wider family of nations - from being unlawfully destroyed. In other words when a nation defends itself from aggression it reaffirms a kinship-based justice that would protect the inclusive family from harm. The image of what the world would have looked like had Hitler prevailed in W.W.II is one even pacifists might find troubling.

If we think of war as a family matter then killing is the ultimate punishment. Just as a naughty child should be disciplined by loving parents so an unruly state must be disciplined by other states. When diplomacy and nonviolent sanctions are not available to restrain a leader like Attila, Napoleon, or Hitler other sibling nations must band together to preserve the human family; utilizing the lawful bearer of arms, the warrior, to preserve the peaceful coexistence of the family of law-abiding states. At the state level no other means of discipline seems viable. This at least is the argument to be made from the perspective of Paul's Love on behalf of war. It is the only one grounded in a justice embedded in the primal paradigm of the human family. A paradigm that perceives the other side not as a hated enemy but as a wayward brother or sister, to be welcomed back, as Lincoln welcomed the defeated South, into the common family.

As we'll see in the final chapter, it's not an argument I would take to be the final word on Paul's Love and war, but it is an argument that honors the sacrifice of warriors like Camus, Keegan, and many of my neighbors and friends, who chose to preserve the inclusive family in ways I cannot. It is also an argument many pacifists like Gandhi and Dr. King accept. Gandhi we recall suspended his nonviolent campaign for Indian independence during W.W. II in order not to cripple the British in their war with Hitler's Germany. This line of thinking, I believe, is one which peacemakers must take seriously, rather than lump all warrior traditions together, as if the conquests of Genghis Khan and Hitler's Third Reich were the ethical equivalent of armed resistance to these tyrants. To say all war is evil – which is I believe true – is not to say tyrants ought not to be resisted – for the sake ultimately of not only the individual nations but also the wider family. Pacifists who refuse to join in the armed defense of the wider family share responsibility for the consequences of war. Perhaps our efforts would have made the suffering less, ended the conflict sooner. Or even made the difference between victory and defeat.

I shudder to think of a society totally devoted to war; a society which had no monks, no nuns, no Amish, no Quakers, no conscientious objectors, no enclaves of resisting peacefulness to preserve the ideal and memory of the functional human family. Yet during times of justified national emergency- far fewer than is generally assumed – the pacifist too bears responsibility for his or her choices. In times of war no one's hands are clean. In one way or another we all participate in the ethical dilemma of war. If I take up arms as the state's lawful bearer of arms to kill, or support those who do kill, the unjust invader I have put aside Paul's Love. I have not shown patience and kindness to other family members. Killing brothers and sisters with or without pity, necessary or not, is not an expression of Paul's Love. If I refrain from taking arms I may allow innocent brothers and sisters to be killed by others. Either way, as Dr. King has said, my hands are stained. Just as Camus takes up arms reluctantly as a last resort, so I must refuse the state's offer to take up arms reluctantly and with deep appreciation for those who do.

Even though I advocate another option, a peaceful alternative to the violence of war, still I must acknowledge the worthy intentions, bravery and sacrifice of the warriors who have in fact preserved my nation and my life style. I must not confuse the intemperate call to arms, the extravagant patriotism that triggers the society's projection of its own unresolved evils onto the hated enemy, with the fortitude of patriots who bear arms in the defense of justice. A justice that is rooted in love for their own nation, and the wider inclusive family.

Chapter

XXV

The Eyes of Gandalf— Seeing Something More

"Do you believe that evil is stronger than good?

Unfortunately, those who commit evil are stronger. One killer with a machine gun triumphs over a thousand sages. It's as simple as that. The killers are armed, and his victims are not...

The night of our arrival in the camp was a kind of gathering of exiles. I thought that the Messiah had come... the Messiah of death. The malefic pole, the destroyer pole...

I compare it to the Revelation on Mount Sinai. It was a kind of anti-revelation. The revelation of Auschwitz was an anti-revelation in the sense that everything this Event revealed was anti-something: anti-Messiah, anti-good, anti-life. It was not simply death, but something more."

Interview with Elie Wiesel, Witness for the Nazi Death Camps of 1941-1944 (*Evil and Exile,* P 26-27, 59-60)

"Love… does not rejoice in wrongdoing, but rejoices in the truth. It bears all things, believes all things, hopes all things, endures all things. Love never ends."

1st Corinthians 13

"The most basic statement of the [Christian] tradition is that there is a double mystery, the dark mystery of evil and the bright mystery of goodness."

David Ford, Cambridge Theologian and Anthologist (*Short Introduction to Modern Theology*), Oxford, P 76)

I

Two of the three basic components of war are now in place. First Radical Evil, Elie Wiesel's malevolent "something more", the anti-revelation, which exists apart from but impinges on the armed conflicts between nations. Second the human component: a kinship based justice implemented by Keegan's humanistic warrior culture. The third basic component, Paul's Love present both in history, and for believers beyond history in God's other world, challenges Radical Evil's (Satan's for Christians) pervasive worldly power. That secluded struggle takes place beyond our conceptual understanding, but its effects are reflected in history in a variety of ways including war.

In the general culture the conflict between Paul's Love and its enemies is portrayed in various forms. In Tolkien's *Lord of the Rings*, in Dante's *Divine Comedy*, in the paintings of Bosch and the late Goya, Sauron, Satan, and the Colossus intrude on our hobbit-like ordinary existence; suggestive evidence of a cosmic clash that spills over into the human imagination, depicting in the artistic realm the unseen adversaries behind war. Just as the Homeric Greeks depicted the dominate forces of their era: domesticity, peace, power, chaos, and war, quarreling as deities above the killing fields of Troy, and the biblical Jews sought to discern the will of Yahweh in their various armed conflicts, so our own culture may gain fresh insight by framing the visible tensions of war in broader, less tangible terms. Much like the good-natured but naïve hobbits of Middle Earth, like Frodo and Pippin, did, deferring to the deeper vision of the wizard Gandalf, who discerned amid the changing fortunes of war the dim shape of the two ultimate adversaries. Philosophers today who would see deeply into the nature of war must cultivate the compassionate and far seeing eyes of Gandalf, in order to discern amid the complexities of national self-interest, justice, suffering, and horror, the cosmic clash between Radical Evil and Paul's Love.

Political, economic, even psychological, factors go only so far in illuminating the more obscure origins of war. After the more obvious causes for war have been explored something is left over. Amid the chaos, rage, devastation, and horrors of every war Wiesel's "something more" manifests itself. Just as I found myself banging a fellow student's head on the stone steps, or punching my undefended friend full in the face as hard as I could, the state at war may find itself drawing on resources beyond its conscious intent. These resources reflect, as I suggested in the last chapter, Wiesel's "something more", the anti-gift that *wants* to inflict harm on human beings. Something or someone who wants human beings to kill one another as extensively and ruthlessly as possible.

The Holocaust, Hiroshima and Nagasaki, and the still looming threat of nuclear annihilation make no sense purely as an unfortunate combination of political and psychological factors. These were purposeful events beyond the will and understanding of the adversaries themselves. No rational citizen chooses to wage war solely to destroy as many human beings as possible. The aim is always to secure the benefits of defeating one's enemy. Security, peace, more territory, an increase in power. There was no public demand in Germany for Hitler's extermination of the Jews, dissidents, and other inferior races. The Holocaust was certainly not a wise strategy to advance Hitler's plans for building a German empire across Europe (at least), and yet despite significant public resistance uncovered by the British historian Ian Kershaw and others, (but very little public protest) and against the advice of his military staff, Hitler pushed on, as secretly as possible with his dream of ridding Europe of Communists, traitors, Jews and other inferior races and groups; even though it diverted enormous resources from Germany's life and death struggle with the Allied forces.

The common rationale for war, which Walter Wink one of my favorite theologians, called "the myth of redemptive violence" does not illuminate war's truly dark side. Each horrific action is undertaken for what are sincerely believed, at least by those involved to be worthy reasons. The exterminators in the death camps saw themselves as advancing the noblest ideals of a resurgent Germany, which had been starved and humiliated by the Allies after W.W.I. They persevered in their arduous task in order to initiate a thousand years of peace where music, art, healthy communal athleticism and folk culture might flourish. Where Germany might take its rightful place among the nations. There was camaraderie and love for one's fellow guards, superior officers, the homeland, and the long-suffering father figure, who was leading them to the promised land. But first the traitors, the deviants, the mentally unfit and the hated Jew, must be dealt with. First the great war against decadence and evil must be won. Then the celebration could begin, and peace, prosperity and honor would follow.

Those who dropped the bomb on Hiroshima for the most part still defend their action. See how many American soldiers it saved? Remember what the Japs did to our boys on Bataan, the torture, the rapes in China and Korea. Remember Pearl Harbor. Yes – drop the bomb! Get the war over. And the bomb was released over an undefended city where tens of thousands of civilians; old men, women and school children died in one blinding flash of heat and light. Three days later without waiting for a considered response to the first attack another bomb was released on another undefended urban center, Nagasaki, bringing the death count to over two hundred thousand human faces, with thousands more suffering from fires, radiation and painful memories. I do not think Americans rejoiced in the killing. For the most part we just wanted to get the war over and were impatient with suggestions to drop the bomb less harmfully elsewhere. Did it have to be dropped on two of the largest cities in Japan to show the war leaders the folly of continuing the war? But there was something more – something or someone who *did* rejoice when the bomb fell. Someone who delighted in the use of the atomic bomb – Middle Earth's legacy of the One Ring of ultimate power? Someone, like Sauron, who still urges us on in the inevitable political conflicts to use the bomb again – and again – and again. Till only death reigns. And the Shadow-within-the-Shadow is king! Over all! Over all!

II

The other protagonist in the cosmic discord of war, the figure for Christians who validates Paul's Love, is Jesus. Using more traditional terms in this theological segment of our argument, I would not however lose sight of our primary subject, Paul's Love, which is cherished by humanists and believers alike. Though Christians use terms like God's Love, God and Jesus Christ somewhat interchangeably, the main thrust of my argument would apply to anyone with a concern for Paul's Love.

I don't know how the triune God, manifest in Jesus, engages Radical Evil in the unseen realm. The struggle between God and the one who entered Judas to impel him to betray Jesus, the one who lives to kill, takes place for the most part out of sight. The part I do understand is that where Radical Evil and Paul's Love converge in human conflict I find Jesus. I can't handle the horrific truth of war and spirit-based violence but Jesus can. He has borne the brunt of Radical Evil on this planet and in God's other world. He is my champion, my God, my savior; the prince of peace I would follow in my personal and my political life.

When the three most common theological arguments that would explain evil: that evil is part of God's circuitous plan, that good always comes out of evil, and that evil is simply the absence of goodness, recede before the horrors of history, I depend on two sources of strength. As a postmodern thinker who accepts a non- monolithic world-view which allows for varied language games, varied truth claims, varied lines of thought I take refuge in Jesus, who rescued me from mental illness and a dissolute life, and who I trust will lend me his Spirit that I might be patient and kind to my sisters and brothers. I also take refuge in the argument of the saints that provides evidence that God's Love is expressed in the compelling heroic lives of individuals. Believers like Jeremiah and Jesus, Buddha and Muhammad and compassionate humanists like Albert Camus, Soviet president and Nobel prize winner Mikhail Gorbachev, and my uncle John Nason who died a confirmed agnostic at age ninety six last week, after a life time of service as college president, U.N. consultant, and tireless worker for charitable causes. A dear man, whose legacy was excellence, not because he promoted his own excellence, but because like Plato and Martin Buber he was genuinely interested in what the other person had to say; drawing from each person, like a good Socratic midwife, his or her own special excellence. Precise in his habits and thinking, uncle John, encouraged others to focus on the issues that mattered to the common human community. A warrior for Paul's Love. Patient and kind in his personal relationships, astute and optimistic in his public endeavors, uncle John is one of the reasons I trust Paul's Love to prevail over evil. Other reasons would include Elie Wiesel, Bonhoeffer, Anne Frank, Corrie ten Boom, and Viktor Frankl who engaged Hitler's radical evil, and yet retained their faith in Paul's Love.

I should note in passing that these two religious arguments for Paul's Love: God, (and for Christians the ongoing Spirit of Jesus), and the witness of saintly individuals, each confirms the other. Without witnesses, martyrs if need be, God is a purely personal option, powerless to confront the world's evils. A loving God without loving followers able to confront Radical Evil is easily dismissed, and Nietzsche is right that the last Christian died on the cross. Without God believers lack the interior resources to confront the horrific events of public life. Both factors, religious faith and saintly individuals, while compelling to believers do not however decisively engage the horrors of war. A thousand saints, as Wiesel puts it, are no match for one machine gun. To effectively challenge the role of warfare in defense of a kinship based justice, Paul's Love must also manifest a credible political response to the myth of redemptive violence. Later I will argue that communal nonviolence offers such a response, but for now we'll pursue our investigation of the cosmic clash between Paul's Love and Radical Evil.

III

If Radical Evil and a kinship based justice have their roles to play in the drama of war, what role does Paul's Love play? What unique methods and goals does Paul's Love employ to counter Elie Weisel's anti-revelation and the easily manipulated human emotions? Here we must observe closely Paul's Love as it actually operates during wartime, seeking once again to advance our argument from what already "is" to what might and "ought" to be.

We've already noted that citizens, during wartime, bond together, sacrifice personal interests for communal interests, and exhibit the virtues of courage, loyalty, and compassion that Aristotle and MacIntyre cherished. Having conducted themselves honorably within the confines of a disciplined and principled military tradition most warriors leave military service feeling justified; innocent of any wrong-doing. Even warriors in what was commonly agreed upon later to have been an unworthy cause: Germany and Japan in WW II, the Americans and French in Vietnam, and the Russians in Afghanistan, have in general been respected for their service in their own countries. Though the war may have been fought for ignoble reasons and precipitated the senseless slaughter of countless citizens - may in fact have had the evil one's fingerprints all over it - still Paul's Love nurtured the warriors with love of comrade and country in battle. After the conflict Paul's Love bonded citizens together in their respective countries as they rebuilt their devastated cities and economies. Even in the midst of the horrors of war Paul's Love works for the welfare of all its children, preserving, healing, and renewing the victims of war, on both sides, as they struggle to rebuild their devastrated cities and economies.

But what of state violence itself? Should Paul's Love utilize the state to protect the innocent and preserve the inclusive human family? Just war theologians argue yes. They argue in effect that God utilizes the power of the state to act as a parent would to punish an unruly child, and prevent him or her from harming other family members. The amount of force used depends how much force is needed to obtain compliance. The greater the resistance to compliance, the greater the force required to compel compliance. Effective restraint must be intensified if sovereign states are to maintain a rough justice among the family of nations. The difficulty with this argument is that parents do not kill their children to discipline them, while states routinely do use deadly violence. It's a real dilemma because if we forgo violence we may leave the innocent to suffer. If we condone violence we transgress the intent of Paul's Love which treats others with patience and kindness. Even if we acknowledge that individuals must sometimes use coercive force, as parents do to discipline children, it would be unthinkable for the parents' right to punish their children, to become a rationale for killing. Killing in any circumstances negates the possibility of an adversary's change of heart and rehabilitation back into the human family. The use of police and prisons while coercive does not necessitate inflicting such life-terminating violence on the offender. That said the dilemma remains and many believers – most in fact – have reluctantly felt impelled to employ violence to defend their nation and the wider world community from what is perceived by both sides to be an unjust attack.

The extent to which a loving God is, or should be, involved in preserving the wider family by force of arms remains a matter of dispute. Many pacifists, like Dorothy Day, and the historic peace churches: Mennonite, Brethren and many Quakers, see God's hand only in political actions that do not condone killing. God is always on the side of peace and reconciliation and does not support or condone wars of any kind. Some, at the other extreme, notably certain medieval popes and Islamic potentates have seen God as a warrior God, acting through a crusade or jihad to destroy the evil enemy, the heretic or infidel. Many modern Christians like Reinhold Niebuhr see God's will preserving a rough international justice by the use of diplomacy if possible and modern weapons of war if necessary. Including rather sadly I think for a disciple of Christ the threat of nuclear annihilation. Thomas Merton, though not an absolute pacifist like Dorothy Day, allows for the possibility of a just war, but has in practice strongly opposed the Vietnam and other wars of his own time. Many Christians – I would be one - follow Gandhi and Dr. King in condoning the use of violence to resist oppression, for those who are not willing to embrace nonviolence as the preferred response to injustice. Still others, represented by the American Catholic bishop's statement on war and peace in 1986, are nuclear pacifists, believing that though just wars have in the past been necessary, weapons of mass destruction make war obsolete. They insist that humankind must turn to nonviolent ways of resolving conflict. They believe that whatever position one may previously have held has become irrelevant in the face of the impending danger of global destruction. At the philosophical or theological level war remains an unresolved dilemma, not only because of the natural diversity of human opinion, but also because of the puzzling nature of the secluded struggle between Paul's Love and Radical Evil.

War remains a dilemma because the conflict between these two ultimate mysteries remains opaque to human understanding, like the muffled cries from a heated argument behind closed doors. One hears the clash of wills but not the particulars of the dispute. Individually either mystery, goodness and evil, eludes our ordinary understanding. Their conflict with one another only compounds the conceptual confusion. Instinctive self-preservation and rationality, as noted in Part I, is confronted by the bright mystery of goodness that altered the lives of St. Francis, Camus, and my uncle John Nason. The dark mystery likewise has oriented the lives of the sun-worshipping Aztec executioner-priests and the death camp exterminators. This doesn't mean we must abandon our search for a worldview that encompasses a reasonable response to the complexities around us, but we should acknowledge the limits of human reason. Limits which ethical philosophers like Kierkegaard, Sartre, and the pragmatists argue leaves the way open for choice – free will - to engage reality in non-noetic ways. Our responsibility as human beings is not to know reality but to act rightly in our ordinary lives on the basis of limited information.

We cannot predict the consequences resulting from any particular course of action. We don't know whether Radical Evil or Paul's Love will ultimately prevail. Paul of course claims love will prevail, but that's a hypothesis, not a certainty. It's part of Paul's faith in a loving world redeeming creator. The escalating intensity of war during the past century suggests a different scenario. Having for the first time in history the means (weapons of mass destruction) and the intent, clearly evident in the death camps and other instances of ethnic cleansing, to destroy all life on earth Radical Evil is exposed as never before in history. An awesome challenge to any humane world-view.

IV

So, the issue is still open; the dilemma still unresolved and those who would adhere to Paul's Love can only choose between the various options their particular culture offers. Acting without full knowledge we must chose to support the collective efforts – violent or nonviolent - that best serve the human family. To avoid pre-ethical judgments based on unexamined emotions and fuzzy thinking, we need to step away from the political and psychological particulars of each conflict to identify the enduring components of war: Radical Evil, family driven justice, and Paul's Love. Radical Evil, utilizing the myth of redemptive violence encourages adversaries to slaughter one another indiscriminately until every last human being on earth is dead. Human justice (defended by Keegan's third warrior tradition) wants only to protect the state from its enemies and return to a peaceful state as soon as possible. Paul's

Love works to prevent war, by reason and diplomacy and as we'll see later by nonviolent communal action. During the war itself Paul's Love is evident at every level to support and heal the victims of war on both sides, civilians and warriors. This is not to say Paul's Love (God for believers) wants war but that Paul's Love is present in the snarled catastrophe of war with its own agenda, bringing patience, kindness and courage to those who struggle with the burden of living in the chaos that is war.

During my two years in the army at the end of the Korean War God's presence guided and protected me from many of the temptations associated with military life. I felt God's Spirit was with me, and honored my decision made in good conscience to help defend my country. Visiting the rubble at Ground Zero in lower Manhattan shortly after the September 11 attack I sensed a strange, even awesome stillness. Standing amid the aftermath – the hole in the city – of the horror and grieving of Sept. 11 I felt the presence of both ultimate mysteries. Contemplating the tragedy in company with my fellow citizens I felt as if we were in a great outdoor desiccated cathedral; a sacred space where the conflicting unseen realities of good and evil impinged on our limited human consciousness, not to shatter but to deepen our faith. As I looked into the eyes of my somber fellow citizens I sensed we shared a common healing; that our thoughts were not of outrage and vengeance but on the mercy of God, who would somehow address the evil that lay exposed before us. It was a time of reflection and worship.

Many commentators and common citizens have felt that war clears away the illusions of civilized life and confronts citizens with the conflicted nature of human existence. Like Frodo's small band of well-intentioned hobbits they've come to appreciate the nature of the ancient cosmic conflict in which they must play their own small roles. May God give us the insight to see clearly into this conflict, and to respond wisely and compassionately to the great needs of our time. Amen.

Chapter

XXVI

Nonviolence — God's
Preferred Response

"The virtues of mercy, non-violence, love and truth in any person can
be tested only when they are pitted against ruthlessness, violence, hate
and untruth... The sword of the *satyagrahi* [nonviolent warrior] is love,
and the unshakable firmness that comes from it."

Gandhi

"Suddenly at a word of command, scores of native policemen rushed
upon the advancing marchers and rained blows on their heads with their
steel-shod lathis [staves]. Not one of the marchers even raised an arm

to fend off the blows. They went down like ten-pins... Those struck down fell sprawling, unconscious or writhing with fractured skulls or broken shoulders... When the first column was laid low, another advanced... They marched steadily, with heads up (until) the police rushed out and methodically beat down the second column... Another column presented itself... Hour after hour stretcher-bearers carried back a stream of inert, bleeding men.... The raids and beatings went on for several days."

Louis Fischer, British foreign correspondent and author, describing a nonviolent confrontation north of Bombay in 1930. With Gandhi himself in jail the march of 2,500 Indian volunteers was led by the poet Mrs. Sarojini Naidu and Gandhi's second son, Nanilal Gandhi.

"The essence of nonviolence is love. Out of love and willingness to act selflessly, strategies, tactics and techniques for a nonviolent struggle arise naturally."

Thich Nhat Hanh, Peace activist and
Buddhist monk (*Love in Action*, P39)

"Buddhist [peace workers] wanted to create a vehicle for the people [80% Buddhist] to be heard and the people only wanted peace, not a 'victory' by either side. During our struggle, many scenes of love rose spontaneously – a monk sitting calmly before an advancing tank; women and children raising their bare hands against barbed wire; students confronting military police who looked like monsters wearing huge masks and holding bayonets; young women running through clouds of tear gas with babies in their arms; hunger strikes held silently and patiently; monks and nuns burning themselves to death to try to be heard above the raging noise of the war. And all these efforts bore some fruit."

Thich Nhat Hanh,(*Love in Action,* P. 39, 40)

I

Looking back our journey began with *1 Corinthians 13*, and the revelation in the ER that despite pain, fear, and death "Love wins!" In Part I we traced the individual's journey as she moved from the rock of Paul's Love to the four stepping stones that carried her across the turbulent waters of ordinary life: Other, Choice, Gift, and seed. Levinas's Other (Buber's Thou); pragmatic Choice; physical, psychological, and spiritual Gifts; and finally, Kierkegaard's uniquely personalized seed. Seed being an individual human being nurtured by the tool-like Choices that lay within one's power to be patient and kind to other human beings, with the assistance at times of sun-like Gifts (not under our direct control) that supported those Choices. The culminating image from Part I separated the overlapping realms of consciousness and the lived bodily life; the first with clear vision standing on shore the second with restricted vision and range of motion as the swimmer-observer adjusted to life underwater.

Moving into Parts II (on capitalism) and III (on war) Paul's Love crossed from the personal realm into the public realm, which presented a whole new set of obstacles. But even in the realm of business, corporations, and armies, Paul's Love challenged human frailty and Radical Evil, God's ultimate adversary, with the species affinity human beings have for their sisters and brothers all over this land. Here in the global human family we were united and enriched both by the things we have in common, and equally important by the things we don't have in common. Our differences of class and color, nationality and gender and all the other distinctions which keep us from finding our role in what Quakers call the Peaceable Kingdom, if seen through the eyes of Paul's Love immeasurably enrich our appreciation for the varied wonders of creation.

At the socio-economic-political level the functional family was viewed as the prototype for all other institutions, notably our economic and military institutions. Evidence was presented that the ethos and ethics of the family (the social equivalent of Paul's Love), despite the conflict between Paul's Love and its ultimate adversary, Radical

Evil, had permeated these tough minded institutions far more than is generally recognized. War especially was seen as a theological stink bomb, a confusion of contending elements including justice, bravery, senseless brutality, and compassion that exposed with puzzling clarity the conflict between the dark mystery of evil and the bright mystery of goodness.

II

Which brings us to our final stepping stone, communal nonviolence, which is Paul's Love's ultimate response to war, and God's preferred option for confronting injustice, oppression and violence. We may approach communal nonviolence in either of two ways; first from a hobbit-like practical street level perspective, or second from the wider wisdom of a wizard like Gandalf. From the humanly astute hobbit-like perspective of a sociologist or political philosopher I might present evidence that nonviolence has worked. I might argue that the 20th century has witnessed an historically unprecedented blossoming of Paul's Love in communal nonviolence which from India to Poland, from the Philippines to Montgomery, Alabama has promoted a kinship based justice in ways consistent with Paul's teachings in *Corinthians 13*. I might point out that in promoting Paul's Love by publicly protesting political and economic oppression over half the world's population – some say two thirds – have during the 20th century engaged in some form of nonviolent action. In two years alone, from 1989 to 1990, thirteen nations underwent successful nonviolent revolutions. A notable exception being China. I might point to successful nonviolent campaigns against even the harshest regimes: Hitler's Third Reich in Denmark, and to a significant degree in all other occupied European countries [see Martin Gilbert's *The Righteous – Unsung Heroes of the Holocaust*, Henry Holt & Co. 2003and Eva Fogelman's *Conscience and Courage,* Anchor Books, 1994], Marco's dictatorship in the Philippines, and the repressive Communist regimes of Eastern Europe. We might celebrate the nonviolent labor struggles, the demonstrations, strikes and negotiations, which ignored the call to armed violence of Marx and Lenin and the nonviolent emancipatory movements that brought women, gays and other marginalized groups into the common family. We might discuss the notable failures of nonviolence – in Vietnam, China, Tibet, and the post- Gandhian Indian subcontinent divided into two often hostile nations. We might discuss why nonviolence seems more effective in promoting social change than in governing the still violence-prone state after changes have been made.

It might be argued that though violence does restrain destructive social tendencies, it has, in our nuclear era, become a dangerous and obsolete means of resolving conflicts. While a typewriter will get the job done, it might be argued creative nonviolence, utilizing the varied complexities of diplomacy, education and dialogue, sanctions and direct nonviolent action will, like a good computer do the job better. And be far more cost effective in alleviating the after effects of traumatic conflict. Rather than leaving the defeated adversary resentfully plotting new outbursts of violence, nonviolent resolutions allow both parties to work out future differences within a social framework that provides for both their needs, which is what happened in Poland where Catholics and Communists peacefully coexist and post-Dr. King America where blacks and whites, despite continuing racial poverty, share a common goal of one harmonious society. While a violent Civil War precipitated a century of segregation and racial hatred, nonviolence in the 1960's paved the way for integration, reconciliation, and a shared vision of the American dream. There are of course major differences between slavery in the 1860's and segregation in the 1960's but clearly nonviolent protests left fewer scars in rectifying a grievous social injustice than a violent Civil War.

Most works on the history and theory of nonviolence view communal nonviolence from this human perspective. But as I look back over Gandhi's career, the Civil Rights work of Dr. King in the South, the democratic movements in Poland, the Philippines, and less publicized events such as the Buddhist nonviolent movement during the Vietnam War and in the Dalai Lama's Tibet I find something else going on. Something beyond the struggle for economic justice and political freedom. I find it significant that in our humanistic, post-religious era, many of the major nonviolent upheavals have involved a critical spiritual component. These were not only works of human justice but were works of the Spirit, works of God. Let us shift from the ground level perspective of the astute social observer to the loftier view of Homeric early Greeks, or the Hebrew prophets, who saw spiritual forces at work in the tangled events of history. Let us share vicariously, impressionistically, the great social upheavals where God's Love confronted institutional oppression, before returning to a more thoughtful mode where we access God-inspired nonviolent movements in the troubled 20th century.

III

Half a world away, half a century ago a nation of 400,000,000 impoverished, backward and superstitious non-Europeans struggle for seventeen years to peacefully expel their more civilized colonial benefactors; relieving the British of the obligation to bear the white man's burden in a foreign land; because in their minds and hearts, and the mind and heart of Gandhi their leader, the universal God of justice and love whom Gandhi called Truth or Rama, had taken up their cause. God was with them. That was their belief. As they sang hymns to God before the marches and demonstrations, and listened to the teachings of their short, big eared, unimposing, gentle Mahatma – great soul - tell them God wanted them to show compassion for their oppressors they found strength to curtail their own unruly natures. They were able somehow with the help of God to forgo Nietzsche's resentment, the frustration of the weak, and endure suffering without inflicting suffering. This they believed was not their own work, but the work of a loving creator whom they'd been worshipping for centuries. God they were convinced had come to be with them in a new way. Without that belief there was no nonviolent independence movement.

Do you begin to sense it? The gentle surge of compassion that throbbed at the prayer meetings in Delhi and later at Montgomery, Alabama and black churches across the south? "A person – plus God – can be somebody!" Over and over the telling phrase reverberated, in black churches reviving the courage of a cowed and cautious people… "Stand up for righteousness," Dr. King heard the interior voice say when he put his head down on the kitchen table exhausted from weeks of death threats and racial abuse. Afraid for his wife and first child. Ready to move North to safety. "Stand up for truth; and God will be at your side forever." And he went back and took up the fight. Ten years? Speaking and marching and preaching. And the quiet ones followed. The poor of the earth. Fannon's wretched ones. Standing up for justice that did not kill. A justice that welcomed back the oppressive brother and sister. A justice that said though I suffer and die for it, we are kin. We are all God's children. Black and White, gentile and Jew, rich and poor, believer and humanist, Muslim and Christian.

In Poland and the Philippines they went to Mass before they took to the streets. Asking God's blessing not to win a contest of arms, but to be faithful. Just to be faithful to the God of love who had entered their lives in new and amazing ways. Jostled together on the streets of Manila calling for the resignation of Marcos the hated dictator there was a new spirit among them. God cared! Let the soldiers arrest whom they will, let the tear gas and bullets drive us back. We will not be moved. God is with us. For four days they marched and sang in the streets — resolute and peaceful. And Marcos reigned. In Poland, after years of repression by a regime which had defamed their beloved church, God had responded. God had shown them a way out of injustice and deception, lies and corruption. There were no soldiers slain, no grieving kin. No bloodied body of the tyrant lying in the street, yet God had heard their cry for justice. The church had been right. The priests and nuns who preached restraint and loving protest had been right! They thanked Jesus and the Blessed Mother for the victory. And brought flowers to the church. Poland and Manila were free at last!

It did not go as well in Vietnam. For twenty years Thich Nhat Hanh and his fellow monks and nuns practiced Buddhist nonviolence in the cities and villages, calling for an end to the war that dragged on and on. Seminars, newspapers, conferences, demonstrations, marches, hunger fasts and the oddly unnerving human bodies sitting in flames. Sitting cross legged breathing compassion out to their violent kinfolk, breathing in smoke. Patient and kind to the end of this phase of existence. Saying please. Please stop the killing. Trusting Buddha, the good nature within would strengthen their witness; would bring peace out of sacrifice. But the war dragged on and in the distance over the burnt land there was laughter. Twenty years and a half million dead, mostly civilians. 50,000 foreign soldiers. Laughter that mocked their sacrifice. "This one was mine! My victory! Death reigns!"

But as the sun rose in the days that followed and the fields were fresh and green, and the monks and nuns took up the healing in the villages, the memory of their struggle, was not forgotten. One battle? What is one battle? The war is not over. The Buddha still lives. We have life. We are poor, but we are not defeated. We did not become like our enemy. We still reach out to one another as we rebuild our country. And remember the days of our trial, when though our efforts failed to stop the war, we preserved our Buddha nature. We were true to our faith.

IV

If war is hell, a destructive craziness, a stink bomb that has confused our conceptual senses we cannot expect philosophy to resolve the dilemma war presents to the advocate of Paul's Love. While peacemakers like Gandhi, and this text, may reluctantly agree that violence is sometimes necessary in defense of a kinship based justice, and warriors like Keegan and Camus wistfully admire nonviolence as the preferred option, the issue is not resolved. Gandhi, it may be recalled, taught that justice defended by violence was preferable to injustice and cowardice. During World War II he called off the national independence movement in India that England might deal with its own oppressive enemy, Germany; a tactical move many criticized for not taking advantage of his enemy's vulnerability. Keegan summarizes this mutual respect position by stating that "Western culture would not be what it is unless it could respect both the lawful bearer of arms and the person who holds the bearing of arms intrinsically unlawful... Pacifism has been elevated to an ideal; the lawful bearing of arms – under a strict code of military justice and with a corpus of humanitarian law – has been accepted as a practical necessity." (*History of Warfare*, P.4,5) While Gandhi might point out that nonviolence with its historical track record in India and elsewhere was more than an ideal he would I believe, find common ground with the position of Keegan and Camus that in our present world disciplined and principled violence and nonviolence each has played a role.

At the philosophic level however the dilemma remains. The destructive chaos of the paradoxical and saturated phenomena – war – precludes human thought from encompassing the logic of Paul's Love and the logic of war in any one comprehensive ethical theory. In fact I would suggest that any theory that does attempt to resolve the tension between Paul's Love and war is flawed. Flawed because such a theory would deny the premise that both God's Love and the Radical Evil of war are paradoxical and saturated phenomenon, with more content than reason can handle. If God and Radical Evil are quasi-conceptual phenomenon any conceptual attempt to make the unthinkable thinkable diminishes their respective natures. It is not that God or Radical Evil are irrational phenomenon, beyond any rational understanding, but that the bright and the dark mysteries intrude on our lives without our grasping their secluded nature; nor their contentious relationship to one another.

Though there's a limit to our conceptual understanding of the two ultimate mysteries, we do encounter them in our personal and public lives. As warriors and peacemakers we each play our varied roles, without working from a completed script. We begin with a few introductory lines, the rest is uncertain. It's not only that we don't know how the play turns out; it's that the elements that impinge on the actors are not clearly seen. Warriors act on behalf of the values of justice and national kinship. Peacemakers on behalf of love and an inclusive kinship. Though the issue is unresolved each culture: violent and nonviolent, will press its own response to war, we all share in the common tragedy. Trying to maintain the bonds of kinship in dark and troubled times.

Dr. King understood the dilemma we face. "After reading Niebuhr, [the neo- Augustinian advocate of just war]," he writes, "I came to see the pacifist position not as sinless but as the lesser evil in the circumstances. I felt then, and I feel now, that the pacifist would have a greater appeal if he did not claim to be free from the moral dilemmas that the Christian pacifist position confronts... While I still believed in man's potential for good, Niebuhr made me realize his potential for evil as well... [he] helped me recognize the complexity of man's social involvement and the glaring reality of collective evil." (*Stride Toward Freedom*, P 81) Having seen evil close up in the vicious responses to their nonviolent movements, Dr. King and Gandhi gave their lives witnessing to the glaring reality of collective love: Paul's Love, nonviolence, *ahimsa*. Political forgiveness. This too is part of the incredible saga of the past century.

Gazing at the modern world from the short end of the 20th century with the optimism of progress, science, and a rational democratic world view one would have thought humanity's dark ages lay behind us. Surely it was clear in the first decade of the new century that enlightened modern men and women had evolved beyond the horrors of medieval warfare and superstitious religiosity. God, diminished by Nietzsche, Marx, Darwinism, and the wonders of science, was truly dead and humanity could face the future with a hopeful humanism. That unaccountably to me is the view that *still* pervades our culture. Two horrific wars, Hiroshima, ethnic cleansing in Bosnia and Africa, and the Holocaust seem to have taught us nothing. How much horror must be un-leased on our poor planet before we admit that reason, science and democracy do not begin to understand the dark realities of political life? When hobbits wander - some blissfully, some nervously - about the shire while orcs and dark riders ravage the neighboring lands, perhaps it's time to take a second look for a deeper conflict behind the unreasonable, chaotic, unscientific, events that threaten the life of the planet. Radical Evil is clearly visible in the historical events of our era.

And yet. So is the face of God acting through the communal events in India, Montgomery, Manila, Poland and elsewhere. And whether or not one perceives God's awesome compassion as Gandhi, Dr. King, and Bishop Tutu in South Africa do, behind these political events one can take heart that Paul's Love, the Dali Lama's compassion, has had its advocates and martyrs. Though the culture of violence permeates our political institutions, the culture of peace, which has its own long history, still remains an option. Not only, as with Thoreau and Tolstoy, as an individual witness of conscience, but as a viable collective response to violence and war.

Religious faith, and the witness of saintly individuals, has remained constant throughout history. What is new in our time is that Paul's Love, the ethos of the family, has become a political reality. Think of India in the 1930's and 40's. For the first time in history a whole nation commits itself to gaining independence by loving their enemies. Nothing like it in history. True the early Christians for the first three hundred years up until the time of Constantine refused to fight in wars or serve as judges where they would be called on to execute criminals. And there are other instances of peaceful communal action: the early Franciscans, the first Quakers, but nothing like the widespread nonviolent movements of the 20th century. I am still overwhelmed contemplating the breakdown of compartmentized ethics Dr. King initiated bringing the Sunday sermons on love and forgiveness into the streets. His words are still in print, still available to energize a culture which has turned a deaf ear to the meaning of the God driven events that confronted the entrenched forces of injustice. "We must love our white brothers and sisters no matter what they do to us... Because the white man needs [our] love to remove his tensions, insecurities, and fears... Jesus still cries out in words that echo across the centuries: 'Love your enemies; bless them that curse you; pray for them that despitefully use you.' This is what we must live by."

What moves me about Dr. King's use of these words from the Sermon on the Mount is that they are spoken not in a domestic or religious setting, but in a political setting. They are spoken into the teeth of racial hatred and violence. It is not yet clear how effective nonviolence can be in international affairs. The few examples I've touched on – toppling the dictator Marcos, the Polish overthrow of Communism, Indian independence – are not conclusive evidence of nonviolence's ability to replace all forms of lawful violence, but they do present a viable alternative. An option that was not there in 1931 when Gandhi was wrestling with the issue of Indian independence. There will still be occasions when peacemakers must say, "Well, let's be the first." Times when they will have to trust, with Thich Nhat Hanh, that out of Paul's Love new and appropriate nonviolent strategies and techniques will arise.

Sometimes, as the Vietnamese and Tibetan Buddhists discovered, nonviolence doesn't achieve its political goals. But it is an option. Something that already "is" which therefore may be pursued as an "ought". Something that is doable, because its been done. Before Gandhi we didn't even have that. Before that we had peaceful individual saints and violent political solutions. Now an option – the politics of forgiveness - that was not available to warriors of the American, French and Russian revolutions is available. The exceptions have made new rules. Its been done. And what has been done can continue to be done. If the 20the century brought fresh horrors – a sobering glimpse of Radical Evil– it also brought fresh wonders – the political face of Paul's Love - for many God's Love - gazing at the enemy as Other, as Thou, as sister and brother. Refusing to suffer injustice timidly, Paul's Love has stood up for justice, for kinship knowing that if the first line of peacemakers falls under the blows of violence another line will take their place. And another. Because Paul's Love despite suffering, or death, or war is persistent. This is my faith; the faith of the advocate of Paul's Love, that despite evil love wins. The Ocean of Light covers the Ocean of Darkness. Love wins!

Lord Jesus, guide us to the next step as we continue across the river the turbulent of life. And though we haven't yet reached the farther shore, be our companion, our guide, our joy, as we struggle to adhere to the love Paul celebrated in *1st Corinthians 13*. For those who cherish the Buddha, or Allah, or the wisdom of their own hearts; may they too adhere to the compassionate impulses that would bond them to the inclusive family. Till we are all one. And only love reigns.

Amen.

Appendix

War, Freedom and God's Will in a Nutshell

"The greatest gift of God, most suited to his goodness, the gift that he most prizes, was freedom of the will."

Paradiso, Dante

"It were better to have no opinion of God at all than to have such a one as is unworthy of [God]; for the one is unbelief – the other is contempt."

Plutarch, Greek biographer 1st century C.E.

I

If Paul's Love is not to become a purely mechanical interaction, coerced and programmed for perfection it must allow for unkind as well as kind interactions. If Cain is to love his brother Abel he must also be free to not love his brother, even to do him harm by whatever means lies to hand. Restrict Cain's freedom, predispose him to interact only in loving ways, and you restrict his love. Over time Cain's followers found the means at hand did in fact grow ever more deadly, until today we possess the means to destroy the entire human family many times over. All this rides not on Paul's Love (or for the believer God), but on freedom. Any morality – God-centered or humanistic – which would hold individuals accountable for their actions, must allow human beings the freedom to choose between meaningful alternatives.

In public affairs citizens are held responsible for their actions. In international conflicts individuals are also held accountable. The world court at the Hague presumes that state leaders may be tried and punished because they as individuals, not the inevitable forces of history, the state or anything else, committed horrendous acts out of their own free will. Even in a world from which all traces of God had been omitted war, free will and evil would still be problematic.

Freedom, not God, is the culprit who created the formal possibility that human beings may choose to harm one another. That they actually make this choice leads to the social realities of strife and war. Which then take on a life of their own. Let me use another example, to clarify the distinction between a formal possibility and a social reality. Before meeting Betty I knew the formal possibility that I might fall in love existed; after falling in love that formal possibility became a daily reality in our long life together. I might still speak of the role freedom played in my relationship with Betty but the formal possibility I'd pondered on shore had been transformed, in the underwater existential world into a committed relationship with a particular person. Betty Jean, the unique individual, sister in the common human family as well as wife and friend, confronts me daily with a plenitude of intriguing complexities. Her face focuses my world.

In the case of deadly violence, the formal possibility of human being #1 doing harm to human being #2, existed before Cain and Abel were ever born. If history had developed at a less frantic pace we might still be clubbing and stabbing one another, but since our accumulated choices – to utilize the material resources available as weapons to resolve our political disputes in the way we did – war is no longer only a formal possibility but has become a social reality. It has acquired a long history of its own within which we must make new choices. With the proliferation of cheap handguns and semi-automatic weapons, today Cain is faced with new options for inflicting death on his brother.

II

I'm not saying that if believers present God as the creator, the dominate cosmic figure, God may not legitimately be questioned about how things are going in creation. These questions however I would argue, must come from those who accept God as the creator. Elie Wiesel has questions he wishes to address to God over the treatment of the Jews in the death camps, but he is clear that he asks these questions as a believing Jew. Humanists have questions about evil in the world, but since they know God only as a formal possibility, it seems to me they should refrain from talking about God as if they knew what God was like. Without a visceral relation to God they really don't know who God is. They – some not all humanists – would speculate on what God is like and then blame God – the non- existent God – for the evils that trouble them. In effect they say they don't believe in God – who doesn't exist anyway - because God either causes war for his own purposes or is powerless to stop war. Either God is a heartless cosmic dictator, or God is an impotent weakling. It's not that believers don't wrestle with the issues behind such characterization, but that we don't characterize the divine in the way humanists – without an avowed experience of God – do. The caricatures of God we hear expressed in the general culture bear little resemblance to the compassionate, authoritative presence millions of us experience in our day to day lives.

To engage a dialogue partner on serious issues one must first acknowledge the partner exists. Then one must be willing to let the partner define herself. One listens to and gets to know the partner over time. One can't say sight unseen, "O I know all about you. I've been hearing about you since I was in grade school." One must put aside the misinformation and false impressions one has received and be open to a real encounter with the partner.

Let us revisit our example. First I fell in love with Betty; then I was accorded the right to question her behavior – and she mine. Then I could engage her in real conversation over real issues that stood between us. For me to have addressed questions to a hypothetical lover, and blame her for shortcomings I'd observed in others, would have been presumptuous. For humanists to blame a God they don't believe in – except as a formal possibility, or a cultural hypothesis – for the evils they see around them, seems a bit like refusing to date someone because he – or she – reminds one of someone else. For me to have said I won't meet Betty, I won't date her - I don't even think she exists! Because she is self-absorbed and mean-spirited like my last girl friend, seems speculative? Premature? Intellectually unwarranted?

For Jeremiah, or Job, or Elie Wiesel to argue with a God they accept and worship is one thing. To blame a God one doesn't believe in for the horrors humans inflict on one another is quite another. I'm not saying humanists may not legitimately question the motives and actions of believers. That's another matter. That both, humanists and believers, hold common values of fairness and justice makes this judgment possible. Pointing out the discrepancy between scripture and the believer's own actions seems warranted; just as I might challenge Communists who deviate from the teachings of Marx, or certain capitalists who misrepresent the stated motives of Adam Smith to justify ignoring the plight of the poor, whom Adam Smith cared about deeply. When challenged, of course, Christians, Communists and capitalists are free to respond by claiming that they *do* adhere to common values: social stability, freedom etc., but if trust in a loving God is not a common value between humanist and believer real debate is thwarted. The humanist has not engaged the God of Gandhi, Mother Teresa and

Dr. King. She has attacked in effect a straw figure spun from cultural misinformation, and perhaps the outdated image of an early Israelite tribal God. Which has been significantly modified since. Perhaps her image of God is based on an unloving and judgmental parental figure. A simple, but unfortunate, case of mistaken identity. If she *hasn't* encountered the God of Mother Teresa, Dorothy Day, St. Francis and Dr. King how can she be so sure God *isn't* the wonderful being many of her followers say God is? After all who do you trust to know the real nature of God? A shrill fear filled evangelist or St. Francis, Pope Francis, Mother Teresa, and the Christians one does respect? Somewhere the Hebrew bible mentions Elijah as the one true prophet among 400 false court prophets. One needs to listen for the best Christian voices not the loudest and most disturbing.

In any event I would argue that freedom, not God, is the formal basis for Radical Evil and war. Whether the human suffering and injustice that history records balances a freewill based Paul's Love is worth it, is still an open question. Despite the optimistic claims of religion and the ominous logic of Radical Evil the issue of whether Paul's Love will prevail over chaos and war is unresolved. But however we assess the pluses and minuses of existence it's freedom not God, fate, or power that creates the possibility for humans to treat each other unjustly. And while the creator may be legitimately addressed for having provided freedom God cannot be held responsible for how the two other basic participants involved in war – Radical Evil and human beings – have utilized their freedom. Betty and I likewise, as parents, must allow our adult children to make their choices in life; and while God remains a more pervasive and authoritative influence both must honor the freedom of their offspring if unforced affection is to animate their relationship. I hope our kids turn out well, but there's no guarantee they will.

I would agree the creator has the authority to outlaw war and injustice, but not without coercing compliance to God's will. God was not coerced or influenced by any outside agent to provide humans with freedom, but once given God like the rest of us must live with the consequences of this critical gift. Despite the sufferings, injustices and the horrors of war, to which freedom may lead I cannot conceive of wishing it otherwise. I'm not suggesting as Leibnitz did that ours is the best of all possible worlds; I would concur with Dr. Schweitzer that while my knowledge of the world tends towards the pessimistic my willing remains optimistic. Dr. King from a paper plate wall hanging, given to me by our grandson John who plays lead guitar in a hard rock band and writes raunchy philosophical novels, says "We must accept finite disappointment, but we must never lose infinite hope. Only in that way shall we live without the fatigue of bitterness and drain of resentment."

Printed in the United States
By Bookmasters

FLOURISHING

families

THE HOME WITHIN

Denise Dziwak

FLOURISHING FAMILIES
THE HOME WITHIN

iUniverse books may be ordered through booksellers or by contacting:

iUniverse
1663 Liberty Drive
Bloomington, IN 47403
www.iuniverse.com
1-800-Authors (1-800-288-4677)

Because of the dynamic nature of the Internet, any web addresses or links contained in this book may have changed since publication and may no longer be valid. The views expressed in this work are solely those of the author and do not necessarily reflect the views of the publisher, and the publisher hereby disclaims any responsibility for them.

Any people depicted in stock imagery provided by Getty Images are models, and such images are being used for illustrative purposes only. Certain stock imagery © Getty Images.

ISBN: 978-1-5320-6159-2 (sc)
ISBN: 978-1-5320-6158-5 (hc)
ISBN: 978-1-5320-6306-0 (e)

Library of Congress Control Number: 2019900206

Print information available on the last page.

iUniverse rev. date: 05/03/2019

"To Roman, Valen, Sofi and Juan Fran.
Thank you for being my daily inspiration
on learning how to love."

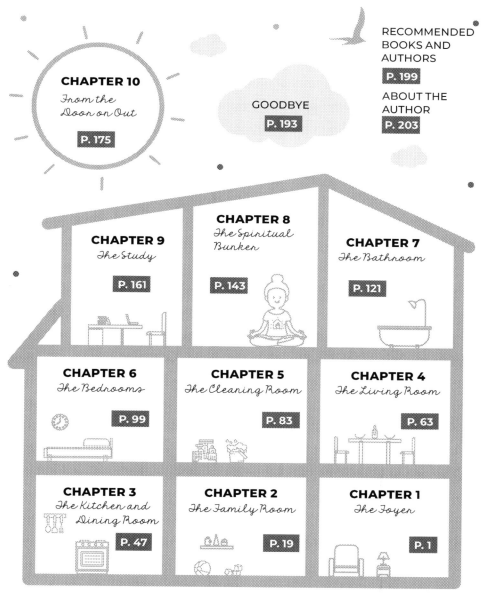

Preface

Welcome to My House

My house always has had its doors open to all who would like to enter. This book was created so that many more people can walk through my house, rest wherever they feel good, discover something they may have lost sight of, admire something beautiful that they can put into practice in their own homes, and share a learning experience together.

With the walk-through of my house in the pages of this book, I invite you to explore within you, discover your own house, and imagine how you would like to build or rebuild it. Some areas in that house may not feel altogether good and will require a redesign and upgrade, according to your values. This is a very healthy process. You'll see how convenient it is to change everything that we need to change about ourselves (beliefs, attitudes, and behaviors) in order to live lives of fulfillment.

At the end of the walk-through, you should be ready to return to your own house, where you will review and rebuild what you wish. In so doing, you'll generate that ideal scenario so that you too may create a flourishing family life.

We'll start at the *foyer*. There, you will get comfortable with and discover the meaning of putting a family together, starting with the mom/dad team. I'll share a guide for the stages of pregnancy and through puerperium, the six-week period after childbirth, to help you design the family you want to build.

We will continue through the *family room*, the area where all the members of the house connect. Sharing, playing, and relaxing together, here we will discover ways to build our family relationships. In this space, learning to communicate with love and to develop our emotional intelligence is key. We will help our children manage their emotions and build a play area that brings us joy and enthusiasm creatively.

Then we will step into one of my favorite areas, the *kitchen and dining room*, where we will discuss physical and emotional nutrition and discover different ways to enjoy as a family.

From there, we'll enter the *living room*, where we welcome relatives and friends who nourish us and bring us new perspectives. We will enjoy their support and encouragement, which will contribute to our family having a sense of belonging in the community around us.

We will then step into a space near the kitchen, the *cleaning room*, where we will discuss order, cleaning, and how we all contribute so our physical space can support our growth and happiness. In this area, we may get help and collaboration from parties outside of the family who enter and become a part of our inner circle. We will discuss relationships with nannies and housekeepers and how they too can be a part of our flourishing family life.

From there, we will head to the *bedrooms*—first, the children's rooms, where we will explore play and the power and magic of storybooks, as well as sleepless nights and the importance of rest. We will discover that the bedroom is a space where we can closely relate to our children, and we will discuss the support we provide for them in their education and learning. Then we will go to the parents' bedroom, where we will explore the importance of rest and intimacy and will connect with that partner in the most private area of our house.

We also will go to the *bathroom*, where we will connect with our own bodies in order to take care of ourselves and stay healthy. We will look at anything from sex-education issues with our kids to how to understand illnesses as the body's unspoken messages, and we will learn to give our bodies a voice as well as caring in order to heal them.

Here we will make a stop on our path to get to know the heart of our house within. I call it the *spiritual bunker*, an immaterial place that can be in any area in the house. In the spiritual bunker, we reconnect with ourselves, meditate, explore the way we are relating to our own interior and with our environment, and recharge with love and inner peace so that we can offer that to our family and the world around us. I will show you secrets about how to achieve that inner peace that is so key to building a happy and full family life. Sometimes this important area may play the role of purgatory, where we can face our darkest sides with compassion and discover what to do to heal what is damaged. Do not be afraid; I promise this will be an unforgettable place. I have no doubt that you will want to give it all your attention when you design your own house.

Then we will go to the *study*, the area where some of us parents pursue our careers. This area also can be staged outside the house—at the office, for example. The study is part of our house within, not only because we spend a lot of time in it but because it is intimately linked to family life. We will discuss the purpose of work and how it can be a source of happiness and nourishment for family life, instead of competition against it.

At the end of our walk-through, in chapter 10, "From the Door on Out," we will explore all that is close to our house and concerns us. We will discover how much we can enjoy and learn outside, the importance of breathing in a different air, looking at things from another perspective, and sharing with our children and partners on another frequency. We will discuss family vacations, outings, and exploration and how to maximize them in order to live more fully and to grow.

Finally, we will say goodbye with the promise to do something with all that we have learned along our journey. That promise will be to your own being, with your soul, who, like your inner child, needs you in order to make the changes and live with more peace, fulfillment, and happiness. My exit gift will allow you to apply what you've learned in your own life.

I welcome you to my house within with all the love and gratitude that having you as my special guest brings to my heart.

Acknowledgments

This book would not be what it is without the patient and loving guidance and instruction of my editor, Mauricio Gaviria. He didn't just fix my spelling and semantics; he took me by the hand and gave me writing notions to depict my ideas in a way that others could receive and understand them. It was not easy for me (the student who always gets straight As) to get my initial texts back full of edits, but that helped me to declare myself a learner again and to plunge into learning something new, improving each day, thanks to his edits. Empowering and organizing my thoughts, he helped me to express my voice without turning it into someone else's. His ideas, questions, and suggestions were invaluable; this book was a team effort with Mauricio.

Thank you to the family I have and continue to build day to day with my husband, Román, whom I love with all my heart. I am grateful for his strength, his patience, and his persistence in the face of each suggestion and question I made and will continue to make. We have been together for more than eighteen years, and this book tells a lot about how we built our family. Our path together has been the inspiration and motivation for me to continue learning and sharing with others this way of flourishing together.

Thank you also to my children and teachers: Valentina, named this way because she was very valiant in being the first daughter of such inexperienced parents. She made us come out of the shadow and invited us to work to heal ourselves. Sofía, meanwhile, propelled us to live with greater freedom and as intensely as all that she is and does. Thank you to Juan Francisco, who brought us his warmth and need for contact, his inner peace, and his sensitivity, which allowed us to explore other ways to be parents.

I also thank my parents, Al and Lauri, and my younger sister, Sigrid. They are present in each of these pages; they are a beginning, a model, and a thousand lessons. I thank them for their love always because being parents is quite a commitment, and they took it on with great generosity.

My father gave me strength of spirit. I owe him my belief that anything is possible, that I can achieve my dreams, and that nothing is impossible if I plunge into learning. He helped me see this path that is life with a lot of compassion. Like me, he continues to learn, and I honor him for doing it because it is not an easy task.

My mother showed me what it is to serve another and to keep an eye out and tend to his needs. I thank her for, among many other things, always being ready to receive me, no matter how late it was, and to caress my tired feet—few words and great acts that speak for themselves about her love and dedication.

Thank you to Sigrid, my younger sister, who always accompanied me and called me to open doors with a lot of learning. Thanks to her, I met my spiritual teacher, who opened the doors to transform me, healing wounds and discovering my potential.

All my gratitude also to Machu, my spiritual teacher, because the path that I have walked was thanks to the door that she opened for me and the tools that she taught me to find well-being and fulfillment in my life. Even though she is no longer physically near, she always guides me with generosity and wisdom, amplifying all that I can learn and give to the world.

Thanks also to my extended family and my friends, among whom I want to highlight my mother-in-law, Sonia, for being available to my children with a great vocation for service. I thank my great friends: Pauli, Sofía's godmother, whom readers will find in so many pages of this book without knowing it. The experiences with her and our conversations taught me to be more loving with myself and my children. Also to my friends in Peru—Debi, Pala, Andre, and Olguita—who made me welcome and rooted for me, from the first idea up to the birth of this book, with their love and appreciation. Last but not least, to Lula, friends since we were two years old, as we continue to grow and learn ways to heal, love, and live lives rich with connection.

With all of them, I continue to exchange experiences, and we keep learning, with compassion and respect for our flaws and always from the unconditionality of love.

Thank you, friends and adventure companions, for welcoming me into your hearts and for being available to grow together in love.

Introduction

What a beautiful experience it is to step into a house where we are welcomed and embraced and where we also can be nourished by learning lessons that make us happier and more fulfilled!

This book is that house, and I will show you everything that I have learned on building a family world in which you can feel love, peace, joy, and union with everything around you. I invite you to step inside as I share my experiences so that you can build your own house within—a space in which time runs at your own pace and where you can be happy and have a fulfilling life with your family.

I'm a "moving expert"—I have lived in five countries and have had different experiences in each one: new people, apartments, neighborhoods, landscapes, and cultures. I've started over in each house with curiosity and uncertainty, always knowing that something was solid and constant—the house that I built within me, my home. I consider myself a nomad, but I always take my house with me. The key to that has been knowing I can choose, decide, take responsibility, and live each day with full awareness.

My house is built upon a particular pillar—the freedom to choose, a freedom that all human beings have. We are free to choose how we relate to what happens to us. Things come with life that we cannot change, such as the color of our eyes. We have the freedom to accept them as they are, complain that we don't like them, or even blame our parents for our genes. But before going to this ridiculous extreme, why don't we just stand in front of the mirror and feel grateful that we have eyes in the first place?

Think about it: How many times a day do you complain? We often choose complaining as a way to relate to something we don't like and for which we don't want to be responsible. I call this behavior the "victim attitude," and it's very common. This attitude keeps us feeling bad because it doesn't offer any solution. Will we continue to complain about what we cannot change? Or will we accept it? It's like fighting the rain; it doesn't make sense. What does make sense is to

change our way of *looking* at things. Instead of focusing on what we can't change, let's focus on what is up to us. It's simple: If it rains, take an umbrella, and thank the sky.

We want to feel good in our house within. It is in pursuit of this well-being that we use our ability and right to choose freely. But this freedom has a cost, and that is to take responsibility for our own lives.

Each of us is the creator of our own inner and outer realities. Even in those instances where we can't change what's external to us, as with the rain, we always create our internal state, and we can always *choose* to change it. Rain can be good or bad—it depends on how we choose to relate to the rain.

The option to choose is what gives us the power to build our houses within. If we don't exercise our right to choose, our house within will be a collage that doesn't answer our own life plans, and we'll eventually allow other people to build our houses for us, which surely won't generate happiness, peace, or love for us. When I invite you to get to know my house, I am inviting you to take responsibility for your own life.

Along with freedom, awareness is another foundational concept of my house, as without it, there is no choice. If we want to change something that happens to us, first we need to know how it will affect us. It's *awareness* that allows us to notice our thoughts and emotions with respect to it. For example, when it rains, we either can say, "This is terrible. I hate getting wet!" or "This is wonderful; there's water for the crops!"

If it rains on the day we had planned to enjoy the outdoors, the rain will be an obstacle to our plans, and we may become sad or upset. But the rain is not the problem; the problem is our inability to accept and deal with reality. If we are aware of whatever generates emotions within us, then we can be in control and will be able to choose thoughts that create a more flourishing life for us.

Being aware depends on our ability to utilize a key tool: the mind. The mind can be a type of flashlight that illuminates one area at a time. While we focus on something, the mind solves what happens automatically, according to what we have learned in the past. When we learn to drive, for example, we focus on each action that it takes to drive—stepping on the clutch, changing gears, releasing the brake, stepping on the gas, looking in the mirrors, etc. At first, this takes up a lot of energy, but once we learn, we do certain things on autopilot until the mind uses the entire automated system. Little by little, we start to drive with ease as we listen to music, talk to someone, or follow instructions from the navigation system. Of course, if something out of the ordinary happen, our minds have the ability to focus on whatever we need to solve the issue, deactivating the autopilot.

A small portion of our minds always operate in the present moment, while many decisions or choices are made in the past, and we repeat them constantly. The drawback of the mind's automated system is that some decisions we make generate discomfort—for us or others—if we repeat patterns we should have learned to avoid. Instead, we should ask ourselves how making those same decisions will affect us in the present. We may think that authority is achieved by screaming, and so we may scream at our children when we want them to do or stop doing something. But if we think about what actually gives us authority—the kind of authority we want to have in our family and important values like peace and respect—surely we would choose something other than screaming as an option.

While in Peru, I learned one of the most caring cultural values. Peruvian parents instruct and reprimand children in a kind and gentle way. It's an indirect communication style, in which respect for each other is paramount. It's a silent pact that I treat another as I would like to be treated. Having done my share of screaming, I've noticed that if I operate on autopilot and don't check myself beforehand to see if what I'm about to do is best, I'll end up shouting things like "Get down from there right now!" The worse the situation, the more calm and poise is required to make sure that things happen as we would like, while caring for those involved.

For example, if we want to mitigate a dangerous situation, then let's think if it's necessary to shout something extreme like "Watch out! You are going to die doing that!" That can create a panic, instead of aiding someone who needs help.

Being aware means that we stop, take at least three deep breaths, and then find a more effective and loving way to communicate or behave. It is a challenge, but it's possible, and the more we behave intentionally rather than on autopilot, the more effectively we will transform those behaviors that make us and others feel bad. If we achieve that, we will bring wellness to everyone.

Awareness, like that flashlight, requires us to take some distance to light the whole and not just one part. At first, the flashlight can be focused on the present act, but if we take a few steps back, we will expand the flashlight's focus and light up other aspects we lost sight of, such as our emotions and thoughts. If we expand our focus, we will become aware and will see that there are other options. Then we will choose the one that is most aligned with our values.

Awareness allows us to understand we have a choice and will feel free to create the lives we want.

My house is constantly under construction; everything is built inside of me and expands toward the outside, the environment. What we want in life changes in time, so we are people in constant need of redesign. To build our inner homes, we need to first realize what we want and then understand how to achieve it. It's a process that starts with self-knowledge and doesn't end; we can express ourselves in infinite ways. In each act, life offers us opportunities to get to know ourselves more and express ourselves in different ways. Our house within and, consequently, our family home will be a structure built based on awareness, our experiences, and lessons learned.

Throughout this book, you may form and reform your own vision of your ideal home. You will understand how you'd like it to be, as well as what is important to build it while feeling inner peace and fulfillment. Our values allow us to operate in the world and make us feel satisfied in what we achieve and the way we behave in achieving it. This is our code of ethics and personal morals. That's why we must understand the way we build our houses. If I want my children to do what I ask, I can't scream commands at them. Then I would not be living or applying values like peace, love, and respect.

Awareness is a great tool for building our houses in peace and harmony. Even though we all have awareness, we do not turn to it as often as we should, which brings regret to our lives. When I fight with my husband and say things that hurt his feelings, or when I make fun of something that one of my children did, I am not generating love but separation. That doesn't mean I'm a bad person, just that I was not aware enough to notice I had a choice between hurting and not hurting. Thanks to awareness in my house within, there is a warm sensation—a type of voice that always says to me, "Easy there. There are valid reasons for what you're doing. Let's try to understand together." It's the voice of love that questions me regarding what I do with compassion.

Being aware of my own self teaches me to develop compassion. *If I want to generate peace in the world, I must start by generating it inside of me.* I achieve that, thanks to compassion. Don't confuse compassion with pity or feeling sorry for yourself or another. Compassion is love, combined with an understanding of your and another's motivations, desires, and interests. I'm always learning to love myself in my house; to achieve it, I have to understand with love (compassion) what I do and what I generate so I can become aware and choose the best path.

MY NOTES

....

....

....

....

....

....

....

....

....

....

....

....

....

....

....

....

....

....

....

....

....

....

....

CHAPTER 1

The Foyer

1

The Foyer

As I open the door to my house within, I invite you to walk through my private space. Take off your coat, shoes, and wristwatch. Leave your cell phone elsewhere. Get comfortable. In my house, you can learn from everything, and in this learning, you can love yourself more and create a world of greater peace and unity. Let's begin this first walk-through.

Family and Its Purpose

A family is a community ("common unity") that is organized with a common purpose. Those who are part of it share values that guide them in relating with each other. Although each family can have its own distinct purpose, three purposes are common to most: (1) sharing, (2) learning and loving, and (3) creating value for the world in which we live.

When I wanted to become a mother, my purpose was to learn to love—love myself and love that part of me who at first could not become a mother. In 2007 I had surgery to remove thirty ovarian cysts. The message that I got from that was that a part of me could not or did not want to become a mother. Before the surgery, I had not noticed that, but that physical manifestation of what was happening invited me to self-reflect and search for what was happening with me. What was I "holding in like a cyst"? After this experience, I had the desire to start a family and began a path of self-knowledge and healing that allowed me to become pregnant with a baby girl one year later.

The most important part of this beginning was learning that in order to become a parent, it was necessary to walk through the path of love—to give love especially to myself and then to my partner and children. Learning to love has been a part of my purpose in starting a family. Although I am not sure what my husband's purpose was, I can assume it had more to do with creating value for the world and transcending through our children's creation and education. By our being together, that also became my objective.

Each couple will feel a different calling when starting a family. For that reason, it is very important that we discuss these questions: Why did we decide to start a family, and what end are we pursuing? There may be a variety of answers. A very practical one might be to populate the world. A more couple-oriented one could be to give and receive love. A personal reason could be to create from the core of our being and leave someone behind who transcends our own existence.

I never asked myself about our common purpose as a couple when we started a family, but I am grateful that the question arrived when conflict surfaced that threatened to dissolve my marriage. In the middle of crisis, I realized that as I had decided to be with someone, I should have a deep and important motivation for it, much more than comfort or convenience. Answering the question of why we want to start a family with our partners is key to joining with a common purpose and to getting through the difficulties on the path.

A Better World

Prior to choosing to start a family, it would be good to reflect on your purpose for having one and to be sure this purpose is intimately linked to who you want to be and the kind of life you want to live. Only when you have compared your motivations, interests, and desires with those of your partner will you be able to identify the common unity—the common purpose—that will guide you from the beginning of and throughout your union. That union will end at some point, either because one of you dies, or you decide to separate.

I know many couples who affirm that their family's objective is solely to raise their kids. But if that's the case, then after the kids grow up and leave the home, will being a couple cease to make sense? I don't judge the sole purpose of raising children as bad; I only invite those couples to ask themselves what joined objective they will have as a couple after their children become independent. Here are some deep questions that can help to clarify the way:

- What does it mean to "raise kids"?
- What results do you hope to obtain with that?
- What do you want to experience while raising them?
- What happens after you are finished raising them?

I firmly believe that building a family goes beyond mere procreation and raising children with health, security, and education. Family is

the very constitution of society and the world we wish to live in. If we create and sustain a family with values such as love, respect, peace, solidarity, compassion, honesty, commitment, freedom, integrity, and others, we will then see those values reflected in our world.

Our inner and outer harmony depend on the coherence of our values. Whatever we live in our inner world must be coherent with what we live with our families, our groups of friends, at work, or in whatever area our lives unfold. We cannot sustain a fragmented life forever; that is, we can't live with certain values in one area and with opposing ones in another.

Starting a family involves establishing a way to live in community, behaving according to our values, and helping our children learn this as well. This way, when we leave home we will translate these values to the world around us, as will our children and their own children after that. This is how our family transcends our relational space and contributes value to the world.

The Couple—Built as a Team

Is a childless couple a family? Of course it is. The bond we establish with someone has as its purpose to love and to create. The bond is a creative process. The *Mahabharata*, an ancient Hindu text, says that your best friend is your *dharma*, meaning your path, lesson, or mission. When you relate to someone, it is because your *dharma* unites you; you two share a path, lesson, and/or mission. You come together with someone to learn from each other, to walk a path together, or to accomplish a mission together.

Starting a family is a special *dharma*—a mission that many of us choose to undertake with our partners. Sometimes a couple's union means creating something other than children together. It can be an organization that contributes something of value to society. Learning to be a couple and keeping each other company is in itself a goal.

There also is the option of raising children without a partner, and that can be a family. Those mothers and fathers who are alone because they so choose or because life circumstances distanced them from their partner would seek to create a different kind of family, and that is perfect. All types of families exist. Beyond how they are formed, what's important is the way we choose to contribute to the world around us.

We've seen that family is a community in which a couple comes together to have children under a common purpose. We can look at that community as a team, where there is at least one but frequently two participants who direct it and are captains—the parents.

If we want to be a team, we need to start by agreeing with our partner on issues such as the following:

- What do we understand as family?

- What values do we want to share?

- How do those values translate into our behaviors?

- Why does each of us want to be a part of this project, which must be aligned with our own deeply personal interests? (Without this last bit, it will be hard to pull through as a couple during the inevitable conflicts and crises that arise.)

Now comes a question with a very elusive answer: What will allow me to achieve what I want? In my case, having a family was always a purpose to be achieved with someone else—a companion on the journey and team, my husband. But the truth is that we each will have our own answers, which may vary, depending on timing and circumstances in our lives.

If we are to build a family with someone else, it is ideal to know what that person wants in building it and what type of family we want to build together. It's like two people designing a house; once they agree that they both want a house, more questions arise regarding how they want it to be, what objectives they want it to fulfill, what style they like, and what priorities they have. My husband and I built it as we went, overcoming questions that arose during crises and conflicts that, at times, even made us move from our house and neighborhood.

The decision to do it was never a simple one. Not only was it economically and logistically complex, but it also meant missing out on certain dynamics we enjoyed, such as a beautiful city, walking to dinner, being minutes from the theater, or the nearby company of two of our children's grandparents. If we moved, we would lose some things and gain others. The decision to move prompted us to ask what was important to us. We needed to consolidate ourselves in our union, so we prioritized the areas where we both felt the most enjoyment and fulfillment.

Through this and other issues, we realized the importance of working as a directive team. We focused on being a team and knew together we would lead our family to grow in awareness and produce positive effects in our world. We also wanted to live certain values such as unconditional love, honesty, peace, joy, freedom, responsibility, integrity, commitment, and humbleness. Not only that, we also wanted the members of this family to develop fully, enjoy their own well-being, and be happy living together.

To achieve all of this, we organized ourselves from a point of consensus and established criteria for authority, where we are parents who choose and make decisions in agreement. We know that each of us has his and her strengths and opportunities, and we take on roles along those lines to make us more efficient in achieving what we want.

Roles

As with a soccer team, role division is key. The first thing to know is that not all of us can do the same thing. If we want to win the match, we have to know that we can't all stay near the goal to block dangerous shots, nor can we all score. The second thing is to identify each person's strengths and interests.

In my family there are issues that, although they are key to our well-being, I am not interested in, but my husband is. If we happen to identify something in which neither of us is interested or that requires a skill that neither of us possesses, then we would have to find outside help.

Choosing a school for the first time for our older daughter was one of those instances in which neither of us knew how to solve the issue. The little we knew regarding education was limited to our own experiences as students (one of us had studied in a religious school and the other in a nondenominational school). To top it off, we went to the same engineering university and majored in the same thing. We weren't exposed, in theory or reality, to the many educational options available nowadays. So we found experts in education who had worked as school inspectors for twenty years, and they knew pedagogical theories as well as their practical application. We discovered with them a great variety of pedagogical options. They helped us to clarify the type of education that we wanted for our children outside of the home and helped to identify our priorities, always taking the temperament and sensibilities of each child into account and what we deemed best for them and for the family. Those experts in education helped us think short, medium, and long term, integrating the choice of school with other decisions that were almost made at that time—such as moving to another country, for example. Thanks to this professional help, we were able to choose with the kind of confidence, poise, and trust that we would not have had on our own.

We also learned so much that when we arrived in the new country, we knew which questions to ask ourselves, what to look for, and what to question when visiting a potential school for the kids. With this experience, we learned that asking for help is also a way to integrate perspectives and redirect the sails of the family boat.

With respect to the roles we had to take on, we concluded they were unavoidable, and that even if we didn't know how to play the roles at first, we would learn them. This applies to becoming moms and dads; at first, we don't know how it's done or how to be parents, but we learn, and that is fun.

We can read and research what it means to be a good "scorer," but we always know that each player has his own unique way of playing, and it only develops by stepping on the field and playing. By the same token, we can read many books on how to be better fathers or mothers, but we will live our own experiences and learn from what feels best and is most useful.

The first step toward choosing what type of dad, mom, or family we want to be is to test our own tools. Only in this way will we know how we're doing with respect to the common goal, our particular roles, and what we need to learn to achieve it.

Learning—the Basis of Everything

Learning is inherent to building a family team—the kind of learning where roles change. When a mother has a newborn, she needs to be completely dedicated to him, but her role as a mother when her child reaches adolescence—when he can generally take care of himself—is very different. Children are new players who become a part of Mom and Dad's team, and as they grow up, they will take on responsibilities according to the level of maturity they demonstrate, their innate abilities, and their capacity to learn. To the degree that each contributes his grain of sand, the team builds trust with each other. It's not necessary for the children to be older before they start contributing; they show their gifts from an early age and can share them with the rest of the family.

My daughter Sofía is very empathic. Since she was very younger, she's made us realize what we were feeling, even before we were aware of it. When she asked me why I was sad, I was able to stop, reflect, and choose how to process that sadness that only she had helped me to identify. Otherwise, I probably would have carried on with my life without paying attention to what I was feeling.

On the other hand, Valentina, my older daughter, has a great capacity to see what others don't see and to question issues deeply. The questions she asks herself have often allowed us to reevaluate our decisions and to be more aware of them. We still don't have answers to some of her questions ("Where is the universe?"), but they allow us to grow as we research possible answers. And this has been the case since she was two years old! It's the same with my youngest child, Juan Francisco, whose personality is the very epitome of tenderness, charisma, and joy. When he does something that he realizes was not okay, it is very hard to reprimand him because he smiles right away and caresses my face, as if he's saying sorry with his gesture. He brings out the tenderness in me, and all I want to do is cover him with kisses. Children provide opportunities for us to learn with them.

To learn means to be open to the new and different, even if it is uncomfortable for us. It also means abandoning our know-it-all attitudes. When we think we know everything, we close the possibility of learning new things. I think even the most renowned philosophers have come to the same conclusion: the more they think about a topic, the more they discover and the less certainty they have about it. The best way to relate to each other as a family (or team) with love is to be willing to learn. When my husband questions a decision of mine, I listen to him and take on the learner's attitude. I then can inquire about his motives and question his reasoning with kindness and curiosity. If my identity and self-esteem are in a know-it-all and an I'm-always-right mode, it will be difficult for me to inquire; in fact, I'll want to argue, persuade him that he is wrong, and show him that it also is wrong to question me.

The reason there is peace in my house within is that I decided many years ago to declare myself a student of life. Because of that, if someone has a different opinion to mine and questions me, I am open to review it. This doesn't mean that someone can convince me through verbal of physical force; if I allowed that to happen, then I would not be honoring myself or my values. The door is always open, however, to peaceful dialogue. Otherwise, I cut that dialogue short because for me, it would no longer make sense. Although it is sad to need to emphasize it, I think it is key to care for our boundaries and to protect our and our family's integrity, while always honoring our values. In chapter 2, "The Family Room," we will see more about how to communicate assertively with love and openness.

The Beginnings of Parenthood

When do we begin to be parents? I believe that we take our first steps as parents from the moment we know about the pregnancy. I'd like to delve into what happens to us during that stage and how we can use it as an opportunity to grow, learn, and evolve. Men and women experience this stage very differently. At first, of course, it's a physical issue, as the woman perceives changes taking place in her body, and questions, which also involve the man, begin to arise.

Let's look at some of these questions:

How do I prepare my body during pregnancy?

Use your imagination to go to those first months of pregnancy. What thoughts populate your mind? What's different about you now? What do you feel, more or less than before? Women might mention changes, "disturbances," or physical imbalances that make them feel uncomfortable. Some women who are pregnant continue with their regular life, but then realize that they cannot because something has changed. They forget about formerly "important" things, feel their energy change, and are more sensitive to smells, flavors, and environments.

When a woman carries a life inside of her, she may choose take better care of herself in a way she hadn't done before. For example, she might stop smoking, or she might avoid certain foods, drinks, or environments that aren't good for her. This is very interesting and surprising to me because we women always have known those things were bad for us. It simply didn't register, or we didn't have a good enough reason to make the necessary changes. Caring for our babies is what prompts us to change. It's something that is beyond all logic, something that guides us and is borne of a very primitive and essential place.

It's my experience that the majority of us women have effected changes in our lives during pregnancy that we never would have considered but for the intention of taking care of our babies. Women who currently are pregnant know this is an excellent opportunity to choose, with awareness, what is best for them and their babies. This should guide their actions.

Those of us mothers who have left that stage behind can ask ourselves, What prevents us from taking care of our lives today as we did when we were pregnant? Let's give ourselves enough rest and eat food that nourishes us and promotes well-being. Let's be aware of the environment, relationships, and activities that are good for us. Men also can learn from this stage and seek wellness, learning from how their wives care for their babies.

Will we have the capacity to be parents?

With pregnancy come many fears. We live with them daily, and they manifest as anxiety, doubt, and questions.

Fears are not absolute truths but emotions that arise from thoughts, which I suggest should be reviewed. Fear can be perceived as a relationship between that which we consider a threat and our resources to face that threat. Analyzing both what we consider a threat and our resources will help us deal with the fear.

Is that fear rooted in a real and present danger, or is that fear a mind trick? To find the answer, we could talk to other people who went through similar experiences, but let's pay attention to what our hearts say and listen to our inner truth. If what I fear is real and present, then I will take preventive action, such as arming myself with resources to take care of that threat. If it is not real, then all I can do is live in the present moment and let go of that unrealistic fear.

A classic fear during pregnancy and even during the baby's first months is the fear of lack of financial support. A few different variables come into play; for example, the mother doesn't want to return to work after giving birth. This provides us the opportunity to take charge and stop worrying.

From a financial standpoint, the practical thing to say is, "I'll spend less or make more." Spending less can mean changes to the couple's lifestyle, and in that case, they must think about what they are willing to change. If the choice is to make more money, there are many possibilities, such as taking on extra work or asking a relative or friend for financial help. Someone's lending a hand doesn't that we are less worthy.

It's not unusual for women who were raised in the women's liberation generation to have heard things like "You always must have a plan B" or "You must be able to do it alone and not depend on anyone, especially a man." These phrases are manifestations of beliefs that have an effect on both men and women and that we experience as part of our personal history.

But let's be careful, as this is another great trap. Let's evaluate where these voices come from—voices that create pressure and fear to self-sustain financially. In my case, I realized that I was trapped in others' ideas and experiences. The fact that I depended on my husband financially in no way said anything about me or my value as person. That's how I was able to ask for and get the help that I needed to dedicate myself to my priority—being a mother and enjoying all that involved. This was a big relief because it meant realigning with my purpose and my values—I had chosen who I did and did not want to be.

How will we stay connected and united as a couple?

Pregnancy is a period of preparation for both women and men. This includes facing their fears with awareness and *communicating* continuously regarding their worries so they, as a team, can figure out what to do. Depending on the role divisions, we may think that certain decisions belong to either the mother or the father. But I firmly believe that team childrearing needs to be aligned to have one vision, and the couple should make decisions as a united front. This involves a lot of communication and dialogue, without trying to convince the other person. Rather, the couple should discuss what worries them, what they feel, what they dream, what makes them restless, and how they can advance together so that they both feel better.

My recommendation is this: *Don't dismiss or set aside conversations.* A conversation is an excellent opportunity to connect deeply with your love and life partner. I have heard many women complain about not feeling accompanied, but when I ask them if they prioritize their romantic relationship, they realize they often don't. In most cases, they simply "wait" for their partner to do something and respond to his needs, wants, and unexpressed expectations. In Spanish we have a saying: *El que calla otorga*, which means "Silence is consent." If we don't express what we feel, want, or need, then we cannot expect the other to know it. Many women still wait for Prince Charming to anticipate and attend to all their unexpressed needs, some of which they're not even aware of themselves. Likewise, some men wait for a woman who doesn't ask for much and who will take care of them as a loving mother would. These are fairy tales that we tell ourselves and that only bring us sorrow. Let's release them and live with awareness. Let's take responsibility, giving and receiving without double meaning or hidden expectations. As we say in Argentina, "Let's put all the meat on the grill," and let's cook together. It's our best option and the most loving one for all, especially our children.

Will we still be the same?

Here we enter the realm of identity. Both for men and for women, pregnancy raises questions about our capacity to be parents, about how this will transform our lives, and about who we are now. "Do I have to change who I am, now that I am a mother (or father)?" This question shakes up the idea we have about our personalities. In my lexicon, this is called an *existential crisis*. "Who am I? Why am I here in this world?" Welcome, crisis! In Japan, crisis is an opportunity. Let's make this an opportunity to learn and create greater well-being and happiness in our lives.

When we make choices with respect to *who we want to be*, I call attention to a very common trap we set for ourselves: choosing with the mind—from the ego self, from that character created by the fear of losing others' love and approval. The behaviors and attitudes that we adopt in order to please others are nothing more than armor that doesn't allow us to feel and connect with reality around us. It's true that such armor protects us from criticism, but it leaves us sad inside because we can't accept and integrate those "undesirable" parts that are a part of our being. I thought that being creative—*flighty, with my head in the clouds*—was a bad thing because that's what I had been told all my life. Because of that, I thought that I had to be more grounded and responsible. But when I became a mother I took off that responsible-woman armor that doesn't think about or do things that are out of the ordinary, and I focused on strengthening that very aspect of myself. I allowed myself to create and have fun with my children and to do crazy things like get dirty, run around without shoes, stand in the rain, jump, dance, and shout at the wind. As time passed, I realized that this was not contradictory to being responsible and that one thing didn't diminish the other. I don't think I would have learned that if I had not experimented with being different or if I hadn't been motivated and inspired by my children.

Perhaps the more conscious choice regarding who we choose to be is simply to respond in the present moment with what we need and wish to express.

Every minute life asks something different of us, both outside and inside of ourselves. Responding from a place of love and peace will allow us to navigate safely and fully. To me, life is more like a river with rapids than a calm lake, which is why I live in awareness of external changes and identify what I need to learn to navigate and enjoy every moment. There will be moments of going over the falls and even a feeling of drowning, but if I am connected to my inner self, I will surface and navigate again—or maybe even swim; why not?

What will happen to my previous life plan—what I dreamed of doing?

I often hear mothers and fathers who still hurt over the life they did not live or that they "lost" when their children were born. When we choose something, we lose something else. This is implicit in each choice in our lives—if I chose to see a movie, maybe I won't have enough money or time left to dine at a restaurant. Something so simple can become complex when what I'm choosing who I want to be in the world.

When I take off that armor that no longer serves me, sometimes I also take off things about the armor that I enjoyed, and that means a loss. If I choose to leave the corporate world because it no longer aligns with what I desire, I will gain time and freedom to act, but I may lose an active social life, trips, nights in beautiful hotels, and training courses through that job. It's all part of the choice. It is harder to leave behind the benefits of the armor than whatever we didn't like about it. Accepting this is key to mourning that loss.

We often dismiss mourning or overlook it, and we hurry to move forward and continue our lives as if nothing happened. This has a collateral effect, which is that the mourning continues. It is there, even if we want to cover it up. The sadness associated with this mourning inevitably will come out at some point, many times as a resignation that puts us in a place of impotence and victimization.

Resignation is nothingness itself—the "I just can't, and the world is against me." Resentment also shows up, usually along with anger and with someone to blame. Neither resignation nor resentment are productive; neither opens us up to learning. If we leave behind something that we no longer want, we also leave behind something we like but that at the time was best for us to do. Accepting this allows us to lament the loss, to weep, and to let that painful emotion move through our bodies. For some, this will take place within a matter of days; for others, it may be months. In any case, let's allow that the pain to flow and not stagnate, with love for our being. It's simply about accepting the process of decision, being grateful for the gains, and weeping over the losses. At the end of the day, we will feel more inner peace.

The path of learning in love means connecting with all that we feel, taking care with love and compassion, and giving ourselves the time needed to process it.

Conclusions

A family is a community with a purpose. Defining it with our partner is key to guiding us, especially through whatever crises we may face. Family is a way of contributing to the world, bringing new values, and learning. In addition to aligning with our partner in a common goal, we form a team that is key to identifying our roles, to giving our best, and to knowing when we need outside help to guide us in issues beyond our capacity. For the team to work at its best, we talk frequently and are open to learning, detaching from the need to know it all.

We explored the start of a family with children and how we can learn to take better care of ourselves as we care for the life that grows inside the mother. We posed the question of how to manage our fears by questioning them. We favor communication between the couple, and we get rid of ideas regarding our identity that we no longer need in order to reinvent ourselves and live connected to the present moment, honoring and accepting what we left behind while welcoming the new.

Proposed Activity

A Game as a Couple

Let's start a conversation with our partners. The goal of this game is to know each other better and to head on the same path. For that, all you need are ten pieces of paper the size of playing cards and a marker to write. Take five of those papers, and write the following questions, one per paper:

- Why do I want to start a family?

- What is the most important thing to me regarding starting a family?

- What fear and what hope arises when I think about starting a family?

- What do I expect from my partner the moment we start a family together?

- What values are really important to me, and what do they mean? (Mention the values and a behavior associated with each one.)

Now:

1. Place the five cards with the questions on a flat surface (a table or the floor), and mix them up. Set the remaining five blank cards to the side.

2. One person will randomly pick up the question cards, one by one, and must answer the selected questions out loud to his or her partner.

3. The other must listen attentively to what his or her partner says and then must say what the speaker has said in his or her own words. If the speaker feels that the listener did not understand the whole message, the speaker must reinforce it until the listener is able to express what the speaker wanted to say, demonstrating that he or she has been understood it entirely.

4. On one side of a blank card, the listener must write a short phrase (use no more than half the card), summarizing or highlighting the most important part of what the speaker initially said and then must read it to him or her out loud.

5. The one who initially listened now must respond to the same question. Do the whole process with the other person—one speaks and the other listens; repeat or express out loud the other's message until it's clear; and summarize it on the other half of the formerly blank paper.

6. Once both have expressed what they've heard and written it on half the paper, both will agree upon and write down one phrase that summarizes what both of them said on the other (blank) side of the paper.

7. Now they move to the next question, chosen again at random. Repeat the same process until all five questions have been answered orally and written down on the papers.

NOTE:

Enforcing fines or "dares" can add fun to the game. Do this, for example, if one person needs a third try to put into his own words what the other said. An idea for a fine can be singing a children's song, jumping on one leg in the shape of the number eight, or giving your partner a loving and pleasant foot massage, three minutes per foot!

The main idea with this couple's game is to align in a single vision each of the partner's feelings, so that both can head toward one single north, and both are willing to travel the same path. This game also allows partners to practice couple's communication in a fun way. The possibility to negotiate important topics will also arise, delving into what each seeks and always listening to one another.

You will always be able to come up with a way to satisfy each other.

MY NOTES

CHAPTER 2

The Family Room

2

The Family Room

Not everyone has a family room—also known as the den or rec room—but we can always make a room (the living room, for example) function as a family room. It's that comfortable space shared by the entire family, where we gather to do what we like—play, read, or watch TV. This is a place of fun that allows us to unfold our creativity and do whatever makes us laugh, feel united, and have a great time as a family. In order for us to connect, enjoy, share, and relax in it, we first need to generate an environment of love and happiness. Because of that, good communication is key, as is handling our emotions with intelligence.

Let's discuss the options that the family room offers us for enjoyment. Having fun is the thing. Fun can be self-generated or externally supported. The self-generated kind often arises from boredom, and we use our creativity to suggest ideas for connecting with others and finding something that is fun for us all. The adults might choose to read a novel while the kids play with their toys, or we all might play Twister or Monopoly. We also might watch a movie together or dance to the rhythm of a song, imitating choreography, like in "Just Dance" on YouTube. There are many options, and all arise from thinking about the kind of mood we want to be in.

There also is externally supported fun. Adults as well as children often choose to entertain themselves with video games; spending time on social media, the computer, cell phones, or tablets; or spending hours in front of the television. This option doesn't generate much of a connection between family members because even if it's a group game, it never allows us to express as much as other options for fun.

I once heard a father say that video games with aggressive content allowed his son to free himself from his anger and to blow off steam in a violent way, without it affecting him or others. This is untrue. Unloading such emotion is only possible when the whole body is active and working, including muscles that generate energy by making hormones flow through the body. Also, it usually requires someone to hold our space to vent our stormy feelings and feel loved and accepted. Violent images in video games or on screen are not a release for us. On the contrary, when we overload on them, we have to find ways to process and purify our emotions. Especially in children, that tension often manifests as fights with other children or through restless dreams.

I'm not saying that video games never should be an option. We don't play video games at our house, but I have tried and enjoyed some— such as the sports or music games, which require an active attitude from me that nourishes me and brings joy to the time I spend with others. It's not so much a question of using or not using video games; it's about consciously selecting what is good for us as a family.

Each game or activity is like a door that we choose to step through— or not. Our children are sometimes interested in doors that we didn't know existed, doors that open through such simple portals as a piece of paper and some coloring pens or a rubber ball. As adults, we can always point out new doors to play together or for our children to explore on their own. Some of the best doors, such as reading, require our company to be enjoyed more and with more trust. Sometimes adults think that only screens of all sizes exist as doors to fun, and we miss out on all the other ones that our children open through numerous activities. We just have to try something new. For example, the first time I tried Twister, I laughed a lot. It's a game I could share when my boy was two years old and my elder daughter was eight years old. All of us had fun and burst out laughing with so many ridiculous falls and tangled hands and feet.

If we try new things, we will discover doors to fun that are always open to share as a family. The more we find, the more options of family connection we will have.

In the family room, we also can play in parallel, which the younger kids, especially, like a lot. While I play with the train tracks, my son builds with Legos, my younger daughter plays with dolls, my older daughter makes origami, and my husband reads a manual on building a model airplane. We're already sharing by being together, and it can be even more pleasant if we turn on some background music that we all enjoy.

Part of this time is making sure that fun doesn't turn into unrestricted consumption. This happens when, for example, we decide to watch a movie as a family, and when it ends, instead of moving on to something else, we look for another movie to watch. At that point, we won't have the same level of concentration, our bodies will be tired from being in the same position, and we actually will become bored. If we watch two movies in a row—not uncommon if we have Netflix—we will no longer be in fun territory but in the territory of excessive consumption.

The natural thing at that time is to do something different. Awareness allows us to keep an eye on our needs and those of our children. Children, regardless of age, need to use their bodies and energy; if we are always sitting, they will be full of accumulated energy and be perpetually jittery.

There is nothing better than building the fun together because if we all decide what we are going to do together, we will have a better chance of everyone enjoying it. Sometimes the idea will come from us parents, but brainstorming with our children is an excellent way for other options to surface. This also allows the kids to add value to the family—to choose and to see that we appreciate their ideas, which raises their self-esteem.

More toys, more decorations, more furniture, and more types of screens are not always what's best in the family room. Let's beware of excess, as it tends to do away with enjoyment. The less we have and the more ample the space, the more possibilities we have to create and use what is within our reach.

My children store their toys in boxes in their bedrooms, but I always leave some in the family room. We rotate their location. We also have a family library, where children's books are at child height so they can grab them when they want. When we are going to spend some time in the family room, I bring in some of the toy boxes and pick some books as reading options. It is really fun because then the family room turns into a type of entertainment store—cars to race, dolls with their clothes and accessories, Legos and other constructions blocks, and sheets of paper and coloring pens. Even the toy boxes can be turned into drums! Each box and its contents offers different ideas; we can go from one to the next, and each of the kids and us parents can choose to do whatever interests us the most. I get a kick out of bringing out the boxes, playing for hours, and then putting everything away, leaving the area free again, as if it were a blank page to write or paint a new story.

What we do and the things we use are important, but what really determines whether we live with happiness and love in this area is the way we relate to each other. Let's see how to accomplish that.

Loving Communication

Loving communication can be summarized like this: *I hear you in order to know you better, and I talk to you in order to love you just*

the way you are. To communicate with our children and partners, the first thing we must do is to learn to listen to each other openly, setting judgment aside and accepting the other person unconditionally, while being conscious that what that person says, thinks, and feels is very intimate and that he or she has good and valid reasons for that.

We can listen when our four-year-old daughter comes to us, crying because her little brother took her toy from her hand and doesn't want to return it. To listen with love, we can acknowledge her emotion (sadness) and offer solace, support, and help to resolve the issue.

First we must appreciate what she says and validate it: "Honey, you are sad because your little brother took the toy. Of course, I would be just as sad if I were in your place."

After that, we can offer (not impose) help: "How would you like to solve it? What can you think of doing to feel better?"

We wait for her answer, and she will probably say something like "I want you to tell him to give it back to me."

Then we can suggest something for her to develop the ability to solve her own conflict: "What if I go with you, and you ask him for the toy, and you can also ask him why he took it like that. Maybe your brother saw you having so much fun that he also wanted to play like you were. Since he doesn't yet know how to ask you for it, he just took the toy from you. What if you ask him to play with you and teach him how to have fun too?"

Sometimes our daughter will say that she doesn't want to share anything, that she just wants her toy. It is then that certain rules of coexistence (which vary per family) will apply. In my family, if a child doesn't want to share a toy, it's fine; she can play with it by herself in her room, for example. But it is not valid for her to use it by rubbing it in the face of whoever doesn't have it. If my children want to share space with another child (sibling or friend), they must be willing to really share in the full sense of the word—to take turns or to come up with a way that both can enjoy the same toy together.

It's also unacceptable for a child to take something from another one without asking permission. We consider that an act of assault and violence. If we are going to share, then all of us can use a toy, and we have norms to do it, such as not breaking, losing, or hiding it. Of course, there are toys for older kids that run the risk of breaking in the hands of the younger ones, which is why, when we are in the family room, we usually don't have those available, or they use them under supervision.

Then there are activities or games that are not appropriate for all ages for many reasons. If I decide it would be fun to do my nails in the family room with the kids, it would be best to think twice because they almost certainly will want to do their nails as well. It may not be a good idea for them to handle nail clippers, nail files, nail polish, and polish remover. The family room is for sharing what we want and what we can share without risk or generating unnecessary conflict.

Loving communication, then, consists of listening while validating the other in his emotion and offering our love (helping him through our actions and by suggesting what to do) so that he can deal with what is happening to him. Fred Kofman, contemporary philosopher and renowned coach,[1] explains that people talk to each other because they want to get something from each other. I agree with him. I have not found a single situation in which I have gotten together to talk to someone without wanting to give something or without expecting to receive something from that person—an ear to listen, some support, or some help.

Sometimes we speak with our children to get to know them better, to know how they are doing, and to be closer to them. The family room is an ideal place for this. Children tend to tell us things while they are playing. There was a time when I would play cards or dice every afternoon with my older daughter, and in that time she would tell me about her friends, school, her fears, and her triumphs and joys. While we played, I connected with the rest of her life that would emerge through conversation. Talking is uniting through language. It's like a dance where we enjoy each person's movements without forcing anything. We parents tend to think we know what our children need and want, even without listening to them. While this may sometimes be the case, this attitude doesn't always help them. Instead, it makes them feel controlled and not highly valued because we don't give them enough space to express themselves.

It took me some time to discover that listening was the way to give my younger daughter space to express herself when she was between two and four years old. I couldn't understand her language and felt that there were blank spaces left in our communication. Little by little, however, I learned that just by staying quiet, concentrating on listening, and asking her questions, I could understand her without hurrying. So too, little by little, she learned to tell me what she wanted more fluently. Even now, she remembers many things and feelings, and she can express them in a way that she could not do at that time.

With children younger than three years of age, language can be a limiting factor, so let's not be in a hurry. If you listen, give them space, and ask them with the intention of understanding (without imposing

---

[1] Fred Kofman is vice president of LinkedIn and author of the books *Conscious Business* and *Metamanagement*.

yourself), little by little they will tell you more, and you will understand them more. The communication experience that I had with my daughter allowed me to learn more about little ones' language. Since before he was two years old, my son already was telling me with whom he had played in his playroom and with which toys. All I had to do was catch some expression—for example, "sand"—and encourage him to keep talking by asking something like "Did you play in the sandbox? Did you use the glasses or shovels?" And he would reply, "Shovel," and mimic how he had played. Building a conversation is as easy as that.

Children learn and enjoy communicating very much when they feel listened to without judgment. An example of that would be something like "I can imagine how angry you were today when Benjamin took your toy away. That must be why you bit him." The first thing to do is to put ourselves in their place, and then show them that biting is not okay—it's not something they would like done to them either—and that there is a kinder option to biting next time, such as telling Benjamin to give the toy back or asking the teacher for help.

With patience, communication opens space, and the family room is an ideal space for that. It allows us to interact and discuss in a loving way that nourishes our relationships and lets our children and partners feel valued and respected.

This is also important for us parents. We sometimes think that we know each other well, and it is precisely for that reason that we lose sight of basic principles, such as treating each other with respect and kindness, which erodes the relationship and is a bad example for our children. I may tell my husband in anger, "You turned on the TV for them again? You couldn't come up with a better idea?" Then I am judging him and accusing him of not caring that his children be nourished with something other than the TV in this family space.

But what would happens if, instead, I said without anger, "Love, why did you think of turning on the TV for them? What was your idea for this moment as a family?" That way, in a pleasant tone and with sincere curiosity, I can understand why he did that, or I can propose something different, such as, "I thought we could take advantage of this moment to connect with each other a bit more and have fun. What do you think of suggesting other ideas in addition to the TV, and then we'll choose together? What if we all dance for a while, or play with dice, or build those train tracks that have been in the box for a while, or maybe even read a bit or drink some tea?"

To summarize, some keys to communicating with love include the following:

- Create a friendly and loving context. This could be defining why it's important for us to talk to each other, what we want to take care of in that conversation (some object, something of value, the relationship, etc.), or appreciating something about the other. For example, "I want to talk to my son in order to get to know him better, know how he is doing in school, and to accompany him in his learning." Or say to your partner, "Love, wow, I so admire your capacity for seeing what others don't see and your sensitivity in feeling and talking about what is happening with you."

- Be very quiet while someone talks, and after listening, put in your own words what the child or spouse has told you in order to know that you understood his message and what he is feeling. For example, "So what happened today was that everyone went to the farm, and your friends were going with their moms, but you weren't? I bet that made you sad. Is that the case?" And then tell your child how that made you feel and what you think about what he told you. For example, "I feel guilty that you felt sad."

- Ask more about what he thinks and feels. For example, "Do you want to tell me what you thought about what happened today and how you felt?"

- Validate and accept what your child feels or thinks. For example, "I can imagine how sad you felt, thinking that I didn't care about your field trip to the farm!"

- Ask what he would like you to do, or suggest something. For example, "How would you like me to help?" or "What would you think about taking time to do something, just the two of us, together right now? We could look at the pictures from the farm so you can tell me all about it."

I know that achieving this is not easy because we often judge and are not receptive. To accomplish it, let's talk about *emotional mastery*. If our interactions are loving most of the time, then that's what will persevere in our family environment and in the example we leave for our children so they can apply it in their lives.

Emotional Mastery

The capacity we have, thanks to our emotional intelligence, to recognize emotions within us and others and process them for our or another's benefit is what I call emotional mastery.

Most of this theory arises from Daniel Goleman's book, *Emotional Intelligence*, which mentions experiments that let children develop their emotional intelligence and how that made them more successful. A child with high IQ (cognitive intelligence) but a low EQ (emotional intelligence) probably won't achieve what he wants, either because he cannot handle his own emotions, or he can't cooperate with others because he doesn't know how to empathize, for example. Even if we have a high IQ and this benefits certain scenarios in our lives, having a low EQ means that we will have problems in managing other essential aspects, such as stress, self-motivation, and self-esteem. There is much to be said about this topic, but we will center on how to develop emotional mastery in order to enjoy our family more and help our children develop their emotional intelligence.

We understand emotions as psychophysical reactions generated in the face of an exterior event that affects us or in the face of something we feel. In order to develop our emotional mastery, the first thing we must do is to distinguish which emotions exist and which are the ones we are feeling. At first, it's simply about defining and putting into words what we feel. This is important for us (especially if we did not have emotional education when we were children) and for our children.

Each emotion is also a treasure that calls us to an action. Emotions ask something of us in order to take us back to wellness. For example, sadness asks us to accept and be grateful for what we lost, anger to set limits and take care of ourselves, fear to prepare ourselves so we do not lose that which we fear losing, and joy to celebrate that which makes us happy. Sadness, fear, anger, guilt, joy, gratitude, and even pride are among the most common emotions. Let's run through a few of them:

- Sadness can be a call to be calm and to acknowledge that which we have lost or think we have lost and to value it and honor it with gratitude. Sadness asks us to go into mourning. We must help our children accept that they are sad, that this is valid, and that crying is okay. How many times have we heard phrases like "Don't cry" or "You are too emotional; I can't talk to you when you're crying like that"? It would be so different if we could accept what is happening to the other person and take care of our own discomfort by saying something like "I'm sorry you're crying. I can see why you're sad, but I don't think this is the time to resolve it. If you'd like, I can stay here and keep you company, or we can talk another time."

Of course, it's a little different with our kids because sometimes they use crying to get our attention—and that's fine too. All bids are valid, and, as parents, we must heed those calls. When the children cry, I think they are sad and that I can hug them and give them love without its meaning that I have to give them what they ask. My son might cry because I won't give him chocolate for breakfast; that's normal, but I will then say to him, "Honey, I know not getting chocolate makes you sad. I'm sorry, love, but that is not good for you at this time, so I'm offering this bread with jelly instead, if you want it." I keep my stance with love, acknowledging the emotion without judging and without trying to change it.

In general, it is hard to deal with sadness. The truth is that sadness makes us uncomfortable. We wish we could change it and remove it from our lives. Some of us even fear that sadness will prevent us from carrying on with our lives or that we will be sad forever. My experience is that if we experience the sadness on time and go through our big and small mourning, crying all that we need, then sadness will pass, and it will leave something beautiful behind—love, gratitude, and a tremendous sensation of empowerment after having overcome such a vulnerable state.

When we do not acknowledge children's sadness or emotions, they may react in one of two ways. The first is to cry uncontrollably or scream in anger in the face of a tiny external stimulus or in the face of the slightest of scratches. The second possible reaction is to hide their emotion and not express a single thing. At times this may be confused for apathy, and if what is being hidden is a fear, then we will think—wrongly—that our child is extremely brave. But a child without fears is not normal; it is most likely that he is hiding his fears to look braver because he thinks his parents will value him because of it. No extreme is healthy, so when the child exaggerates, let's identify the opportunity to hear and attend to him before he goes to the extreme.

If the child never shows his feelings, then we must pay attention to how we see and value him. Most likely, a child doesn't express his emotions because he doesn't feel or think that he can—his parents are somehow preventing him from doing so. For that we must take action with ourselves more than with him directly. Doing so is very easy if we become aware of how we talk about our children to friends and family and how we describe them— it's exactly in this way that they perceive themselves. There are opinions regarding our children that will support them and others that will not.

I believe my daughter is very skilled in math. She can come up with great strategies to resolve her problems, but if I only see that quality in her, and it's the only one I talk about in front of my friends and family, then she might feel that she *has* to be good at math. She will put pressure on herself and be afraid to fail in math, thinking that if she does, I may stop appreciating her. Likewise, if I said my daughter was really calm or even "good" as a baby because she didn't cry, that might inhibit her from crying and expressing her discomfort.

Sadness is also a great companion to love, so let's help our children feel and honor it. We can even show them our tears—that's healthy; there's no need to hide them. But if our pain is too deep, and we need to cry until we scream, then don't do it in front of the kids. They are impressionable and may feel unprotected. When sadness is too strong, it's best to express it in intimate spaces with our partners, relatives, friends, or even on our own.

- Fear, one of the most common emotions, tells us that something of value to us is at risk, and it calls us to protect it. We can look at fear as the equation between a perceived threat and the resources we believe we have to face it. I intentionally used the words *perceive* and *believe* because emotions are based on thoughts (or *fantasies*), not reality. For example, a lion's roar in the jungle can represent a threat to my life, and because of that, I feel fear—a valuable fear because it calls on me to protect myself by hiding or running. But if I'm a lion hunter, then that same roar may generate excitement and joy rather than fear, and instead of running, I will follow the sound to pursue it. What is a threat to one is not necessarily so for another.

We often don't acknowledge all the resources we have to face the threat. We can help our children handle their fears by acknowledging and exploring their fears with them. They need us to help them increase their resources so they may live with less fear. A simple example is putting pads on their knees and elbows for their first skating class, or floaters for their first swimming lessons, or suggesting they ride their bikes on the grass when they ride without training wheels, just in case they fall.

- Anger is like a mix of sadness and fear. It tells me there is the risk of losing something valuable and that someone is not respecting my values or my personal boundaries. We get angry when we think that someone crossed our boundary, the limit of decency, respect, trust, or property. I get upset when someone is late for an appointment with me because that shows a lack of respect for my time, and his tardiness interferes with my schedule, causing me to cut the meeting short, which is not ideal. Anger is almost always outward, and it invites us to set a healthy boundary and repair what's damaged. The most important question we must ask ourselves when we get upset, regardless of what has upset us, is what we will do with that which has angered us. There usually is no way to change the behavior of the other person or events that are outside of our control and affect us. What we can do is prevent something similar from happening again, and we also can learn to behave in a way that generates well-being in the face of what bothers us.

When someone's late to meet with me, I can choose to wait only fifteen minutes and then leave if the person hasn't arrived by that time and go about my day. I will have lost that meeting, but I won't feel like the victim of someone else's actions. I also can decide not to set meetings with that person again or to communicate that I will not accept his tardiness for a future meeting.

Anger often hides sadness. When we move beyond anger, we can discover what we have lost and, having identified it, we can do something about it. Maybe our daughter is deeply upset because her brother cut her doll's hair, and her doll will never be the same again. We can help her complain to her brother with love and accompany her during her sadness. Sometimes parents can repair or replace what our child has broken or lost but not always. When we cannot do it, all we can do is mourn and feel gratitude for what we had and for what we still have.

If it is the adults that face anger, the best thing to do is to use "the mirror" resource. When we are upset with someone or at something, let's ask ourselves, *What is bothering me about myself in this situation?* Almost certainly, the answer will lead us to an action that will fix the situation.

It angers me that my neighbor parks his car so close to the boundary of my parking spot because that doesn't let me open my car door. But what bothers me about myself in that situation? It bothers me that I've never told my neighbor to please park his car correctly, and it upsets me that I have never told him how it affects me that he parks so close to the line that marks what belongs to me. Or perhaps I did tell him and got no change in attitude from him, so what probably upsets me about myself now is that I was not able to file a formal complaint through legal means, or maybe purchase some orange cones at the hardware store and place them there myself, or simply accept that my neighbor will not do what I ask of him and that there is nothing left for me to do except to find myself another parking spot that meets my needs in order to be at peace. *If I respond to what upsets me, I always have the option to overcome it.*

- Guilt is similar to anger; it's a type of anger at oneself. Guilt says, "I did something that was not good, and I feel bad about it." Guilt also includes a bit of sadness, and it is a very useful emotion to bring love and compassion. By acknowledging our mistakes, we can learn to love ourselves. Guilt also allows us to repair or correct the wrong we did, and if we cannot repair it, we can at least learn not to do it in the future. The mere act of acknowledging a mistake, accepting ourselves, trying to repair it, and asking others and ourselves for forgiveness is already a positive thing.

- Shame doesn't make us feel good at all. It has its roots in nothing but judgment—we're not as we should be, we don't do things as we should do them, or we don't have the things that we should have. To feel ashamed is to feel inadequate in being, doing, or having, but the shame is not real because it is usually based on a critical and destructive opinion of ourselves. The best thing to do when we feel shame is to identify that opinion, value judgment, or destructive belief and where and when we learned it, so that we can cancel or change it. If we learned it from someone, then we can relearn it according to the present moment. If I went to a party dressed in cocktail attire, and everyone was in jeans and tennis shoes, I can feel shame when I see that I don't fit in—but I can also laugh at myself and at the mix-up, take off my high heels, forget about my dress, and join the others with a positive attitude.

  Children feel shame too, but adults must observe that sometimes what they feel actually is fear. The shame they might feel is a call for us to reinforce their self-esteem and confidence. A child may feel embarrassed to walk into a new house with people he doesn't know, and in that case our company can provide reassurance. Singing in front of people also can be embarrassing, so maybe we need to strengthen the child's self-esteem without pressuring him. We can let him know that we love to hear him sing and that other people would be lucky if they could hear him too.

  I always gave my children the choice to say no, but I also let them know that they were valuable, whether they did or didn't do what they were afraid to do, and that I loved them regardless of their choice. Shame originates in the fear of being inadequate, of making a mistake, or of being rejected by others. If we can nurture our self-esteem and that of our children and never measure it by good results or our mistakes, then we will always come out well.

- Joy provides us with pleasure and invites us to celebrate it and express it however we want. If we don't express or value joy, we won't fare well because covering up our joy is like saying to ourselves that being happy is not good and neither is showing it; to do this is to deny our very being. In our guilt-oriented culture, we often think that if we are happy and someone else isn't, we should not express our joy for fear the other person will feel bad. We may even think that we don't deserve joy, which is worse. Let's always realize that we deserve joy and well-being, and instead of hiding it, let's share it and express it! If we are next to someone who is not happy, we can use our own positive energy to help him or her feel better or simply spread our joy. The great thing about children is that they are great emotion "imitators"; they feel whatever surrounds them. If the child's mother is anxious, the baby will be upset, and if she is calm, the baby will be at peace.

With age, we understand that we feel differently than others do, but even so, our "mirror neurons" capture the emotions of someone else or the environment, and we feel that which surrounds us. Emotions are contagious, so let's feel joy in order to spread it.

When we see our children happy, let's acknowledge that and provide them the opportunity to express it—dancing, singing, or doing whatever they like to do to celebrate. We sometimes see our children so excited that we want them to stop and calm down—I get that. But before that, we must acknowledge that they are happy and offer them a way to celebrate and express their happiness. "If you can't beat them, join them," as the saying goes. That's something that has worked for me. When my children come up with something funny, they repeat it and repeat it, laughing more each time. Instead of calling them to order—a nearly impossible task in this situation—I join in the joke, and I enjoy that more than if I'm the party-pooper. (More so, what need is there to be that?) In general, we have to accept that when we want to cut the party short for others, it's often because we fear losing something that is valuable to us (we're jealous). If I acknowledge, listen to, and process that fear, then it will disappear, and I will be able to enjoy and let others enjoy.

- Enthusiasm is like an anticipated joy. It asks us to prepare for something and to do something. If we don't do it, the enthusiasm may turn into fear and paralyze us, or we may feel sad for having lost the chance to carry it out.

- Gratitude is what we feel when we appreciate something or someone. It calls for us to acknowledge and express it. It's what we do, for example, when we go to a friend's house and bring a gift, even if it's a simple note with a happy face on it, thanking him for his friendship and company. Gratitude is one of the most transformative emotions because it can help us change the rest of our emotions, including anger and sadness.

- Pride, also at times known as confidence, is that sensation that arises when we love and value ourselves. Pride calls for us to appreciate ourselves out loud, to acknowledge ourselves for all that we are and for how we behave. Appreciating our children is vital for them to feel proud of themselves, so they can set out to do what they wish to do in life without fear of failure or rejection.

Pride is nourished at home when we value how special each person is and when we say good things about everyone. We shouldn't nurture it only in our children but with our partners as well. It can be just a small gesture, action, or word, as everything that we admire touches and inspires us.

I admired my four-year-old daughter's empathy and caring when she saw how sad her brother was when he broke his toy. She gave him a hug and helped him fix it. To see such loving behavior makes me proud as a mom and inspires me to do the same. It's also good to acknowledge and be proud of how our children handle such uncomfortable emotional states as sadness and anger. I recently was surprised that my older daughter wrote some very sweet and heartfelt poems about how much she loved me and missed me and how sad she was when I was away on a trip. As I read the words she wrote for me as a Mother's Day gift, I was touched and couldn't have been more proud to see how she expressed her emotions through poetry with so much love. I thanked her and acknowledged such creative and emotionally mature behavior.

Emotional mastery requires us to recognize and acknowledge emotions and to understand what they ask us to do. We need to help our children take care and sometimes suggest the course of action. If my daughter is sad over a loss, I will offer her a hug so she can cry and tell me how much she appreciated what she lost. If my son is angry because he doesn't have something, I will acknowledge his anger and offer him help; for example, by replacing whatever he doesn't have with something different or simply by helping him connect to the sadness that is almost always behind his anger. I also can teach him to set a boundary with love when someone attacks him. The key is to recognize, acknowledge, understand with love, and act in kind. This is true not just for ourselves but with others as well, as we often feel what others feel and can assist them in acknowledging their emotions and taking charge of them. That connects us to others; helping also fills us with meaning and pleasure.

In love, emotions are doors to learning. By recognizing and inquiring what emotions ask of us, we can take care and provide greater well-being for ourselves. Our children will need a bit of help from us at first to achieve whatever their emotions are asking, but eventually they will learn to provide that for themselves, and that level of autonomy will always allow them to get back to peace and well-being on their own. Emotions also leave an open door for us to solve interpersonal conflicts in the best way. Let's look at some of them in detail and what we can do to enjoy our

Denise Dziwak

home in peace and harmony, even during the most difficult and uncomfortable moments.

Negotiations with Love

A conflict is a situation in which two or more people want the opposite thing or are in scenarios that mutually exclude themselves. Let's imagine a very common family conflict: We go to buy a carton of ice cream for everyone, but my older daughter wants strawberry, my younger daughter wants lemon, and my son wants chocolate. We have a conflict because no carton of ice cream has those three flavors, and we are not going to buy three different cartons of ice cream to make everyone happy.

Conflict is natural, and it arises in our lives all the time. It is not something bad, in and of itself. Because we often don't know how to handle it peacefully and lovingly, we may look for ways to avoid it. Let's see how we can get through conflicts with more strength and happiness. First of all, we need to be *aware* that we are facing a conflict. Sometimes we only realize we are going through conflict after we are already arguing, and temperatures are rising.

Here's another very common family conflict: It's Friday night, and I want to go out to dinner, but my husband would rather stay in and watch a movie. He wants something very different from what I want, and in between all this is the management of a resource that is very scarce for both of us: time. In this type of situation we may try to convince the other person of our option, or we may give in and submit to the other's wish. And if there are more than two people in conflict, we often opt for a vote, an option that always ends with someone feeling bad. Voting, as Fred Kofman says, is like three wolves and one sheep deciding what to eat; it's unlikely that the sheep will come out of the conflict unharmed.

The truth is that none of these is a good way to solve conflict. We can only solve conflict by negotiating with love and respect. To that end, three premises are infallible, according those who have applied them and my own experience. Let's see what they are.

1. A successful negotiation is one in which we all win and satisfy our interests.

When we can't have what we want, we must go beyond what we want. For example, in my Friday night scenario, we would ask each other what we want. My answer was to go out, and my husband's answer was to watch a movie at home. Then, to understand each other's motivation, we would ask, "What will your choice give you? What's important about it for you?" I would say that I want some alone time with him so we can talk and enjoy a delicious dinner together. He'd say that going out for him means changing his clothes when he would rather stay with his comfortable outfit and be with me in a private setting without people around. More than anything, my husband chose staying in to watch a movie because of the kind of environment he wanted, and he strengthened his argument by adding that someone recommended a really good movie that promises to bring laughter and tears.

2. Together we can create a solution to satisfy both of our interests.

We each have to see how we can come up with an option that meets both of our needs. Maybe we will choose to order sushi delivery and to eat on our terrace. I would get some alone time with him while enjoying a good meal, and he won't have to change clothes and will get the privacy he wants. After eating, we can choose to watch that highly recommended movie. In fact, we could watch the movie while we wait for the food, pause it when it arrives, and then finish watching it after we eat. This plan would meet everything that each of us wanted deep down, and it is very likely that we would both agree to it.

Such a scenario has happened to my husband and me many times. The truth is that the solution is not always the same. Answers and motivations surface from each of us that we would have never imagined were important for the other when we ask, "What's important to you?" My husband might say that he'd rather not go out to a restaurant because his stomach hurts, and he's not hungry but that he would love to accompany me, if that works for me, or we could order food just for me, and he would have some tea. As long as we talk, there will always be positive options for both of us.

3. There is always a deeper interest beneath a request.

Let's solve conflicts by acknowledging those deep interests and talking in order to understand the reasons for our wishes. It is easier to find a solution when we know each person's true interests.

There are times when resources are limited, like with buying ice cream and sharing toys. Our children may get into conflict because they want to play with the same toy at the same time. We can understand why that toy is important and perhaps offer an alternative so that both satisfy their interests, or we can arrive at a solution like sharing, whether playing together or taking turns. In this way, each will have the toy at different times. Of course, they may say, "I wanted it now, not later," and in that case, we can do a raffle or ask how we can compensate the one who takes the later turn—possibly giving that person more time with his turn or giving something special while he waits.

Parents tend to want to solve children's conflicts in the fastest way possible so that they don't get angry or fight. This is impossible because conflicts will always exist. Instead of avoiding them, the best thing we can do is to help children solve conflicts without overexercising our authority. It's better if we teach them to understand what each one wants before they fight so that both can decide how to be satisfied. If we realize that our children cannot decide on their own, then we can help them with ideas—but always with the understanding of how each of them feels and seeking what makes both of them happy.

Let's go back to the case of the ice cream. When it comes to such a conflict, we will have to negotiate. We won't decide on the *best* flavor of ice cream but on the one that will satisfy everyone to an acceptable degree. One person's reason for wanting ice cream may not be the same as another's. Maybe my son, who wants chocolate ice cream, would be satisfied with a chocolate candy bar and would leave the ice cream decision up to his sisters.

Finding a way to solve each conflict is a challenge, and it's one of the most beautiful lessons I've had in my couple and family life. While I accept that there are times that I want to decide by myself, period ("without anyone bugging me"), I also admit that in those cases I always end up realizing I can't do it that way: What I want is to be with my family. I want to share, want us to do something together, and don't want to be by myself. We don't always have to be in agreement, of course. In conflict of opinions, it's perfectly valid to be in disagreement and at peace at the same time.

We adults and the children both like to impose our own opinions and be right: "Lemon ice cream is the best!" "Going out to dinner is better than staying home and watching a movie!" Being right means that I want my opinion to be worth more than the other's (self-esteem weighs in here). The good thing is that we can always agree that we both are right, accept the other with his own tastes, and live together in peace and harmony. By listening to each other, understanding one another, and doing our best to collaborate with each other, we always have the opportunity to meet somewhere beyond opinions and particular desires.

When I enter into negotiation, I want to help the other person and help myself. If the other person is not there, I will never achieve anything. In fact, *many conflicts tend to dissolve instead of being resolved*. With the mere fact of not opposing the other person but showing genuine interest in helping and understanding him, I arrive at an agreement without any obstacles. When children see their parents argue, when they see that each of them is trying to bend the other to his or her will, they feel uncomfortable and afraid. Children don't like to see us upset

or not speaking nicely. This is one more reason to become aware and care for children by learning to solve conflicts with love.

Solving conflicts with love and openness allows us the possibility that the members of the family will live with happiness and peace. That's one of the great values of the family room: It's the space to share, have fun, communicate with love, and learn to deal with our emotions in the best way, especially in moments of conflict.

Proposed Activity:

The Emotions Game

The object of this game is to teach children what emotions are and how to recognize what we feel. Additionally, we will show them how to handle their emotions in a way that will generate well-being for all. It's best if we play parents and children together. That way we can cheer on the kids and show them that we also feel what they feel. Game duration is about thirty minutes.

This game is a very good option for moments of conflict or when we are feeling bad about something and don't know what's going on within us. It brings us closer together and shows us that everyone experiences similar feelings and emotions at different times, and we can help each other feel better.

What do we need?

Masks. We can make them or use the ones that suggested here (next), but don't feel restricted to these. Think about the many emotions that you and your family go through daily at home and in other scenarios, like the park, school, or work.

What will we do?

We each choose a mask at random, put it on our faces, and start an improvised monologue around what we feel in made-up situations. We express what we would like to receive from our loved ones in that state of mind and in that made-up situation. And then we talk about what we would do to help those who would feel the same thing we do:

- I feel (happy, sad, scared, excited, guilty, proud, at peace, affectionate, upset) when (suggest a situation that generates the emotion mentioned).

- When I feel (name the emotion), I would like my friends and family to (name the action) with me.

- If you felt (name the emotion), I would like to (mention something you would do to help that person feel better).

If you play with very young kids (two and younger), it's recommended that you express yourselves through paint or imitation, since you can't always expect words from them. It even will become fun for you adults to express yourselves without talking and use signs or take a blank sheet of paper and draw an answer.

MY NOTES

. . . .

. . . .

. . . .

. . . .

. . . .

. . . .

. . . .

. . . .

. . . .

. . . .

. . . .

. . . .

. . . .

. . . .

. . . .

. . . .

. . . .

. . . .

. . . .

. . . .

. . . .

. . . .

. . . .

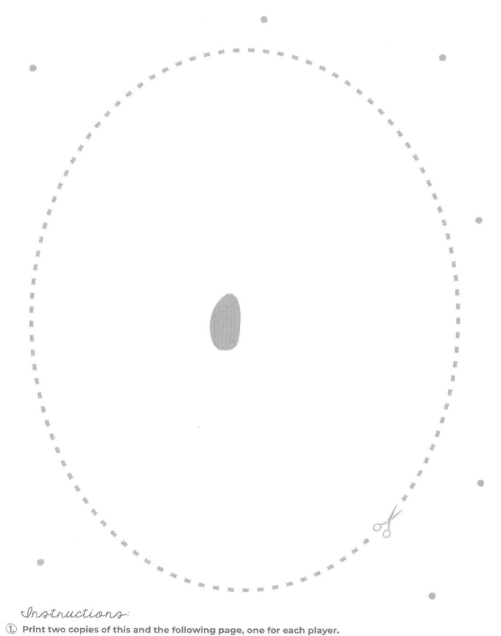

Instructions:

① Print two copies of this and the following page, one for each player.
   Note: the size of the page should be such that the dotted oval covers your kids' face.
② Cut through the big dotted oval and the small circle in the middle (this is where the nose fits in)
③ Cut and paste the eyes and mouth into this big oval to make the feeling face.

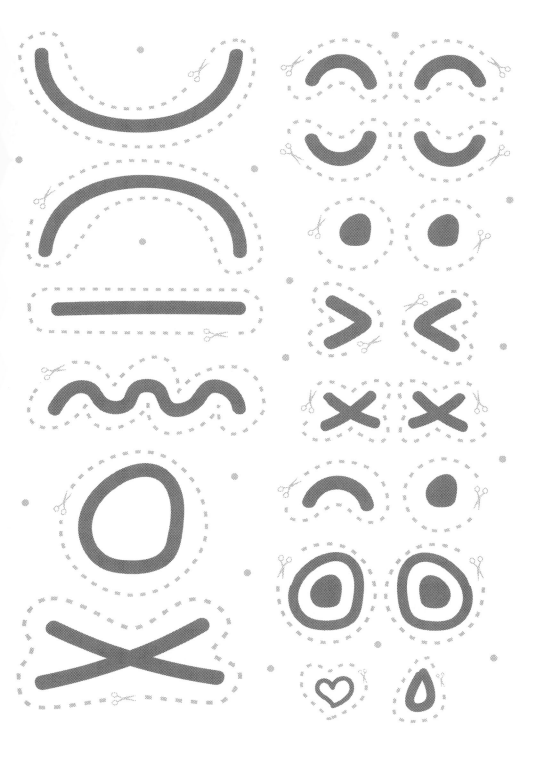

CHAPTER 3

The Kitchen and Dining Room

3

The Kitchen and Dining Room

Come with me to the kitchen and dining room, my favorite places in the house. I enjoy preparing delicious recipes, smelling the aroma of something recently baked that reminds me of my grandma, and setting a beautiful table to receive whoever is joining us for a meal, but what I appreciate and value most is that this space is where we spend time as a family, eating, sharing, and nourishing ourselves with healthy food that allows us to live fully. Because of that, my kitchen and dining room are a sacred space.

In my house, the kitchen, where we prepare meals, and the dining room, where we eat them, are joined as one because I believe that both rooms have a special power to gather the family. Regardless of where your family eats their meals, take time to discover and make the most out of both rooms. Whether it's just Mom, Dad, and kids, or we have guests—grandparents, uncles, aunts, or friends—the kitchen and the dining room are places of connection, contact, and enjoyment.

Time to Eat Well

Have you eaten when you're stressed and in a hurry? Have you eaten while thinking about what you haven't done yet today? Have you attended to a task as you were eating? If so, you probably noticed afterward that that meal didn't go down well or that it gave you indigestion. That same food likely would have gone down better if you'd eaten it in peace while enjoying the company of your loved ones.

We seem to go through life quickly, and many times we eat as if by reflex, without stopping to think about what or when we eat. We only think about finishing as soon as possible so that we can continue the

activities of the day. In doing so, we forget how important it is to eat with awareness and at regular times.

Sitting down to eat calmly is good for us and for our children. If we give food the time and special attention it requires, our children will too. I have a friend who was worried because her two-year-old daughter didn't like to eat.

"Regardless of what I make for her to eat," my friend said, "she eats very little before she wants to go play."

"What about you?" I asked. "Do you eat well?"

"No," she answered. "Sometimes I pick on something on the go, but I don't have time to sit down, except to feed my daughter. When I'm in the kitchen, it's to prepare and eat something quickly."

"Maybe that's not helping your daughter to eat well," I suggested.

She decided to change her habits and started to make good food for herself and her daughter and to formally sit down to eat with her.

"It was hard at first," she later told me, "because it demanded time that I'd dedicated to other things, but then I discovered that cooking the food, enjoying it at the table, and sharing that space with my daughter—and even cleaning the kitchen and leaving it organized— changed everything."

Her daughter started to eat well, and my friend stopped living in a hurry. Moreover, she felt healthier and had more vitality because she was nourishing herself properly.

Let's give ourselves that time. Let's prioritize the time to have breakfast, lunch, and dinner with family or friends. Let's think about what to eat, put some dedication into making it, and enjoy not just the meal but the conversation after it. To give ourselves that time is to make a parenthesis in the middle of the noncommunal rhythm of each day, one that will benefit our nutrition and health.

Ideally, try to eat with your children and spouse once or twice a day so you can share the enjoyment, but even if you are by yourself, make cooking and eating well a priority.

Sharing—the Basis of Happiness

In the movie *Into the Wild*, an adolescent decides to live by himself and not depend on anyone, but when he almost dies due to intoxication, he realizes a key thing: *Happiness is only real when it is shared.* I firmly believe that, and it's from that place that I choose to build a full and happy life, sharing it with other people—my children and my

husband, other relatives, friends, coworkers, and anyone with whom I cross paths.

The kitchen is an ideal place to share as we prepare the food. Depending on kids' ages, they can help out with small tasks, such as setting the table or even helping us cook. To enjoy this time, don't rush, and set aside perfection and requirements regarding order and cleanliness. For me, this phase of preparation produces a lot of pleasure. When my children or my husband don't help me, I make up stories, as if I were cooking on a TV show, and I comment—into the "camera"—on the necessary steps of preparation. ("All of you at home can make this delicious family recipe.") I always end up laughing so hard by myself that my children and husband want to participate in the "show," and all of us to have a good time together. You don't have to put on a cooking show, but eventually you'll find your own way to relax and have fun while cooking delicious and nutritious food or setting the table in a beautiful way.

My mother-in-law told me that even when her children were still babies and could barely hold a utensil, she still laid out a napkin, silverware, and a glass for them, just as she did for the adults. At first I thought that was a waste of time and energy because she'd have to wash those things, even if the kids hadn't used them. Then I understood that it was a way for everyone to feel a part of the meal, and so I also adopted this custom in my house. Sometimes enjoying and sharing a meal requires that we get rid of rigid ideas regarding efficiency and order.

We definitely need to sit at the table *together*, even if it's not always easy with small children. As parents, we also need to make our schedules and priorities flexible. At my house we have dinner between six thirty and seven o'clock, which I never would have imagined doing when my husband and I were dating at twenty-five years of age. Back then, having dinner before eight thirty was much too early for most people of our age in our culture. Every country or culture has its own schedule, but regardless of that, children generally need to dine early so they can go to bed early as well. For that to happen, adults may need to postpone finishing late-afternoon tasks or jobs, and do them after the children have gone to sleep. These are small efforts toward being together as a family, but they are worth it.

Discussing with Harmony

When we gather to eat, we seek to spend time together. That's why I recommend that the children stay at the table for a few minutes after they finish eating. It's also valid, though, to be more flexible now and then, and let them leave the table while the adults continue eating

and talking. It may be hard to get through the entire meal, especially with small children, but we can try to spend as much time together at the table as possible.

Having a conversation is an art that we learn together; we look into each other's eyes and listen with appreciation. When we talk at the table, let's seek harmony, the kind of harmony that has nothing to do with strict order or silence but with a constant flow of interaction. Contact, listening, and basic rules (such as not interrupting whoever is talking) are key here. Of course it's not easy to carry on a conversation when children are young—they talk and eat at the same time, unconcerned if someone else is talking—but as parents, we can avoid getting exasperated when we notice that the conversation is not going as we would like. Eventually, we can achieve a conversation flow and take turns speaking so that both adults and children can express themselves and listen to each other. We adults can discuss our own matters and include the children in the conversation in a way they can understand (according to their ages). It's not good for adults to take over the conversation with worries and topics that children cannot understand or that can even frighten them.

For harmony, think about the layout of the seating, especially if there are more than two kids, if one of them still needs help with eating, or if they tend to fight about anything. We could try to seat them together so they can learn not to bother each other, but I prefer to avoid that, so I stagger their seats between my husband and me. In this way, we can help out with food, give hugs to the one who needs it, and keep our eyes and attention on the one who is speaking. Once children get used to a certain place at the table, it gives them a sense of security, and they won't want to move from that spot. We can show them, however, that it's okay to change. We won't need to do it all the time; it's enough for us to try one combination one week and then another on the next week, until we find the one that is best and most comfortable for our family.

Technological Distractions—That Unnecessary Evil

I love technology. I was born and raised with it and have incorporated it into my life. I'm still learning how to use it and benefit from it, however, without having it interfere with my connection and relationship with people, especially within my family. Even though I know the virtues and advantages of modern technology, I don't allow the TV, tablets, or phones to sit at the table with us. When the phone rings, we generally ignore it. If we need to answer, we first ask permission to do so from the others. If a phone call interrupted a

conversation with one of our children, we always apologize after we hang up and then give them all our attention.

Interrupting a conversation can offend a child's sensibilities. Let's put ourselves in their place: We are sharing something intimate or exciting with someone when that person, without a thought, leaves the table to answer his phone. When he hangs up, he returns to the table and doesn't even remember that we were sharing something important. These small actions and carelessness can erode bonds, so let's pay attention to strengthen instead of deteriorating them. We are not required to answer the phone every time it rings during a meal. It's our decision, not that of the person who calls. We can check the caller ID to see who is calling and then decide if we should answer.

We have a relative who tends to call insistently, always claiming that it's urgent, but then we realize that it was of minor importance that didn't merit our interrupting lunch to answer him. That's why we've opted to return his call only after we get up from the table. It's common sense not act on autopilot but instead to be conscious of the moment that we are sharing with our families and not take away from its being a priority.

The same goes for the TV and tablets. If I allow my kids to watch while we are all eating, the act of eating will take a back seat, and nobody will connect with the person next to him. When I was a little girl, we had a television in our kitchen, and when my parents turned it on during a meal, it was horrible. It made me feel like I was alone, even if my loved ones were sitting next to me. Fortunately, they finally took the television out of the kitchen, and we were able to get back to eating and sharing our lives and experiences. I also remember going to many friends' houses as a kid, where an adult always had the TV on. That bothered me a great deal because I felt that it came between me and other people, especially if we were eating.

When children are young and are so restless, it's tempting for us parents to put a cell phone or tablet in their hands because it's an easy solution for us to talk without being interrupted. I confess that I've done it (and still do) so they can eat while being entertained or so that I can finish eating without so much noise when they are excited. The tablet magically brings momentary silence and peace, even though I know it's not good and that I am only buying time that will cost me dearly later.

Even if it is uncomfortable, it is better to withstand the kids' yelling and excitement until they calm down, and then eat in peace with them, maybe with a new incentive, such as a new topic of conversation or a lovely story. Children, especially the younger ones, have short attention spans and little ability to remain still, so they need to have

change and to explore new things. Adults can offer them those changes without resorting to electronic devices that quiet them and cut the connection with them. If we do use such devices, it should be as a last resort and not as a mealtime routine.

Consider this fact: It's been shown that we eat more and worse when we watch TV at the same time because when we don't pay attention to what we're eating, which means it is more likely that we won't adequately digest what we consume.[2]

Food and Romance

Sharing food helps us to connect on a deeper level, but we also can use it to strengthen our relationships and add to our intimacy and communication time. Partners might make up recipes to please each other, cook together, or create a special environment around food, with candles and music. This is perfectly compatible with our children, and most of the time we will be able to share our romance when children are present. I was blessed to witness, from childhood, the close and beautiful relationship my parents had as a couple. Thanks to them, I understood that being in love can last more than forty years if both people keep creating romantic moments when cooking and eating together.

Remember that we are all free to create our worlds, and we also have the ability to maintain romance and nurture intimacy. Let's not believe, however, that romance and intimacy are reserved for the bedroom. We can also create and strengthen those bonds in the kitchen as well, and it takes very little to do so. It's enough to look at each other when we talk, to cheer with a glass, and to be grateful that we are together and that there is food on our table. At my house, it is special for my husband when I prepare his coffee and warm his bread, which is what he likes the most in the morning. He also cooks for me and makes a special effort with the grilled fish and veggies that I enjoy so much. Part of the romance is making and sharing something the other person will enjoy, and this takes place in the kitchen! All that we give to our partners must come from unselfish love, without looking to get something in return, not even reciprocity. Ideally, we should do it before we are asked for it or before we get a love complaint.

Our children like to see that we love each other, that we are romantic, and that we take care of each other. Feeling that love that we have for each other gives them a sense of security. Of course, sometimes

---

[2] Studies done by Leann Birch, PhD, professor of Human Development and Family Studies at Penn State University. Read more about this topic at http://www.ncbi.nlm.nih.gov/pmc/articles/PMC2678872.

they also get jealous and want to get in the middle—that's good and normal—so let's include them so that they feel that they are part of that Dad-and-Mom union.

You Are What You Eat

Let's talk about what we eat. This topic is of great importance in my life. I've been interested in nutrition since childhood, and I think that interest was derived from conflicts that my relatives and I had regarding food. I saw their worry and fear when my sister barely ate; she would not eat the balanced diet my mother prepared for her. I also saw how my father would diet to lose weight but then engage in unbridled eating when he was anxious. I would get my parents' approval when I ate everything put before me and more approval when I had seconds. In my teenage years, I wanted to be thin, so I decided to stop eating—to the point that I had to get medical help so I would understand that not eating was bad for me. I had to learn how to eat according to my real needs and not according to pictures of models in magazines.

I dieted until I was twenty-eight and kept a firm eye on my food and what my body looked like. Around that time, thanks to a spiritual growth path that arrived along with pregnancy, everything changed for me. That's how I started to *eat to feel good*, and I identified which foods contributed to my goal and which didn't. I stopped eating and drinking some of them and noticed the difference. I began to read and taught myself. I internalized information and also consulted nutrition specialists from various fields like Ayurveda and macrobiotics.

Ayurveda, along with traditional Chinese medicine, is the oldest science of health. Developed in India thousands of years ago, Ayurveda recognizes three *doshas* or biotypes—*vatta*, *pitta* and *kapha*—in people and the nutrition that helps balance each one of them, according to the way nature's elements (air, water, fire, and ether) exercise their power. If the body is in balance, it tends to stay healthy on its own and to heal in case of illness. Ayurveda is mainly vegetarian and uses many spices that work as medicine for each *dosha*. A remarkable doctor and expert in this discipline was Carmen Frigerio, who, along with Ana María Raíces, wrote *Recetario Ayurveda* ("Ayurveda Recipe Book"), a book that explains the basic concepts of Ayurveda and provides menus and recipes for each *dosha*. If you're interested in this type of health science, you can find more references in bookstores or in wellness centers, such as the Chopra Center (http://www.chopra.com), where they combine treatments like massages, nutrition, yoga, and meditation to improve quality of life.

Denise Dziwak

The other nutrition trend that I explored and recommend is macrobiotics, developed in Japan and later brought to the West at the start of the twentieth century. It's based on the balance between yin and yang. All of us have yin and yang elements in our bodies, and it's necessary to balance them through food so we can maintain an equilibrium that allows us to minimize the body's efforts. In this theory, foods are graded on a scale of yin and yang, where, for example, sugar is on the yin end, and meat or salt is on the yang end. (That's why when we eat something too salty, we then feel like eating something sweet, to balance ourselves.) The inconvenient part, according to macrobiotics, is that in going from one end to the other, the body works too hard and produces a lot of waste that needs to be processed and eliminated. If we remain in the middle of the yin/yang scale, however, we will be healthy and balanced. This balance is individual, according to our biotypes—those who are very yin will need more yang foods, and vice versa.

My family and the birth of my first daughter were my motivation to learn more about these topics. It was one thing to experiment with my body and health and another to do so with her little body and health. At first, it seemed logical to take sodas and sweets out of her diet, but what basis did I have to limit red meat or dairy in her diet? At that moment, and thanks to conversations with my husband, I realized I needed to consult nutritionists to be better informed about a one-year-old's nutritional needs. Many times, especially during her first year of life, I tended to be radical with my choices. What previously seemed healthy to me, I then saw as harmful poison.

The more I knew about a topic, the more I wanted to take care of all of us at home. I explored ongoing options so we would continue to enjoy our food. Besides being nutritional, what we ate had to be pleasing to the taste buds and look attractive. As a chef, my mother-in-law helped me with that a lot. Although my whims sometimes made things hard for her, she always prepared food that was very healthy and very tasty, which was not entirely common where we lived at that time.

Becoming aware of the foods that truly nourish us brought many favorable changes to my family's eating habits. I'd like to invite you to try some of the following ideas and consider them as something fun, not as a rules to be rigorously adopted.

I do experiments; for example, I won't eat added sugars for six months. During that time, I observe how I feel, and I decided what was useful to me during this time and what was not. Another experiment was to eliminate sodas from the house. We drank them only when we went to events or places outside the house. This is a very healthy recommendation because the amount of sugar, synthetic

sweeteners, and chemical compounds that these drinks contain can affect, for example, the absorption of calcium in the body. We might also cut out packaged sweets and replace them with home-baked cakes and cookies, which provide us yet another experience to share with our children. We can experiment with taking some type of food from our diet and replacing it with another. For example, we might cut out dairy—especially if we have allergies or excess mucus—and instead get our calcium from eating broccoli or almonds. All of these experiments allow us to discover what our bodies need and how to provide that in different ways.

A friend once said to me, "Don't tell me the ingredients of those cookies because I don't want to know. I just want to enjoy them." At that moment, I realized that many of us don't want to know or become aware of what we eat because we think that will take enjoyment away. I can tell you from personal experience, however, that those two are not mutually exclusive. All you need to do is explore and be creative, and you'll achieve a balance between food that's tasty, healthy, and fun.

My personal motto is this: Grow in awareness for a better world of love, peace, and unity. I also apply that when it comes to eating. I want to know what I'm eating and take charge of my choices.

During my childhood, I was very fortunate that my parents were always interested in healthy food, and they experimented a lot. They shared their ideas, and I continued to explore when I grew up. Paying attention to our nutrition in order to feel good is the example I want to set for my children as well. Then they later will be able to decide on their diets, according to their own standards.

Today, my children prefer drinking water to drinking soda. When we lived in Argentina, my older daughter carried her water bottle to birthday parties because many times, only sodas and artificial juices were served, and she didn't like that. In the Peruvian culture, people seem more aware of healthy nutrition, and meals tend to be prepared using fresh and natural foods, which expands healthy options for the kids.

The body of knowledge on nutrition is constantly evolving. There are interesting findings daily—for example, the relationship between certain foods and intestinal health and how that affects the body or the brain. Other findings suggest how we can cure physical and mental ailments just by changing our eating habits. For example, I follow a type of diet based on genotype, which was developed by naturopathic physician Peter D'Adamo. Following this nutritional plan has healed my allergy problems without medication and allows me to have optimal energy and feel fulfilled. This nutritional plan is based

to a large degree on each person's blood type. It seeks to empower beneficial genes and silence negative genes in each person, which are inherited from our parents.

The studies compiled by Dr. Natasha Campbell-McBride in her book *Gaps, Gut and Psychology Syndrome* are very interesting as well. She tells us how, through nutrition, she helped her son overcome autism, and she suggests dietary changes to heal illnesses like schizophrenia, depression, dyslexia, and allergies. Her studies on the relationship between gluten (wheat protein) and digestive ailments brought me to eliminate gluten from my diet. When I did, I felt, for the first time in my life, that I could eat without my abdomen becoming bloated. This is aligned with my genotype diet; according to my biotype, gluten consumption is not recommended.

We can all experiment with different eating options at home to feel good and to be in physical, mental, and emotional balance. Our relationship with food and knowing how much nourishment we get from what we eat depends on our experiences with our diets. We adults must help our children in this regard.

Tips to Enjoy Healthy Meals as a Family

Here are some ideas for you to experiment with at home. I hope that you will notice positive changes with them and that they will allow you to fully improve the experience of eating and sharing as a family.

Recommendations

1. Effect changes in your nutrition little by little. Be the example for your children, and explain the reasons for the dietary changes to them.

2. Focus on changing your habits where you have the most control—at home and in school lunches. Be more permissive during special occasions, such as birthdays, outings with grandparents, friend's invitations, or eating at a restaurant. When your child's friend comes over to our house, remember to ask about any food allergies he or she might have. Likewise, when your child visits another home, communicate openly regarding any dietary restrictions.

3. The best way for children to eat healthily is for them to be hungry at mealtime (so avoid offering something to eat at any time) and for the food to be healthy. Don't offer children too many options from which to choose. This has a very simple yet important explanation. In my house, one of the children usually doesn't like the menu of the day, and in that case, we offer whatever is available— for example, leftovers from the day before—but we won't prepare something new. It's not just

about the food and healthy eating; it's also about boundaries and what we are willing to accept. If we had only one child, we might make more exceptions, but with three, that's not possible—I'd basically be a short-order cook!

4. Design a weekly menu that you know will be good for everyone: diverse, nutritious, and one that you can make according to your time and activities. Be flexible; it's okay to change some things. The idea is not for it to always be the same but for you to be able to change it every now and then. That way, you and the kids won't get tired of always eating the same thing. You might prepare the menu along with your children, playing with food and varying flavors that each of you likes the most. This will make everyone feel included, and creating it together will also make it fun.

Ideas to Improve Nutrition

1. Avoid processed foods and juices. Most prepared food is not as healthy as what we prepare ourselves with fresh foods. When my older daughter was six years old, I gave her the following advice: "Read labels, and only eat it if you recognize all the ingredients." With that, we scrap about 90 percent of the products available for purchase at kiosks and the supermarket.

2. Reduce your sugar intake, especially the added sugar found in sodas, juices, cookies, and all kinds of processed foods. Use sugar from fresh and dry fruits, or substitute it with more natural sweeteners, like brown sugar, honey, and sweeteners that don't alter blood sugar, like agave, coconut syrup, malt extract, and stevia. Natural sugars are preferable to synthetic ones, such as saccharine, aspartame, sucralose, or cyclamate.

3. Reduce your starch intake, especially wheat, due to its similar effect to sugar and for its gluten, which has been shown to have a negative effect on the

brain and for allergies. We can replace starches with foods like quinoa or amaranth. Also, consume more vegetables, fruits, and foods rich in omega-3 and omega-6, good fats found in foods such as fish and avocado.

4. Choose organically sourced vegetables as well as meats, like free-range chickens or animals from farms that favor sustainable practices and respect toward animals.

5. If you choose a vegetarian diet, be careful not to add too much milk and flour. Opt for organic legumes and whole grains instead. Be careful with food combinations so you can better absorb vegetable iron. Don't forget about vitamin B12; seek oils that contain this key nutrient. If you decide on a strict vegan diet, make sure you know how to replace and combine foods so that you don't suffer any nutritional deficiencies.

6. Make your afternoon/evening meal the lightest one, and try to eat it as early as possible. That way, you'll give your body more time to return to a fasting state and finish digesting what you have eaten before sleep.

7. Eat at least two hours before going to bed, opting for vegetables and proteins, especially for the children, and avoiding sweets.

The kitchen and dining room is a space for meeting and connecting, and it contributes to the construction of the kind of family we want in a very significant way. Creating and preparing meals as a family is fun, and when we sit down at the table together, we take the time to look into each other's eyes and listen to each other while we nourish ourselves with healthy food. The aromas from the kitchen will remain etched in our memories, along with the hugs and laughter that we shared, so create an environment in which everyone feels special and welcomed while you all take care of your bodies, minds, and souls.

MY NOTES

. . . .
. . . .
. . . .
. . . .
. . . .
. . . .
. . . .
. . . .
. . . .
. . . .

. . . .
. . . .
. . . .
. . . .

. . . .
. . . .
. . . .
. . . .
. . . .
. . . .
. . . .

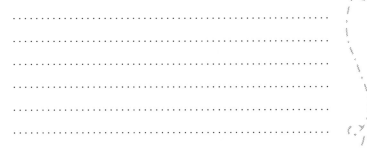

CHAPTER 4

The Living Room

4

The Living Room

Of all the spaces in our houses, we probably welcome friends and families mostly in the living room. It's a place to relax and share without the need to associate it to particular activities or chores. In almost all cultures, getting together with others at home involves entertaining whoever visits by offering them something to drink or eat. Enjoying food and drink with those we love and who love us gives this space meaning.

But there are also personal interactions with a background. Let's explore together in this part of our walk through the house. It's wonderful when someone visits who's outside of the family nucleus. This person brings his history, his way of looking at life, and his codes and values and shares them with us. This allows our family the opportunity to look at life through that new prism and learning new ways of being. It even gives us the opportunity to change something in our family culture if we believe it to be good for us. To know, learn, and grow together is fascinating and enriching.

With an Open Heart

In order to appreciate that which is different and to learn from it, we need an open-heart approach: We must have the willingness to hear the other person without judgment and so we can appreciate, value, and understand him with empathy and compassion.

A while ago, a great friend told me that she valued my capacity to listen to her compassionately and without judging her.

"It makes me feel good," she said, "because I know I can be myself with you, and you will love me no matter what I do. I trust you enough to open up, feel vulnerable, and tell you my wins and losses with inner peace. I think this is an innate ability you have—it's not something that can be learned because, in my experience, all human beings judge one another."

Reflecting on what she told me but contrary to her opinion, I concluded that every human being can be loving, compassionate, and totally accepting of another human being. The reason is simple: We are born with that ability, and it is also a *need*. Babies are one example. A baby accepts whoever wants to take care of him, regardless of who it is. The baby doesn't notice skin color or if that person is pretty or ugly, and he doesn't care if the person is more or less intelligent or rich or poor. When we were babies, all of us accepted what life gave us at the time, and we never showed a judgment of distinction between us and others. We came from a uterus where unity is a physical reality, and when we exited, we expected the same: unity.

As we grow, however, we begin to perceive ourselves as different from the rest.

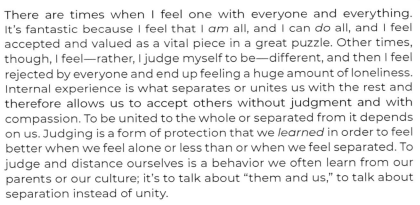

There are times when I feel one with everyone and everything. It's fantastic because I feel that I *am* all, and I can *do* all, and I feel accepted and valued as a vital piece in a great puzzle. Other times, though, I feel—rather, I judge myself to be—different, and then I feel rejected by everyone and end up feeling a huge amount of loneliness. Internal experience is what separates or unites us with the rest and therefore allows us to accept others without judgment and with compassion. To be united to the whole or separated from it depends on us. Judging is a form of protection that we *learned* in order to feel better when we feel alone or less than or when we feel separated. To judge and distance ourselves is a behavior we often learn from our parents or our culture; it's to talk about "them and us," to talk about separation instead of unity.

In my family, there was a lot of judgment at first—a lot of separation awareness. My dad would proudly say, "You are a Dziwak," as if I were better than others. I would hear how he judged others who had more money or less intellectual capacity or less physical beauty. But in spite of his judgments, I also saw how he and my mother could become friends with a lot of people and help everyone without looking at their situation. My parents carried their own history and probably are different now, but those judgments and behaviors were part of the experiences that made me think of myself as someone who could be united with or separated from others.

Years after growing up in this environment of judgment and differences between one another, my friends would praise my compassion and my ability to accept others unconditionally, which is ironic to me. I also have to recognize that this perception doesn't represent me 100 percent because I often judge other people and distance myself from those I don't like. Now, however, I am conscious of it, and when I realize that I am judging another, it hurts me. It hurts me that we cannot see the light that there is in each of us and that we cannot see our own capacity to love. Each person has his stories, and the worse he feels about himself, the less he will be able to love others—and judgment operates more within that person and governs his attitudes and behaviors.

So when you invite someone new to your house and therefore into your family, accept that person as equal to you—as someone who can love, be happy or feel pain, judge or make mistakes, and feel afraid and uneasy.

I know that opening our hearts is not easy because that means finding ourselves face-to-face with our fears. Sometimes we fear that the other can hurt us, and that's why we don't open up. The heart is like a room where all the love, happiness, and peace in the world is housed, but it also contains sadness and pain. We cannot open the door and step into that room without the possibility of finding one or the other. We can close our hearts, but if we do that, our lives will not be full. How will we feel alive if we don't allow ourselves to feel? Let's open our hearts and let the other come in.

By opening up to the new—to those people and their different worldviews—we also feel a natural need to take care of ourselves. To be open and loving doesn't mean to stop honoring our values and morals. If I invite a friend and her husband to my house and at some point she gets angry and hits her husband, I will interfere.

I will tell her, "I understand your feelings, but I do not share your way of behaving, and I cannot allow that in my home."

I would do the same—and with even more reason—if the violence were against me or my children. I would not accept it. When facing such a situation, you might say you don't want that friend in your life, but I will make the effort to set boundaries with that person to help her realize her mistake and so she can change. It would be selfish of me not to show her what she is doing wrong; it would be like denying her from the start the possibility of changing and improving.

People can change. They just need someone to point to what is hurting them and what can be changed and then make them feel loved during the process of change. By neutralizing my friend's violent outburst, I am honoring values like unconditional love and respect for life.

I've been in friend gatherings where I have said things like "Girls, I love sharing with you, but I cannot be a part of this conversation. If we are talking bad about someone who is not here, I'd rather not be here either."

"You're exaggerating," someone has said. "We are only talking about what bothers us."

And I've answered, "I thought you were talking about someone else, but, if you'd like, let's talk about what is going on with you regarding that person. I think that's great; that way we can help you see what you do or don't do when that situation continues to present itself to you."

Other times, they've said, "Jeez, it was a joke."

And I haven't hesitated to respond, "I didn't think it was funny. In fact, I thought it was hurtful, and if I were that person that you are discussing, I wouldn't like for you to joke about me like that, especially if I'm not around."

Of course, I have lost friends ... but all of those, in the end, were not the ones I would have wanted next to me.

When we invite someone to our house, we are saying, "You are welcome," and that doesn't just mean that we are accepting and valuing that person as he is. We also have a tacit commitment: "I am going to listen and open my heart to you." Because of that, it is very important for us to really want someone in our living room and to know why we have invited that person.

Better to Be Alone than in Bad Company

To invite and welcome someone has a meaning and reason. Each of us must define that meaning and intention as well as honor it. I haven't always done this, which is why many times I ended up in uncomfortable situations with people who, deep down in my heart, I didn't want to invite into my home. That doesn't happen to me much anymore because when I invite someone to come in, it's because I want to get to know him and give him a place in my life, even for a moment. And in that moment, I seek unity with that person and want to learn about how that person lives. Surely there will be something about his experience that will enrich mine.

Why am I inviting him to my house? This sincere question determines what I choose to do and not do. For example, there are times when I don't invite in the mom or dad of my daughter's friend who has come to play because I am not available to give the parent my attention. It is important to recognize that *to invite* means to be available for the other person.

If we have other priorities, it is better not to invite the person. Imagine if you'd just given birth. It's natural for close friends and relatives to want to visit and meet the baby, but neither mother nor father are able to welcome everyone at any time. I didn't want to do anything but rest, sleep when the baby allowed me to sleep, and live those days in total family privacy. My body hurt, and I didn't recognize myself in it. The process of breastfeeding was a physical and emotional challenge for me. When I made the mistake of allowing too many people to visit, I felt invaded. I didn't want to greet anyone or talk to anyone; I just wanted to seclude myself. Obviously, that wasn't good for anybody.

Always check both your physical and emotional availability before inviting someone to your house.

If we invite someone we really don't want to invite, it's almost certain that while he is with us, we won't treat him very well and won't accept him openly and compassionately. Many of us tend to reject and exclude when we don't feel comfortable. "Better alone than in bad company," as the saying goes, and that fits well here. Woe to the guest who falls into the web of an insincere invitation.

Creating Community

When we know why we invited someone to our living room—when we invite him with awareness and an open heart—something wonderful and magical will happen: We create community, a group of people who share a language, location, values, projects, and dreams. *We join our guests, and we create bonds beyond our own family.*

Each encounter creates a bond with another person, and this, in turn, creates a bond with others so that we all start to unite. It's wonderful to feel a part of that network because it gives us security. It also shows us that there is a place in the world where we belong and that belongs to us. We are in union, not in separation.

With each interaction between us and our guests, we build ideas and new ways of seeing things. This, then, spreads to our actions inside and outside the house, thus transforming the world in which we live. If we get together and learn to love with more freedom, then the world will be like that as well. If, however, we get together and talk negatively about others, and we distance ourselves from those we do not like, then that will create separation, fear, and war.

Belonging has both light and shadow. In its light, we identify with those with whom we have things in common. In its shadow, we feel different, and this separates and excludes us from other communities. I don't feel that I am part of any unique or static community; rather, I *become a part* of one or another at various times. I look at myself as a part of a whole that I call life.

Maybe the way to not exclude others is to feel part of something small, immediate, and similar to us in the present; something that, at the same time, is part of something bigger that we will access in the future, and we will interact with those who are not that similar to us today. As life passes, we all change, and in this change we feel comfortable with different groups of belonging. I would like to believe that through books like this, we can make the world a community of love and compassion, where there are no external or internal boundaries.

Tribe and Maternity

If I learned anything when I became a mother and, later, a coach and therapist to other mothers and fathers, it's that we cannot do it alone. In her book *Maternity: Coming Face to Face with Your Own Shadow*, Laura Gutman says that Mom and Dad are not enough to raise a child on their own. She suggests a return to living in "tribes," a model that prevailed before nuclear families and that still exists in communities that are less influenced by the economic system that prevails in the world today. As a woman and mother, it is easier for me to understand that during pregnancy and puerperium (the roughly six weeks after giving birth), we need companions—grandmothers, teachers, therapists, friends, or sisters who have been through what a mother goes through and can understand us and give us love and, most of all, a hand.

My husband, who felt how my energy was concentrated on the baby, also needed his own group to understand him and explain to him that what he was going through was natural and would pass. Although he would not get back the spot he had before the baby arrived, he would have a new role, a beautiful and different one.

I met one of my best friends when I brought my three-year-old daughter to her first day of preschool. For me, it was a time of transition because I had just arrived in the neighborhood and had moved in to an apartment where I could not cook because the gas had not been turned on yet. Without knowing me, she invited me into her house, along with her two-year-old son and another friend with her little girl. That's how our story began. The warmth, love, and support that I felt at that time when everything was new for me was huge, and I give thanks for it. I have always taken in others and, at that time, I needed to be taken in. To this day, I remember it and cry from gratitude.

Eventually, we created a tribe, a community of parents with small children. Although we all were very different, we shared the upbringing of small children and the challenges that this entailed.

Parents need help, not just with the basic things, like preparing food or cleaning the house, but also with deeper aspects, such as learning to educate their children. It is important that our children receive love from different people in different ways, and when we open our living room, we allow our guests to come in with their love for us and for our children. In my experience, many of those guests are now part of the family. I have friends who are "sisters," "aunts," or "godmothers." By any name we want to give them, our guests are sources of love and learning for us and for our children.

I Don't Force You; You Don't Force Me

We already know that if we are going to welcome somebody, we should do it with an open heart. Preparing a special meal to offer, setting a beautiful table, fixing up the house, and dressing up to receive the person can be part of it, but if it's someone we trust and feel comfortable with, everything can be different. I have very close friends who I greet in my pj's and for whom I love making their favorite juice. I give them some cookies I've just discovered or share a cup of the delicious chai tea I invented years ago and that I still make to entertain.

When we expect company, it is good to prepare our children for it, telling them who is coming. That helps them feel comfortable more quickly when people they don't know arrive. It's also a good idea to ask our children who they would like for us to invite, and let everyone decide. And when we are the guests at another house, we can give our children ideas, such as taking something (for example, a drawing they made) to represent the gratitude and love we feel for those who open the doors of their house to us. This type of detail, along with some kind of food, dessert, or a small gift for the house, are valuable symbols of appreciation. Everything counts when it comes to giving of ourselves, both when we are hosting and when we are guests.

I recommend that when we're preparing for visitors, we should take care so that we don't exaggerate the importance to the point of causing stress. If I have to spend the day cleaning the house every time I'm having someone over, very soon I won't want to have guests again. At the beginning of my husband's and my relationship, we had a very different way of getting ready for guests. He liked to have everything scheduled, taken care of, and ready. I was always more informal but would worry more—and still do—about the flavor and presentation of the food than about the general appearance of the

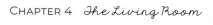

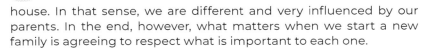

house. In that sense, we are different and very influenced by our parents. In the end, however, what matters when we start a new family is agreeing to respect what is important to each one.

Ever since I was a little girl—and many people have criticized me for this, including my family—I've never forced anyone to do anything. I don't force my kids to greet, say goodbye, or kiss anyone—family or not family—in any situation. This whole having-to-kiss-people thing bothered me so much as a girl that I decided not to do that to my kids. I will never forget how horrible it was for me to kiss my paternal grandmother, from whom I never got anything resembling affection. Each time I kissed her, I would see her warts and then feel how her thick hair would pinch my cheek or lips. It was unpleasant. I trust my children's intuition and sensitivity to greet people in one way or another, and I will let them do it however they want, without forcing them to do anything.

Not forcing anyone also means affording guests the opportunity to choose not to eat or drink something we offer them. If we see that they do not like something, that means we're getting to know them better, and the next time we invite them over we will offer something more in line with what they do like. On the other hand, if I want to suggest something, I will do it openly but without imposing. "Would you like to play cards? I know a super-fun game that might interest you." Or I might say, "Why don't we go to the balcony? It's a very nice time of day to see the park."

Maybe the most important aspect of *not forcing* is not forcing myself to adapt beyond my capabilities. For example, my body doesn't work well if I eat dinner too late, which is why, although it may not be normal for my guests, I tend to invite them to a tea that is a dinner at the same time. I know my habits, and the results have never been good when I've forced my body to do something that doesn't feel right, so I almost never do that now. It's the same with my kids: They have their rhythms and preferences when it comes to meals, and even when we have guests, I respect them.

To Have Fun, Share, and Enjoy

Having guests is the chance to connect with others, have fun, have a good time, and enjoy. For me, there is nothing better than a chat with a girlfriend without thinking about time, along with some tasty tea and listening to the kids playing in the background. I like talking to my guests a lot—getting to know them, seeing how they're doing, and hearing about their lives, passions, and interests. I'm amazed by everything I discover and how much it inspires my own life.

But many times I also prepare for a visit by having ideas for playing with dice, cards, or games like Charades. Sometimes I play music, and we dance; sometimes I hire a salsa instructor to make us all dance. To have fun with our guests, we can have ideas on what would be fun to do together and to create an ambiance that encourages having a good time. When proposing a game or activity, allow the mood to flow and perceive what's best for whom. Karaoke is also one of my favorites, and it's really fun for the kids; they often end up stealing the show. What's better than sharing the fun and games with them? The adults often want the kids to be entertained among themselves so that we can talk about "adult stuff." But there is a time for everything, and I think it's important to go with the flow in any situation. Sometimes the children want to present a show they put together or show us the lair they built. That's beautiful because we see how they created something out of nothing, with their imaginations and togetherness, and then share it with us.

Keep in mind the ages of the children who come to visit. If a two-year-old child comes to visit, and my daughter is at that five-year mark where she doesn't want any of her toys or dolls to be touched, then we'd better put them away before they are "in danger." Let's also invite our children to bring out other toys as they hide their favorites and encourage them to lend and share them while playing with other kids.

I love to have boxes of toys to bring out for each occasion, taking into account the ages of the kids who come over—I make the boxes by selecting toys appropriate for different ages—and at the same time, I offer them an ideal place to play with them. Not all areas are good for play; my bedroom once was destroyed after the kids built "subterranean lairs" in it. It's better to prevent situations that may be uncomfortable or put us in a bad mood, which takes the fun away for the kids and the adults. Defining what works and what doesn't is key; that's why I recommend doing it *before* the guests arrive.

One issue with children is electronic games. Parents often have different ideas about these toys. Some of us see them as a break for us, and it's true that sometimes they are a very effective "electronic pacifier." My idea is to not abuse this easy resource. Children have a lot of energy and imagination, and what they can accomplish when they get together with others is wonderful. The electronic pacifier can numb their energy and mine their creativity and imagination. When they play with tablets, possibly sitting next to each other but playing singly, it seems a waste of an excellent opportunity to form bonds and develop their creativity.

What happens when the guests bring the electronic device? It's very common for the guest's children to bring their tablets or electronic

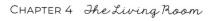

games. In those cases, I talk to the parents to see if they think it's better for us to encourage the kids to have fun without the electronics. If we don't agree, I tell my children that their guest will be busy for a while and available later. I don't think it's great, but I respect each parent's decision. My friends already know what I think about electronics and what my house culture is like, which is why they've often told their children not to use their phones or electronic games when they visit our house.

By handing our children the phone or tablet, we are passing on the message that they need something outside of themselves to have fun, which will make them dependent on somebody or something in order to feel good. In the future and in other environments, that may create people who are unsatisfied and incapable of being happy because they never discovered how to make themselves happy. It can sound extreme, but it's something I see already in some children and adolescents, and it breaks my heart with sadness.

Let's think twice before we resort to technology as a source of fun. There are so many fun alternatives. Teenagers, for example, can get hooked on building a tree house or a car with bearings with a dad who likes mechanical stuff. We can invite them to do something that will benefit others, like selecting toys and wrapping them as gifts to give to children with lesser means at Christmas, or doing arts and crafts to sell for a fund-raiser for a cause. Everything works to inspire our children, regardless of their ages, as long as they are doing something more than staring at a screen.

It is also a good idea for children to interact with other children of different ages. Some mothers and fathers look for children of the same age to play with their children because they think this will help the kids avoid getting frustrated. But life is not like that; there is wealth in diversity. We should make contact easy, not limit them. Younger kids love to stick with older kids who do super-interesting things. This allows the older ones to express their tenderness and their ability to take care of the younger ones. Of course we also should keep an eye out to avoid any abuse—verbal, social, physical, or sexual—from older kids to younger ones.

Grandparents—Those Special Guests

Because they are a very important part of our family and because there is a greater intimacy with them, a visit from the grandparents transcends the social space of the living room. Grandparents are like extensions of the parents, more relaxed and willing, in general, when they come to enjoy their grandchildren. The invitation to share with the grandparents is a very special one because the mere fact of coming in contact with them increases the love flow toward our children.

If you ask me to remember a moment in childhood when I felt eternally loved and could be myself, I would say, without giving it a second thought, that it was when I was in the company of my maternal grandparents. My grandmother's love was magical—her soft skin; the sensation of warmth and protection that I felt as I sank into her arms and chest; her baby-powder scent; her peaceful heart. It all would calm me. When my grandmother hugged me, nothing bad could happen to me. Just thinking about it even now makes me feel protected and loved. I've never stopped feeling that she loves me, even though she's no longer here, and that is something that has given me support in many difficult moments. With my grandparents, I could be myself. There were no rules about how to wear my hair or clothes—sometimes I wore sports pants and elegant shoes; I laugh just thinking about it. I could climb trees as high as I wanted to, hide wherever I fit, run, and jump. With them, I felt total freedom and as if I could go beyond the limits of my own imagination. If this could be the same experience and memory for our children with their grandparents, why not do everything in our power to encourage it?

When we become parents, we may clash with our own parents with regard to the way we raise our children. With love, they will want to give us advice, but we often see their advice as criticism. Instead of becoming closer to them, we want to distance ourselves so they don't impose their ideas and their own way to raise kids on us.

My parents, my mother-in-law, and I have big differences regarding how to raise my kids, but today, I listen to them more because I no longer feel threatened by their opinions, nor do I see it as criticism. Now I know that their opinions and recommendations are simply their way of loving. Moreover, the gratitude I feel for their presence with and commitment to their grandchildren is infinite.

For us as parents and for our children, grandparents are extremely valuable. Grandparents, for example, sometimes help with raising the children, and this is convenient, especially because they lend a hand when we don't have anyone to help us. That used to cause stress for me because I would feel that if I let the grandparents in too much, they would change everything, and I'd be giving them authority to criticize my way of parenting. On the other hand, if I didn't do it, then I would be missing out on their love and care, so I would debate between both scenarios. After three kids and after sometimes living thousands of miles away from the grandparents and other times living only two floors from them, I have a different perspective. Now I want to invite them over more often so that my children can incorporate these wonderful beings into their lives.

Grandparents are important because they lend us a hand in childrearing, but they are extremely important for various other reasons. For our son, his grandparents are *possessions*. In general, grandkids do whatever they want with their grandparents, and their possessions responds positively, reaffirming their self-esteem. It doesn't matter what the grandchild does; the grandparents will support him unconditionally because they have fewer expectations and projections about him than the parents do. The grandparents' expectations were already deposited in us, their children, and whether we met them or not doesn't matter anymore. Now they can enjoy children without this expectation. Moreover, grandchildren give grandparents the opportunity to heal and to parent once again without that stress that inhibits spontaneity and intuition in many parents. Grandparents have experience, but nobody is evaluating them. They are "weathered," and the comments of other people don't stop them from being who they are in essence—so much so that we may ask ourselves, "Why wasn't my father like that with me?" Maybe it's from that question that we find a third reason that grandparents are so important—they allow us to heal our relationship with our parents. With the passing of time and the lessons that both they and we have acquired, we can talk again about certain topics and arrive at new agreements. We especially can forgive mistakes and understand with love and compassion in order to build something new together.

My recommendation is for grandparents to share on their own (without the parents) with their grandchildren as much time as possible. The children will have their grandparents 100 percent available to them, and there won't be that competition that can arise between parents and grandparents. It's very good for them to have privacy to build their own relationships with their grandchildren. Without losing sight of this, when we are all together, we should be conscious of how we treat our parents and in-laws because our children see that.

My maternal grandmother didn't worry about how she dressed us or did our hair. I don't know why; maybe she simply dressed us with whatever she had at hand, or maybe she dressed us and combed our hair differently because she had a very different idea about beauty than my mom. Whenever my grandmother got me ready, I felt perfect and didn't feel the need to comb my hair or use tennis shoes instead of regular shoes when I wore sports clothes. I didn't care about that as long as I could play! While wearing dress shoes, I had fun sliding as if I were skating on my grandmother's tile floor. That happiness only lasted until I heard my mother criticize my grandmother for the way she dressed me and did my hair. For my mom, that was not okay. I wanted to defend my grandmother and tell her that I was happy, but I didn't. For some reason, I felt that my mom didn't accept the freedom I experienced in Grandma's house and that meant she also didn't accept my free and careless spirit. That's when I began to set that part of me aside and express it outside of the house, where I knew I wouldn't be criticized or excluded.

Even as an adult, I would not allow myself to express those characteristics that were so *me* because I felt it wasn't right or that I wouldn't be valued. But after some therapy, coaching, and working on myself, I let all of that go. Today I feel free again, as I am. I want my children to be who they are and for their grandparents to allow that and encourage it. My lesson learned from this experience is this: Don't criticize the grandparents in front of their grandchildren. That's like telling the kids that something of theirs that they love very much is not good and that will hurt them. It would make them think that their parents don't value that part of them that expresses itself naturally with their grandparents.

This logic may sound a bit convoluted, but think about it: What were your parents like with your grandparents? How did they behave? That determined their own experience with them. You likely will find things to emulate and other things to avoid. The sum of all those reflections and experiences is what makes inviting the grandparents to spend some time at your house so enriching and positive for all.

"Adopted" Family

Sometimes in the living room, we share so much and so intimately with people outside of the family that we end up establishing relationships with them of a familial nature. For example, I have friends that are "aunts" to my children.

With their love, culture, and ideas, these close friends enrich our family very much. We don't want only blood relatives for our children. In fact, there are instances when, even though there is unconditional love, we cannot find a way to relate well enough to blood relatives.

My parents had some friends my grandparents' age who became substitute grandparents to me. I still remember that couple; I felt they were like my grandparents. She would cook for me with love and welcome me with cozy embraces, while he would tell me stories that I loved from the Old Testament or *The Odyssey* and *The Iliad*. It was so interesting and fun for me to be with them. They were truly like second grandparents. I also had a "godmother grandmother," who was my mother's godmother. Besides my maternal grandmother, she was the "other grandmother" who was the closest to me. Thanks to her, I also got to know much more about my family, my mother's story, and my grandmother's story. It was like finding out where I

came from. It is so important to have someone to tell us about our own history!

Those friends we "adopt" who become uncles or aunts and grandparents expand our worldview and provide us other experiences of love. Our children can receive love in so many ways and surely will draw upon those memories and sensations when they need to do so later on. Providing our children different experiences than those that come from the family nucleus is a great act of love to offer them.

Ideas to Welcome Guests
with Love and Joy

In the living room, we discovered that to learn from others, we must have open hearts, be compassionate, and leave judgments aside. This is key to finding ourselves as part of community and feeling like we are part of something bigger that supports us in the task of being parents. Finally, we saw the importance of including the grandparents in our family so that we and our kids have more opportunities to receive love in different ways and to learn to give it that way as well.

Throughout this chapter I told you how much I like to entertain those who come to my house and how much I enjoy sharing and having fun with my guests.

Here are ideas you can put into practice or that might inspire you so you also can have the best experience with your guests.

Ideas for Adults-Only Gatherings

- Guests often want to bring something to a gathering, so allow them to do so. One can bring drinks; another can bring the dessert or something to go with the coffee. ;

- Suggest board games, and play in teams. These can be card or dice games or team games like Charades. Scrabble or Pictionary also are good choices. A deck of cards or some dice will offer a variety of possibilities for fun.

- Prepare surprises, like inviting a salsa instructor, or have karaoke installed and ready to start the show. It's also a lot of fun to have a dance competition. Put "Just Dance" on YouTube and do the choreography. The idea is to have fun, and you'll surely laugh at yourselves too!

Ideas for Gatherings with Adults and Children

- Everyone needs his own space and way of interacting. Children generally don't enjoy our long conversations about topics they don't understand. Allow them their space. If you want them to eat with the adults, include them in the topic of conversation and then let them go play.

- Don't expect children to behave like adults—they *aren't* adults and don't have to be so. Suggest board games, costumes, dolls, Legos, cars, or balls, depending on their age. It's a good idea to have these games ready before the guests arrive.

- Respect schedules. Children have a limited time to be awake, especially at night, and even more so if they are young. To force them to stay awake, although it may seem like they are having fun, possibly will disrupt their sleep cycle and their routine for the following day.

- If there are many small children at the gathering, it's a good idea to have a slightly older cousin or friend (or a babysitter) who will suggest games and can care for them while the adults chat or play their own games. All of this depends on how you want to experience the gathering. Ask your guests ahead of time so you can prepare the right context.

Ideas for Children-Only Gatherings (When Your Children Are Inviting)

- Small children sometimes don't tell you that they miss their moms or that they feel bad. Help them feel at ease in your house. Show them where the rooms are, especially the bathrooms, and where the adults will be and who you are so you can assist them when they need it. They need to know that they can ask you to call their parents if they want you to.

- Prepare your children for the visit by thinking about which toys or games they will share with their friends. If there are games they do not want to share, it is better to not have them available so there is no conflict. The more you prepare your kids, the more confidence and enjoyment they will have.

- Do something fun with them. Make cookies together, paint with watercolors or crayons, or play with Play-Doh, clay, or colored dough.

MY NOTES

....
....
....
....
....
....
....
....
....
....
....
....
....
....

CHAPTER 5

The Cleaning Room

5

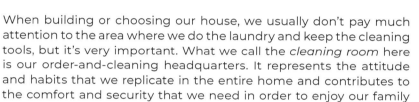

The Cleaning Room

When building or choosing our house, we usually don't pay much attention to the area where we do the laundry and keep the cleaning tools, but it's very important. What we call the *cleaning room* here is our order-and-cleaning headquarters. It represents the attitude and habits that we replicate in the entire home and contributes to the comfort and security that we need in order to enjoy our family life in harmony.

Cleaning tasks and habits are very important because they denote an internal order that allows children to learn and grow, feeling secure. They live in constant surprise in the world and discover it every day, but while they grow, they also perceive expected dynamics that provide them security, such as bathing in the morning or at a certain time in the evening, eating on a particular schedule, reading a book before bedtime, or knowing that they will find their cars in the blue drawer and their building blocks in the yellow one.

Let's walk through issues like cleaning, collaboration in the home, order as an element that benefits learning, and the people outside the family who help us in domestic chores. All are key issues for us to enjoy and learn together.

Five Reasons to Promote Order and Cleanliness

When I was a kid, my mom would be after me, saying, "When you get home from school, take off your uniform, and hang it up so it doesn't get dirty," or "Don't leave everything all over the floor." These and many other instructions formed habits in me. Years later, these cleaning habits helped avoid arguments with my husband. Even though each of us had a different idea of what "clean" and "orderly" meant, both of us agreed that maintaining cleanliness and order habits would prevent our losing the house key or domestic accidents from shoes left in the middle of the floor.

I recently recalled some of the great advantages to order and cleanliness:

1. *Keeping order keeps us in order* and invites us to begin and to be in movement, creating and building. Many of us associate disarray with laziness, and it can make us lose motivation.

2. *All of us want to feel welcome*, and order invites us to be welcome and to share, instead of our wanting to take off running in the face of chaos.

3. *Order prevents arguments* because we know where things are, adults and children won't fight over who left what where.

4. *Order saves us time and money* because it allows us to find everything quickly. We know what we have and what we don't, and in this way, we avoid buying something that we already had.

5. *Order helps us prevent accidents*. In the kitchen, for example, we keep cutting tools in places that are inaccessible to children. We also can easily identify when some food is expired. Additionally, order prevents us from tripping over things on the floor and hurting ourselves

Order as a Way to Learn

An orderly, clean space is a safer space to live in because it prevents accidents. When everything is in its place, we don't waste time looking for utensils or tools to cook or fix something in the house. This is especially important for children because the house is also like a school; it's where they learn everything from the sound certain objects make when they touch, hit, or drop them to the shapes and sizes and even language itself. Before a child understands the concept of numbers, he must make associations like big/small, near/far, inside/outside, now/later, and high/low and to distinguish between series and patterns.[3] He can learn all of that and make discoveries in the different environments of the house. Keeping objects in order or, better yet, tidying them up along with the kids, allows us to fill the home with stimuli for learning.

For example, we can organize two groups of objects in front of our kids. Each group must have the same number of objects. One group will have small objects very close to one another (small paper balls,

---

[3] You can learn more about this at http://www.scholastic.com/teachers/articles/teaching-content/early-math-how-children-learn-about-numbers.

bottle tops, corks, or buttons), and the other group will have bigger objects that are farther away from each other (tennis or soccer balls, shoes, or pillows). When the child has looked at them, ask him which group has more objects. If the child chooses the group of bigger objects, you will know that he can differentiate between proportions but not the concept of numbers yet. We can continue to stimulate him, little by little, without pressuring him, with games in which he learns to organize, compare, and categorize.

We used to think that we could teach counting by repeating and memorizing, but actually that is not enough. There are more creative options for counting using our own houses, its spaces, and its objects as a fun "learning lab."

Order gives us clarity to think, learn, decide, and relate to ourselves and others. There is a saying that goes, "As it is on the outside, so it is on the inside." Sometimes it's enough to put our own physical space in order to also achieve mental and emotional order.

Cleanliness That Renews and Brings Abundance

Our house is the special place where we can spend an enjoyable time. When our spaces are clean, they give us ideas for something new. And who doesn't like to try something new? We can get used to different cleanliness standards, according to the place we find ourselves in and according to our financial capacity and our time availability. If it's summer, and I'm on vacation in a beach apartment, I won't expect the floor to be impeccable. I will even tolerate there being sand in certain areas at certain times of the day. In the afternoon, however, when we all return from the beach, take showers, and put on clean clothes, I want the area to be clean and renewed so we can be in tune with the sensation of cleanliness that we have in our bodies and spirits.

Cleaning ourselves has to do with renewing ourselves, with taking out what no longer serves us and creating space for the new. When we clean the house—and more so when we take out what we no longer use and what is broken or very old—we are making space to create and live different experiences that provide new moments of enjoyment and learning as a family. This helps both adults and kids to leave behind what isn't useful anymore and what we've moved beyond in order to welcome something new and different.

For little children, the task of donating their toys to other kids can be terrible. They require a certain emotional maturity to detach from those things that, although they don't use them anymore, they enjoyed very much in the past. I used to do a toy purge when my kids were not at home. I would leave the toys that I considered appropriate for their ages and that contributed to their learning. (I must admit that the noisy toys were the first to go.) I also looked to see which were broken and which were worth repairing to keep at home. I would donate the toys in good shape that my kids no longer used and would throw out the damaged ones as well as those that I considered would not be useful to my children or any other child.

Donating toys has always been very important to me. As my children grew up, I told them about other kids who didn't have many toys and how nice it would be to give something from all the things they had. Little by little, they started to tell me on their own that they wanted to give some of their things as gifts. My older daughter often chose one of her toys to give as a birthday present to a friend of hers. She would wrap it herself and put a card on it, even if I had already bought another gift. I thought it was lovely and generous of my daughter to give both gifts. When children are very young, they can regret giving away a toy after they've done it, so it's best to help them understand the full meaning of giving a gift.

To free up and give space to the new, I live in constant review, donation, and reorganization, not just the toys but also furniture, decorations, utensils, and clothes. To me, it is important that if something new comes in, something else goes out. If I buy myself a pair of jeans or a pair of shoes, then I give another away. Not all my friends, especially not the ones who love shoes, agree with this. Some of them have surprised me by giving me, for no reason, things that I had not asked them for but that were very useful to me. Getting rid of something generates a void that will then be filled with something else, material or immaterial, whether we seek it or not.

The idea of cleaning and letting go of what we no longer use is not only an issue of order; it has to do with the concepts of *flowing* and *abundance*. In nature, everything flows, is transformed, and changes constantly. The same happens in our bodies, and when something doesn't flow well, we become ill. It also happens with things—what doesn't move, gets stuck and rots. Abundance is believing we will always have what we need in order to be well. Because of that, we will not be able to have abundance if we do not let go of our material attachments.

Life has confirmed to me, time and again, that when I give, I receive, and when I let go, new things arrive.

Cleaning the house and taking out whatever is no longer useful or is in excess allows us to create a flow of abundance, enriching our lives and those of our children.

We Are All Responsible

Our children must know that we are all responsible for our physical spaces, our things, our clothes, and our toys, and that we all should care for them.

Children see parents as models; each of our attitudes becomes a reference for what is or isn't acceptable to them. If they see that we leave clothes on the floor, we will hardly be able to ask them to pick up their own clothes and put them in the dirty clothes bag. We also won't be able to ask them not to throw trash if they see us committing that act, such as throwing a receipt from the tollbooth out the window. Our actions carry messages. If we put our things away but make a mess of the newspaper in the living room, we send the message "I only care about what is mine. I don't care about what is shared." It shouldn't surprise us, then, if someday we see our child stepping on his brother's toys while he takes care of his own.

If children see that we wipe the bathtub dry when we get out of the shower, put the cap back on the toothpaste, close drawers after taking something out, and pick up our dishes after we finish eating, then they will do the same. This has two great benefits: (1) If we all collaborate, it will be easier to keep order and cleanliness, and (2) we are teaching our children that all things are valuable and that taking care of them is a way to honor and show gratitude for having them. They can learn values like solidarity and commitment to the community.

It's better to arrange the toys together while singing a song, instead of running after the children, reprimanding them, and, in the end, picking up everything by ourselves, which almost certainly will make us tired and angry and affect our availability for our children.

I know I'm not the most industrious of women—far from it. It is precisely because of this that I seek everyone's help, including that of my children. I try to be as practical as possible, creating environments with few things, having only elements that are easy to clean, and keeping them organized and put away to avoid getting them dirty. With respect to clothing, for example, I buy the kind that doesn't require ironing or hand-washing and that, ideally, is inexpensive so I don't stress if it gets ruined. I apply this standard to myself and to the children.

It is key to take care of our things and ourselves because everything that we have is the consequence of an action and effort that we must honor. Before six or eight years of age, our children can't completely understand that most of the people in the world are extremely poor and that, unlike us, they don't have a house or clothes, and they can't eat whenever they are hungry. Being able to have time, education, and money to buy a book and read it is a privilege. If our children understand that what they have is, to a large degree, their parents' (or grandparents') work, they will learn to appreciate and to take care of what they gave. Again, this is not something they will understand with a speech from us. We need to teach them to share and care for things by being the example, through our own actions.

People Who Work and Live with Us

Some of us get help with household chores from domestic workers, who take care of cleaning, washing and ironing clothes, cooking, tidying up, and even taking care of our children. The biggest reason to count on their service is that they lighten the load and allow us to concentrate more of our energies on enjoying our partner and our children and, in time, on working and achieving professional fulfillment. It's important for each family to know the reasons and objectives in hiring someone to help with the house. What type of help do you expect, and what are you willing to give in order to get that benefit?

During the time that he or she is at our house, that person will be part of our family. Whether she comes only a couple of days a week to clean or she lives at our house, it is important for us to accept domestic workers as a part of the family system. They interact with us and our children and that means that we will form bonds with them; there even will be a sense of belonging. Many of the maids, nannies, and gardeners that have been at my home have taken pride in working with my family and have felt part of something special. This has always been very reassuring for us and has shown us that they have not arrived at our house with the simple intention of finding a job but also with the intention of feeling good as people, offering us their virtues, and creating bonds of solidarity and respect with us.

The benefits of outside help go beyond house chores. It's about a human being who, while feeling good in our family nucleus, will share all her being with us, her experience, and her gifts for enriching all our lives. A maid brings a lot of learning and well-being to the family. She brings her dreams, her needs, and her virtues. If we welcome her with love, she will share the best of herself with all of us.

I have lived with wonderful people from whom I have learned much, and I am happy that my children are exposed to other ways of seeing life. They see people with talents that I don't have, and they receive affection from people other than the members of the family nucleus. When I've left my children in someone's care, I've always known that

Denise Dziwak

that person will give all she can to care for them, as if they were her own children, and that is something that is only possible with love.

In this dynamic we get emotional benefits, but there are also costs (nonfinancial) to take into account. A very common one is that we lose a bit of family privacy. It's up to us how much privacy we allow ourselves to lose. When starting the relationship with the maid or nanny, it's good to explain how the daily routine will be and where and when we will need her. We will also set schedules for work and for being in certain family environments.

It's always important to talk with this new person, asking her what she likes to do in her free time, what she feels is missing from her life, how she envisions work at our house, and what her experience has been with other families. That way, we can think about how to help her channel those wishes by inviting her to do concrete and productive activities in her free time or breaks. Neither employer nor employee wants her to be sitting in the living room, bored, watching TV or cooped up in a room. It's best to have these conversations alone, without the kids, because the worker may bring up topics that children don't understand or that can affect them. Every boundary implies an order of times, topics and places that we, as parents, will have to establish so that all of us who live together have more enjoyment.

We must also invest time and energy in this person's training and qualifications. This process will allow us to create a relationship with her and, in time, let her see what we want her to do and what we expect from her. I'm not just referring to specific tasks, such as keeping the kitchen clean, but also to emotional aspects, such as the way in which she treats our children. This is just as important as cultivating respect and consideration in our children. I've seen cases where the children mistreat the maids, demanding things without respect, for example. Part of our roles as parents is to set the limits for what we believe to be good for all. It is also good to give the maid certain authority so that she can set limits and for the children to recognize and accept them.

When I often hear about conflict in the relationship with the maids, it has to do with boundaries. When we feel that limits or boundaries are becoming blurry, it's important to mark the playing field well. If we don't like something the maid did or said, it's best to talk with her and to share our reasoning and what we expect to change or happen in the future in similar situations. It's important to know on which points we agree and which we don't. If there are points that are very important to us but not for the maid, then there won't be a lot to negotiate. I use the same communication and negotiation principles with a maid that I use in my job or with my husband.

Differences may also arise regarding the maid's or nanny's treatment of our children. We once had a babysitter who lied to my two-year-old son to prevent him from having a tantrum or getting upset. She told what we would call "white lies," such as saying, "There is no more cereal," when there was, but it was not time to eat, or saying, "Your mom is not here," when actually I was but was busy working. I didn't like this, and I decided to talk with her to understand the reason behind her little lies. Then I explained to her that I had two important elements for raising my children: (1) Boundaries are for taking care of people, and (2) it's good to express all emotions, even the more uncomfortable ones, such as anger and sadness.

The babysitter understood and was also surprised to later discover that my son's tantrums would dissipate shortly after telling him the truth. She discovered that a child can learn a lot when expressing his emotions in front of an adult who can accept him and offer him her affection at the same time.

I am used to living with a domestic worker, as I have done since childhood. My parents taught me to treat this lady who worked at our home with humility, respect, and admiration. They were my example regarding how to treat her and integrate her into the family. As an adult, that has allowed me to value this help and at the same time has taught me to foster relationships built on respect and mutual affection. In my childhood, the maid was responsible for keeping the house clean, cooking, and washing and ironing the clothes, but she also had a role that was not explicit—to be company for us, to play and have fun with my sister and me when we were still little.

Additionally, I saw how my mom would help her with her chores at times and how she taught her many things, listened to her like a friend, and was even on top of her material needs. She also would often bring some small gift for her or her family.

This was my model, and, with gratitude for my parents, I see that it is still the best possible one. Before I had my children, a maid would come to my house once or twice a week, and although the emotional bond and the time I shared with her was not a lot, I always sought closeness with that person and tried to understand and satisfy her needs, as well as offer her all I could in terms of teaching, clothing donations, things for her house, or simply an ear to listen. Then, when I had children, another maid came to live with us, and since then, my experiences with them has always been very positive. As if they were angel-sent, people have come into our lives who have supported us in a wonderful way and have helped us maintain our family's well-being. When it came time to go, many of them left transformed and grateful to our family. I still keep in touch with them, and although their leaving saddened me, it also made me happy because their lives were transformed for the better and to greater well-being. Some of them even left to start and enjoy their own families.

Of course, there have been relationships that did not work out, but that is also fine because everything has been useful in learning and growing in love and awareness.

If it is within financial possibility, domestic help can be a great relief. I know many mothers who stop working to devote their time to the kids, which means less income and a possible reason for not hiring a maid or a nanny. Sometimes this works very well because the mother enjoys and feels good doing all the chores or sharing them with her husband. But I've also heard cases in which parents in these circumstances feel frustrated, angry, tired, and powerless. In this case, the healthy thing to do is to ask what they would like; maybe they can reroute and adjust their decisions to the way they are. Sometimes it can be better to spend less time with the kids but know that these hours will be higher quality and give them more attention, instead of spending all day tired, frustrated, or depressed due to their lifestyle.

The key here is to know ourselves and to monitor our decisions so we can reroute whenever we need to. If we choose with awareness, we will never regret, and if we make a mistake or if something doesn't work, we know that we can choose again as many times as we need to do.

Taking Action: Wellness Test

We have seen how order and cleanliness are necessary for us to feel good with our physical environment and how this contributes to encouraging a space of fun and learning. We've also discussed how all of us are responsible for taking care of our space and how a clean and orderly place allows us to enjoy and learn more. To clean doesn't just mean to dust but to renew ourselves and to let things flow without attachments or accumulation to the point that energy and abundance stagnate. We let it flow instead. We explored the concept of domestic help and how we can design our lives to maximize our well-being. We know that the people who help us will become part of our family system and, therefore, are part of our responsibility. All of this together allows us to build and strengthen our family, with values such as respect, collaboration, solidarity, gratitude, and commitment as a foundation.

I invite you to take the following test that will allow you to identify if your physical space and the things that make it up contribute to your family well-being and what to do to improve it.

Rate each of the following phrases from 1 to 5, with 1 being very much disagree, 2—disagree, 3—agree a little, 4—agree, 5—totally agree.

1. My house is so tidy that I can find everything easily, from scissors to any of my children's toys.

2. I feel like enjoying my house when I am alone as well as when I am in the company of friends and family. Each environment offers me a space of pleasure and enjoyment.

3. My house is safe, especially for my children, and in it everything can become a great world of learning.

4. I am very pleased with the cleanliness of my house and things, and it doesn't take much effort to keep it this way.

5. There is space in my house; things flow; they come in and go out without stagnating. I don't accumulate things.

6. Everyone at home collaborates in the tidiness and cleanliness to the extent of our capabilities.

7. I have the domestic help I need, and that allows me to live more at peace and to enjoy more. If I don't have it, it's because I choose not to have it and to prioritize other aspects (financial, for example).

8. (Answer only if you have domestic help.) I have a relationship based on respect and affection with the person who works at my home. I am satisfied with her contributions.

Based on your score, reflect and respond:

What's working well?

....
....
....
....
....
....

What could be improved?

....
....
....
....
....
....

What will you do to improve it?

....
....
....
....
....
....

How and when will you do it? (Make a plan with deadlines and execute it.)

. . . .

. . . .

. . . .

. . . .

. . . .

. . . .

MY NOTES

. . . .

. . . .

. . . .

. . . .

. . . .

. . . .

. . . .

. . . .

. . . .

. . . .

. . . .

. . . .

CHAPTER 6

The Bedrooms

6

The Bedrooms

In the bedrooms of the house we can play, learn, rest, pamper each other, and be in touch with ourselves and the people closest to us. This is where we get comfortable, where we are barefoot or in pajamas, where we drop on the bed and read or to the floor and play. Because of this, we only bring our most trusted people to the bedrooms, because we are inviting them to a more intimate and special place. The bedrooms also represent that essential place inside of us where we build the confidence and self-esteem that make us feel valuable and loved.

Secure Attachment for Our Children

In the privacy of the bedroom, we can build strong bonds of love with our children, which will help them during infancy and will prepare them for their adult lives. When I talk about attachment, I'm referring to the *need* to feel connected to another human being. I say *need* because I believe human beings were not born to live in solitude. We require bonds in order to enjoy our lives most fully and to be happy. Here it is important to note that children *depend* on bonds of love in order to grow with integrity and fulfillment, while adults no longer strictly *need* those bonds, although we do enjoy them, and they enrich our lives.

So that we know in more detail what our children need and how to build ways of loving, let me tell you a bit about psychologists John Bowlby and Mary Ainsworth's attachment theory. According to them, children experience four possible types of attachment. *Secure attachment* is where the child knows his mom will be there for him when he needs her, even if she is not with him all the time. *Anxious attachment* is where a child thinks his mom will leave and won't return, and he will lose her. Therefore, he pays a lot of attention to her, and when he "feels" that his mom is about to go, he becomes anxious, scared, and wants to possess and keep her. *Avoidant attachment* is where the child feels his mom is not there. Therefore, he decides to distance himself because he believes that his mom's unavailable presence is more painful that her absence. Finally, there is *disorganized attachment*, which sometimes is the anxious kind and sometimes the avoidant kind, which makes the child feel constantly insecure. This isn't necessarily the biological mother but the *mother figure*, which can be the father, the grandmother, caretaker, or whoever has had the strongest bond with the child since birth.

Attachment is not only built in childhood but throughout life, which is a positive thing because we can renew our relationships with the children and keep supporting them that way. Many times adults experience insecure or avoidant attachment, which makes us feel empty or anxious when there is no longer a father or mother who can help us. That's why it is important for us adults to also build that bond of love and support with ourselves at the same time that we learn to do it with our children.

The mere fact of sitting down on the floor to play with our children opens a door for them to invite us to do more things with them. Kids observe our reactions to what they do and will surely share and tell us what is happening in their lives outside of the home. In this case, for example, we will favor secure attachment. Moments and situations like these are very valuable opportunities to get to know more about our kids, to understand what they need, and to help them learn what they require in order to achieve whatever they need.

When my older daughter was around three or four years old, she showed insecure attachment behaviors, and that led us to understand that she needed to feel more trust in my love and more physical contact, in addition to words, in moments of crisis, so that her anxiety and fear would not increase, and she would build greater inner confidence instead. Although I sometimes notice that she is more vulnerable than her siblings, after years of being present in the way that she needed me to be, she built her self-esteem and confidence, which now allows her to endure moments of anxiety, fear, or loneliness much better, even when I am absent.

Following are some ideas to build secure attachment with our children:

- Above all, listen to them.

  Carl Rogers, psychologist and creator of person-centered therapy, said, "One of the experiences that transform a person the most is feeling heard, seen and perceived completely without judgement or reservation."[4] This is especially evident in our children. We need to know how they feel and to know them just as they are, not as *we want them to be*. This had been important since birth. Each child has his own way of communicating; each one emits his own signs, and parents can interpret these signs by paying attention and listening to them. Children also change, which is why it's good for us to keep observing how they transform with each learning. Each child will require something different from us, and that is exactly what we will need to hear with greater attention.

My older daughter wants exclusive time with me; she wants to play or do arts and crafts while she tells me what is going on with her friends at school. My other daughter asks me for patience and compassion; she wants us to run around the park together, to laugh, dance, and sing out loud and for me to value how she is. My son asks physical contact from me, to enjoy music with him or play ball and for me to follow him in his games (in his own way) and to value our time together 100 percent and without interruptions.

- Give them quality time without interruptions.

There's an Argentine children's song by María Elena Walsh that says:

I want time but time unhurried,
Play time, which is the best.
Please give it to me loose,
And not locked inside an alarm clock.

Quality time—that's what our children need. It's not necessarily about dedicating eight hours a day; it can even be forty minutes, but they must be precious minutes. The time we spend alone with them should not have adult rules; it should be a time when we are totally available for them and for whatever they want to do with us. When kids feel that they have all our attention and time, their self-esteem increases because they know that they are important and valuable. We can find that moment of quality time in the bedrooms. It can be painting, playing ball, playing with little cars, working puzzles, reading storybooks, playing with dough, putting on costumes, making bracelets, or even helping them with their homework—that is, without pressure, impatience, or too many rules. Let's leave those adult structures out of this space, and try to be as light as they are and curious as to what can emerge by being alone with them.

---

[4] Carl Rogers and Richard E. Farson, *Active Listening* (Chicago: University of Chicago, 1957).

- Support them and offer them options and resources so they can open up and experience the world, developing all their gifts.

One of the most important tasks we have as parents is to offer our children the world, to invite them to play and to explore it so they can see what excites them the most, what challenges them, and where they can develop their gifts. If we are with them, looking out for them, and keeping them company, they will feel more confident to venture out and try. Just as important is to be with them when they get frustrated and to encourage them to try again, without pressure or judgment.

My daughter Sofia loves music, but when she was four years old, she was embarrassed in front of other kids in violin class. Seeing what was happening, my husband and I would take in turns in going with her, sitting down beside her and the other kids, and taking the class like any other kid so she would feel secure and have fun as she tried.

There will also be other activities that at first will be fascinating to them, but then they will get tired and want to do something else. Let's allow them to change activities so they don't get bored, but let's also take care that the reason they change the activity is not that they got frustrated with trying to do something. Let's also make sure that the toys or activities are age-appropriate, so that we don't require them to do something that is beyond their capabilities. For example, we can help them, without their noticing, to build that puzzle that is hard for them, so they will gain confidence and learn to do it on their own. We can also let them win when we play board games, as these small wins give them confidence and will also help them later to know how to lose. All of this is like teaching them to ride a bike: We hold them until they no longer need us, and they discover that they can do it on their own. All new things will be like that, and they will need us more or fewer times, according to the child and the activity.

- Share activities that we also like with them. Let's not force ourselves because they will notice.

This is a lesson I learned, paradoxically, by force. I tried to play dolls with my daughter, but this was extremely boring to me, and I would start to yawn while thinking about what I would do when the game finally was over. Of course, my daughter would notice and feel like I wasn't really playing with her or doing what she wanted, which made her sad and upset. Only when I accepted that playing dolls was boring for me was I able to suggest other options to her or to transform that game into something that I would also like, such as taking the doll to the park for a stroll.

Children can read between the lines and even if we try to cover it up, they will notice how we play with them—if we are excited and having fun or if we can't wait until their game is over. The latter can make them feel less valuable because they will associate our annoyance with their person, when, in reality, we chose to play the game badly. Let's choose carefully, respecting not just their preferences but also ours so that we can maximize fun for all.

In the face of an anxiety or fear situation, a child who has developed a secure attachment style will be capable of calming himself, listening to himself, honoring himself, and taking care of himself. If he feels loved, the child can take care of himself and will grow with self-esteem and confidence. His vital security is that he will never lack love, and if he feels that that love is there, the pain, frustration, or challenge he faces won't matter as much, and everything will be all right. That absolute confidence in well-being beyond the experience allows us to express ourselves freely as adults, manifesting all our being without fear and giving ourselves the chance to flourish.

Helping kids to develop secure attachment, to feel confident in themselves and with greater self-esteem, is the biggest gift that we can bestow on our children.

Learning and Education at Home

Bedrooms are also the places where our children learn. In each action, they are learning and playing at the same time. When they are babies, they repeat the same action time and again; when they are a bit older, they build Legos, dismantle them, and build them again. In the bedroom they reinforce knowledge acquired in school (by doing homework, for example), and it is there that parents have the opportunity to support their outside learning at home. With this, however, we must be careful not to force or demand too much. Instead, we must help them develop the abilities they need in order to learn.

It is key, for example, that children understand what a responsibility is and what it means to commit to something, respect it, and honor it. The commitment can be represented by homework or picking up toys after playing. Commitments that are respected and assumed consciously help us build trust in each other. Likewise, we can help them so they can achieve what they want (homework, games, or activities like soccer or ballet).

At our house, my older daughter often was stressed because she thought she wouldn't get to her ballet class on time. We understood together that we had to prevent that from happening again, and the first agreement we made was to define the time to leave the house. We set an alarm clock to alert us when it was time to get dressed for her class. But that was not enough because I was not always available to do her hair, which she would take a lot of time to do. Additionally, it never failed that just as we were about to leave the house, she would realize that she was hungry or thirsty, but she wouldn't have time to eat or drink anything for at least two hours. We desperately would run to prepare something for her to eat on the way. I would suffer, thinking that the food would get her all choked up when she did her ballet workout. There were the tears, screams, and anguish that not getting there on time would generate for her, and the sum of all of those emotions ended up getting to me too. And to think that all of this was perfectly avoidable with just a bit of planning and organization!

How freeing it was when we gave her her own watch, and she was able to keep track of time herself instead of depending on me for everything. We also made a list of all aspects to check, including if I would be home to do her hair that day. All of that gave her confidence and peace. Of course, there were days when that anxiety and those tears ended with her saying, "I don't want to go to ballet."

In those instances, with firm love and a hug, I would say, "I understand you're upset and that you would have liked to do everything differently. Still, you're going to your class, and the next time we will do it differently. I will go with you." Hand in mine, she'd be on her way, at first with a little anguish and then calm, seeing she wasn't alone. Accepting a mistake, overcoming the upsetting consequences, and taking charge of changing the future are key aspects. Supporting our children in their learning is part of our job as parents.

School and Homework

It's the same with what they learn at school; sometimes we will have to give them support by reinforcing activities at home, such as helping them incorporate number concepts by giving them organizing and classifying tasks. Here, again, the idea is *not to demand* but simply offer them a space to develop new abilities.

The same goes with homework. Many families stress and suffer together. There are kids who, although they are very capable in math, are not aware of time or how to get organized to do homework at a certain time. In that case, we must accompany them and help them learn to organize their time to do it before it's too late. It may be that other children are not that capable in math, and in that case, it will take more time and patience on our part, as well as helping them to do the exercises, for them to understand. What parents are called to do depends on each child—the ease or complexity of each subject for him and his capacity to do the homework in the way the school demands and on time.

Realize that our roles as parents is to help children acquire abilities that they need to learn, which is very different from teaching them math or literature—that's what school is for. We can help them get organized, remind them that they have homework to do, and keep tabs and be available for them if they need our help. We can even give them ideas or make suggestions at the time they are doing their homework, but always let them lead the activity (never us). Additionally, this will create an excellent opportunity to tell them about our own experience with homework or with certain subjects when we were their age. If we tell them that a certain subject was hard for us, they might sigh in relief and realize that they don't need to be perfect.

Let's tell them about how we felt that day we went to class without having done our homework, what happened, and what we would do if we could relive that situation.

When I was nine or ten years old, I could not do a certain homework assignment, which was to draw something related to *Don Quixote*. When I told my mom about my frustration, she took my pencil and notebook and created a drawing that looked to me as if had been done by a professional artist. I was shocked and surprised, but I also felt that I was not enough because I would never be able to draw like her. Instead of freeing me or helping me, that put more pressure on me because it was very clear that the teacher would know that I did not draw it. How would I explain that I hadn't been able to do the homework and that my mom had done it for me? I remember the sadness and disappointment in myself that this caused me. At the time I didn't know what to do, but now I understand that I needed for my mom to accompany me in my frustration and help me draw without caring about the result. I needed her to help me know that I was valuable and that, regardless of the result, the important thing was to try and to learn in the process. I needed her to do anything except draw it for me. I know that all she only wanted to help me, but the result was worse. For many years, I believed that I could not draw until, as an adult, I discovered that I had my mother's gift of drawing and art.

We parents have the opportunity to support our children in the same way that we would have wanted to get support from our own parents. My parents were demanding when it came to academics. I received few compliments for successes but many criticisms for failures. Getting a grade of eight out of ten was bad for them. I experienced things from threats to send me to a school for "dummies" if I didn't study and get good grades, to the questions, "Why not a ten?" or "And how did the rest of the kids do?" After that, and after having been exposed to new ways of educating and loving, I learned to support my children in a different way.

Some ideas to support our children with love are as follows:

- My child is valuable and doesn't have to show me that he is.

  My child doesn't have to be the best at math, soccer, or anything. I love and value him. I know that he will have a place in the world, even if it's an effort for him to learn a second language, math, or geometry. My child already has all the wisdom and internal capacity that he needs. Learning experiences are there so that he can manifest them and bring them to life. He is not an empty glass ready to be filled with knowledge; he has within him a whole knowledge that is ready to be awakened under the right stimuli. I want to help him to learn, and I want him to learn much more than concepts. I want to teach him how to hold the pencil instead of drawing for him.

- I respect my child's learning preferences and timing.

  I value that my child has his own timing and virtues. Some may awaken before others, but that doesn't mean I will focus on what is missing. I will support him in everything, especially stimulating his strengths. There are children who learn to count at the park by counting little branches or leaves; others prefer using colored blocks. It's all good.

- The best lesson I can offer my child is experience and a compassionate look of acceptance that will tell him that I believe in his potential.

  The most important thing is for my child to understand that I love him and value him beyond anything he may do. I have enough patience and love to understand that some things will be hard for him. When he feels powerless for not achieving something, I will be there to value his effort and to make him see that it's okay to fail and to try again as many times as he needs. If I am present in a compassionate way and motivate him, that helplessness can transform into optimism and confidence instead of turning into sadness, frustration, and anger.

- I understand that the best way to learn is by playing and making things interesting and fun, and that will be my focus in helping him.

  When my children tell me what they are learning in school, I curiously look for other references to support their lesson—books, videos, or doing some activity that relates to it.

When we give our children our unconditional support and nurture their learning experiences, they will want to undertake their own homework and projects.

This generated a pleasant surprise for me: When my daughter Valentina was eight years old, she took a physical education class in school that sought to generate empathy with people with physical handicaps. A week later, while on vacation, she collected funds to buy wheelchairs for poor people. She learned how to use PowerPoint and created works of art, and she gathered art from other children and used them for an auction. She sold them all. Moreover, Sofia, at barely four years of age, asked me to "work" at home; that is, to play number blocks with her, paint and draw, or read books to her dolls. And Juan Francisco, at two years old, would suggest we sing his daycare songs together and for me to put a costume on him and start the music. Each one asked to keep experimenting, learning, and unfolding his or her potential. They are wonderful initiatives that I alone would not have been able to suggest.

To learn in this way really generates a connection with our children that many times happens in the intimacy of the bedrooms, where we can contribute a lot to their self-esteem and confidence. Additionally, for us adults, it will be healing to relive those learning experiences from another point of view. My daughter gave me math lessons, and that's how I realized I'd always liked it and that it was fun to solve a math problem in a creative way, seeking the best strategy when we only know addition and subtraction.

Extra Support

In some instances, our children require more support than we know how to give them, and we must consider seeking someone who can help with specific situations. This might be game therapy to overcome emotional problems, like anguish, frustration, anxiety, fear, or anger; problems relating to others; or tutoring in math, French, or any other subject.

In our case, we discovered that we needed to help Valentina develop emotional intelligence, so we turned to a therapist who could help her unblock her contained emotions and manage them instead of holding them in. It's also something that helps us parents support her in her emotional learning, and we keep learning along with her.

It is good to seek outside help but without overreaching. Sometimes when faced with their children's learning inconveniences, parents immediately turn to therapies and school support, without experiencing frustration, which is also part of learning. We should be patient when looking for outside learning alternatives and identify if it's a deficit in the ability to learn, a lack of suitable stimuli, or simply a normal evolutionary limitation (to be expected) for the age of our child. Let's remember that there are ranges of possible abilities for each age. My daughter was not able to jump with both feet at three years old, but that doesn't mean that she needs body therapy. It took her longer to achieve it, but today her dance teachers praise her elevated corporal awareness.

"All in due time," my grandmother would say. In these fast times, let's resist the need to solve, and instead let's tend to the need to understand what is happening and how we can support our children. Sometimes the best support is *not doing anything*. I should mention here that psychology speaks of "progression and regression," meaning that every development in the learning process is progress, and every step back or impediment in achieving something that could already be achieved is a regression. The mistake, in my perspective, is to believe that learning is linear, and that once we learn something, we never forget it and will apply it for life. Is that true? Let's think, for example, about the number of times we trip over the same stone, thinking we've learned the lesson and that there will not be a next time. Even if we don't want to, very soon we will again trip over the same stone. I believe that learning is not linear but spiral, and throughout our lives we will go through certain issues, time and again, in different ways, learning something new each time. So if our child knew how to count, but suddenly he forgot, we have no reason to think that it is a step back, just that it is part of his learning. Etymologically, in Spanish, "to learn" means to let go in order to take it back up again, and this is true for certain concepts we forget or set aside in order to take up a new, maybe more evolved one. Let's have a curious and accepting perspective when it comes to "back steps," and instead let's focus on what our child will learn with each new opportunity.

When Night Falls

At night we want and *need* to sleep. Parents as much as children need restful sleep in order to process the experiences, emotions, and lessons of the day. Further, when we sleep, the body generates hormones that help children grow and adults regenerate their bodies. The greater the activity during the day, the greater the need for rest. High-performing athletes, for example, need to sleep ten hours to be able to process the metabolic waste from training and to produce enough protein and red blood cells for the following day's activities.

This happens to all of us to a greater or lesser extent, so it's key to *teach children to sleep.*

This learning to sleep is a controversial issue. There are those who say that sleep is a natural response to tiredness, something that was evident in olden times, when there were probably not that many lights or activities to keep people awake. But nowadays many things keep us up, even beyond what is healthy. It's very common to see overstimulated kids who have trouble going to sleep at the end of the day because they've spent too much time playing with their tablets, or they stayed up watching cartoons, or because playing with their friends went longer than it should have. And sometimes it happens when parents stay chatting with friends, and so children keep playing, even when it's time to slow things down. Their bath time routine, dinner, story time, and relaxation is then shortened so much that it no longer has an effect. Adults also may be overstimulated. It's not that easy to sleep when we go to bed while chatting until the last minute or when we work on the computer in bed until just before we turn off the light.

In her book *Thrive*, Arianna Huffington, founder of *The Huffington Post*, speaks of her experience in reeducating herself to sleep. She thought that she didn't need to sleep much, four hours would suffice, but all she was doing was damaging her health, to the point that she almost died due to lack of sleep.[5] Do you remember the last time you stayed up late watching a TV series or because you went to dinner and dancing, and you went to bed at dawn? How well did you sleep? What was your energy like, and how well did you feel the following day?

Sleeping well doesn't just have to do with the amount of sleep but with having sleep that is truly restful. Not all types of sleep provide us rest and repair; that depends on how deep the sleep is. Today we can measure brainwaves while sleeping to identify the type of sleep that is most restorative. It is known, for example, that delta brainwaves encourage deep sleep. We need at least 20 percent of this type of sleep. Children need a greater amount of REM (rapid eye movement) sleep, in which brainwaves are fast and encourage dreaming, which is key for the cognitive development of children because that's how they record what they learned in memory; at the same time they recover in order to learn new things.[6] The time we put children to bed is also important because there is more REM sleep before midnight.

---

[5] You can see Arianna Huffington's interview at http://efectonaim.net/arianna-huffington-la-defensora-del-sueno, and her experience in her book *Thrive*.

[6] *Brain Basics: Understanding Sleep,* National Institute of Neurological Disorders and Stroke, http://www.ninds.nih.gov/Disorders/Patient-Caregiver-Education/Understanding-Sleep.

The earlier they sleep before midnight, the more time they will have to process what happened during the day and to learn. For babies, naptimes are also important to encourage greater REM sleep.[7]

How many hours do our children need to sleep? Here are suggestions from the National Sleep Foundation:[8]

Age	Recommended	May be appropriate	Not recommended
Newborns 0–3 months	14 to 17 hours	11 to 13 hours 18 to 19 hours	Less than 11 hours More than 19 hours
Infants 4–11 months	12 to 15 hours	10 to 11 hours 16 to 18 hours	Less than 10 hours More than 18 hours
Toddlers 1–2 years	11 to 14 hours	9 to 10 hours 15 to 16 hours	Less than 9 hours More than 16 hours
Preschoolers 3–5 years	10 to 13 hours	8 to 9 hours 14 hours	Less than 8 hours More than 14 hours
School-aged children 6–13 years	9 to 11 hours	7 to 8 hours 12 hours	Less than 7 hours More than 12 hours
Teenagers 14–17 years	8 to 10 hours	7 hours 11 hours	Less than 7 hours More than 11 hours
Young adults 18–25 years	7 to 9 hours	6 hours 10 to 11 hours	Less than 6 hours More than 11 hours

The best thing we can do for our children is to encourage them to sleep and for the number of hours they most need, according to their ages. So that everyone, children and adults, sleeps better, take the following into account:

- Keep sleep routines consistent each day, including the routine prior to going to bed (taking a bath, dinner, and reading) and the time of going to sleep. The body gets used to things and that helps with falling asleep. When we and the kids are tired, let's not hesitate: It's no longer time to read one last story. It's best to set time limits. One alternative is to make up stories with the lights off or to sing, which will prepare them and help them sleep because they will feel accompanied and secure.

- During the hours prior to sleep, let's favor relaxing activities, like reading or taking a bath, instead of physically or mentally stimulating activities, like action games on a screen or working on office issues, or contact or physically exerting games and gymnastics.

---

[7] For further detail, I recommend reading *Healthy Sleep Habits, Happy Child,* by Marc Weissbluth, MD.
[8] National Sleep Foundation, http://sleepfoundation.org/excessivesleepiness/content/how-much-sleep-do-babies-and-kids-need.

- Eat light and at least two hours prior to sleep. Avoid foods that are energizing (sugar, cacao, caffeine) or that are difficult to digest (fats, complex carbohydrates).

- Use the bed to sleep and relax and not to watch television, work, or talk on the phone. That way, our minds and bodies will associate bed with sleep.

The same advice applies to adults, with the additional recommendation to turn off the cell phone at least one hour before sleep time and not leave the phone next to the bed so we don't succumb to the temptation of checking messages and emails at night. In my house, we also decided not to have television in the bedrooms, and although we sometimes work at the bedroom desk, when night falls, everything is closed, turned off, and cleared, and the bedrooms are transformed into places of relaxation.

Sleepless Nights and Night Terrors

Theories regarding dreams are great ... until we face our baby or young child not sleeping or sleeping at intervals. That's where all theories end and questioning begins:

- "What if we bring him to sleep in our bed with us?"

- "Is cosleeping good or not?"

- "What if I breastfeed him or give him something to drink?"

- "Is he hungry?"

- "Is he upset because of something that happened to him during the day?"

We ask these questions because we want to solve "the problem" that prevents our child from sleeping when he needs to.

Find your family's own sleep routines and dynamics. If the only way you or your kids can sleep is to all sleep in one room, do it—or throw five mattresses on the living room floor. These surely will be temporary solutions. It all depends on what you are willing to do or sacrifice as parents. I recommend the book *Healthy Sleep Habits, Happy Child* by Dr. Marc Weissbluth, who offers various strategies for good sleep, each one with its pros and cons.

Teaching our child to sleep in his own bed requires effort on our part. Often we have to get up from our own bed and accompany him back to his, as many times as he gets up. This is something that won't always find us rested or in the best disposition, but it's key that as conscientious parents, we ask ourselves—from the bottom of our hearts—*what we believe to be best for us and for our children*. If we lack sleep and that bothers us, or if it makes us irritable and puts an end to whatever patience we may have during the day, then it will not be good for anyone. On the other hand, sometimes it's preferable to "sacrifice" some nights to "save" the rest.

I doubt there is one single answer for how to teach our children to sleep. I believe we need to experiment with a strategy for a while and see how we feel with it, what results it brings and at what cost, and then decide if it works or if we should look for another strategy. It was useful for me to experiment with a bit of everything with my three kids in order to learn, while always trusting in my inner wisdom as a mother.

As I write this, I still have two- and four-year-old kids, and many times there are four of us sleeping in the same bed—and I think it's great. I even get to enjoy the cuddles in the morning as we wake up. On the other hand, I will not let that change from a temporary exception to a habit because I like my personal and couple space in bed.

They Don't Exist, but They Are Definitely There

Around three or four years old, when kids start with night terrors, it is important that we are present, keep them company, and help them sleep again by telling them a nice story that will fill them with safety and love.

At home, we've had strong, sometimes frightening night experiences. There are times that I dream something awful, and I hear one of my children scream and start to cry, and soon after, the other comes to my bed, crying. I don't know why this happens, but when it does, I meditate and pray to *clear* the house ambiance and calm myself and my children. On scary nights, some people light candles and pray to guardian angels, and others teach their children to breathe and imagine themselves with them in nice places. It's all useful if we do it consciously. Even if there are things we do not understand, we adults always should offer our presence and support to our children.

I know how maddening not sleeping can be. I spent a lot of sleepless nights and went from being upset with my children and with life to accepting that I could not do much on the worst nights, but somehow I could handle the consequences of not sleeping. Sometimes we will be able to regain some hours of sleep during the day and reprioritize our activities, depending on how well we slept.

The key thing is to take care of ourselves both at night and during the day, and the result will be a mother or father who is more available, loving, and patient with her or his children, as well as being an example of personal care and responsibility of our own well-being.

Stories to Grow, Learn and Find Peace

I have always liked stories and tales of all types. When I was very little, I would ask the adults to tell stories to me—the longer the story, the better. I could spend hours listening and wouldn't tire. Perhaps because of that, I intuitively started to make up stories that to tell my children before bed to help them process what was happening to them and to bring a little bit of light to the somber parts that might be roaming around our family environment.

Stories help children understand the reality in which we live in a symbolic or archetypal way. It is very likely that we are all jealous, and that sometimes we want to behave like the witch in *Snow White* and send the sweet, innocent princess we envy to her death. Of course we don't do it, but to read or play the role of the bad girl in the story helps us to experience our own "shadows" safely, without fear of rejection or judgment. Sometimes we don't even recognize our own shadows or lights, but stories have the power to show them to us, like when we identify with characters and perceive that we have their talents too.

Kids between three and four years of age start to feel fear because they understand, for example, that the "bad" mom, the one who sets boundaries, and the "good" mom, the one who has fun with them, is the same person. To understand that makes them see that they are also "bad" and "good." Since they cannot integrate or accept the bad child in them, they project it with their imaginations, and fear it. They really fear the bad they have inside, but it can take them years to integrate it completely. Some adults still continue to project outside that bad in them.

With stories, we can help children to manage their fears. When my older daughter was three years old, I made up stories for her about the times before the bad one was bad or the times after the happy ending. The idea was to see both characteristics in one character, who would change, learn, and grow, according to how he would behave. In those stories, there was always a compassionate character who would help them be at peace with both sides. Actually, that character was me as the mom.

To help us create these types of stories, we can show characters who feel disapproved of, rejected, or diminished and give reasons why they would start to do bad things until they became the bad ones. These bad ones see that they always lose and that happy endings are reserved for the good ones. They see that they can't continue in this way, or they won't have the good luck of someone compassionate arriving and giving them an option—to ask for forgiveness and repair the damage so they can go back to being who they were before they turned bad … or the other option: to disappear forever. The compassionate characters were in charge of reminding them of all the good they had and of their real value. The option of asking for forgiveness and taking responsibility, or not doing it and disappearing can seem drastic, but it also reveals the power of mercy and love. We can all choose right (or wrong). Even though each choice has consequences, it is never too late to choose again.

We can take these tales to the real world and take advantage of the time before bed to ask forgiveness for something bad we've done and to say thanks for something good we experienced during the day. The children will probably not say anything at first, and in that case, we can do it ourselves as an example. In my experience, after a while my daughters expressed issues that we had not discussed during the day; they came to light at that time of reflection because of the stories and their characters' situations. Maybe it was feeling totally accepted that allowed them to talk about something they previously had kept secret or preferred not to tell, which many times would cause them nightmares.

We can use stories as a resource to talk about what is happening without mentioning it directly and to pass on our own wisdom. If we find it hard to make up stories or tales, we can check out books from libraries, where there are many stories for learning; for example, on potty training: *Potty* by Leslie Patricelli. The classic tales, like those of the Brothers Grimm (*Snow White*, *Sleeping Beauty*, *Hansel and Gretel*), can help us to talk with our children and ask them things, such as:

What do you think happened to the witch when she was little for her to choose to become a witch?

What problems do you think the prince and princess have, now that they are together?

The possibilities are endless. We can also see the witch and the princess in us and in our children, pointing out both the light and the shadow. I would tell my daughters that I identified with Belle from *Beauty and the Beast* because of my courage and desire to help those who at first seemed to be frightening and despicable. This is great until courage makes me forget about myself or until I try to transform someone who doesn't want to be transformed or hasn't even asked me for it. Or until I meet a beast who could hurt me, and I get too close because I only see his good side. We can all find ourselves in the symbolism of the story and learn from it.

Bedrooms offer us all of these moments of intimacy to reflect and find other ways to love our children so they can develop confidence and self-esteem. It's from that connection with them that we can help them in their learning so they can take steps that will fill them with self-confidence. Many things tend to happen during the night, but above all, we want to encourage rest because it is vital for the wellness of all, children and parents. All of this happens with a lot of presence, listening, company, and unconditional support.

Bedrooms represent a place where we love our children by supporting them in their development and where we are responsible for their well-being and ours as well.

Taking Action: Here's an activity that will allow us to know ourselves more as and to design our roles as parents to give our children our best.

In the privacy of your own bedroom, ask yourself:

1. How would I like my child to describe me when he grows up?

2. What are my beliefs and principles regarding my children's education?

   ....

   ....

3. How aligned are my principles and the way I behave with the way I want to love my children?

   ....

   ....

4. How well do we sleep at home, children and adults? What could we improve?

   ....

   ....

5. What do I commit to doing in order to better align myself with my values and principles in order to love my children and to increase the well-being of children and parents at night?

....

....

6. Do I need outside help to meet my commitment? If so, who will I contact to help me?

....

....

Write in a concrete way the promises and actions that you will fulfill so that the answers given above cease to be an ideal and become what's real.

....

....

....

....

....

....

....

....

....

....

....

....

....

....

....

MY NOTES

....
....
....
....
....
....
....
....
....
....
....
....
....
....
....
....
....
....
....
....
....

CHAPTER 7

The Bathroom

7

The Bathroom

The bathroom is a space where parents and children share intimately and where the kids get in touch with their bodies. Having a bath, for example, helps us to wake up in the morning or to relax at the end of the day, and it's a time to have fun and share with the kids. Having a bath and other cleanliness and wellness habits we associate with the bathroom help us stay healthy and prevent illness.

Connection with Our Children: Intimacy and Fun

When kids are young, at least one adult helps them in the bathroom. If parents approach those times with calmness and without hurrying, there can be a lot of intimacy and fun. When children relax and play, they invite us to participate in their lives; they deeply want us to do it! To children, taking a bath has nothing to do with cleansing but with experimenting, playing, having fun, and spending time with Dad or Mom. Even the older ones who no longer need us to bathe them often ask us to keep them company while they shower. Sometimes they might ask for help, just to keep us nearby because they want us to be present and *available*.

To be available means to be 100 percent at their service, watching them, and listening to them attentively. When we are available, we are not thinking about what we have pending or what happened that day at the office. Children benefit if we don't hurry them and if we let them experience sensations like shampoo on their heads and soap sliding down their bodies. Letting them shower alone reinforces their sense of autonomy and power. Of course, we parents should be there to supervise and keep them company but not to correct them on how to shower properly. Here, it's about having an experience without expectations so they can learn with love.

We don't need sophisticated toys or super-creative ideas for bath time. Shampoo is enough, as with it, we can create soap suds to make beards and moustaches. Little ones love to play with soap suds, and while we obviously won't let them eat the soap or shampoo, it won't hurt them to experiment by putting a bit of foam on their mouths. They also can play with empty cups or pretend they're getting into the ocean and swimming, while we help them float by holding them up. If we want them to familiarize themselves with water and learn to swim, the bathtub is the ideal place to do it.

We can play with them by making bubbles under the water with a straw or by pretending a waterfall is spilling over their heads when we pour water over them. We also can experiment with the water temperature before they get in so they can feel the difference, and at the end of the bath, we can leave them in the bathtub while it drains so they'll see they don't go down the drain with the water. What appears most basic to us is an opportunity for children to learn something, to have fun, and, above all, to receive love from us, which is what they need most.

Of course, before we engage in all the bath-time activities, we parents need to have time to prepare ourselves to be available; only in this way will we be carried away by the children's spontaneity and their constant curiosity. We should turn off the cell phones, close the bathroom door, and have everything at hand before starting the bath and devoting ourselves to the enjoyment. If we are worried about time, we can set a timer to let us know when to finish. This will give us the peace of mind to know that we are not overextending ourselves, and it will signal the end of bath time for the kids. To mark the beginning and the end of bath time, we can have a routine; for example, saying *hi* and *bye* to the water. Although we may not be able to bathe our kids every day or may not always feel like doing it or have the patience for it, when it *is* bath time, we should give it our all. Giving our loving presence without demands on time allows them to feel sure of our love and therefore of their value as people.

Ideas to Reinforce Your Relationship with Your Children When Bathing Them

1. Take enough time. That way, children will feel that their personal hygiene is important and that *they* are important to you as well.

2. Become curious again. Explore simple things with them, such as smells, textures, or soap bubbles and shampoo. Invent games, taking care to avoid underwater scares or slips and falls in the shower or bathtub.

3. Make use of bath time (or shower time) to tell them about issues of sexuality and how to care for their private parts.

4. Use your hands to caress and massage them. Put oils or lotion on them while you sing to them. For older children, massage their feet, hands, and back.

5. Listen while they talk or sing. Share that moment by giving them the freedom to discover and learn.

Cuddles to Love and Heal

Cuddling children at bath time is a privilege that lasts only a few years, so make the most of it. Even though they will allow us to give them a back rub or foot rub when they're older, our actions during their first years will nourish them and help to build a close relationship, both emotionally and physically. Some children are more sensitive than others and will want a soft and sustained touch. Others will be less sensitive to touch and will want more strength in our hugs or our caresses and massages. Discover that with each experience with them.

I did not know how to enjoy my first daughter, Valentina, during the first two or three months of her life. Besides changing her diaper, I didn't know what to do with a baby so small—she ate, slept, and cried. I was very grateful for the instructions of pediatricians and therapists, who taught me how to relate to her (and later, with my other children) through physical contact. I began to do physical exercises with Valentina each day to stimulate her muscles and played music while my husband and I caressed her. That also gave her dad another opportunity to connect with her. With my second daughter, Sofia, it was harder to be in touch and achieve peace and tranquility because she was more active. From the time she was born, we carried Sofía like a kangaroo. Perhaps that's why she immediately felt secure enough to go out and explore the world. She started crawling at four months, and nobody could stop her! I took advantage of bath time, diaper changes, and sleep time to hug her and hold her as close as possible. When my son, Juan Francisco, was just fifteen days old, I had the loveliest opportunity in the world—a massage and reflexology workshop that we started, along with other mothers and newborns. I learned a Bengali lullaby, and although I still don't know what the words mean, I sing it to him even now, and when he hears it, he lies down on his back and stays still or gives me his little feet to massage.

Massage is therapeutic; it heals because it gives love and balances the body's energy so the organs work better. There's nothing like a good massage to loosen cramps or congested airways. He still asks me for massages, and I gladly give them. Perhaps it is due to this experience that Juan Francisco is so physically affectionate. He often comes to wake me in the morning, lies on top of me, and brings his face close to mine with softness and sweetness, barely touching me; it's delicious. This has happened since he was two years old. I know he probably won't do it any longer by the time he's seven, so I will enjoy it while it lasts.

Numerous scientific studies have noted the positive effect of massage for kids. One that impressed me was "Juvenile rheumatoid arthritis: Benefits from massage therapy," published in the *Journal of Pediatric Psychology*,[9] which stated that after getting a massage, children who suffer from rheumatoid arthritis (a very painful disease) experience an immediate reduction in anxiety and cortisol (the hormone associated with stress) levels, and after thirty days of massage, they report even less pain. Many other cases like this show that massage increases oxytocin (the hormone associated with happy states) and the feeling of peace and happiness.

Sadly, there are also studies on the effect of the lack of physical connection in abandoned children or children of unavailable parents. What gives us hope is that, as human beings, we learn and transform all the time, and we can regain or obtain what we didn't have. For example, babies who can't be with their mothers from birth because of a health issue can recover from that lack of physical contact later on, either with their mothers or another person who "mothers" them. Even adults who lacked caresses and love in childhood can heal that lack with the help of someone who gives them love in the present.

Cuddling our children is a pleasure for us and for them. It's a way to give them love and to communicate how much we appreciate and love them. Looking them in the eye while they enjoy our cuddles is an act of intimacy and love. I would not want any parent to miss out on such an experience. We can provide this for our children so they know they are loved and so they remember that during turbulent times. Those cuddles will give them a secure place, a memory of unconditional love to draw upon when they feel sad, lonely, or helpless. With each cuddle we will build a loving home in their bodies.

Educating about Sexuality

Physical contact is key for children because through it, they feel loved and learn how to take care of themselves. I will always remember Isaac, a pediatrician I appreciated and cared about very much. When

---

[9] T. Field, M. Hernandez-Reif, S. Seligman, J. Krasnegor, W. Sunshine, R. Rivas-Chacon, S. Schanberg, & C. Kuhn, "Juvenile rheumatoid arthritis: Benefits from massage therapy," *Journal of Pediatric Psychology* 22 (1997): 607–617. Extract from http://www6.miami.edu/touch-research/ChildMassage.html.

Sofía was born, he said to me, "You know that you have to caress her entirely, right?"

"Sure," I replied.

He looked at me and said, "Also the private parts, and the fewer clothes, the better."

Blushing, I asked, "What? Are you sure?"

"Yes," he insisted. "If a child is not touched in any part of her body since birth, she will not recognize it as her own, and that can create a great internal disorganization later on, such as not taking care of that part, and she even may be more exposed to abuse because of it."

Years later, when my son was born, I asked Isaac if I was to do the same thing with a male child.

"Yes, ideally until he, by himself, can touch all his body parts."

Because I was raised in a different time and with a different paradigm, I was totally embarrassed. In my house, nobody *ever* spoke to me about sexuality. I first learned about sexuality from books and through a "progressive" teacher who discussed the topic in school.

The knowledge of the body and sexual education can start after with newborns, and the setting for that is usually the bathroom. Adults care for children and send the message that the body is valuable— that we care about it and that we should take care of it. When I took classes in sexual education for parents, I understood how important it is to discuss all of that with them from childhood. We cannot close our eyes to such important things as teaching our children the value of their bodies. We must start by telling them the actual names of their private parts, without resorting to diminutives like "your pee-pee" or, for girls, her "front" or "flower." Why is it so hard for adults to say *penis* and *vagina*?

Children have to feel secure about each part of their bodies. There is nothing that should make them feel ashamed. To ensure this, we parents also should not feel ashamed. If we do, it's time to work on our own issues to free ourselves from the outdated taboos that prevent us from helping our children. If it's hard for an adult to talk about his genitals or if he's afraid to touch them, he's probably hiding his fears. We acquired many of those fears in childhood, and they arose from false beliefs. The problem is that we could never talk about them with anyone. Only to the degree we are able to discuss them and bring them to light will we realize that we are limiting our capacity to live in greater contact with our own bodies and to have awareness, which is a benefit to children and to us.

Children also feel sexual excitement when they come into contact with their sexual parts. From perhaps age four or five, we may see them experience the sensations that touching themselves produce, and there need not be a problem in that. We can tell them that it's okay to touch themselves but not when they are with other people or when their hands are dirty because they can get an infection, especially the girls. The lewd or negative connotation regarding sexual activity is the fruit of our own negative mentalities or hearing negative comments and warnings about it. How can adults enjoy their bodies or the intimate sexual act of love if they learned that all of that was forbidden and bad? Let's not do that to our children; let's do everything in our power so they can feel good about their bodies and their sexuality.

Let's help our children to know their bodies, to know that they are their own, and that it is their responsibility to take care of their bodies. Telling them that nobody should touch their private parts and that they must not show them to anyone are the first messages in teaching them to take care. When my daughters were three or four years old, I told them that those are very delicate parts, that they belong to them and nobody else, and that part of their bodies is like a very special possession that they love very much and don't want someone else to ruin or break. I also explained that only Mom or Dad could clean or check them there, and in some instances, with their parents' permission, a doctor, nurse, caretaker, or relative could also do it.

It is also important that we teach children to identify the physical differences between men and women. It's likely that they will ask us about that when they see their brother or sister naked or when they see babies or pregnant women. If they don't, some child psychologists recommend that adults bring up the topic and talk about it, and I agree.

In her book *Latents*, about the upbringing of children between six and eleven years old, Maritchu Seitún comments that for children to be able to enter the sexual latency stage, they need to have experimented with their sexual organs in the previous childhood stage.[10] She makes a point that I love, and I think it's key for us parents—before our children become teenagers, let's take the opportunity to teach them all we want them to know as a model for health, morality, and values in general. If we teach them that the sexual act is a result of knowing and loving each other, then they will think that way regarding sexuality. When the idea to have sexual relations arises, they will be able to look to what they learned from us when they were young and make more informed and better

---

[10] Maritchu Seitún, *Latents* (Buenos Aires: Grijalbo, 2015).

choices. We can make the most of it while they still listen to us, planting the seed of concepts that will later represent a safe place for them—one they will always start off from and return to. The advice and experiences we share with them to give them security won't always keep them clear of dangerous situations (because defying limits is part of an adolescent's omnipotent attitude), but it surely will increase the odds that they will take better care of themselves and keep them safe.

It's interesting that while parents will see their children naked when they are young, the reverse won't work. Why? Given that our private parts are bigger and different, our bodies can scare them. Sometimes, male children get scared when they see Dad's genitals, or they even may feel "less than" because theirs aren't like his. It's a little different with girls, but after three years of age, it is not suitable for us to show ourselves naked in front of them and certainly never both parents at the same time.

Children can suffer psychological damage if they see, hear, or are present during sexual acts. They will not be able to understand it or put words to it until they are of a certain age.

When it comes to sexuality issues, information is power, and offering it to our children in a way that is understandable for their ages will empower them to protect and take care of their bodies.

When Illness Speaks

The bathroom is also a space associated with health, that state of balance in which the body works in an optimal way. When there is an imbalance, we become ill. Illness often upsets us and makes us feel vulnerable because we can't carry on with our lives in a normal way. And when our children get sick, we may feel even worse than they do because their illness can make us feel powerless, and it scares us. Parents tend to find a way to eliminate symptoms—headaches, stomachaches, and fever—as if by overcoming the symptoms, they can continue with whatever they were doing. But it doesn't work that way.

Symptoms of disease are warnings; they are ways that our bodies communicate an unmet need that generated an imbalance and then an illness. At times, the illness also provides the context for us to learn a key thing in our lives. Exhaustion, for example, lowers our defenses, and we tend to get sick. Instead of taking cold medicine, maybe we should take a break, rest, and reflect on what we did to get to where we are. Some illnesses are not that easy to decode, and we can't find their cause, but we can almost always see them as an opportunity to learn something in the present moment.

We should understand some illnesses as soul processes and treat them as such. If we don't listen to those messages that provide us the opportunity to grow and face them, then the disease and its symptoms will remain present, and there will not be a single antibiotic or other medication that will help.

If we get sick, we must take the time to connect with what our body is trying to tell us—what is it asking of us that we are not providing?

Ten minutes is enough to reconnect with our bodies and listen to them—this can be the most powerful and effective "medication" in the world. Detecting what the imbalance is won't be enough; we must also decide what to do. Our bodies are communicating with us, and we must commit to change and to give them whatever they are asking for. This will not be easy because other issues in our lives and other priorities compete with our bodies' messages.

Listening to our Bodies

Here's a simple way[11] to connect with your body and to understand the meaning of the illness so you can take care of yourself as you deserve. This process doesn't take much time, and you can do it almost anywhere. The important thing is to be alone in a quiet place.

Step 1: Feel. Get in touch with your physical body. Concentrate on what you feel in your body. It is easier if you close your eyes and breathe deeply, filling your abdomen with air. Imagine that you direct the breath toward the spot where you feel the disturbance or tension, or, while you breathe, place one hand

---

[11] This technique is derived from an integration of therapies like focusing and inner bonding. It can be put to practice each time you feel some symptom of disease—pain, discomfort, a cold, or muscle tension.

on the part of your body where you feel discomfort. Let your body know that you are there, *feeling it*. Imagine that that discomfort is a part of you that has a consciousness and that needs to be seen, heard, felt, and cared for.

Step 2: Let your imagination show you images about that sensation. You can zoom in on something in particular and then zoom out to see the bigger picture. Let the images happen. If nothing appears in your imagination, give that sensation shape and form; it can be something that you think represents it, from a sharp rock to a little green monster—it all counts.

Step 3: Have a dialogue with that part of your body that is in pain. You can establish a mental dialogue or write it out, if you prefer. Close your eyes to hear the answer, and write it automatically. It will help if you ask the question while writing it with your dominant hand, and answer it while writing with your nondominant hand so that you can access the right hemisphere of your brain, which is the creative side. Establish a dialogue, saying something like "I have been feeling and observing you, and I came to hear you, to know about you. What do you want to tell me? What am I doing that is making you feel like this? What do you need me to do in order for you to feel better?" Listen or write.

Step 4: Commit to make the change that your body is asking you to do. Sometimes that commitment can be immediate, like drinking water or taking a break. Other times, it will be something of greater reach, like changing your diet, getting more sleep, working out, or doing yoga. Check with that part that this commitment is enough, "Is this enough for you? What else can I do for you today?" If there is nothing else, finish. If something else comes up, go back to step 3 and pick up the dialogue again.

Illness in Our Children

Although we cannot ask our children's bodies what they want to tell us, we can stop to observe what they are experiencing and identify what could be interfering with their health.

When children become ill, I often hear explanations like "He caught it at school." I feel sad. This is as if we are missing a big part of the movie and, with that, the chance to become aware and learn to love ourselves. Although it is always possible for children to catch a virus that roams in closed spaces that they share with others, let's ask ourselves, Why do some get sick and others don't? Is it due to lowered defenses, stress, or changes in their lives? What is preventing my child from being healthy and protected by his immune system?

The reason for the illness can be something as simple as a change in diet, or it can be combined emotional factors, such as if they are starting longer days without their parents; experiencing a greater demand of attention on learning tasks; facing a first encounter with a social environment, such as starting school; or that at home, everyone is in such a hurry and "crazy" with daily routines that they don't take time to rest, enjoy, and communicate with each other. There are numerous possibilities, but only to the degree that we pay attention will we be able to realize what makes them sick. When we identify it, we can change it. If what we identify leads us to conclude, for example, that it's too soon for our child to feel safe starting kindergarten, then we can decide to wait until he acquires the confidence he requires, without pressure or hurry from anyone, especially from those he needs the most: his parents. Perhaps our older children need more leisure after school or less external stimuli—like visits, going out, television, or video games—and more contact, listening, and the company of parents and adults who love them and are ready to hug them.

The process of connection with the illness of our children is similar to our own, except we observe, feel, and listen to the little one. Here, it is important not to put our words on to the child. When one of my daughters was sick, the pediatrician would ask me, "Did she tell you it burns, or do *you* think it burns?" Or "Who said 'stomachache'? You or her?"

Sofia would say, "My tummy hurts," every time she wanted a hug. I later understood that her tummy didn't really hurt. This statement started when, faced with her sadness, I asked her, "Does something hurt? Your tummy?" Instead, I should have connected to what was happening to her and hugged her. This "emotional short circuit" that I created put words in her mind that did not correspond to what she felt and needed. It's sometimes better to ask, "Is something bothering you?" If children say yes, then we can go a bit further and ask, "Where? Show me with your hand," or "What's that discomfort like?" And then we can offer options such as, "Does it itch, burn, or tickle?" Or simply, "Does it feel weird?" This allows us to encompass something that neither of us can name.

If our children are very young, they won't be able to answer the question, "How can I help you?" But if they are five years or older, it is likely that they can answer, and it's at that age, we can give them the chance to choose what they need. You may be surprised with how quickly they begin to accept responsibility over their bodies.

With babies, we can't have a dialogue, but we have the advantage that their emotional bodies are open and connected to everything, especially the mother. Children share the emotional body with their mothers (like a cord that joins them in feeling and identity) until they are eighteen to thirty-six months.[12] Thanks to that, we can "feel them" and do the same exercise I proposed above, this time with the child's body. The answers will come from inside of us, but they will be connected to the baby. In this case, blockages can appear, generally associated with our fears as mothers or fathers, that won't allow us to connect, but we can always ask someone close to us, who is more calm and confident, to help us connect with the baby, to help feel him, and to give him what he needs.

Besides questioning him regarding the origin of the illness, we must help our child when he doesn't feel well. We can choose to go to a medical center in the middle of the night, or give him a steam bath and wait until he is better the next day, or call the family doctor to consult him. It's a good moment to ask ourselves if we count on the help and support of professionals or if it is time to change and choose other paths than traditional medicine, such as homeopathy. Changes that help us find solutions at the source and go beyond the actual symptom are welcomed.

In my experience, I've gone to the doctor for an emergency only a few times, and when I've had to do it, it has been precisely as a consequence of my intuition. I only went two times with my first daughter to a nearby medical center, but I did it more from my fear and feeling powerless than because of a real need. I wasted time and felt drained upon leaving. I learned that there is nothing more important than listening to myself.

---

[12] Laura Gutman, *La maternidad y el encuentro con la propia sombra* (Barcelona: Editorial Planeta, 2015).

The Experts—to Whom Should We Turn?

Perhaps due to my personal history, my training, or my love of freedom, I always questioned myself regarding what I should do and, instead, researched what was best, according to each moment and each situation in my life. I've also put this into practice with my children and their illnesses. When I decided to do (or stop doing) something, people close to me always asked, "And your pediatrician let you?" At first, I would answer, which made me feel uncomfortable because it was as if I had to explain and validate my choices with an "expert" or with someone who seemingly had more "authority" than I, as a mom, to say what was best for my daughters.

Who Knows What's Best for a Child?

There is nobody better than the child to know what is best for himself. We tend to believe that children are less wise or less capable because they are young or have fewer words or less life experience, but they are much more in contact with their survival instinct, with life, and with how to care for it. And they are less tainted by beliefs and social paradigms regarding what is right or wrong in each situation.

So the first and most important opinion is the child's. Although many will tell you a child cannot tell you what he needs, we need to realize that it takes a lot of love, trust, and open-mindedness to listen to a baby and decode his message. For that, it is necessary to *release preconceived notions and ideas about what we believe is right*. Deep in her heart, each mom and dad who is in touch with the children knows what the child needs from the first moment of life. Many mothers and fathers, however, have lost touch with their essence, and that's why it is so hard to listen to the essence of another being.

To listen to a baby or child and thus identify what is best for him is a great opportunity, and we always have it on hand. We should ask ourselves, "What is the most loving thing I can do for my child at this time?" The hardest thing, without a doubt, is to wait for the answer without first running out to find someone to answer *for* us. Sometimes the internal response will be to take him to a doctor who can offer us a diagnosis; if that is what we hear on the inside, then trust that. In order to know if our inner voice is from the soul or the mind, notice how the answer makes us feel. If the answer creates anxiety, guilt, fear, depression, or insecurity for us, then it is not very trustworthy. But if the answer makes us feel deep peace, security, and love in our hearts, then it is the right one, even if it contradicts those who believed they knew everything about the topic in question.

I find more and more open-minded doctors who endorse endless possibilities and give the parents freedom to make important decisions regarding their children. A diagnosis is not a sentence. Like all loving beings, *a good pediatrician listens*, and when he notices that the parent speaks from fear, he questions, instructs, and helps to dissipate doubts and concerns so that the parent can make the best decisions without fear ahead. A good pediatrician also offers appreciation, opinions, and options, without making them sound like absolute truths, which is also a gesture of humility and of a desire to share a dialogue, instead of wanting to convince or impose.

A good pediatrician also shows a deep compassion and acceptance toward the parents who consult him. He doesn't expect them to follow his recommendations, and he values whatever the parents have done until the time they came to consult him.

When going to a pediatrician, let's ask ourselves what we are looking for in him. What we seek should go beyond his medical training and experience as a professional. It's not always the titles or specialties that give credit to a person's life experience and wisdom. I don't go by external opinions, such as, "He is the best specialist in the country." To me, that's just nonsense. I have found excellent young and mature professionals in medical centers, hospitals, and private practices. Some were recommended; others weren't. I have one way of finding what I want in a doctor, and that's following my heart and asking myself, Does he treat my child and me like sensitive human beings? Does he listen, value, and esteem us, and does he accept us with love? Does he want to help us selflessly and want to give his all? If I feel the doctor meets those characteristics, then I trust that I have an excellent professional who will accompany me in deciding what is best for my children.

Pediatricians are excellent allies, but, in the end, we parents must decide the best course of action, having listened carefully to what our child needs. Perhaps someone joined us on this listening process, but nothing replaces the voice of the soul.

Alternatives to Traditional Medicine

I suffered from low-back pain and allergies for many years, but I don't any longer, and it's been years since I've been sick. This is thanks my discovering ways to for my family and me to stay healthy.

Once we learned to listen to the diseased body, it's time to discover options to help it heal. Note that I said "to help it heal," not "to heal it," because the body that gets what it needs returns to balance and health on its own. Understanding that is key. I did not believe it until I gave myself permission to put it into practice and let it happen.

My lower-back pain was not cured by spine surgery or with painkillers or anti-inflammatory medicine. My lower-back pain disappeared after a single Touch for Health session, in which a therapist gave me a massage to balance my energy meridians and told me why I had an imbalance. It was only when I understood the cause of my pain on a mental and emotional level that I was able to keep myself healthy and not have these types of problems.

My husband and I had resorted to traditional medicine to resolve problems like coughing, bronchospasms, and colds for our first daughter. She was only eight months old and was taking antibiotics, nebulizations with corticosteroids, and various other medications and procedures. After two months, we decided to try something different: homeopathy. We could not explain what happened, but it was like a miracle. Our daughter healed and from then on didn't get sick again. Without needing to know much, homeopathy made perfect sense to me as an alternative, and we and our other children also were treated through homeopathic methods. It is of great benefit to use a way of healing that respects the body and doesn't affect any of its parts—kidneys, stomach, liver—as commonly used medications can.

To heal and stay healthy, we also introduced changes in our diet that helped us stay balanced (see chapter 3). Now there are many books and articles about healthy nutrition, and in this sea of information, there are opposing ideas. When I wanted to inquire about homeopathy, I found different stances about what is and isn't scientifically proven. The same is true of acupuncture, which the Chinese have practiced for thousands of years, even to doing surgery without anesthesia, while we Westerners, due to our worldviews, still ask ourselves if there is proof of its effectiveness and benefits.

Remember that we parents are responsible for taking care of ourselves and our children, and health comes with the internal connection of giving ourselves what we really need. Sometimes we will need to take antibiotics; other times, we can use homeopathy medications or acupuncture. My intention is to open the doors to new ways of healing so you can explore and decide, based on your own experience. We can consider the opinion of experts, but, in the end, it is our responsibility, and taking charge of our bodies depends solely on us.

Take Out What Doesn't Work

We still have one topic that is no less important to our health than the others: digestion. In the bathroom, we take internal waste out of our bodies through feces and urine. Many of us, including our children, suffer gastrointestinal discomforts, which take us to the bathroom to eliminate what is no longer useful to the body. Sometimes the body eliminates too much, and we cannot retain anything; sometimes we retain too much, and we cannot release what no longer works for us.

In these instances, we should ask ourselves what these imbalances symbolize. The child who throws up without stopping is saying *no* to something that should be nourishing him. It can mean an intolerance to a certain food, but if the situation is recurring, then there can be emotional issues. It can be a fear or maybe something the child "cannot pass" in the relationship with his parents and siblings, at school, or with his friends; therefore, it's thrown back out.

The same thing happens when our bodies can't absorb what should be nutritious or when we can't release what no longer works; this might be some idea that is "blocking" us on the inside. Working metaphorically helps us to find what we can do to return to balance and heal.

In this sense, we should take two times in particular into account with kids. The first is when they learn to be without diapers. Many times we take them off too quickly, before the child is ready for it, and the consequences will be negative. The child will get frustrated, and that will create unnecessary pressure, including prolonging his peeing on himself. By not wanting to be without diapers, children can retain too much due to fear, which can enable infections.

My older daughter stopped wearing diapers before she was ready because I let myself get carried away by social pressure. ("Now that summer is coming, take the opportunity to get rid of diapers.") In the end, with homeopathy and returning to diapers for a few more months, everything went back to normal, but it was not good to put what others said above what my daughter needed.

The second time is when kids, especially little girls, learn about pregnancy and babies. Between three and four years of age, they realize that they are female and think they can be moms. If we have not explained it to them, they could fantasize that babies come out where feces do, and then they may get scared of going to the bathroom. At that age, it is recommended to teach them to differentiate the body's orifices and their functions. We can explain it using metaphorical language, with sensitivity and trying to be as direct as possible. Something like "There is a 'door' for urine, which is in front, and there is another door for poo, which is behind. And there is another door that moms have when they are *older* [exaggerate this part so they don't identify with it], and that's where babies, who are in a little bag inside, come out. The baby knocks on the door when it is ready to come out, and the mom and dad go to the clinic. Then the door opens, and the doctor helps welcome the baby to make sure everything is okay."

Girls can look at and touch their sphincters and recognize them. When they know that they *won't* have babies and that poo is not like having a baby, they will feel free from unnecessary fears. They can play at having them but not *believe* that they will have them—that's the key. With boys, it's clearly easier: They have two well-identified "doors," separated from one another, and because of that, there is no possible confusion. Still, some boys of around three may think they have a baby inside because they are learning about sexual difference. We should explain the difference between men and women, and ensure them that they do not have a baby.

Meanwhile, sometimes our children need help to say goodbye to that which used to be of the body and no longer is. If they are little, they can watch their poo, say goodbye, and then flush the toilet themselves. If they are older and have problems with constipation, maybe we need to assist them in letting go. It will help, for example, to play with Play-Doh, pretending it's their poo and that they are squeezing it until they take it out.

Although there can be an endless reasons for them to release too much or retain too much, something emotional generally is associated with it that we can help them put into words to regain balance.

When Leaving the Bathroom

When we leave the bathroom, we are calmer, clearer, and more purified than when we went in. We often get the best ideas in the bathroom. It is here that we let go of what doesn't work and are ready to absorb the new; that's why it's as important as any other place in the house.

Its importance lies in keeping ourselves healthy, taking care of ourselves, and knowing our bodies so that we can educate our children about that, and they can take care of themselves as they grow.

We saw that the bathroom is a space of a lot of intimacy, and we can turn it into a place to connect with our children, playing or giving them massages and cuddles. We explored that each imbalance or disease carries a message from which we can learn to love ourselves and that our intuition takes precedence over experts because, in the end, we care the most about our health and that of our children. We also associated the bathroom with letting go of what no longer works or is not good for us.

Taking Action: "The Healthy Little Tree" is an activity to do with our children and to help us heal

Using the metaphor of how a healthy tree feels and how a sick one feels, this is activity will help our children and us connect with the disease using artistic expression and understand what we need in order to heal.

There are two possibilities for carrying out this activity. The first is to do it with four hands along with your child (ideal for kids between two and four years old). The second is for your child to do it on his own, and you do it along with him (ideal for kids five and older). Choose the one that works the best.

Draw two trees, one healthy and the other sick, and develop the following dynamic, using the steps mentioned below. You might need to help younger kids draw; they can indicate to you what they want to show. You don't want this activity to be about how they draw, so help them out as much as needed.

MATERIALS

- Two sheets of paper for drawing
- Crayons or colored pencils
- Colored paper or old magazines to tear up
- Scissors

Note: If all you have is paper and colored pencils, that's enough; it will just be more fun for kids to do this collage-style.

Step 1: Tell a story.

Tell your child the following story (you can get creative and add details to the proposed script): "This little tree has the same name as you—James. It feels just like you and wants to tell you what is happening with its leaves, shape, trunk, and colors. For that, we will help it express itself by drawing it and showing its leaves, its colors, and helping it to tell us whatever it wants to tell. On one sheet, we will draw it how it feels now that it is sick, and on another, we will show when it feels good and happy and it has energy and the desire to play. While we draw, it will tell us how to help it be well again."

Note: If your child's illness already has passed, especially if it was important, do the activity to liberate traumas and elaborate on what already happened.

Step 2: Show the healthy tree.

On one sheet, draw the tree when it feels good, happy, and content, when its body is healthy with energy and strength. Children can draw, color, and paste different colored paper and magazine trims like a collage, if they want to. If the kids are older and know how to write, they can use words to describe what it feels; for example, in its leaves or trunk. Talk about what the tree likes to do when it feels well, asking your child something like "When you and your tree feel well, what do you like to do?"

Step 3: Show the sick tree.

On the other sheet, draw the sick tree. Help your child with guiding questions, such as:

- Is the tree the same, or does it have a different shape and color? Draw it how it is now that it feels like you.

- How do you show what the tree is feeling now? Maybe it looks like some color or paper that you want to glue or draw.

- What do you think this tree needs to be like the other one that feels well?

Step 4: Compare and commit.

Look at both trees at the same time and relate them to the child who feels sick, mentioning what you will do for him to feel better.

Write a promise for the sick tree or letter saying what you will do for it to get better, or simply draw on it what you will do for it to feel better.

CHAPTER 8

The Spiritual Bunker

8

The Spiritual Bunker

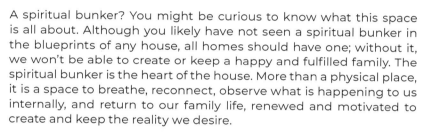

A spiritual bunker? You might be curious to know what this space is all about. Although you likely have not seen a spiritual bunker in the blueprints of any house, all homes should have one; without it, we won't be able to create or keep a happy and fulfilled family. The spiritual bunker is the heart of the house. More than a physical place, it is a space to breathe, reconnect, observe what is happening to us internally, and return to our family life, renewed and motivated to create and keep the reality we desire.

The spiritual bunker allows us to take care of ourselves so that we can, in turn, give our all to our family. Stepping into the spiritual bunker is similar to when race cars make pit stops to change tires, clean the driver's helmet visor, refuel, and check that everything is working well or make the necessary adjustments. Some cars, in order to gain advantage, decide not to make these pit stops, but because the race is long and demanding, they generally suffer great wear and tear in the long run and will have to stop for a longer period of time—and that means they'll lose the advantage they had or, worse, break down and be forced to abandon the race.

Our life as parents is a bit like that car race, in which each does the best he can. But in order to give our best, we need to stop and check our "cars." In the spiritual bunker, we pause to check our bodies, minds, and emotions. There, we fix whatever is not working and refuel (love) in order to resume the race. This will allow us to keep going without discomfort and with fluidity on a track, where we will sift through whatever obstacles arise more easily. When we reach the end, the entire family is the winner.

To approach the spiritual bunker, we will discuss freedom, responsibility, and awareness, as well as easy tools for growing in awareness and for making decisions that will provide wellness for us and for our families.

You might have read something like this in psychology magazines or in self-help books, or you might have heard it in a spiritual teacher's conference. What I call the spiritual bunker touches on other personal-harmony concepts and trends. For the purpose of this book, I will share the result of my studies,[13] personal life, and professional experience with clients and friends. This chapter is in accordance with spiritual ideologies. It's all about how to live in order to achieve peace, happiness, and love in our lives. Let's start this experience together.

Freedom: Learning How to Choose

My grandfather used to say, "First things first." The first thing we will do is to discuss ourselves because everything we will see later is derived from there. As I've mentioned, human beings are born free and stay free. Some call this condition *free will*. The question is this: Free from what and for what? We are *free to choose*. We can choose what to do with what happens to us. We can choose what to do regarding our inner world—thoughts, emotions, physical sensations—and we can choose what to do regarding the exterior world (what others say to us or what the weather conditions are, for example).

If it's raining, we can't make the rain stop, but we can use an umbrella or enjoy playing in the rain. This example seems trivial, but it is profound. Most of the time we focus on what we cannot do, and in this way, we become victims of our own circumstances, instead of focusing on what we can do and become heroes and protagonists of our own lives.

There are always *at least* two explanations as to why what happens *happens*, and both are equally true and valid. For example, if I have an apple in my hand, and I let it go, the apple falls. The apple fell for various reasons. Someone might say the apple fell due to the force of gravity, which is true. Someone else might say that it fell because it slipped from my hand, which could also be true. Someone else could say that the apple fell because I got a hand cramp, and someone else might even say that the apple simply fell because I let it go. Of all the explanations, there is at least one over which I have power: I let

---

[13] The readings that have contributed to the development of my idea of the spiritual bunker are many. Among them are the following: *Being and Time* by Martin Heidegger; *Por la senda del pensar ontológico* by Esteban Echeverría; *The Tree of Knowledge. Biological Basis of Human Understanding* by Humberto Maturana and Francisco Varela; *Existential Psychotherapy* by Irvin Yalom; *Man's Search for Meaning* by Viktor Frankl; *The World as Will and Representation* by Arthur Shopenhauer; *Essays* by Michel de Montaigne; and *How to Know God* and *The 7 Spiritual Laws of Success* by Deepak Chopra. Also, literary works such as *War and Peace* by Leo Tolstoy; *Thus Spoke Zarathustra* by Friedrich Nietzche; and Ancient Greek authors, like Heraclitus and Plato.

it go—because I could have decided *not* to let it go. There is another over which I have power, not in the present time but in the future: I got a hand cramp. If I know that I often suffer from cramps in that hand, then I could hold the apple with the other hand.

We can always choose how to explain what is happening to us, and depending on the explanation, we can do something about it or not.

Freedom is an essential value for me, and because of that, each time I feel that my freedom is limited, I experience annoyance, pain, anger, or powerlessness. These emotions have been so strong in my life that I researched them to discover how to handle them. I then discovered and built my spiritual bunker, where now I take time to reflect on everything—how happy I am, what makes me lose sleep, and what options I have to create peace and happiness in my life. I use the word *create* because I believe that happiness is an internal feeling and not a response to environment. To see that happiness is not determined by material things, it's enough to observe the happiness of children, playing, smiling, and in good spirits, even when they live in a state of extreme poverty. *Our happiness is determined by our own will to create it.*

In his book *Man's Search for Meaning,*[14] doctor and psychologist Viktor Frankl recalls his experience as a prisoner in Auschwitz during World War II. Although he was totally deprived of his freedom, he discovered he could be happy and at peace with himself if he could find meaning in his situation. The hope of reuniting again with his family motivated him to stay alive, and, despite everything, he kept putting into practice his gifts and talents as a doctor to help those who suffered along with him. Thus, he teaches us that to find meaning in our lives, serving those around us is the best way to put into practice the freedom we were born with and never lose. "Man is not fully conditioned and determined but rather determines himself whether he gives into conditions or stands up to them," he says, regarding human beings.

Often, we parents find ourselves in front of situations where we think we cannot choose. One of the worst situations we face are the illnesses of our children (see chapter 7). There is no greater feeling of powerlessness than that of being beside a child who is suffering due to a disease that we do not know how to cure. However, that powerlessness is not lack of power because we can always learn from that illness and from that situation. We can always understand why it came into our lives, and we can take the necessary actions to prevent it from happening again. In any case, we can always do the best we can in the present moment, serving our child with love, with

---

[14] Viktor Frankl, *Man's Search for Meaning* (Beacon Press, 2006).

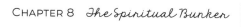

all our presence, and without guilt or reproach (for them or us). Love is what heals, and acceptance of what is what allow us to love without judgment or boundaries.

Responsibility—the Ability to Respond

Freedom goes hand in hand with responsibility, which we can understand as the ability to respond to challenges that come our way. Although we won't always have the same ability to respond (some challenges will overcome us), the important thing is to focus on what we *can* do and not what we cannot do. This way, whatever happens to us, we can *always* choose how to respond. Only in this way will we live from a place of unconditional responsibility.

In his book *Conscious Business*, philosopher and business consultant Fred Kofman states that one of the key abilities we need to be happy and live in peace is unconditional responsibility. He says human beings decide not to be responsible when they fear accepting their own guilt or are singled out as guilty. And in this, adults react just like little kids. When a toy breaks in my house, it is very unlikely that someone will say, "I broke it." I generally hear, "It broke." Why? My children don't want to assume responsibility; that way, they avoid being punished. The finger that prosecutes rejects before understanding, and the fear of feeling rejected or misunderstood prevents us from taking responsibility.

When I identified that unconscious behavior that affects both children and adults, I stopped placing blame. I no longer blame whoever does something I consider wrong. I no longer blame someone who damages something that is special to me. Although it may make me angry or frustrated, I ask that person what he or she can do to fix it and to prevent it from happening again.

Instead of reprimanding my children for breaking something, I always acknowledge their emotion and mine, including their fear of punishment. "Are you afraid I will punish you for this? I won't. I know you didn't do it on purpose." Or if he did it on purpose, I say something like "Are you afraid I will punish you? I won't. I understand that you were so upset that you threw the toy, and it broke. And now that makes you sad too. I'm sorry the toy broke. How about if, when you're upset, you throw something that won't break or damage anything else instead, like a pillow? Do you think you could do that?" Next, I show him by mimicking how to express anger in another way, so as to not hurt anything or anyone and not hurt himself either. I can also say things like "I'm sorry about what happened. I can image how sad you must be due to what happened," or "I would be furious too if I broke my favorite toy. I can image how you're feeling." That

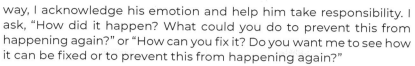

way, I acknowledge his emotion and help him take responsibility. I ask, "How did it happen? What could you do to prevent this from happening again?" or "How can you fix it? Do you want me to see how it can be fixed or to prevent this from happening again?"

I can also express my anger or sadness but without blaming my son for that because the emotion is mine, not his. "I am sad because now my iPad is broken, and I don't know if it can be fixed. I understand that you didn't realize that when you broke it. It would be really nice if you apologized to me and helped me fix it or for us to talk about how to prevent this from happening again." Maybe I would take him with me to get my iPad fixed instead of going to the park, without blaming or reprimanding, as a simple consequence of the break.

To Avoid Guilt, Start by Not Blaming

Let's acknowledge that we were wrong, just like our kids, and with a lot of love, let's take responsibility for our freedom to choose what to do in the face of what happens.

What parents face moments like this, they say to me, "Denise, I agree, but how do I do that thing of acting with love in situations like that?" I understand them because it's still hard for me to act with love at certain times. But it's enough to just start doing it, and each time we will be more aware and loving in how we react in these types of situations.

Realize that when we blame, we are not taking responsibility for what we ourselves must do with what someone else did. One time, in a situation in which I was exhausted, I screamed at my daughter, "What? Now what?" I thought she would ask me for something else when I already was feeling collapsed. My daughter didn't say a word, and without understanding why I had screamed at her, she started to cry in anguish. My husband, who heard and saw what happened, approached her and said, "Mommy is tired; that has nothing to do with you. Why don't you tell me what you need, and let's see if I can help you." Thanks to his reaction, I realized my mistake and was grateful for his support. My daughter didn't want to ask me for anything; she just wanted to tell me about something that happened to her at the park.

That night, after the kids were asleep, I spoke with my husband and thanked him. Again, he behaved with compassion, acknowledging what I could have been feeling at the time and also reaffirming his support if something similar should happen again. The next day, I talked to my daughter, apologized, and explained that my reaction had nothing to do with her. "If it's okay with you," I said, "I could fix my mistake by taking you out for some tea, and you can tell me all that she wanted to tell me."

Sometimes adults make mistakes and behave opposite to the values they want to experience as a family. In my case and my husband's, it's usually things like yelling at the kids or making threats in order to manipulate. My husband and I know that's not good and that it's aggressive, but we also know that there are times when, due to emotion and anger, we do it without being aware. Our agreement to help each other is that whoever observes the mistake doesn't question the other but directly intervenes in a loving way, behaving as he would want things to happen.

At the end of this chapter, I will provide you tools so that you can behave with love and start to inhabit and use your spiritual bunker, but first, I'd like to tell you a brief story:

There once was a master of Aikido in Japan who was teaching his disciple the martial art to resolve conflict and avoid fights. The student would practice and try to attack the master, but the master would always leave him on the floor. Exhausted after the end of practice, the disciple asked the master, "Why do you never fall?"

The master answered, "I do fall; it's just that I get back up so quickly that you don't even notice. And each time I get up, I feel as much peace and harmony as before I fell." That left the student surprised, but from then on, he was able to see how his master would sometimes lose stability and regain it, almost as if it were a normal and expected thing.

We can achieve something very similar in our spiritual bunkers—get back up after falling and regain serenity. It requires practice for us to be compassionate and for us to give ourselves the time we need to fail and try again.

The Path of Consciousness

Consciousness means "with knowledge"; it's awareness of ourselves, of others, and of the situation we are in.

In the same way we avoid guilt, we avoid being aware due to fear of being judged or guilty. That's why the majority of tools to grow more aware invite us to observe what happens to us without judging it. That's what mindfulness does, for example. It's about observing without emitting our opinion on what we think or feel, both on a physical and emotional level. It's as if we went on to become the observers of our lives—as if it's a play, and we are playing a role. Although it's a very simple concept, you can find more theory about it in a book by a mindfulness precursor, Jon Kabat-Zinn, titled *Mindfulness for Beginners*.

The concepts associated with awareness seem very simple, and they are—in theory. What's hard is putting them into practice. One of the reasons for that is simple: We are beings designed to survive; that's why we seek pleasure and avoid pain. This can be summarized with a phrase I learned from Fred Kofman: "What tastes good doesn't always do you good, and vice versa." After eating a delicious piece of chocolate cake, we have two options: to continue eating or to stop there. If we become aware, we will probably realize that it would not be good to eat that extra piece. Nevertheless, our bodies are designed to favor temporary pleasure and the present time, which means that saying no to the second piece of cake is an act of awareness and will.

In this we are a bit animalistic, although animals generally don't eat until they feel bad. We cannot say the same of human beings. With food, the explanation is genetics. We have thousands of years of famine registered in our DNA, and because of that, our genes are designed to choose fatty foods with a lot of sugar—those were the types of foods that helped us survive in the past. The same happens with our aggressive or defensive reactions. We have a history of danger from predators and not being able to control nature's effects, so our first reaction is to defend ourselves or to attack when faced with a possible danger. Today, however, many of those dangers and threats have ceased to be real.

Let's look at the brain as an organ with three layers. The first and innermost, the one we call the "reptilian brain," is the most primitive, and its function is to help us survive. It gets activated when we're faced with a possible threat, and it secretes hormones that generate changes on a physical level, such as carrying more blood to our legs and arms so we experience fight, flight, or freeze when in danger. The reptilian brain allows us to act before thinking. When faced with a possible attack by a bear in the forest, we fight with whatever we have on hand; we hurt it and escape.

Today the problem is reacting without thinking, for example, when your child breaks something you love or when your partner says he won't come to an event that you think is important. In these situations, to your reptilian brain, your son or partner becomes the bear, and your reaction is primitive—to fight. Fortunately, there is a second layer in the brain that envelops the reptilian brain, called the limbic system. It's the result of our evolution as mammals, in which we've acquired the instinct to preserve the species and protect ourselves, as well as feelings like love and brotherhood.

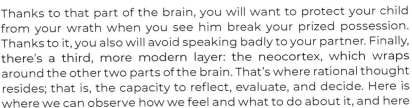
Thanks to that part of the brain, you will want to protect your child from your wrath when you see him break your prized possession. Thanks to it, you also will avoid speaking badly to your partner. Finally, there's a third, more modern layer: the neocortex, which wraps around the other two parts of the brain. That's where rational thought resides; that is, the capacity to reflect, evaluate, and decide. Here is where we can observe how we feel and what to do about it, and here is where we become aware.

Awareness is our ability to use all the parts of the brain in a coordinated way and to choose our well-being and that of those around us. Without it, there can be love but not always loving behavior; many times we can hurt that which we love. Without it there is no capacity to repair and return to inner peace. The path of consciousness or awareness is to choose to realize what is happening to us so we create greater well-being in our lives. Although everything in this book is about that, now you will see how you can do it in the most intimate part of your being. Another reason to have a spiritual bunker is that in it, you will be able to grow in awareness.

The Connection Within

In order to be aware, we need to see and feel ourselves from different perspectives. How? By connecting with ourselves. A large part of what we know as emotional intelligence has to do with this. It's about being conscious of our emotions and understanding the way we feel, think, and behave in life. It's about directing all of that in pursuit of love, peace, and our well-being and that of those around us. And that's also what the spiritual bunker is for.

In the houses I've lived, I've always dedicated a physical space and time to this. I create in it a place that gives me enough peace to go inside my own being. Today, I feel there is no longer such a need for a physical space because I carry it inside me; I have developed the habit of being in constant connection to myself. Nevertheless, there is always a time in the day when I delve deeper into this and reconnect in order to recharge with love and peace. That's the time of the day that I step inside my spiritual bunker.

Today, my spiritual bunker has a physical space—my study. But for a long time, it was a small space beside my bed, where I would sit and meditate. I have friends who are much more experiential and who prefer to live experiences that help them gain awareness, such as exercising, traveling to mystical places, or simply going to their neighborhood church; these are other shapes for the spiritual bunker that are valid. Because it's about a space that is primarily interior, it's fine for the spiritual bunker not to be in a physical space of our house.

We might establish our spiritual bunker when we are in touch with nature, the energy of which helps us to connect to what is happening to us and to obtain the wisdom we need to take care of it.

In my case, the sea and wind are the nature elements where I establish my spiritual bunker. When I get in the ocean, I feel its strength and feel as if it's cleansing me inside and taking out everything that bothers me. When I get out, I feel I have renewed strength to take care of things. I go to the ocean every time I can, and when it's not possible, I imagine being there.

I must go to my spiritual bunker every day. I invite you to do it as well. If I don't take a moment to write about what I feel or what is happening inside of me, for example, I will be much more reactive at home, outside, and at work. I will become more "reptilian." I have a tendency toward routine that makes me feel secure (sometimes I'm a prisoner to it), and because of that, I always keep the same breathing, meditation, and writing practice as a way to become conscious of what is happening with me. I need to return to my spiritual bunker daily in order to purify and recharge with self-love and be able to give it to others.

The place doesn't matter; what must be present is the importance of achieving internal connection—that should be the constant. With this clear, let's set aside ideas such as, "Being emotional is bad," or "Strong people don't cry." These thoughts have made us emotionally incapacitated, and they prevent us from feeling and recognizing our emotions and those of others.

Emotions

In the chapter 2 ("The Family Room"), we discussed emotional mastery. Here, we will see how we can manage our emotions in order to feel fulfilled. Most of what is presented here comes from the *inner bonding*[15] and *focusing*[16] techniques. We can work and act upon only that which we know and can distinguish. Just like Eskimos are able to distinguish between hundreds of different whites in order to live

---

[15] Inner bonding, created by Dr. Margaret Paul and Erika Chopich, is a method to lovingly take care of yourself, share your love with others, and have the ability to take responsibility for your own feelings and behaviors. A book to use as reference is Margaret Paul's book *Healing Your Aloneness: Finding Love and Wholeness Through Your Inner Child*.

[16] Focusing, or experiential therapy, is a psychotherapeutic technique that uses the patient's ability to pay attention to feelings and wishes that are not expressed with words. The term was introduced by psychotherapist Eugene T. Gendlin, disciple and collaborator of Carl Rogers.

in the snow, we will need to recognize our emotions in order to work with them in favor of our well-being.

There are five basic emotions, named because we can recognize them even in the facial expressions of babies: joy, fear, sadness, disgust (or aversion), and anger (or rage).

With a very original premise, Disney Pixar's movie *Inside Out* describes how emotions work and how they affect our experience. Besides being very entertaining, I recommend this movie because it can help us to understand how, for example, a rainy day is different when we feel sad than when we feel happy. It doesn't depend so much on what we experience but in how we feel on the inside when we experience it. And although we cannot avoid emotions, we can manage them, and that skill is key to our well-being.

As I write these lines, I feel a mix of joy and calm that allows me to write from a place of connection to my wisdom and life experiences. I also feel hungry, and although that is not an emotion, I know it's important because if I don't tend to my physical needs, it can generate a negative emotion in me that prevents me from maintaining this state that benefits my writing and allows me to put into words the message I want to pass on to you.

Emotions and physical sensations are alarms that tell us what we need. As the free and responsible beings that we are, we must act in order to give ourselves whatever we need. Because of that, the first thing we should do is take the time to decipher which feeling, sensation, or emotion we feel. The body is one of the most direct routes to emotions because it doesn't have any rational filter. In this sense, a discomfort in the stomach can also indicate anguish. If we ask that anguish what it wants to tell us, perhaps it will reply that we are pressuring ourselves more than is healthy for us so that we can finish a job on time. Maybe we are running around all day to finish tasks when we are already too tired.

Many times, we generate the emotions we experience. We generate that anguish from always being in a hurry to meet acquired outside commitments—no one forces us to do so. The choice to free ourselves from that anguish is within us; it's as simple as taking the time for a break and not hurrying or pressuring ourselves so much because, in general, we know these are not life-or-death commitments. We can be responsible when faced with our emotions.

There are emotions, however, that don't depend on us. We don't cause the loss of a loved one, but we feel profound sadness when it happens. In that case, what works best is *presence*—accompanying ourselves with love, connecting to what we believe gives us love in life (in my case, the divine in me), and feeling that we are not alone in facing what is happening to us. Sometimes we can find the company of someone who loves us and offers the affection we need. Life, or God, or however each calls it works through all that exists.

Sometimes it's good for us to research why we do and believe what we do and believe. This allows us to see patterns that repeat and to give them meaning, and it also gives us the option to choose differently. I may think that if I achieve everything on my list of goals and pending tasks for the day that I will be more productive (and therefore, valuable) than if I don't, but surely one thing is not necessarily the cause of the other. I am sure that this way of thinking comes from my childhood. I can see that in the past, maybe I needed to be accepted and loved by my parents, but today I don't need that to feel and know myself as valuable. I can change that belief and forget that I need to fulfill obligations in order to be valuable. When I have a case at work that reminds me of that childhood situation, I ask the client to imagine what he would do if he discovered that his six-year-old daughter's stomach hurt because she couldn't finish all that she was expected to do. In general, parents realize the situation, listen, and take burdens away from their children, instead of blaming or forcing them to do what they expect them to do. The idea is to treat ourselves, our emotions, and our feelings as if they were our children, and then, with love, give ourselves what we need to feel loved, secure, and happy.

The Further Inside, the More Spiritual

The words *spiritual bunker* are charged with intention. A bunker is a place where we protect ourselves from a possible aggression. When we enter a bunker, we isolate ourselves from the world and don't know what happens beyond the walls around us.

We all need to feel secure and protected. It's not about knowing we are safe between four walls; it's more about feeling cared for in a space created by us for ourselves, a space where we connect to what we think, feel, and need in order to make our lives flourish with happiness and fulfillment. By putting our own spiritual bunker to work, we will discover that we are not alone. The more we connect with the deep part of our beings, the more we connect with the love that flows through all of us, with what unites us as human beings. "We are spiritual beings having a human experience," Teilhard de Jardin, a French Jesuit philosopher, used to say. After that, our bunkers should be spiritual places, a place for us to connect and for our spirits to blossom.

Whether we believe in God or not, we all have access to a state of consciousness where we can feel that part of us, and that connects

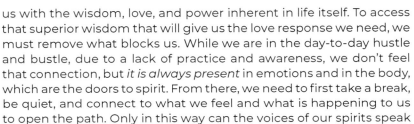
us with the wisdom, love, and power inherent in life itself. To access that superior wisdom that will give us the love response we need, we must remove what blocks us. While we are in the day-to-day hustle and bustle, due to a lack of practice and awareness, we don't feel that connection, but *it is always present* in emotions and in the body, which are the doors to spirit. From there, we need to first take a break, be quiet, and connect to what we feel and what is happening to us to open the path. Only in this way can the voices of our spirits speak and guide us to whatever is best for us.

This spirit manifests through us in the form of our bodies, thoughts, and emotions, and it is my belief that it always wants the best for us. Some of us call it God; others, love. The best may not always be what we want or what gives us pleasure. Many times the best is what is hard, what takes effort, and what doesn't make sense. But there is always meaning here, and it is up to us to find it by being connected to spirit and transcending the physical, mental, and emotional planes to keep evolving.

I believe that life is good, makes sense, and is forged in the love of the spirit that creates it. Spirit is there to be and expand as love itself. And like that love, we are also here to expand ourselves and generate more and more love. It is for this purpose that we live through different experiences. Much of my learning had to do with recognizing that I always have been and always will be loved, even if I didn't always have love from who I wanted and when I wanted it. Today, I feel totally contained in love and supported by something greater than myself, which is always available and present. That allows me to trust in me, in my value, in my greatness of spirit. Mine is not a special case; we all have been and always will be loved. If you connect to your emotions, if you express them with love, if you also connect to others from an open heart, then you will be able to realize that you are loved, just like all other beings.

Our children need our learning in love as examples of life, and they also need our freedom, our responsibility, and our consciousness. If we are there for us, then we also will be there for them and that provides them well-being. If we want them to be happy, then let's teach them how to be happy by being happy along with them.

Now that we already have the knowledge and some techniques to take care of our happiness, it's time to put them into practice in our own spiritual bunkers.

Taking Action: Creating Your Spiritual Bunker

The following is a guide for you to make your own spiritual bunker. This space, which is both physical and of time, will be different for each person. You may or may not already have a practice that brings you close to your spirit, but in order to reach the benefits that the spiritual bunker affords, it's important to know that it must be a habit, something that is not sporadic but constant. The spiritual bunker is the heart of the house precisely because it never ceases to be. Our ability to feel, to love, and to become aware reside in it. So let's get to it!

1. Separate a span of time that you will dedicate every day, exclusively, to connect with yourself. It can be thirty minutes or an hour. It can be before you start your day, in the middle of the day, or at the end of the day. You decide.

2. Once you have the time span defined, find a physical space. If it's a prolonged time, choose a space in your home where you won't be interrupted. It can be your room, the balcony, or outside, ideally in a space where you are in touch with nature.

3. Let everyone in your house know that at that time, you would like to not be interrupted. Sometimes it's hard with young kids, but in this case, you can get support from your partner, a friend, or your older children. In that space, you can incorporate elements that favor your ideal attitude and mood to connect with yourself. Maybe it's using candles, lighting incense, or playing music.

4. Meditate. In your space, while alone, find a position where you are comfortable so you can be still and feel. You can focus your attention on the breath, or simply close your

eyes and "scan" your body. Relax. Relax each large and small muscle in your body. You will now begin a journey through your body, and for that, you may need to put your hands on your abdomen while remaining aware of your breath; be aware of how your abdomen inflates and deflates like a balloon when you inhale and exhale.

With your eyes closed, mentally scan your body from the bottom up. Start with your toes, and then, slowly, go up through the soles, instep, ankles, calves, knees, thighs, and hips. There, you will encircle the pelvic area, the coccyx and gluteus. (Continue breathing.) Now go up to your lower abdomen, and scan it until you end up in your lower back. During this journey, visualize your tissues, your bones, your organs. Now, continue going up through your waist toward your upper abdomen and the highest part of your back. Continue mentally scanning your body, moving on to your thoracic cavity, chest, dorsal, shoulder blades, neck, and shoulders. Always remember to keep your body and muscles relaxed. You are bringing them oxygen, their balm, through your breath. Now go down through the arms, elbows, wrists, hands, and fingers. Then, going back to the base of the neck and with a 360-degree movement, visualize your throat, trachea, the muscles in your neck, and your cervical vertebrae. Now is the time to get closer to the head. Go up to it from behind, border the scalp, feel your hair, and then go into your skull. Visualize your brain, visualize its right hemisphere and its left hemisphere. Slowly exit the skull and observe your face—your forehead, eyebrows, nose, cheeks, jaw, and your mouth and tongue. Relax your tongue, and let it rest. You are now centered.

Note: If you know a particular breathing technique to calm your body and mind, use it. If not, it will be enough to focus on your breath. For those who have very active minds, a type of breathing called *Nadi Shodhana* can be of much use: Cover your right nostril with your right thumb and inhale through the left. Finish inhaling, cover the left nostril with the index finger of the right hand (which you already have on your face), remove your right thumb, and exhale through the right nostril. Then inhale through the right, cover the right with your thumb, and

exhale through the left. Doing this between five and ten times will help you connect internally.

5.   Once you are done with step 4, choose to do something that you feel complements your inner connection. It can be to write what you feel or think. It can be to talk with yourself mentally or in a low voice or out loud.

If you choose to simply think, that's fine, but it's not the best. Thinking doesn't help much because it's harder to see ourselves and have a dialogue with our inner selves that way, unless we have a lot of practice in this. Additionally, when we think, we tend to disconnect from the body. Connecting with the body is key for understanding ourselves and choosing.

If you think the writing option is good (it's the one I use), keep a diary and write questions to yourself, as if you were writing to your inner child, who is simply a way of seeing your sensitive side, your soul. For example:

- How do I feel?

- How would I like to feel?

- What am I doing or thinking that makes me feel like this?

- What can I do to feel how I want to feel?

- Am I protecting something by thinking or behaving as I do? (Whatever we do that bothers us always has a positive reason behind it.)

- How many other ways can I achieve that without feeling bad?

In your diary, you can ask life, God, your higher self, or your guardian angel (all of them represent the consciousness that loves us):

- What can I learn from this?

- What is the most loving thing I can do with myself (or with my children, spouse) regarding this issue?

- What would be in my highest good?

6. Close your practice with self-directed gratitude for giving yourself the opportunity to be better and therefore able to be a source of love and joy to your surroundings.

CHAPTER 9

The Study

9

The Study

In my study, my life's professional purpose takes shape. It's where I practice my profession, where I work doing what I'm passionate about and through which I make my family's livelihood. It doesn't matter if this place is in or out of my house; it's part of my *house within* and is intimately linked to my family life.

The study maintains the house's aesthetic, even if we change the décor, looking for it to have more or less light or to be isolated from noise and the usual action. We design it, seeking to feel good while working in it.

To achieve a good relationship between work and family, we must first demolish the paradigm of work as an activity separate from family or as something that we must "go out" to do, as well as a paradigm that is associated with the masculine role—the man in a suit, holding a briefcase, says goodbye to his family in the morning and is only reunited with them at the end of the workday. This paradigm was established in our minds in the 1950s, when the man's role was reduced to breakfast with the family, going out to work, and returning from work to eat, relax, and sleep.

Even though that image still occupies part of our mental paradigms, today we are creating a new model in which we accept many other ways to work, where the office can be fixed or mobile, in or out of the house, and women and men both want professional development. Today, work is part of who we are, a manifestation of our beings that seeks professional fulfillment. With our work, we want to contribute to the world with a part of who we are. Through our work, we reflect our qualities and essential values.

That's why I believe that our jobs, just as with the time and space when and where we carry it out, must be integrated into our family life. We will come into conflict if we do a job that we don't like or are not passionate about; if we believe that we are not very good at it and feel frustrated; if we feel that what we do doesn't positively change somebody's life; or if we feel that we are not getting fair financial remuneration to provide for our needs and those of our family. If any of these factors show up in any way, then we know that something is not right.

I've heard many people refer to their jobs by saying things like "You can't have it all," "At least it's an honest job," or "It's what's there for me." These phrases indicate something needs to be done and changed. If we don't make a conscious effort toward integrating this space of work into our lives and in our house within, we will close this part of our being that fights to come out until, deaf to its screaming, we will drown it—and with it, part of ourselves. Each time I hear someone say things like "My work is good, but I'm not passionate about it," I feel that his inner voice is screaming, asking me to help it come out and to reconnect with his passion and with what he loves.

We may make financial reasons as our excuse not to change, and we justify our frustration with phrases like "It's what puts food on my family's table." But this is a very limited argument. All we have to do is explore a bit to discover other jobs that we are passionate about *and* that can provide financial support. Sometimes we may realize that it's not necessary to find *another* job but rather to change the way in which we do the one we have, as we look for it to connect with who we are and what we love.

I invite you to use figure 1, below, as a tool to design your own study, so that your job is incorporated into your house within. The circle of "What I'm passionate about" is for that which you love, what you enjoy so much that you lose sense of time, and with which you are so in tune that it's like nothing around you exists. When we do what we love, we enter a state of flow in which our energy is focused and in which we perform at our highest because we enjoy it.[17] When we love what we do, we are filled with energy instead of getting depleted from it by the task in hand. It's like when we make love: We enter that flow that brings us to ecstasy and then leaves us feeling happy and fulfilled, without emotions of anguish and with a renewed sense of energy and body relaxation.

The circle of "What I do well" refers to those activities that are easy for you and that "flow" for you because you are an expert in them or because you learn them easily. That's why you should discover, recognize, and value what you are good at.

---

[17] Mihály Csíkszentmihályi, *Flow: The Psychology of Optimal Experience* (Harper Perennial Modern Classics, 2008).

Denise Dziwak

Once when I was teaching a workshop about life purpose, I realized that not all of us know what we do well. I thought this could be because nobody ever congratulated us or singled us out for something. To discover it, we must review which tasks we do daily with ease. Maybe it's the gift of listening to others and understanding them, cooking well, being good with numbers, expressing beauty through the movement of our bodies (through dance, for example), or being good at meditating. Whatever it may be, we will always find something, and we are called to share it with others.

Then there is the circle of "What the world needs," one of my favorites and where I put a lot of attention. The idea here is to decipher what we need as human beings and what our children, families, and friends need. In this area, I ask myself (or better yet, ask them) what their desires, dreams, and unmet needs are. I could also investigate what would make people happier, and the answer would complete the space of this circle. Because every person has a different way of interpreting, this exercise is very enriching; each one of us will have his own answer.

Finally, there is the circle of "What they pay me for." We can write some jobs or roles that we've done and for which we've been remunerated. If we offer the world what it needs, and we do it with passion and skill, we will be paid for it because a lot of people will find value in what we offer.

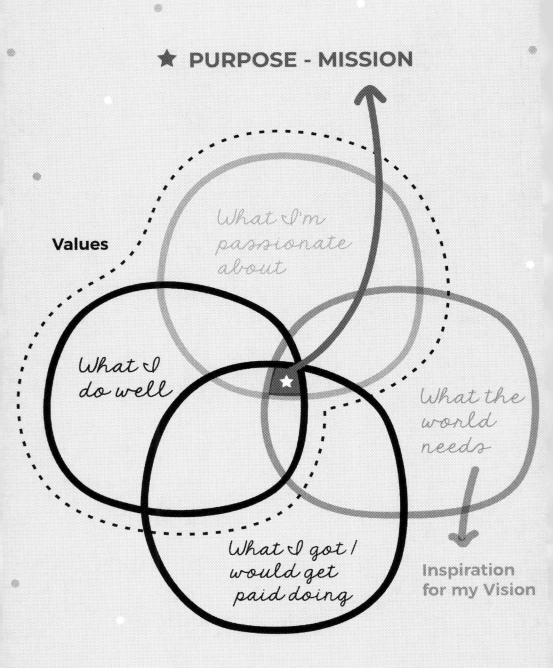

★ **PURPOSE - MISSION**

Values

What I'm passionate about

What I do well

What the world needs

What I got / would get paid doing

Inspiration for my Vision

Figure 1. The Purpose Model

It's important to understand the terms associated with work, such as *vision*, *purpose*, and *mission*.

Vision is something to achieve, a goal or a desired state, while purpose is the way in which we will achieve it. Our life purpose is like a great mission, in which we seek to leave the world a little better than it was when we found it. In that purpose we will have one or more missions that we will accomplish at different times. Here, we will use the word *mission* to designate that assignment that life gives us to fill some need in the world around us.

Just like a soldier's mission can save a village in danger, the mission of a human being can be to bring happiness to children. When we are working on what we are passionate about, what we do well, and what the world needs, we will receive remuneration from the *universal law of cause and effect*. This law states that every action has an associated reaction. The Hindu call this principle of action/reaction *karma*. Sometimes we find the word karma linked to negative acts and its negative consequences for us. But there also can be a positive karma, depending on what the action generates. Because of that, when we give love to the world, we also receive it. That's what our job is about—finding what we want to give to the world.

In figure 1, our values limit what goes inside or outside of each circle. Values are principles that guide our actions and are the engine for them. Honesty, unconditional love, freedom, peace—all of those are values, and they indicate the route that we will follow to carry out our life purposes and all our missions. Along my path, I may find a way to give the world what it needs, but if a certain way is in conflict with my values, then I will not achieve my mission because I would go against my integrity.

To better understand what is proposed in figure 1, take this book as an example. I'm passionate about connecting with people, communicating, creating, expressing, and teaching. I have done it throughout my life in different ways. One of those ways is writing, and even though I am not an expert in writing, I know I have the skills to do it. I'm committed to the writing process, and I've discover that it's easy for me because it is part of what I'm passionate about.

I believe that the world needs happy families that live life with as much fulfillment as I've found in mine. My vision is to create a world founded on love, peace, and unity, and my purpose is to help others (and myself) to grow in consciousness. Of course, I hope that many people read this book and find it useful. My greatest remuneration will be to have positively influenced your life. That's how this book becomes a mission: to inspire parents to create a family life with love, unity, peace, and happiness. This fits perfectly with my life purpose of helping to grow in consciousness and my vision to create a better world.

The key to making our work respond to our vision, purpose, and mission is to know ourselves. We must identify our passions and virtues, and ask ourselves what the world needs—what would make it a better place in which to live, what would make people happier, and how can we do something about it? It's in this sense that the study constitutes a great window that allows us to interact with the external world and contribute to the lives of others. It is in the study that we express our life purposes; because of that, it is a vital space of our house within.

A Window to the World

The study also is a place to which we will invite our children. We open the doors to our workplace so they can enter, see it, explore and discover it, and ask us why, for what, and in what way we use this or that. Children love all of this; they want to know what their parents do, and they need to find meaning in that. This is as important as the time we spend with them in other instances. When the child sees that his parent has gone to work and that he returns at the end of the day, satisfied, at peace, and fulfilled, the child will realize that what his parent was doing while he was not with the child was good. In this way, children find meaning for their parents' work.

Children are extremely perceptive; they are the first to see life's incongruities. When we are not congruent or something is in disharmony, children detect it immediately and will manifest it with a simple question, like "Why are you always tired?" Or with one that digs a little deeper, like "Why don't you want to play with me?" With our choices and actions, we adults are an example for our children, and we communicate the type of life they can have now and in the future. Because of that, if we adopt a victim stance, we will not be taking care of or honoring our potential for service to humanity, and our children will feel that neither they nor their potential is valuable enough. On the other hand, if we value ourselves, they will also value themselves.

To value ourselves means to honor our passions, virtues, and gifts in pursuit of building a better world.

This doesn't mean that our jobs should be something super-distinctive or special. It's not only about what we do; it's about how we do it and for what. I can work cleaning windows and be happy. I can feel a great amount of satisfaction and pride in seeing how I give the window that crystal-clear look, and I can tell my child how happy I am because, thanks to my job, others can enjoy a clear view of the world around them. In that, my child will get an example of commitment, see that what I do has a goal, and see that there is honor in my task and that it requires discipline and good effort.

Of course, the opposite also could happen. If my work is not honest, if I take advantage of people or am dishonest, then my child will see that as the example. He will want to imitate me, and, worse yet, my behaviors may be in conflict with his own sense of morality, which he gets not just from me but from the people around him. The possibility is always there, as it happens in the book *Matilda* by Roald Dahl, that our child questions our ignoble acts. He also can question us when he notices that we do something different to what we preach. When this happens, we should listen to what the children have to say because we often don't realize what is happening to us or that we are doing wrong. We need these "difficult" questions that leave us dislocated, like "Dad, why did you lie to the police?" When this happens, it might be time to review what and how we do what we do.

To find our balance in this sense, we must set boundaries—to know when our job is a source of energy, vitality, purpose, and meaning and to know, conversely, when we are being drained and getting exhausted. If it drains us, we can put an end to it and change it to prioritize what we need. The first thing to realize is that something is not right. The easiest thing for that is to ask ourselves how we feel with regard to our jobs and if we feel that our jobs are integrated into our lives so that they live in harmony. If we feel too much demand or are tired or stressed, let's ask ourselves why. Are we dedicating a lot of time and energy to work and too little to caring for our bodies? Do we have moments of leisure and recreation? Do we feel lack of desire to work and avoid being in our workspace through activities that don't fulfill us?

In this process of reflection, let's explore the reasons for what is happening with us. Often, we will discover that we are centered on doing what we believe we must do, instead of expressing ourselves as we really are through our work. This is very common in women who become moms, because they adopt the socially accepted (but erroneous) idea that they cannot do both things well (work and be mothers) and that they will always have to sacrifice one of the two. I believe each case is individual and unique, however, and that we can design what is good for us mothers.

I'm interested in your finding your passion and carrying it out as mission. Your fulfillment as a person depends on this. When we focus on something we are passionate about, we feel honored, and we will feel how the energy flows our way for the rest of our lives. Because of that, if we feel exhausted and unhappy with what we do, let's cut the time we dedicate to superfluous tasks and focus on that which, for us, really makes a difference in the world. And if we are avoiding

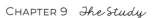

our jobs, then the best thing to do is take some time and space to explore what we are passionate about and to see how, through that, we can pour our virtues in pursuit of giving the world what it needs.

We are free to choose where and what to give our focus; that's why I invite you to review this space and re-create it in pursuit of a better life for you and those around you.

Full-Time Mom and Dad

Some of us make the temporary or permanent choice to dedicate ourselves to being full-time moms or dads, without having a work activity at the same time. At one point in my life, this was my case, and it corresponded to my model of purpose. I love getting on the floor with my daughter and creating fantasies by playing with her. I love going out for a walk and getting in the hammock with her in the park and feeling the wind caress my face. I love to cook and invent the most delicious and nutritious menus for her and the family. I rediscovered how much pleasure it gave me to then take a nap while hugging or getting together with friends to chat, plan, and share. It was something that came naturally to me, where intuition and learning came together. And even though it was not the only thing I did then, as I also was studying to become a professional coach, being a mom was my "job." I was happy doing it, and it took up a big part of my house within. The only thing that created conflict for me, as it happens with many other parents, was when I was asked, "What do you do? What's your job?" And I would answer, "I'm a mom." The person would respond with laughter of disbelief or irony or, worse yet, would ask me, "And what else do you do?" It was as if she couldn't believe that I had chosen to do that one job—to offer my being to the world. At those times, I felt bad—until I connected with my highest truth inside: "I am worthy, and I express my value and my being through what I do. It doesn't matter what others think. What matters is what my heart tells me is best for me and for my family right now."

With the changes that come with time, life offers us different scenarios. In the middle of them, we can choose different jobs, according to how we evolve and what we want to express in each moment. Everything has its own perfect time. Every job is dignified if we do it with love, if it is founded on values, if we are passionate about it, and if we put our best effort and dedication into it.

The study is the place where we live out our values and where we strengthen our identity, which also corresponds with who we are in other environments. There, we can live and show values like service, respect, integrity, freedom, commitment, discipline, perseverance, peace, and love.

Activity

Discover Your Purpose

Duration: 1 hour

MATERIALS

white cardboard or paper
colored pencils
2 Post-it Notes packets, 3 x 3
music that helps you connect inside and a private space

Take some time to connect with yourself. Try to have at least one hour without interruptions. Put on your favorite music, and breathe, inhaling and exhaling deeply for a few minutes.

On a big sheet of paper or white cardboard, draw the four circles from figure 1 and write what corresponds to each area: *What I'm passionate about*, *What I do well*, *What the world needs*, and *What I got/would get paid doing*.

For each circle, do a two-minute brainstorm (time it with a watch). Write each idea on a Post-it, and stick the Post-it in the circle where it belongs. Don't judge the ideas; let them flow (the crazier, the better). Look for quantity, not quality.

Put the ideas in order, maybe grouping them under a certain title or allowing yourself to include new ideas, based on what you are putting in order.

Now, look to complete the intersections. Take two ideas at a time, one from each circle, and find relationships between them. Write these relationships on new Post-its, and put them in the intersections.

When you're done, dedicate five minutes of brainstorming to proposing activities, jobs, or even businesses that could come from the relationships you made in the intersections. For example, if you love meditation and are also good with technology, and you love programming and think the world needs peace, then maybe an idea will arise to develop an app for people to learn to meditate. And if you're also passionate about music, then maybe that can become part of the idea.

Take note of what stayed or can stay in the center, where all the circles unite. From that, write your purpose in one phrase. If you can't do it, don't worry; take a picture to register the final result as the sum of the Post-its.

To enrich this exercise, you can share your results with different people you trust—friends or relatives. Ask each person what they do; maybe you find common points and get ideas about how to put your purpose into practice.

When you've finished the exercise, answer this question: What did I learn about myself in this exercise?

Write a promise you make to yourself, based on what you discovered in the exercise, in order to align your life with your purpose. To fulfill it, have at least one concrete, measurable action, with execution time, and write it clearly. For example: "I will find out if there are businesses or people who are in the field of my mission and decide if I would rather do something on my own or apply to one of them. I will do it before March 11."

MY NOTES

....
....
....
....
....
....
....
....
....
....
....
....
....
....
....
....
....
....
....
....
....
....
....
....

CHAPTER 10

From the Door on Out

10

From the Door on Out

In this chapter we will discuss all that we experience as a family outside of the house—that which we can only achieve by stepping out of our own physical space. Often, we need to breathe new air, which renews us and allows us to take some distance and see our own lives (and what happens to us) from another perspective. We generally designate weekends and vacations for that—a time to get out of our routines, have fun, connect as a family, strengthen bonds in a different way than we do daily, enjoy new places and flavors with those we love, and create bonds with friends and other relatives before returning home, renewed after an experience of joy and learning together. That's the magic of going out.

A Different and Special Place

When I was a child, I was lucky that both my dad and my mom took time off during the three months of school vacation for my sister and me. The beach was our destiny par excellence, and because of the good times I had—and now continue to have with my husband and children—it is still the best place in the world to me.

It was a time without stress or hurry, with a lot of presence and dialogue with Dad and Mom. It was a time to make new friends and a time for different activities, like horseback riding, jet-skiing, or jumping on the bed. The beach was a synonym of time off to play freely with snails, rocks, and sticks and to build secret lairs or do arts and crafts with shells and then sell them to other tourists. Going to the beach on vacation meant sharing all of this with Mom and Dad, who were not busy with their jobs. I would see them relaxed and contemplative, and I liked seeing how they enjoyed going out to dance together, play tennis, or simply rest and sunbathe in a lounge chair. At the beach, I also had more time with my sister. Many times

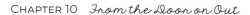

we didn't have any other option than to play together, so we would team up and have a lot of fun (although, of course, we would also fight). Because of all of those memories, I value that time and space outside of the house so much; we would create a new home and a new way of relating to each other. That's why I now try to provide my children with a similar experience, especially in the sense that their parents have all the time and availability for them.

Your spot might be different than mine. Perhaps you like to go to the woods, the country, or the mountains. If you like being in touch with nature, you might prefer to go camping. You might like to learn about different cities and cultures; your ideal vacation might be exploring a city's historical downtown. Each option of a place is as unique and special as we are, and it's suitable for experimenting with "being out."

To give ourselves that chance to go out, change air, be together, and experience something new seems like a great opportunity to learn and grow together in love. And the best thing is that it all starts to happen the very moment we close the door of our house and get into the car to travel.

When Being Bored Is Fun

Because the idea is for us to share as much as possible, I have a simple recommendation: Choose a car that's free of screens and video players incorporated onto the seats or the dashboard. On vacations, it's enough for my husband and me to have a radio in the car so we can hear music; that way, we will favor conversation and make space for games, like counting cars of a certain color or games like I Spy—activities that fuel creativity and connection with others. If the car has a video player, we use it in moderation to produce a different context. While it's true that it distracts the kids and keeps them "entertained," it also reduces the possibility of interaction among all of us. Technology takes over entertainment slots to a large degree, and it's fine to do without it from time to time, especially when we are on vacation or trying to have an enriching weekend. It's even valid to do without cell phones, for the simple reason that it is good to be bored. For adults, going on the freeway for hours is a natural space to meditate with open eyes. On the other hand, being seated with nothing to do—not even a cell phone to check messages, hear music with earphones, or watch videos—is the best way to leave behind everyday thoughts and worries and to let what's important emerge: connecting with ourselves and with those we love and value most.

Boredom is like a mix of tiredness and mental and physical annoyance that we experience when we don't have anything to have fun with. It's an uncomfortable and unpleasant state, especially for our children.

When they say to us, "Dad, I'm bored," they are asking for us to do something about it—to entertain them, to get them interested and motivated. Experiencing that boredom in the car is good because it forces us to unite in a creative search that takes us all out of that state.

Sharing moments of boredom with my kids has surprised me in a positive way. We hear them talk when something surprises them or when they find something strange on the road, or they talk more about something that happened to them in the past and how they felt or still feel about it. It's beautiful to be able to talk with them. Around four years of age, children start to tell us stories about their friends or tell us fairy tales they heard and things they learned in their nursery or school.

In the car or any place, boredom provides us the opportunity of chatting, which is a treasure because our children feel loved and appreciated then. As parents, we can make the most of boredom by giving our children ideas on how to find ways that will bring them happiness and make them feel good under any circumstances. Being bored is an excellent opportunity for human beings to connect with others and create something—a game, a conversation, a moment of love. It might not be easy for us at first, especially if our children get into a fight while we are traveling. But my experience is that if we overcome that first discomfort of our new environment, we will find new ways to relate and enjoy.

To Plan or Not to Plan—That Is the Question

While planning our outings and trips can make us feel at ease, it does take away flexibility and spontaneity. Some travel plans obviously require preparing and planning. In some instances, we need to buy plane tickets, make hotel reservations, or rent cars and apartments. For that, technology is our ally, and we will find various options on the internet and through trip apps. The important thing is to use our judgment with them.

When we've chosen a destination and start to arrange our trip, apps begin to offer us things that might not have been part of our priorities—guided tours, tickets to shows, restaurant discounts, and so on, which become temptation. They are catchy options that promise to save us time and money but that can also displace the expectations and initial plans we had. Even worse, it can end up creating an agenda for a trip for which, at first, we didn't want to have schedules and stress. What if, while on a trip, we find something unexpectedly that really catches our attention? We feel conflicted because if we decide to go for the option that fate gave us, we will not be doing the planned activity (and for which we might already have paid).

In general, when we are with children, we often feel like extending some plans because we don't want that moment to end or cutting others short when we discover that we are all tired. It also might happen that if we have babies or young children, it's difficult to throw caution to the wind for fear of getting stuck somewhere with the kids "crawling up the walls." (That fear, however, was not real.)

No matter where we are, how big or small the place is, or how many plans we have, we will always find fun ideas to connect with that present moment, and that will take us out of the passing boredom we might experience. Maybe that's why I love to go to the beach; once there, we have no other plan than to see what we come up with. We might want to play in the waves or float on a calm sea, according to the moment and weather conditions and the ocean. We can relax, look at the sky, and find shapes in the clouds, or we might make up games with our children that include jumping and running or building castles, tunnels, and volcanoes in the sand. If the beach is your destination, I assure you that you will always find alternatives. You will be in a different place, and that will be inspiration enough to find something to do.

When planning your outing, make sure that the destination is suitable for all—a space that everyone can enjoy. Some places are preferably for adults—they tend to be peaceful, quiet places where activity offerings for children are few to none. Exposing the kids to such a place seems like torture for them and for parents because everyone will be uncomfortable and stressed, and nobody will enjoy being there. If you have small children, it's best to think about kid-friendly places, where, ideally, other families with children also go.

Exploring options and deciding what is best for all will give more of a guarantee of enjoyment. As our children grow, we can try other scenarios with "low risk." Before going to see Paris museums for a week with a three-year-old, I would go to a local museum and see how it goes. I love Paris and its museums, but if I went with my four-year-old daughter, Sofia, who loves nature and open spaces to roam free and explore, she would not enjoy it—at least not until she's older. If I were to go alone with Valentina, who is eight years old, loves art, is more observant, and can dedicate hours to the same subject without getting bored, I would enjoy that. Each child and each age have their peculiarities that change everything.

Planning doesn't guarantee that everything will be perfect or that we will arrive at the perfect place, but we always have the option to improve experiences in the moment and to learn what we like and don't like in designing our experience outside of the house.

Around the Corner

It's interesting to explore, discover, and learn something new when getting out of the house. For that, it's not necessary to go too far; we'll have that experience just by going out to the street, to the park, or to a friend's house.

Little kids love to play at other houses because they find a new world in them. At first, they may need to get acquainted before they feel secure and comfortable, for which our presence without pushing them to do it is ideal. We may need to go with them to the playroom the first time and discover something together—for example, by our taking a toy and showing them how interesting it is. Once they feel secure, they will continue exploring and playing on their own. And if the scenario is a park that they don't know, we can take a little branch and make it into a magic wand or a sword, or suggest a game of hide-and-seek. I have a lot of fun playing with the kids, and when I suggest a game, everyone is into it, becomes friends, and wants to join, and after a while the imaginary world that we've created provides the momentum for them to continue playing and offers a perfect chance for adults to distance themselves to rest or chat with other adults.

Sometimes a change of air is enough for adults and children. It's like when children are babies, and we bring them close to the windows so they can see, get some air and sun, and change their mood that way. It's exactly the same with us adults. Before I began to write this chapter, for example, I went out to the balcony of my house and looked out to the park at the pigeons and squirrels. I became inspired and recharged with ideas and energy to write. I did it without realizing or planning it; I simply needed to go out and get some air and fill myself with something new and lovely so I could later share ideas with you. In this sense, we also have a connection with the spiritual bunker. The park can become our ideal space for our spiritual bunker—that place where we get air, talk to ourselves, get refreshed, change perspective, and return to reality reenergized.

Children and adults can get tired of going to the same park every afternoon, so there's nothing better than thinking of other fun alternatives in our city. When was the last time you went to the historical city center? Children are impressed by the old buildings that have tall ceilings and the way their voices echo off the walls. They might be fascinated by a soldier guarding a palace or government building, in full uniform, with sword and boots. Every city has at least one museum or historical place of interest that you can explore.

Going to a history museum and seeing a mummy or dinosaur bones can be a total adventure.

One of my best memories of childhood is when my parents would take me to see new things, like a big lake with ducks that I'd never seen that was only twenty blocks from my house. Or the time they took me on a speedboat through the Tigre Delta in Buenos Aires, and I saw houses with docks and transport speedboats, which I thought were incredible.

We don't need anything other than to go out and explore a new place that inspires us and the kids. Sometimes we let ourselves get carried away by routine and what works for us, and we don't notice that we begin to get annoyed. We engage in an activity reluctantly because "it's what there is to do," and we don't realize the new possibilities. There are also theaters, old commercial passages, boardwalks, peaceful streets to walk and have some ice cream, bookstores with children's sections and activities, theme parks, and public libraries with cultural agendas for all. We don't have to wait for a vacation or the weekend to seek these spaces; we can do so day to day. Let's stay open to options that are always available to us. We only need to use our creativity and look beyond our routines.

For What and with Whom We Go Out

Everything we do is because of and for something. That's why when we go out, we take a minute to know what we are looking for, where we are going, and why we will be there. There is always a good reason that gives our decision meaning, but if we see there isn't one (which can also happen), it will be better for us to stay home. Going out takes effort and energy, so before doing it, let's think about our reason for going out and who really needs to do it.

I have had such a bad time every time I have left the house without a valid reason that I have reached the conclusion that I actually needed to stay home. On some occasions, I forced myself to go out because I thought my kids needed it, but doing that was definitely a mistake, and I ended up exhausted.

Sometimes the need is real; other times, it is *created by an idea* we have but that doesn't fit with the present moment. In order to make a good decision, the best thing we can do is connect in the present moment with what we love and need and with what our children love and need.

Outings and trips with other families or friends require coordination and certain logistics. All of us have different tastes and needs, and the more we know ourselves and share what is important for us, the

Denise Dziwak

better the outing will be. If we travel with another family, we plan with a certain degree of flexibility and independence so that each family has a margin of choice.

Our family shared a vacation at Disney World with friends, and it was a spectacular experience. We went to many attractions as a group, but we also agreed that there would be moments when each family would visit what they liked the most. This was ideal because our children and their children weren't the same age and didn't have the same tastes. Thanks to that decision, I experienced the parks like a little girl. My daughter wanted to go to every roller coaster, and I decided to go after her and tried everything. On some I felt panic and knew I would never go again, but on others, I died of laughter and enjoyed the sensations, like falling through a waterfall and ending up totally wet. I love fantasy and felt that I really explored Mars on a rocket and flew over the seven wonders of the world. I also loved the musical shows. Along our adventure walk through the park, we found a rhythm with which both of us felt comfortable, and we shared fun experiences.

Safety is also key when we travel, and both parents and children should consider it a priority. In open spaces filled with people, always holding hands with the kids is ideal, so as to not risk losing them. We always allow, however, for getting lost and agree before we start out that the first to do is immediately notify security personnel that a child is lost and state his or her name.

When we go out—to the supermarket, for example—I always give my kids guidelines, like "If you don't see me, go to a guard or a cashier." And I point out who the guards and cashiers are. Or I tell them that if we get separated, they are not to move from a spot previously determined by all of us so that I can find them. From the time they were very young, whenever we were on vacation, my children knew the name and address of the hotel or the place where we were staying.

During that trip to Disney, there was a moment when we lost sight of one of the girls, who was barely four years old. We notified security right away, but the scare quickly passed because we found her in the spot where we had agreed to meet in case that happened. It was a useful experience to remember that that can happen to us at any time and to remember how important it is to be prepared.

But let's keep in mind not to instill fear into the kids with phrases that sound like a threat because that fear will prevent them from having a clear reading on what they feel and intuit at the time, which will make it difficult for them to take care of themselves and enjoy the vacation experience. Let's simply give them clear instructions when we are in places with a lot of people so they feel safe. If they are very young, we can put necklaces with the parents' names and contact info on them or always have them in the stroller and very close to us. Being prepared will give us all peace of mind so that we can enjoy the trip.

Nature Calling

We don't need big plans or exotic faraway destinations to breathe new air, change perspective, recharge, and enjoy. Nature, which we are a part of, is an excellent source of peace, energy, and connection with ourselves and with those who join us. To be in contact with it reminds us that we are a part of something very big that transcends and contains us. To feel a part of that makes us feel loved as human beings.

Natural environments have benefits for people's physical, mental, and emotional health. Pure air and contact with the earth, plants, and animals promotes the production of hormones that reduce stress and benefit the quality of our sleep and rest. There are astounding documented cases in which contact with nature has healed diseases. In Alaska, for example, there is a beautiful practice that allows serious illnesses to heal. The method is called *grounding*, and it consists of getting in touch with the earth through the feet or the whole body in order to let it heal the person.[18]

The green in nature relaxes our sight after hours in front of luminous screens—televisions, computers, cell phones, and tablets—and being in contact with earth frees negative energies because it acts like a great receptor and transmitter that helps us even out our energies, providing us greater harmony. The mere act of being in a natural setting teaches us and our children many things. Thanks to their innate curiosity and ingenuity, children are capable of reading nature's signs. They appreciate, connect with, and incorporate themselves into nature in ways that adults sometimes forget or set aside because, for example, they don't want to get dirty.

In my teenage years, I hated beach sand. The discomfort that grains of sand produced on my skin made me feel like the beach-and-sea plan was not perfect. Years later, with the arrival of my children and the change that this entailed in my way of experiencing life, I began to relate to sand the way they do. Today, I throw myself on the beach without thinking and don't care if sand gets stuck all over my whole sun-lotion-lathered body. I even rest my face directly on the sand while I sunbathe, something that before would have horrified me.

---

18 You can read more about "Grounding," Dr. Mercola's article, at this link: http://articles.mercola.com/sites/articles/archive/2013/10/19/grounded-documentary.aspx. The related documentary is on YouTube: http://youtu.be/b8b_lg2z8Nc.

Now I perceive contact with the sand as a wonderful cuddle for my whole body, and I know that I can always take a shower when I leave the beach.

As a teenager, I backpacked through the south of Argentina and experienced the mountains and woods with a group of friends for twenty days. For the first time in my life, I found myself bathing in the freezing-cold water of the creeks and using dirt as the only mechanism to naturally shelter myself from the sun. Who needs sunblock when you have so much dirt on your body after trekking entire days through the mountains? The experience of being without technology or a phone for so many days and just connecting with nature and other people in a similar situation was incredible. I also lived through an extreme survival experience when, coming down from a mountain, I distanced myself from the group and got lost. I had to wait, completely alone in the intensity of the landscape, until finally, after four hours that seemed never-ending, they found me. Those days in nature also allowed me to develop human relationships beyond the comfortable social context because I was forced to share everything with the group of backpackers. Even though not all of us knew each other well, and there was not always sympathy among all the members of the group, we had to share food and the heat of the single fire in the cold at night. Nature has the power to present us with challenges and to place us in situations of scarcity and abundance, making us develop a sense of community and making us feel a part of something superior that transcends us.

Today, I don't need big trekking excursions. It's enough for me to go out of the city for a few hours to walk in the country, through a beach town, or along a short mountain trail. That ends up being enough for me to notice a change of rhythm and a different perspective on life. To me, this is almost like drinking water. I need it, and I do it for my health.

Another benefit of visiting rural populations or those far away from big urban centers is getting to know its people, who often have another concept of time and whose treatment of others tends to be more relaxed and warm than what we are used to getting in the cities. Contact with country-, mountain-, or beach-town people impresses a calm upon us and helps us to see ourselves from a more pleasant and relaxed angle.

Nature also offers us settings and opportunities to learn about life and experiment in the company of our small children. When spring comes and flowers bloom and animals give birth, we can talk to our children about the cycle of life. That's a way to comfort ourselves and understand that we are also a part of that cycle that constantly renews itself. We can talk to our children about how they change

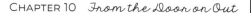

Denise Dziwak

and transform and about how beautiful it is to be with them in this process.

I grew up in a big, cosmopolitan city, but, fortunately, my grandparents lived in a more peaceful neighborhood, with parks full of huge green spaces and open to all. My grandparents worked with their hands, which was quite an experience for me. I helped my grandfather build a clay oven, and he helped me build a house for Pepi the turtle, who is still alive. I also had fun with my grandmother, helping her at the house. I would water the plants, feed the stray cats, and give bread dipped in milk to the hundreds of wild birds that would make a line on the roof when it was time to eat. At my grandparents' house, I could have dirty hands and clothes without being judged as disobedient, misbehaving, or rude.

As parents, we can ask ourselves how we relate to nature today. Let's ask ourselves how often it would be best to be in nature, what "nature plans" we would enjoy, and what outings we liked when we were children that we would like to do again with our families. Let's go look to recover those outings and give our children the opportunity to live and enjoy them as well. Let's rediscover nature along with our kids. Being next to a river, on the grass or in the sand, looking at the sky, wading in the ocean, or feeling the cold and texture of the snow are experiences that give us a lot of peace and harmony. If we can share these experiences with our children, then we will also give them peace and confidence.

Here are some ideas for going out of the house without needing to think about long vacations.

Activities from the Door on Out

If you go to the club every weekend or to the beach, the park, or the mall, why not choose one weekend to go to the city's historical center? Consult a tour guide in your city and explore places you don't know. Make it a "travel in time" and visit museums, churches, buildings, restaurants, and old theaters. It's fun and refreshing to pretend to be a tourist in your own city. You can design a route to tour, and you'll discover charming experiences that you will then be able to repeat with friends and other families.

If you choose to go out to the same park as always, then do it as if you're all kids. Take off your shoes, step into a sandbox, and feel the sand between your toes, or walk barefoot through the grass and feel the earth. Enjoy getting on the ground and looking at the sky or treetops with your children. Get on the swings with them and rediscover that playtime in the open air.

To give the park experience another color, have a picnic. Kids love making food with their hands, even if it's just pieces of fruit. The change of air and having no rules for eating is quite an experience for them—and nothing happens if the mayo drips from the sandwich! Kids love the ritual of putting the blanket on the grass, laying out the picnic things, and tasting

everything, even things they have not tried at home. They like to share with others and eat a little of everyone's food. Sharing, innovating, and stepping out of the daily meal routine with a picnic is as easy as going to the park near the house.

If you travel to the beach, mountains, country, or a foreign city, explore without getting exhausted. Be flexible with each person's tastes and needs. Do what you want, not what a tourist guide or a friend who's been there says you should do. Nothing is what it should be. You, as a family, make it as it is, so pay attention to what everyone feels and needs in each moment.

Activities from the Door on In

Some friends tell me that they don't know how to "drain their kids' batteries" when they don't go out, especially in areas where the winter season is long and cold. Here, the best thing we can do is to explore and give our imagination free rein. Remember that being bored is a great opportunity to strengthen ties and make discoveries that take us all out of that bored state. Our minds are powerful and can take us to many beautiful places. For example, if you have a terrace, go camping on the terrace. Take advantage of a starry night to look at the sky and identify constellations. On a sunny day, you can pretend you're at the beach. If you don't have a terrace or the weather prevents you from doing activities on it, dance along to "Just Dance" choreographies on YouTube, build lairs under a desk, or make tunnels with pillows and sheets. These are good alternatives to expend energy, have fun, and share a connection with your children.

Try cooking together. Kids love it, and it is super-easy. It doesn't have to result in a delicious dish; it's more about having fun in the process and ending up a bit sticky and covered in flour. Prepare yourself mentally for the mess, and set up a special moment for that so you don't stress over anything.

Art, of course, is always welcome. With big papers, paint, crayons, or colored pencils, make murals and spread the paint on your hands and feet. Kids love that. You might also make

shapes or cut them out of old magazines to create a collage. Use rice or sugar as decorative elements.

Another way to go out while being at the house is to undertake a building project, perhaps a structure of a certain complexity with Legos or something a bit more challenging, like building a Lego car, plane, or boat.

Our children's aptitudes, tastes, and talents will blossom and strengthen when they engage in these types of activities.

MY NOTES

....
....
....
....
....
....
....
....
....
....
....
....
....
....
....
....
....
....
....
....
....
....

Goodbye

Goodbye

It was a pleasure to have walked through all the spaces of this house together, a house that is now also yours. Having been together while learning, reflecting, and choosing how we want to create our family makes us "purpose siblings," and we share a dharma, that path of learning and mission.

We both have a commitment to ourselves and with the world—to choose with responsibility by exercising our freedom and awareness and to create a family united in love and peace, a family where we accept its members' differences, valuing them and encouraging each one to develop fully with everyone's support in order to be who we want to be—and can be—in the world.

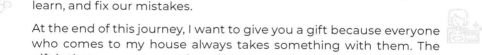

This book creates a bond between those who read it that grows and creates a web of families who listen, have fun, enjoy every moment, and express themselves. These families have essential moral codes, like absolute respect for others, respect that leads us to treat each other with love and without violence. Love allows us to notice when we move away from that model of peace and allows us to regulate, learn, and fix our mistakes.

At the end of this journey, I want to give you a gift because everyone who comes to my house always takes something with them. The gift is that you can create happiness, peace, and unity in your family. You've gone through all your spaces and environments, and in each one I proposed ideas and activities for your own house. Perhaps you already put them into practice, or perhaps you have not felt like it yet and are waiting to finish reading to do so. That's fine; just remember that each one of those activities is an invitation to put into practice what we've discussed—playing with masks to better understand our emotions, as I said the family room; drawing a tree that allows us to identify what makes us sick and how to heal, as I said in the bathroom, or meditating in your spiritual bunker to recharge and return with more clarity and energy to your daily life. If you have not experienced some of this, you can do it now. And what better way to do it than sharing with your partner, children, or friends and, in doing, multiplying the positive effect it will have.

This bond that connected us won't be cut because it is woven in the heart. It's the bond that will allow us to continue learning to create happy, connected families that love and enjoy each other. These families are the cells of a new culture that will make this world a better place—that's how important it is to work toward creating the world in which we want to live.

Remember that besides creating, you also can recreate and learn again. My husband and I have changed a lot in our eighteen years together and have created and recreated many times and many versions of ourselves and our family. Each time is better because we gain more awareness, which allows us to enjoy more and live with greater fulfillment.

Every time that you are offered something to learn that resonates inside and that you think can guide you toward your inner happiness, I encourage you to take it. Why wait? Happiness is inside each one of us, and each learning experience allows us to uncover it a bit more and live it out fully—with all the love that entails.

I hope you continue to visit me—maybe again through this book or maybe through my website (www.denisedziwak.com). I will wait for you always with an open door and a heart ready to receive you.

I leave you with this poem that I wrote, thinking of you:

I'm made of foam, I'm made of salt, I caress your skin when I fly.

Does my flight amaze you? Take my reins and come fly.

Temper the thread, my ball of yarn embraces your soul in love.

It's yours and everyone's to play and heal with.

Don't fear the sunrise; it will convince you with its kindness.

You are beautiful, eternal, loved from the sky,
from the earth, and from the sea.

Come with me to play; tomorrow you can rest.

Activity

A Promise for a Better World

I invite you to make and keep a promise. Write it in first person and in the present time. For example:

- I meditate daily for five minutes to be in peace and to be grateful for my wonderful life.

- I listen to my children, accepting them as wonderful beings that seek my love, especially when they express themselves through crying and screaming.

- I seek intimate moments with my partner to fall in love, time and again, in different ways.

- I set electronics aside when we are together as a family in order to enjoy human contact.

Don't forget your promise; keep it. You have everything to achieve it.

. . . .

. . . .

. . . .

. . . .

. . . .

. . . .

. . . .

. . . .

. . . .

Recommended Books and Authors

Motivated by an immense love that transcended me and filled with courage, I started a path of learning that I will continue to follow until the end of my days. Being a learner, I have shared this book with you with the intention of inviting you to raise questions that can help you choose with awareness and freedom.

Each person has a unique path of growth and learning, and each person life shows step by step where to go. Because of that, this book tells us what and how to do things in order to be better parents and more conscious people. That *what* and *how* will be borne of an individual search that each one of us can do. I only aim to motivate that search.

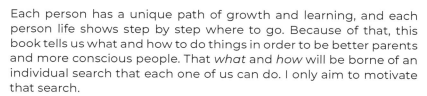

I am an eternal learner and can see that there is a lot of theory and research behind what I have been learning. I love to soak up ideas and make them go through my mind, my body, and my spirit in order to adopt and personalize those that resonate within my soul. Although I began to read to see which flag I could fly and follow, today I read to nourish and inspire myself and to choose what works for me.

Some of these theories I've found in authors that I'll mention next, to whom you can turn if you wish to dive deeply into them. Each one offers various ideas; some will resonate more within you than others. Some will even have the power to generate anger or indignation, something that is very good because it will force you to question yourself and identify whatever there is of that author in you that you don't like or that makes you uncomfortable. What seems most important to me is that we take these readings and authors like a proposal and an invitation and not like a mandate or an obligation. Beyond their words and the tone in which they speak, let's seek and stay with what we are interested in incorporating to have a more loving and healthier life.

Authors with a Philosophical Disposition

- Viktor Frankl—all his works. I cannot conceive of my life without rereading his book *Man's Search for Meaning* at least every couple of years. It's an example of infinite love and transcending personality; it is the anchor of the real and omnipresent spirit. With him, I discovered the triangle of freedom, responsibility, and awareness that guides my steps, always asking me for that which gives my life meaning. The most important question that I am grateful to Viktor Frankl for is this: "For what am I doing what I am doing?"

- Sergio Sinay—an author recommended for those who seek existential theories aligned with logotherapy philosophy.

- Carl Jung—a master without whom I could not recognize what today I call "the shadow," that part of me that is not conscious and that I reject and that has a powerful aspect. As soon as I can accept it, I will appropriate it and use it in my favor.

- Socrates, Aristotle, Heraclitus, Parmenides, Plato. The Greeks are always current. Even after so many centuries, they still ask us the best questions we could ask ourselves about our lives.

- Buddha, Lao Tzu, Jesus, Saint Francis of Assisi, Hindu gods from sacred Vedic texts, Mother Teresa, Gandhi, Paramahansa Yogananda, Elizabeth and Mark Prophet. They have all dedicated themselves to instruct in the spirit.

Authors and Sources of Personal and Spiritual Development

- Dr. Margaret Paul—great teacher who provides a unique, easy, and deep framework to be who we want to be. I highlight her books *Healing Your Aloneness* and *Do I Have to Give Up Me to Be Loved by My Kids?* The latter is a personal work guide for every parent who wants to choose a path of learning in love.

- Deepak Chopra—incredible in his ability to unite and synthesize the path to spirit and give us tools to achieve it. I think I've learned more about Buddhism by reading his novel *Buddha* than consulting or reading a thousand other sources and books. There is nothing simpler or more powerful than the path of meditation with a mantra and breathing in order to find that point of union with spirit.

- Rafael Echeverría—*Ontología del lenguaje* and *Por la senda del pensar ontológico* are two books that made me look at the world in a different way and allowed me to question who I wanted to be in that world. They are works that offer snippets and basic knowledge on philosophy.

- Fred Kofman—From the book *Metamanagement*, I recommend that you read at least the introduction, where he talks about the process of the transformation between the beings we think we are and the ones we really are. Suggests excellent ways to face this process and to relate to others, be it a business or any human group. The tools he shares for that are very powerful and vastly exceed the corporate environment.

- Daniel Goleman—We should all know his book *Emotional Intelligence* and, ideally, develop it in us and our children.

- Daniel Siegel—His book *Mindsight* tells us how everyone, at any age, can update his or her emotional intelligence and how to do it by adapting the brain in order to create a life of greater fulfillment.

Parenting Authors and Books

- Laura Gutman—*Maternity: Coming Face to Face with Our Own Shadow* explains how the baby expresses what the mom feels and how she can recognize and accept it, thanks to that.

- Jean Liedloff—*The Continuum Concept*. I was able to connect with the power of my intuitive upbringing by reading of her own experience living among Amazonian tribes.

- Maritchu Seitun de Chas—*Criar hijos motivados seguros y confiados* and *Capacitación emocional para la familia*. I don't think there is a better source when we want to learn to be more loving with our children.

- Carlos González—*Kiss Me! How to Raise Your Children with Love*. Upon reading it, we can connect to the importance of love over prefabricated ideas in the upbringing of our children.

Of course, there are many more references, but these topics are key. If you would like more information and references, you can contact me via my website (www.denisedziwak.com), and I will be happy to give them to you.

About the Author

Denise Dziwak was born in Buenos Aires, Argentina, on February 15, 1979. In 2001 she graduated with honors as an industrial engineer from the Technological Institute of Buenos Aires and, in the company of her husband, Roman Zaobornyj, traveled to Venezuela, working for Procter & Gamble, where she forged a ten-year corporate career.

Specializing in marketing, she led the training of thousands of executives at the regional level and worked as an internal consultant, incorporating design thinking to P&G in Latin America. In parallel, and since the beginning of her career, she has worked as an independent entrepreneur; she organized business simulation competitions among prestigious universities in Argentina (ITBA and UDESA) and developed start-ups like AldeaX, an online community; Live Connect, video streaming for urban journalism; and Florecer del Alma, an online community to grow in consciousness. She has delivered classes at universities in industrial engineering and ontological coaching.

After becoming a mother and having ventured into energy-healing therapies, angel therapy, and Touch for Health, she decided to leave the corporate environment and become certified as an ontological coach and coach in neurolinguistic programming (NLP). She has worked as a spiritual teacher, inner-child therapist, and life coach for several years. In 2015, she incorporated coaching and consulting to executives and companies, becoming a conscious business coach with Fred Kofman and working for organizations such as Ronald Career Services Group, Vistage, Axialent, and BetterUp.

Together with her husband, she has built a beautiful family with three children (Valentina, Sofia, and Juan Francisco) and their cat (Pisco). They are her source of motivation and learning. Denise is passionate about people and culture and has lived in several countries (Argentina, Venezuela, Guatemala, Panama, and Peru). She loves outdoor sports in contact with nature, like running, walking, trekking, skiing, and sailing. She has practiced and studied yoga for almost two decades, and she enjoys learning as much as she does teaching about spirituality, meditation, philosophy, and psychology. She also enjoys dancing, acting, and singing.

Today, she lives in Panama with her family and works in person and online. From her website she offers resources so that women, as leaders of our culture, learn to connect, transform, and make their lives flourish, as well as the lives of those around them.

You can contact and consult Denise through her website, www. denisedziwak.com.

Printed in the United States
By Bookmasters